day trips® series

day trips® from tampa bay

first edition

getaway ideas for the local traveler

anne w. anderson

gpp® travel

Guilford, Connecticut

All the information in this guidebook is subject to change. We recommend that you call ahead to obtain current information before traveling.

Editor: Amy Lyons
Project Editor: Heather Santiago
Layout: Joanna Beyer
Text Design: Linda R. Loiewski
Maps: Daniel Lloyd © Morris Book Publishing, LLC.
Spot photography throughout © Delmas Lehman, licensed by Shutterstock.com

ISBN 978-0-7627-7937-6

Printed in the United States of America

contents

day trip 03

day trip 04

day trip 05

about the author

Anne W. Anderson has explored the Tampa area for more than three decades and has written about Florida's West Coast for the *St. Petersburg Times* and Tampa Bay Newspapers, Inc. A graduate of Eckerd College in St. Petersburg and of the University of Alabama, Anne is an instructor in the College of Education at the University of South Florida, Tampa, where she studies literacy and children's literature. Born in Idaho and transplanted from Wyoming, she and her husband live in Safety Harbor, Florida, with kids and grandkids nearby, except for one son who returned to the mountains and lives in Colorado. She is also the author of *Insiders' Guide to Greater Tampa Bay Area*.

acknowledgments

This book is not my work alone.

Yes, I did the digging and the exploring and the final piecing together. But all I did was to write about what was already there—about what other people have created.

So cheers to every visionary who said, "Let's build a ___" and then turned swamps into beautiful gardens and massive theme parks, blank building walls into canvases for detailed murals, and old railroad depots into community centers and museums. Cheers also to every visionary who said, "Enough building! Let's preserve this piece of land as it is," and left us natural playgrounds in which to hike and paddle and be. Thank you for giving me plenty of material about which to write.

Cheers also to all the community hosts who have welcomed me into their visitor centers and chamber offices, whose enthusiasm for their town or city has been palpable during telephone calls, and who have created attractive and informative printed materials and websites about the good things going on in their neck of the woods.

More particularly, cheers to Amy Lyons, who has overseen this project, and to the many people at Globe Pequot Press who transformed my raw material into a proud-to-hand-it-to-people book; to Kathy Plank for helping me to stay organized and accurate; to my family and friends who have understood my absences; to my son, Daniel, for helping me pull the maps together; to my husband, Lee, who loves exploring back roads and byways as much as I do—and who keeps me well fed when I'm in writing mode; and to the Source of all vision, creativity, enthusiasm, and ability.

This book reflects your work as much as it does mine.

introduction

Write a book about day trips from the Tampa Bay area?

Love, love, love to! In the 30-plus years we've lived here, we've spent countless weekends exploring the Central Florida area. We love learning about how other people live and seeing what they have created with imagination and hard work.

So outlining 25 trips was easy. Going back and retracing steps in some cases, and discovering loads of new places, was a fun reminder that we need to do this more often.

Some things haven't changed—Lu, the hippopotamus our children fed 30 years ago, still lives just a few miles north of us in Homosassa Springs Wildlife State Park. Today, other children marvel at this four-footed former movie star playing in a Florida river. Some things have changed. Cypress Gardens has been absorbed into LEGOLAND near Winter Haven; Shrek has moved in next door to Mickey.

The hard part was deciding what to leave out. There is much, much more that could have been included—but then this guidebook might have required a forklift to load into your car! Use this book as a starting point, and see what else you can discover at each of these destinations.

In the meantime, consider that you can drive no more than three hours in any direction from Tampa to discover natural wonders, real live mermaids, real live manatees, mega theme parks, ancient ruins, an Elvis-was-here spot, underwater treasures, Florida birds and other wildlife, medieval jousting, an international raceway, award-winning beaches, water sports and fishing spots, and loads of historical and artsy places to go and entertaining things to do. From sand-between-your-toes play in the real world to out-of-this-universe play in imaginary worlds, the mid-section of Florida surrounding Tampa offers something for everyone. Getting to each of these sites can be half the fun; so, for those who enjoy meandering, we've added some stops along the way.

North: To the northwest of Tampa lies a string of Florida state parks and preserves with thousands of acres offering hiking, biking, kayaking, canoeing, and birding opportunities. Less strenuous adventures take travelers from a fantasy world where mermaids play, to an inside-the-fishbowl perspective on Florida's natural resources, to a back-in-time look at the first peoples in this area. Directly north, you'll find skydiving and swamp-festing, early 19th-century history sites, and a glass-bottom boat paradise; to the northeast, art and antiquing adventures abound.

East: How many people in the world live next door to Cinderella's Castle, Hogwarts School of Witchcraft and Wizardry, or the Lost City of Atlantis? We do! So it only makes sense that we include these destinations on the list of day trips from Tampa, yes? But that is not all that lies east by northeast from Tampa. In this section, we'll explore the biggies, and we'll also visit International Drive, with its smaller theme parks, themed dinner theater productions, upscale shopping and restaurants, top-name entertainment—and Orlando itself, with its art galleries, lovely gardens, and more.

South: Southwest Florida was the winter home to some of the most innovative thinkers of the late 18th and early 19th centuries and to one of the biggest circuses of the day, and their legacies live on. To Tampa's south you'll find vast nature preserves, an international raceway, a muscle car mecca, the "granddaddy of 'em all" rodeo, castles, art galleries galore, and a circus that's always in town!

West: Cross Tampa Bay by any of the four bridges spanning it and you'll find a plethora of places to go and things to do—world-class white sand beaches to sun on, waterfront parks to play in, museums and one-of-a-kind art galleries to visit, palatial hotels, and one of the world's largest Greek communities outside of Greece to explore. Nor do you have to stop at land's end—you'll find information in this section about the famed Florida Middlegrounds fishing hot spot. We'll end up back in Tampa, with one chapter devoted to a day trip starting from St. Petersburg and visiting our neighbor across the bay.

So let's pack up the sunscreen, hats, walking shoes, insect repellant, jacket-just-in-case, camera, this guidebook, and—oh, yes—sense of humor and spirit of adventure. Ready? Let's go!

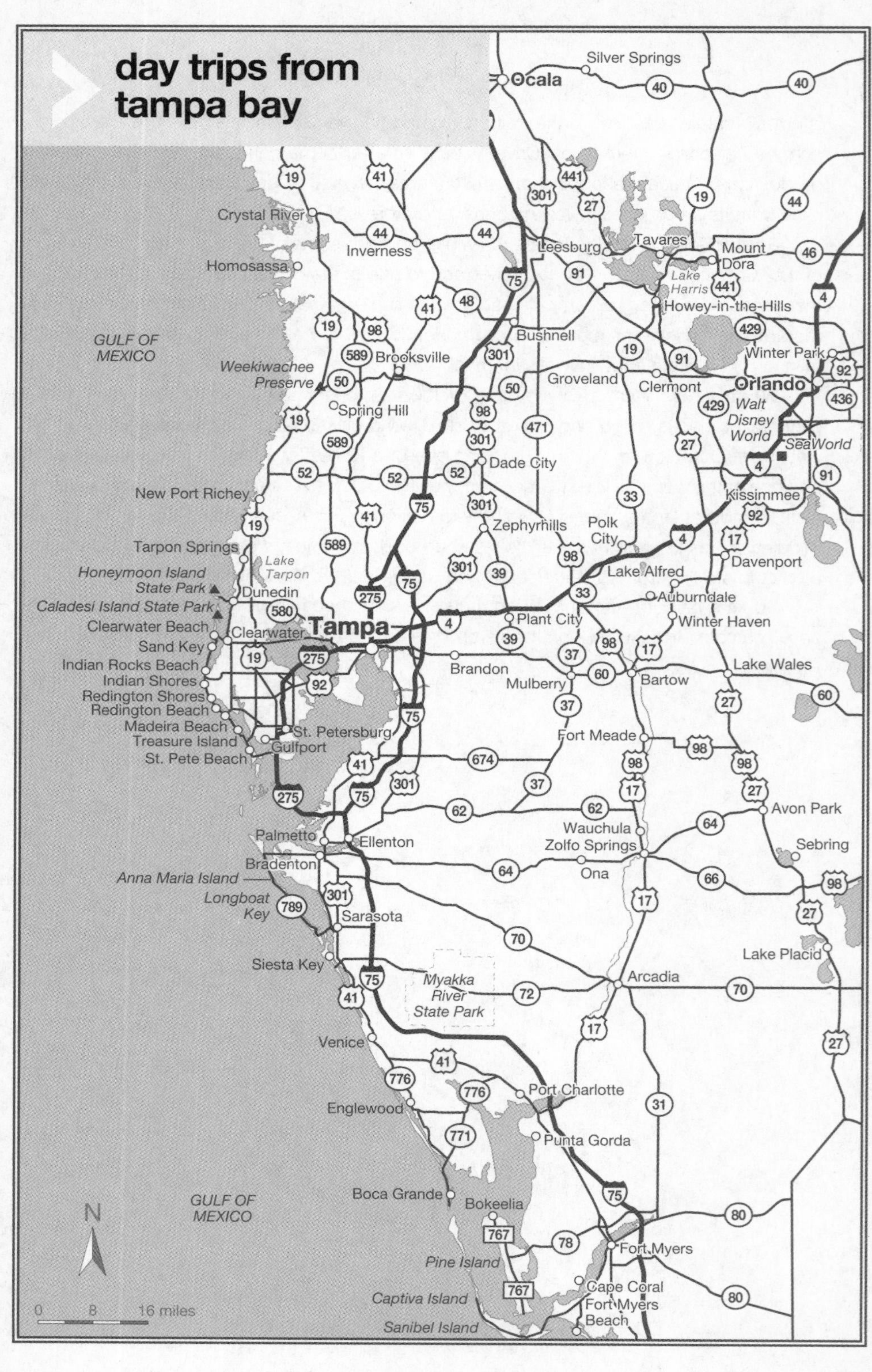

day trips from tampa bay
Ocala
Silver Springs
GULF OF MEXICO
Crystal River
Inverness
Homosassa
Leesburg
Tavares
Mount Dora
Lake Harris
Howey-in-the-Hills
Bushnell
Brooksville
Weekiwachee Preserve
Spring Hill
Groveland
Clermont
Winter Park
Orlando
Walt Disney World
SeaWorld
Dade City
New Port Richey
Kissimmee
Zephyrhills
Polk City
Tarpon Springs
Lake Tarpon
Honeymoon Island State Park
Caladesi Island State Park
Dunedin
Davenport
Lake Alfred
Auburndale
Winter Haven
Clearwater Beach
Clearwater
Tampa
Plant City
Sand Key
Indian Rocks Beach
Indian Shores
Redington Shores
Redington Beach
Madeira Beach
Treasure Island
St. Pete Beach
St. Petersburg
Gulfport
Brandon
Mulberry
Bartow
Lake Wales
Fort Meade
Avon Park
Wauchula
Zolfo Springs
Palmetto
Ellenton
Bradenton
Anna Maria Island
Longboat Key
Sarasota
Ona
Sebring
Siesta Key
Myakka River State Park
Arcadia
Lake Placid
Venice
Englewood
Port Charlotte
Punta Gorda
Boca Grande
Bokeelia
GULF OF MEXICO
Pine Island
Fort Myers
Cape Coral
Fort Myers Beach
Captiva Island
Sanibel Island
N
0 8 16 miles

using this guide

Day Trips from Tampa Bay takes travelers full circle, starting to the northwest and circling clockwise: northwest, north, northeast, east by northeast, east, southeast, south, and west. Each day trip is no more than three hours away, in normal traffic, from downtown Tampa. While there are hundreds of places we could have listed, these represent a variety of destinations selected to appeal to a variety of travelers. Most sections list ideas for other adventures, too. Some places have actual visitor centers; others have virtual visitor centers accessible online. Either way, be sure to phone ahead during the week and plan accordingly.

And, while the title of this book is *Day Trips from Tampa Bay,* the two sides of the bay have very different histories and personalities. People from Tampa come daytripping to St. Petersburg and vice versa, so the last section includes trips within each city.

hours & prices

Because hours of operation and attraction prices change according to season, these are listed only in general terms. As most attractions charge an admission fee, this book only notes if something is free. Remember to call ahead to get the most up-to-date information and to ask questions about specifics.

pricing key

The price codes for accommodations and restaurants are represented as a scale of one to three dollar signs ($). You can assume all establishments accept major credit cards unless otherwise noted. Again, contact the locations directly to confirm the most current prices.

accommodations

The price code reflects the average cost of a double-occupancy room during the peak price period (not including tax or extras). Please also note that during peak season in some areas, a two-night stay (or more) is required. Always check online or call to find out if any special discounts are available.

$	Less than $100
$$	$100 to $175
$$$	More than $175

Note: Most destinations are serviced by chain hotels and restaurants. These generally are not included in the listings for each chapter, as chain hotels and restaurants tend to be uniform across the country. We have listed chain hotels and restaurants only if local alternatives are not available or if the local franchise is unique in some way. The lodgings and restaurants highlighted are typically local to the area. In smaller communities, this may mean limited numbers of rooms available and older establishments. Call ahead to be sure your needs will be met.

Superior Small Lodging (superiorsmalllodging.com) lists smaller inns, vacation rental homes, and bed-and-breakfasts throughout Florida.

restaurants

The price code reflects the average price of dinner entrees for two people (excluding beverages, appetizers, desserts, tax, and tip). You should usually expect to pay less for lunch and/or breakfast entrees, when applicable.

$ Less than $20
$$ $20 to $40
$$$ More than $40

driving tips

The City of Tampa stretches from one end of Hillsborough County to the other. Directions in this book are written starting from downtown Tampa, but driving times could vary by as much as 45 minutes, depending on where in Tampa you start your trip.

- Plan your route before you head out. GPS devices are nice, but sometimes they get confused by similar-sounding names and outdated information.
- Go to fl511.com to get information about possible traffic problems and travel times anywhere in Florida. Click on the appropriate region, and also note the scrolling red notes regarding construction, delays due to sporting events, etc.
- You can also dial 5-1-1 for real-time traffic info. Just don't try to do this while you are actually driving, please!
- Florida has a few toll roads. Be sure you have cash on hand or have purchased a Florida Sun Pass (sunpass.com) or other local pass.
- Beach areas often are accessible by crossing drawbridges, which open to let sailboats pass through. Allow extra time for trips taking you over drawbridges.
- Florida law requires bicyclists and horseback riders under age 16 to wear a helmet.

highway designations

Most highway designations are standard: Interstates are I- followed by a number; state roads are SR followed by a number; county roads are CR followed by a number. US and a number designates the pre-interstate federal highway system. Even numbers run east-west; odd numbers run north-south.

In a few places, it can get tricky. US 19, for instance, splits as it descends into Pinellas County. The result is two different roads labeled US 19A, as well as US 19 itself. US 19 also acquires various names as it passes through different counties. In these cases, we will use the names in addition to the number. In some areas, what used to be a state road has been or is in the process of being turned over to the county. Usually, the road numbers have remained the same, but some older maps and map programs may show SR while signs may read CR.

travel tips

general hours of operation

Hours for restaurants, shops, and attractions are given in general terms. Holidays and seasonal changes may mean extended or shortened hours or days. Smaller businesses may list hours, but may need to be flexible in keeping them. It is always best to call ahead before you go.

seasonal issues

More and more, Florida is becoming a year-round tourist destination, so some places may vary prices by seasons where other places do not. September–October and April–May are usually off-peak months. Many theme parks offer Florida residents discounts on annual passes—some even offer residents of neighboring states special discounts. Check visit florida.com/resident for resident and non-resident specials, and ask each establishment what specials are available at any given time.

Florida's sunshine sometimes comes in the liquid variety. Plan ahead by packing sunscreen and an umbrella! Winter in Florida can mean a frosty morning or two. I've had to scrape frost off my windshield, but I have never needed a snow shovel or tire chains.

sales tax

Florida's state sales tax rate is 6 percent. However many counties have added anywhere from 0.5 to 1.5 percent to the state rate, so the sales tax charged may vary from county to county. Additionally, Florida allows counties to charge up to an additional 6 percent tourist development tax on hotel and motel rates.

where to get more information

Day Trips from Tampa Bay covers a variety of destinations, but there is no way it can cover them all. Most counties have local tourism bureaus, which offer a wealth of information online, by mail, or in person. Historical societies, libraries, and chambers of commerce are other good sources for more particular information. I've listed several main resources below, but check individual chapters for other, more specific contact information.

visitor centers

Many coastal counties have two or three distinct population corridors. One corridor runs along US 19 on the west side of the county. Another corridor runs along US 41 in the middle of the county, and a third runs along I-75 on the east side of the county. Some day trips don't try to cover both sides of the county in the same day, but we have listed the visitor center in both day trips. We have noted where up-front driving directions do not take you to the visitor center first. More and more, visitor centers are putting their larger presence online. In those cases, chamber of commerce offices sometimes function as visitor centers.

bicycling

BikeFlorida.net lists a number of trail rides throughout Florida and offers tips for riding various sections of the trails.

birding

Great Florida Birding and Wildlife Trail (GFBWT). floridabirdingtrail.com. This 2,000-mile self-guided highway trail, a project of the Florida Fish and Wildlife Conservation Commission, lists more than 500 spots to view Florida's birds and other wildlife in their natural habitats. This book notes some of the sites in each area we visit.

canoeing & kayaking

ClubKayak.com. clubkayak.com/cfkt/index.shtml. This website offers detailed information about kayak and canoe trails in Central Florida.

Florida Paddling Trails Association. floridapaddlingtrails.com. The FPTA's website lists more than 150 canoe and kayak outfitters (commercial guides, sales, and rentals), 61 paddling clubs, and 13 trail associations in Florida. Look also for interactive maps and information about the 1,600-mile Florida Circumnavigational Saltwater Paddling Trail—think the Appalachian Trail by sea. Some segments are along coastal counties visited in this guide.

fishing

For more information see **TampaBayCharter.com,** which lists charter captains, boat ramps, tide charts, and boat-accessible restaurants in the Tampa Bay area.

Coastal Conservation Association Florida. ccaflorida.org. The CCA is a fisheries advocacy organization. Scroll to the bottom of the home page. The last link on the left rail is "Fishing Guide Directory." It will take you to a map of Florida. Click on the county or area to bring up a list of guides and charter captains.

Florida Fish and Wildlife Conservation. (850) 488-4676; myfwc.com. In addition to must-know info about fishing licenses and regulations, you'll also find loads of information about youth conservation centers, Florida wildlife, invasive species, and more on the FFWC website. Two things to note: 1) Fish with a licensed guide or charter captain, and you may not need a personal fishing license. 2) Unless you are with a licensed guide, you need a saltwater fishing license to harvest scallops (myfwc.com/fishing/saltwater/regulations/bay-scallops).

Florida Guides Association. (321) 454-7285; florida-guides.com. FGA members are licensed and insured, put safety first, adhere to a code of ethics, and respect the environment. Look for the Fishing Guides Directory tab for a list of guides in various areas of the state.

golfing

Visit Florida/Golfing. (866) 972-5280; visitflorida.com/golfing. Call the toll-free number or visit the website for the State of Florida's official guide to more than 1,000 golf courses around the state. Look for special offers on this site, too.

history

Florida Division of Historical Resources. 500 S. Bronough St., Tallahassee; (800) 847-7278, (850) 245-6333; flheritage.com. From a listing of the Historic Landmark signs posted throughout Florida to information about underwater archaeology, the Florida Division of Historical Resources has a wealth of guides to enhance any day trip. In particular, look for their listing of Heritage Trails, which include Black, Cuban, Women's, Jewish, World War II, Native American, Civil War, and Florida Spanish Colonial Heritage Trails. Publications listing relevant sites are available for each trail. They also have an excellent Kids' Site.

Florida Public Archaeology Network. 207 E. Main St., Pensacola; (850) 595-0050; flpublicarchaeology.org. The Florida Public Archaeology Network offers a greater understanding of Florida's historical past, including underwater archaeological sites.

Trail of Florida's Indian Heritage. (877) 621-6805; trailoffloridasindianheritage.org. This project traces Florida's Indian heritage from pre-recorded history to modern times. A downloadable map features 54 sites around the state.

parks & recreation

Florida Department of Environmental Protection/Office of Greenways and Trails. (850) 245-2052; dep.state.fl.us/gwt/default.htm. The Office of Greenways and Trails manages the 110-mile Marjorie Harris Carr Cross Florida Geenway, which runs from the St. Johns River to the Gulf of Mexico, and other state greenways, blueways, and trails. Look for maps and other information on this website.

Florida Division of Recreation and Parks. (850) 245-2157; floridastateparks.org. Florida's state park system is not only one of the largest—160 parks, 700,000 acres, 100 miles of sandy beaches—it's also one of the best. Florida State Parks System is the only two-time recipient (1999 and 2005) of the National Gold Medal awarded by the American Academy for Park and Recreation Administration—and was a finalist again in 2011. More than 60—almost a third of those parks—lie within the area explored in this book. We will highlight several, but we can't list them all. Check their website for even more state park adventures. Florida state parks, with a few exceptions, are open 365 days a year from 8 a.m. to sunset. The hours may be different for visitor centers, museums, and historic sites, which also may be closed 2 days a week. Admission fees vary, as do the facilities and programs.

Florida Forest Service. 3125 Conner Blvd., Tallahassee; (850) 488-4274; fl-dof.com/forest_recreation/index.html. The Florida State Forest Service manages state forest lands, many of which have camping sites, horse and bike trails, boat ramps, and other services. Interested in geocaching? This site lists geocache sites on state forest lands.

Southwest Florida Water Management District (SWFWMD). (800) 836-0797 (Florida only); swfwmd.state.fl.us. Five water management districts in Florida manage the state's water supply, protect water quality and natural resources, and oversee flood protection plans. SWFWMD manages water issues for most of the counties through which we will pass and owns 360,000 acres of public conservation lands, many of them Florida Wildlife Management Areas. You'll find lots of information about camping, fishing, and hunting on these public lands on the SWFWMD website. The other two water management districts managing lands visited in this guide are the St. Johns River Water Management District (lands near Orlando: sjr.state.fl.us) and the South Florida Water Management District (lands near Fort Myers: sfwmd.gov).

US Fish & Wildlife Service. (800) 344-WILD (9453); fws.gov/refuges. The US Fish & Wildlife Service manages federal lands such as the national wildlife refuges and recreation areas noted in this guide.

northwest

day trip 01

up, up, and away:
new port richey; dade city; zephyrhills

Pasco County, Tampa's neighbor to the north, is one of Florida's Gulf Coast coastal counties with three distinct population corridors. I'm including it in the Northwest section because that's where we're heading first: to the coastal cities along the Gulf of Mexico. After that, we will loop through Pasco County via its two east-west state roads, SR 54 and SR 52. The loop makes a nice out-for-the-day kind of drive through some countryside; you can easily do the loop in a day with dabbling stops here and there. Or head to just one spot and stay the day—or even the weekend. Head to another spot next time and enjoy a different aspect of Pasco County.

This trip takes you first to New Port Richey, Pasco County's largest city, and to the Gulf of Mexico. Then we'll head east to historic Dade City for some antique shopping and history lessons before heading down to Zephyrhills then to Land O' Lakes. Oh, by the way—up, up, and away doesn't just mean hit the road. It literally also means up—as in ballooning and skydiving! Got your spirit of adventure with you? Good—let's get going!

new port richey

If things had turned out a little differently, New Port Richey might have been the East Coast movie capital. Back in the 1920s, movie stars like Gloria Swanson and Ed Wynn not only stayed here but bought property and built homes here. A swank movie theater was built, and Paramount Pictures considered opening a studio in town. The Great Depression undid

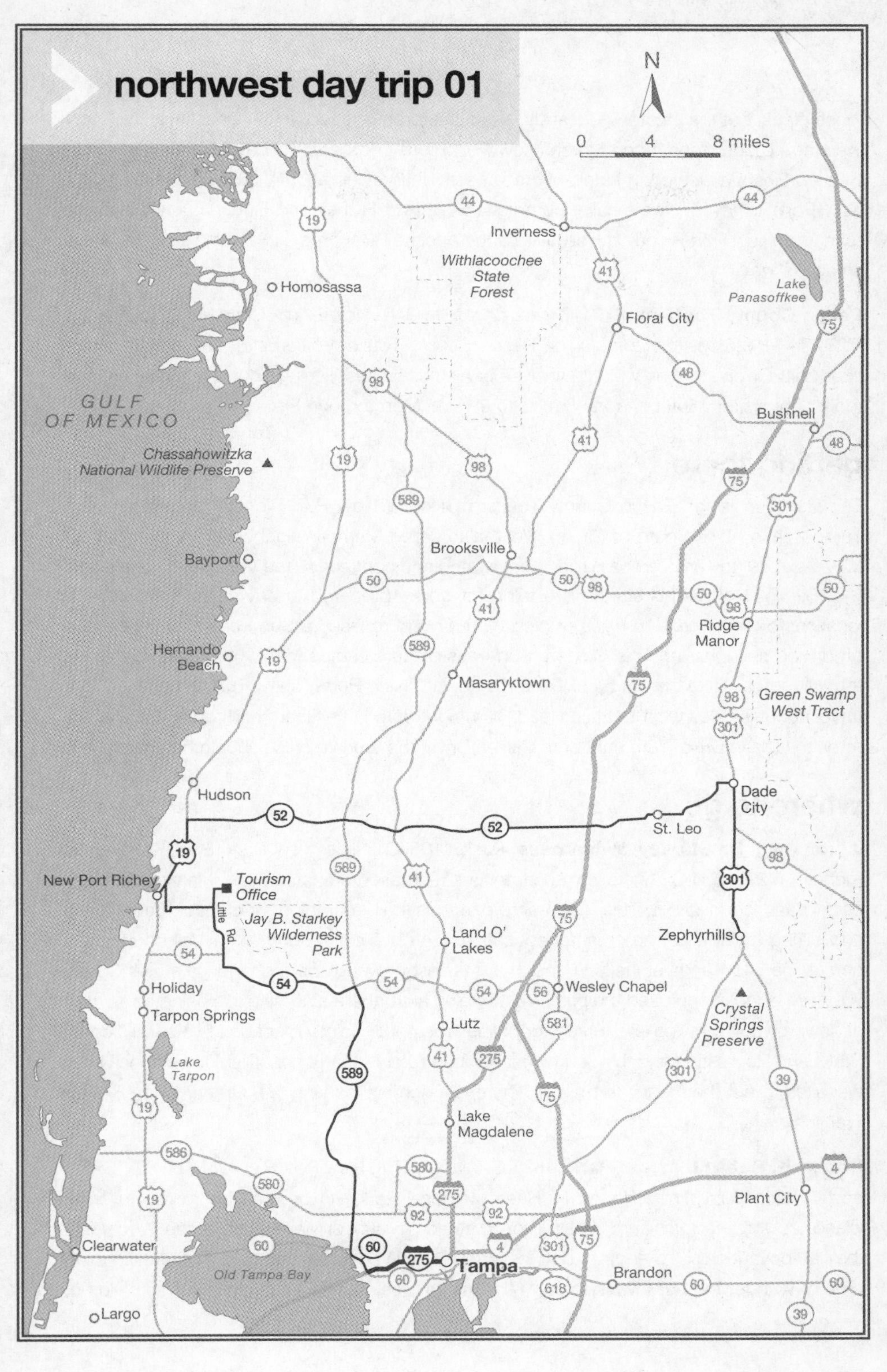
northwest day trip 01
N
0 4 8 miles
GULF OF MEXICO
Chassahowitzka National Wildlife Preserve
Homosassa
Inverness
Withlacoochee State Forest
Floral City
Lake Panasoffkee
Bushnell
Bayport
Brooksville
Hernando Beach
Masaryktown
Ridge Manor
Green Swamp West Tract
Hudson
Dade City
St. Leo
New Port Richey
Tourism Office
Little Rd.
Jay B. Starkey Wilderness Park
Land O' Lakes
Zephyrhills
Holiday
Tarpon Springs
Wesley Chapel
Lutz
Crystal Springs Preserve
Lake Tarpon
Lake Magdalene
Plant City
Clearwater
Old Tampa Bay
Tampa
Brandon
Largo

those plans, but the theater still stands. Newly restored, the Richey Suncoast Theater hosts live stage productions. Each March, New Port Richey hosts an 11-day festival, the Annual Chasco Fiesta, celebrating its history (see Festivals & Celebrations). Just up the road from New Port Richey are the smaller communities of Port Richey and Hudson; just down the road from New Port Richey is Holiday and the Anclote River area—this listing includes these areas, as well.

Pasco County Tourism. 8731 Citizen Dr., Suite 340, New Port Richey; (800) 842-1873, (727) 847-8129; visitpasco.net. The Pasco County Tourism office staff can help organize your visit. Or check their website for lists of historical sites, fishing spots, art galleries, and more. The visitor center is open 8 a.m. to 5 p.m., Mon through Fri.

getting there

Our first stop is the Pasco County Tourism Office in New Port Richey. From downtown Tampa, take I-275 South to SR 60 West (also called Memorial Highway). Merge onto SR 60 via exit 39 (toward Tampa Airport/Clearwater) and continue to the Veterans Expressway/ SR 589 Toll North. This stretch is a toll road, so be prepared to pay cash at a couple of locations over the next 16 miles—unless you have purchased a Sun Pass (see the section on driving tips in Using This Guide). Sun Pass holders can use the outer lanes to bypass the tollbooths. Take the SR 54 exit (exit 19) toward New Port Richey. Turn left onto SR 54, travel about 8 miles west to Little Road. Turn right onto Little Road, and follow it about 4.5 miles to Citizen Drive. Turn right onto Citizen Drive; the tourism office should be on your left.

where to go

J. (or Jay) B. Starkey Wilderness Park. 10500 Wilderness Park Blvd., New Port Richey; (727) 834-3247; swfwmd.state.fl.us/recreation/areas/starkeywilderness.html or portal.pascocountyfl.net. This 8,300-acre park has it all—camping, horseback trails, hiking and biking trails, an environmental education center, a playground, volleyball courts, and horseshoe pits—and yet it sits in one of the fastest growing spots on Florida's Gulf Coast. We have hiked in and used the primitive camping area; there's nothing like being awakened at dawn by cows lowing and turkeys gobbling. The park is jointly managed by Pasco County Parks and Recreation and the Southwest Florida Water Management District, so check both websites to get the most information. There is a nominal parking fee. Great Florida Birding Trail #73.

Robert K. Rees Memorial Park. 4835 Green Key Rd., New Port Richey; (727) 834-3252; portal.pascocountyfl.net. Robert K. Rees Memorial Park sits on the Gulf side of a small island just off the mainland, making for spectacular sunset views. But before you toast the flamboyant finish to another day, enjoy the sandy beaches and designated swimming area or wander the boardwalk through the mangroves. There is a playground for children, a shower, restrooms, picnic tables and grills, and a small rock-based canoe/kayak launch. There is a nominal parking fee. Great Florida Birding Trail #72.

West Pasco Historical Society Museum, Inc. and Library. 6431 Circle Blvd., New Port Richey; (727) 847-0680; westpascohistoricalsociety.org. The building dates back a hundred years; many of the artifacts date back even further. Local history buffs will find displays to browse, including a typical 1900s Pioneer Parlor, and a small gift shop. Open Fri and Sat from 1 to 4 p.m. (closed June and July) and Tues from 10 a.m. to 1 p.m. (year round).

what to do

fishing

Pasco County has loads of lakes, rivers, and other waterways, and saltwater areas open for fishing. Most Pasco County parks and state and national preserves allow some sort of fishing. See the fishing section in Using This Guide for information about licenses, and hiring charter captains and guides.

scuba diving & snorkeling

Scuba West. 6815 Tower Dr., Hudson; (727) 863-6911; scubawest.net. Florida's Gulf Coast boasts loads of places to scuba dive and snorkel. From deep springs that form the headwaters of rivers to off-shore artificial reefs teeming with aquatic life, many of the must-see places in Florida are underwater. Scuba West offers equipment, instruction, training, and diving adventures. Call them or stop in to ask about local places to dive.

theater

Richey Suncoast Theatre. 6237 Grand Blvd., New Port Richey; (727) 842-6777; richeysuncoasttheatre.com. The first film shown at this theater, built in 1926, was a silent movie about the Florida land rush of the early 1920s. Today, the building has been restored and hosts major community theater productions of Broadway musicals, concerts, and other performances.

The Show Palace Dinner Theater. 16128 US 19 North, Hudson; (727) 863-7949; showpalace.net. This dinner theater destination spot has been around for decades, and it continues to produce Broadway musicals and revues and to host concerts and other performances.

where to shop

The Market Off Main. 6241 Lincoln St., New Port Richey; (727) 849-4940; marketoffmain.com. Part produce stand, part cafe, the Market Off Main sits on the Cotee River—they also rent kayaks—and sells free-range eggs, raw honey, spices, herbs, and other goodies in addition to fresh produce (organically grown, when available). The cafe part offers light lunches (until they are gone), ice cream, coffee, and desserts. Open 9 a.m. to 7 p.m. (6 p.m. on Sun).

where to eat

Caposey's Whole Works Restaurant. 5250 Green Key Rd., New Port Richey; (727) 842-4307; caposeys.com. Caposey's serves breakfast and lunch year round; during "snowbird season" they are open for dinner, too. Nothing fancy here—buttermilk pancakes, patty melts on rye, liver and onions, beef tips, fried chicken or shrimp—except maybe the Moo's (mousse) Cakes and other desserts. But the atmosphere is upbeat—cows are everywhere—and the food is good. Open 7 a.m. (8 a.m. on Sun) to 3 p.m. year round. Open until 8 p.m. Mon through Fri during the late fall to early spring. Pets are permitted in the outdoor covered dining area. $.

The German Restaurant. 2616 US 19 North, Holiday; (727) 937-7400; the-german-restaurant.com. From schnitzel prepared any number of ways to sauerbraten and goulasch, the German Restaurant, named one of Florida's top 400 restaurants by *Florida Trend* magazine, features authentic food meticulously prepared by Chef Uwe Kaspar. Imported German wines and beers—and some American choices, too—round out the menu. Check the website for music nights! Open for dinner only, except on Sun when they also are open for lunch. Closed Wed. $$–$$$.

Zen Forrest. 4148 Rowan Rd., New Port Richey; (727) 372-9545; zenforrest.com. With elegantly prepared entrees originating in China, Japan, Korea, Thailand, and Vietnam, Chef Victor Wang terms Zen Forrest a Pan Asian restaurant and a healthy one, too. Their fried rice, for instance, is made with both jasmine and red rice and lots of veggies and herbs, including ginseng; and they offer gluten-free, vegan, and vegetarian options. Watch their website for special event information—recently they offered a limited-attendance wine-and-food-pairing dinner. Zen Forrest serves lunch and dinner Tues through Sat; they are closed Sun and are open for dinner only on Mon. $$–$$$.

where to stay

Quality Inn Suites and Conference Center. 5316 US 19 North, New Port Richey; (727) 847-9005; qualityinn.com/hotel-new_port_richey-florida. Located on US 19 North near the area's largest mall, the Quality Inn Suites and Conference Center offers a guest laundry area, an outdoor pool with a hot tub, and an on-site restaurant serving breakfast, lunch, and dinner. $–$$.

dade city

Dade City and neighboring San Antonio and St. Leo sit among the rolling hills of eastern Pasco County. At various points in its history, Dade City's commerce has been based on lumber, turpentine, cigars, and, today, citrus—especially kumquats! Each January, the city hosts the Kumquat Festival when the ovoid orange fruits are jellied, candied, crushed and baked into cookies, pies, breads, and more. Dade City is also known as one of the state's best antiquing spots and holds a monthly Classic Car Show. And on the first Thursday of each month there's music in the streets from 6 to 8 p.m.

Dade City Chamber of Commerce. 14112 8th St., Dade City; (352) 567-3769; dadecitychamber.org or visitdadecity.com. Both websites list places to eat, accommodations, and attractions. They are open Mon through Fri from 8 a.m. to 5 p.m., and they have brochures and other information available.

getting there

From New Port Richey, travel north on US 19 North to SR 52 (also CR 52). Turn right onto SR 52 and travel east about 27 miles. Just past St. Leo (you can't miss St. Leo's Abbey), at Happy Hill Road, SR 52 takes a couple of jogs northeast and east and becomes 21st Street. Follow 21st Street to Meridian Avenue, turn right, and you should be in downtown Dade City.

where to go

Dade City's Wild Things. 37245 Meridian Ave., Dade City; (352) 567-9453; dadecityswildthings.com. What happens when exotic animals' owners can't care for them any more? Or when native wild animals are orphaned or injured? Often, Stearn's Zoological Rescue and Rehab (stearnszoological.org) steps in. While many animals can be released back into the wild, others cannot. Dade City's Wild Things, a sanctuary zoo, offers an up-close look at exotic and native animals that have found a permanent home here in Pasco County. Open Tues through Sat from 9 a.m. to 5 p.m. Food concessions are available. Reservations are recommended.

Giraffe Ranch. 38650 Mickler Rd., Dade City; (813) 482-3400; girafferanch.com. Would you love to travel the world to see exotic animals, but can't quite come up with the time or money? Giraffe Ranch, a wildlife preserve and game farm, is home to Austrian Haflinger horses, Irish Dexter cattle, giraffes, camels, and more. Take a 4WD safari tour or ride atop a camel. By reservation only.

Pioneer Florida Museum and Village. 15602 Pioneer Museum Rd., Dade City; (352) 567-0262; pioneerfloridamuseum.org. Several area buildings, including a train depot, a schoolhouse, a shoe repair shop, and others, have been relocated to the Pioneer Florida

Museum and Village Grounds. Learn how Florida's early residents lived—check the calendar for cane syrup demonstrations, tractor pulls, quilt shows, and more. Open Mon through Sat 10 a.m. to 5 p.m.

what to do

Green Swamp West Tract. 13347 Ranch Rd., Dade City; (800) 423-1476, (352) 796-7211; swfwmd.state.fl.us/recreation/areas/greenswamp-west.html. This 37,350-acre tract of wilderness preserve includes 46 miles of hiking and biking trails, 60 miles of service roads open to equestrian use, a small boat ramp into the Withlacoochee River, campsites, and picnic facilities. Some of the trails are part of the Florida National Scenic Trail. During hunting season, all or part of the tract may be closed. Great Florida Birding Trail #64.

where to shop

Downtown Dade City Shopping District. visitdadecity.com/shopping.html. The website lists 43 different boutique and specialty shops ranging from antiques to quilting items to a feed store (as in for farm animals). Public restrooms are available. Allow plenty of time for strolling.

where to eat

Kafe Kokopelli. 37940 Live Oak Ave., Dade City; (352) 523-0055; kafekokopelli.com. Kafe Kokopelli is housed in what once was a Model T showroom and repair center—but you'd never know it from the vine-covered exterior and the unique, eclectic decor on the interior. The food is like that, too—stalwart favorites like prime rib, shrimp, and chicken but creatively cooked and combined with eclectic herbs and sauces. They are open Tues through Thurs from 11 a.m. to 9 p.m. and from 11 a.m. to 10 p.m. on Fri and Sat. $$–$$$.

Lunch on Limoges. 14139 S. 7th St., Dade City; (352) 567-5685; lunchonlimoges.com. Technically, it's Williams Lunch on Limoges, but most people refer to it as Lunch on Limoges. Yes, as in Limoges china. Served on tables in what used to be the men's department of what still is Williams Fashion Store, owned by a member of the Williams family since 1908. And they're only open 11:30 a.m. to 2:00 p.m. (last reservation at 1:30; closed Sun and Mon, May through Oct). But don't plan on just popping in. You'll need to make reservations to ensure a spot. $$.

Pancho's Villa Mexican Restaurant. 32804 Pennsylvania Ave., San Antonio; (352) 588-3037; dexknows.com/business_profiles/pancho_s_villa_mexican_restaurant-b69236. A not-very-big restaurant in a not-very-big town with a very big following! *Chile rellenos* (stuffed chiles) battered and fried, *chile verde con nopales* (green chiles with prickly pear) simmered and served—you get the idea. Open every day from 11 a.m. to 9 p.m. (10 p.m. on Sat). $–$$.

Pearl in the Grove. 31936 St. Joe Rd., Dade City; (352) 588-0008; pearlinthegrove.com. An intriguing name, an intriguing menu—and a Golden Spoon nod from *Florida Trend* as one of Florida's best new restaurants. "Homemade slow food" is what they call it; think Southern/Soul/Cajun/French/American. But they're kid-friendly, too; if peanut butter is what your child wants, they'll serve up a PB&J. Open Wed and Thurs 5 to 8 p.m., Fri and Sat 5 to 10 p.m., and Sun noon to 3 p.m. $$–$$$.

where to stay

Hampton Inn Dade City–Zephyrhills. 13215 US 301, Dade City; (352) 567-5277; hamptoninn.hilton.com. This just-built Hampton offers a complimentary hot breakfast, swimming pool, business center, free high-speed Internet access, and more. No pets. $–$$.

Lake Jovita Golf and Country Club. 12900 Lake Jovita Blvd., Dade City; (877) 481-2652, (352) 588-9200; lakejovitagolfcc.com. Rent a villa at the Lake Jovita Golf and Country Club and become a Stay-and-Play Guest with membership privileges during your visit. Lake Jovita has 2 top-rated courses, a tennis center, fitness center, and swim area. The Clubhouse serves lunch and Sunday brunch (open to the public) and dinner (members only). $$$.

Travelers Rest Resort and RV Park. 29129 Johnston Rd., Dade City; (800) 565-8114, (352) 588-2013; travelersrestresort.com. Just in case you can't find enough things to do in Dade City, the Travelers Rest Resort and RV Park has a USGA 9-hole golf course, tennis courts, bocce ball courts, horseshoe pits, and 6 lakes to fish in. Pet friendly. $.

zephyrhills

Directly south of Dade City, on US 301, lies one of the world's largest drop zones. No, the residents aren't incredibly clumsy—Zephyrhills is home to Skydive City, where people jump out of perfectly good airplanes and float down to earth under clouds of billowing silk. Zephyrhills is also home to the bottled water company of the same name. To the west of Zephyrhills, Wesley Chapel has become synonymous with Saddlebrook Resort; further west, and bringing us full circle, is Land O' Lakes, home to—among other things—a number of clothing-optional resorts.

Zephyrhills Chamber of Commerce. 38550 5th Ave., Zephyrhills; (813) 782-1913; zephyrhillschamber.org. Look for the Chamber of Commerce Welcome Center in Clock Plaza. You'll find area info here, and a shady spot or two from which to watch life go by. During the fall and winter, the Welcome Center is open Mon through Fri from 9 a.m. to 4 p.m.

getting there

From Dade City, drive south on US 301 South (also US 98 South and Gall Boulevard) about 10 miles. To get to the Chamber of Commerce Welcome Center, turn left on 5th Avenue. That's it! You're there!

where to go

Crystal Springs Preserve. 1609 Crystal Springs Rd., Crystal Springs; (813) 715-9707; crystalspringspreserve.com. Founded by Nestle Waters North America, bottling Zephyrhills-brand water, Crystal Springs Preserve is a living laboratory where groups come to learn about "Florida's most precious resource: water" and about the environment that supports the preservation of water. The site includes an education center, butterfly gardens, spring-fed pond, river boardwalks, trails, and more. The preserve caters to area schools and other educational groups, but also hosts Florida Master Naturalist courses. Gather 14 other nature lovers or call to find out if there is a group you can join for the day.

Florida Estates Winery. 25241 SR 52, Land O' Lakes; (813) 996-2113; floridaestates wines.com. Stop in for a sample of locally made wines and browse the gift shop. Every other Saturday, Florida Estates Winery hosts a Wine Festival and Market with crafts, homemade goodies, live music, and more. Check the website for upcoming wine festivals, classes, and other special events. Picnickers welcome. Open 11 a.m. to 5 p.m. daily.

what to do

Ballooning. blastvalve.com/Balloon_Rides/USA/Florida_Balloon_Rides. Skydiving a bit too adventuresome? Floating above the Tampa Bay area in a hot air balloon is a tranquil way to experience a loftier perspective on the world. Blastvalve.com lists several companies offering balloon rides across Florida, including several in the Tampa Bay area. Most flights start in northern Hillsborough County and end in east Pasco County or thereabouts.

Skydive City. 4241 Sky Dive Ln., Zephyrhills; (800) 888-JUMP (5867), (813) 783-9399; skydivecity.com. Go tandem with an experienced jumper, try a wingsuit—think flying squirrel—or practice swooping at Skydive City. It's all good. In addition to an on-site cafe, bar, laundry, and shower facilities, they offer camping (RV hookups and tent camping) and trailer rental on their 14-acre property.

where to eat

Cafe Fresco & Bakery. 27209 SR 56, Wesley Chapel; (813) 333-1200; cafefrescobakery .com. Serving breakfast, lunch, and Sunday brunch, Cafe Fresco serves soups, salads, burgers, wraps, and 6 (!) kinds of fries. The bakery side keeps the sweet tooth satisfied with homemade pies, cupcakes, tarts, and other goodies. Open Mon through Sat 8 a.m. to 2 p.m. and Sun 9 a.m. to 2 p.m. $–$$.

Flaco's Cafe. 5347 Gall Blvd., Zephyrhills; (813) 788-3585; flacoscafe.com. Authentic Cuban cuisine begins with café con leche and Flaco's Spanish omelette in the morning and ends with *arroz con pollo* (yellow rice with chicken) in the evening. Or maybe a chorizo and egg breakfast sandwich on Cuban toast in the morning and *ropa vieja* (shredded beef) in the evening. Check the website for daily specials and coupons. Open every day at 7 a.m. Sun to Tues, close at 3 p.m.; Wed to Thurs, close at 8 p.m.; Fri to Sat close at 10 p.m. $–$$.

where to stay

Saddlebrook Resort. 5700 Saddlebrook Way, Wesley Chapel; (800) 729-8383, (813) 973-1111; saddlebrook.com. With two 18-hole Arnold Palmer signature golf courses, 45 tennis courts, an elite athlete training facility, a 5-acre ropes course, bike rentals, fishing spots, and walking and jogging trails, there is every enjoyable reason to keep fit and trim. Afterwards, reward yourself with a visit to the European-style spa, relax in one of the 3 swimming pools, and dine in one of several on-site restaurants and bars. Children have their own activities in the S'Kids Club. $$$.

Clothing-optional resorts. Several clothing-optional resorts are located near Land O' Lakes. The two listed here are among the largest and/or oldest in the United States.

Caliente Club and Resorts—Tampa. 21240 Gran Via Blvd., Land O' Lakes; (813) 996-3700; calienteresorts.com/tampa/destination.html. Hotel rooms, casitas, condos, and villas surround 3 small lakes. The resort area features a white sand beach, swimming pool, tennis courts, children's playground, and more. Dine at the Caribe Grill and Bar or at the Calypso Cantina. The full-service Spa Sereno is also open to the public. $$–$$$.

Lake Como Naturally. 20500 Cot Rd., Lutz; (877) 879-5253, (813) 949-1810; lakecomo naturally.com. Lake Como has been a resident-owned, family nudist community since the 1940s. Guests can rent a travel trailer or motel room, pitch a tent, or bring their RV. There's a pool, tennis courts, and a clubhouse, with activities ranging from darts and billiards to bridge and yoga. Dining options include the Bare Buns Cafe and Butt Hutt Bar. $.

day trip 02

where mermaids play:
spring hill

spring hill

Spring Hill, a quiet, unincorporated community on Florida's Nature Coast, is home to one of Florida's oldest tourist attractions, the mermaid shows at Weeki Wachee Springs. For more than 60 years, highly trained women and a few men have performed in one of Florida's largest first-magnitude springs for audiences who come from around the world. Next door, Buccaneer Bay, Florida's only spring-fed waterpark, lets visitors swim in the springs, play on waterslides, or drift lazily in a tube. The immediate area, which includes Hernando Beach and Bayport, also offers scuba diving, snorkeling, canoeing and kayaking, scalloping, fishing, golfing, and a chance to step into the Florida wilds.

Hernando County Tourism Information Center. 31085 Cortez Blvd., Brooksville; (800) 601-4580, (352) 754-4405; naturallyhernando.org. The Hernando County Tourism Information Center's website contains a 4-page restaurant guide with a good map, a list of hotel/motel accommodations, bike trail maps, and lists of golf courses, antiques shops, and other places to go and things to do in Hernando County. To reach the Tourism Information Center, follow the directions for Weeki Wachee Springs State Park, but turn right, instead of left, onto Cortez Boulevard. Follow Cortez Boulevard several miles, pass under I-75, and look for the center on your right. The Tourism Information Center also mans a Welcome Center kiosk at Weeki Wachee Springs State Park.

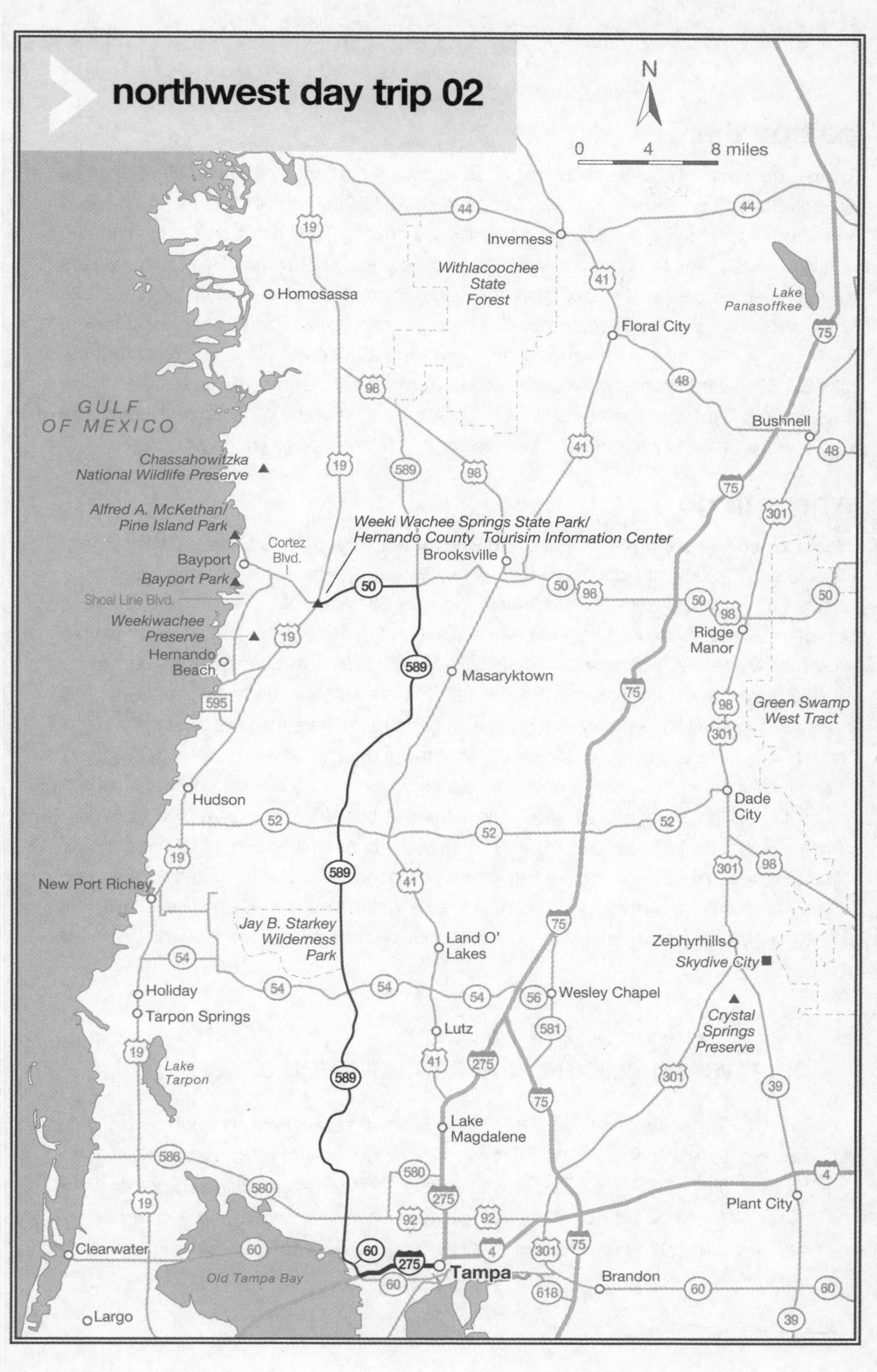
northwest day trip 02
N
0
4
8 miles
GULF OF MEXICO
Inverness
Withlacoochee State Forest
Homosassa
Lake Panasoffkee
Floral City
Bushnell
Chassahowitzka National Wildlife Preserve
Alfred A. McKethan/ Pine Island Park
Weeki Wachee Springs State Park/ Hernando County Tourisim Information Center
Cortez Blvd.
Bayport
Brooksville
Bayport Park
Shoal Line Blvd.
Weekiwachee Preserve
Ridge Manor
Hernando Beach
Masaryktown
Green Swamp West Tract
Hudson
Dade City
New Port Richey
Jay B. Starkey Wilderness Park
Land O' Lakes
Zephyrhills
Skydive City
Holiday
Wesley Chapel
Tarpon Springs
Crystal Springs Preserve
Lutz
Lake Tarpon
Lake Magdalene
Plant City
Clearwater
Tampa
Old Tampa Bay
Brandon
Largo

getting there

There is no official city center in Spring Hill, so the directions here take you to Weeki Wachee Springs State Park. From downtown Tampa, take I-275 South to SR 60 West (also called Memorial Highway). Merge onto SR 60 via exit 39 (toward Tampa Airport/Clearwater) and continue to SR 589 Toll North; this becomes the Suncoast Parkway. Both stretches are toll roads, so be prepared to pay cash at several locations over the next 40 miles—unless you have purchased a Sun Pass (see the driving tips in Using This Guide). If you have a Sun Pass, you can use the outer lanes to bypass the toll booths. When you reach exit 46, take SR 50 toward Brooksville/Weeki Wachee. Turn left onto Cortez Boulevard, and follow it west about 6 miles until it intersects with US 19. Turn left onto US 19 South/Commercial Way and follow the signs to Weeki Wachee Springs State Park, to your right.

where to go

Weeki Wachee Springs State Park and Buccaneer Bay. 6131 Commercial Way, Spring Hill; (352) 596-2062; floridastateparks.org/weekiwachee/default.cfm or weekiwachi.com. Located at the intersection of US 19 North and SR 50, Weeki Wachee Springs has been part of the Florida State Parks system since 2008. But its history goes back more than half a century. Since 1947, mermaids have frolicked in the Weeki Wachee Springs, performing for visitors who come from around the world and sit in a 400-seat underground theater that looks into the springs. Typically, the mermaids perform 2 different shows, 3 times a day (1 show twice; 1 show once). To appreciate what these aquatic athletes do, try holding your breath for 2 minutes while diving down more than 90 feet. Or try eating underwater! Animal shows feature an up-close look at Florida wildlife. A short riverboat cruise on the Weeki Wachee River also is included in the admission price; boat cruises begin mid-morning and run throughout the day. Buccaneer Bay offers swimming in the springs, a tubing area, and a water play area for children ages 6 and under. A water slide area is open seasonally. No pets (except service animals). No food or drink may be brought into the show park—where

oh, give me a home where the dinosaurs roam?

Yes, that's a 110-foot-long and 48-foot-high brontosaurus cousin on the west side of US 19 just south of Weeki Wachee Springs State Park. The gray novelty building, built in 1964 as a Sinclair gas station, now houses an auto service center. Look for the smaller pink dinosaur statue, built in 1962, nearby. This critter can't decide if it's a brontosaurus or a stegosaurus, but seeing as how it's pink, it probably isn't either.

simple concessions are available—but picnic tables and a pavilion are available at Buccaneer Bay.

what to do

boating, canoeing & kayaking

Even beginner paddlers can navigate the quiet, shallow waters of the Weeki Wachee River or the small lakes in the Weekiwachee Preserve. More experienced paddlers and boaters will want to explore the estuarial waters rimming the Gulf of Mexico. Or hire a captain who really knows the area to take you out for the day. Tip: Hernando County's Park and Recreation Department's website (co.hernando.fl.us/parks_rec) has downloadable information about both freshwater and saltwater boat ramps, dive spots, and canoe trails. Of particular importance is the map of offshore navigational markers, rocks, and other obstructions.

Paddling Adventures. 6131 Commercial Way, Spring Hill; (352) 597-8484; paddlingadventures.com. Paddling Adventures runs the canoe and kayak concessions inside Weeki Wachee Springs State Park. They are located inside the park at the rear of the parking lot. Rent a canoe or kayak or launch your own at Weeki Wachee Springs State Park, then paddle your way down 7.5 miles of the Weeki Wachee River to Rogers Park. A shuttle service picks paddlers up and brings them back to the beginning.

Weeki Wachee Canoe & Kayak Rental. 8021 Darts St., Weeki Wachee; (352) 597-0360; floridacanoe.com. From US 19, continue west on SR 50, which then becomes CR 550 and follows the Weeki Wachee River a couple of miles. Look for the Weeki Wachee Canoe & Kayak Rental on your right. They suggest allowing 2.5 hours or more after being dropped off to paddle your way to the pickup point.

Weeki Wachee Marina. 7154 Shoal Line Blvd., Weeki Wachee; (352) 596-2852; weekiwacheemarina.com. Don't want to paddle the Weeki Wachee River? Rent a small boat instead! A family-owned business operating since 1975, Jim Lanier's Weeki Wachee Marina offers 14-foot to 16-foot skiffs with small outboard motors for up to 8 people. Idle your way to the Bayport Pier and back and fish along the way. They also rent canoes and kayaks and do boat motor repair.

beaches & parks

Alfred A. McKethan/Pine Island Park. 10840 Pine Island Dr., Spring Hill; (352) 754-4027; co.hernando.fl.us. Most people call this Pine Island Park. Drive out on a 2-lane road that looks like it's going nowhere. At the end you'll find palm trees and sea oats, sandy beach and swimming area, volleyball area, small playground, concession stand, picnic area, shower and rinse stations, and restrooms. There is a parking fee, and parking is limited, but that means the beach is never overcrowded. Great Florida Birding Trail #66. The park generally is open 8 a.m. to 8 p.m.

Linda Pedersen Park/Jenkins Creek. 6300 Shoal Line Blvd., Spring Hill; (352) 754-4027; hernandocounty.us. Pedersen Park is on the Weekiwachee Preserve, a 6,000-acre piece of wetland marshes and quarry lakes previously part of area mining operations. View the preserve from a 40-foot-high observation tower or hike, bike, or canoe your way around. There is a beach area, restrooms and showers, picnic tables, and other amenities. Great Florida Birding Trail #68. The park is open sunrise to sunset.

fishing

Fishing's good in western Hernando County. Tarpon cruise the waters off of Hernando Beach; redfish, snook, trout, and more await the avid angler. Bass and bluegill fill freshwater creels. See the fishing section in Using This Guide for information about charter captains and guides.

Bayport Park. 4140 Cortez Blvd., Spring Hill; (352) 754-4027; hernandocounty.us. Catch it and cook it? You can! Bayport Park sits right on the Gulf of Mexico and features a boardwalk and fishing pier, boat ramp, picnic tables, and grills. Great Florida Birding Trail #67. Open 24/7.

Hernando Beach Bait & Tackle. 4211 Shoal Line Blvd., Hernando Beach; (352) 596-3375; hernandobeachbaittackle.com. In addition to stocking a full line of live and frozen bait and assorted tackle, the Hernando Beach Bait & Tackle also repairs rods and reels. Check their website for a list of charter captains and party boats.

Jenkins Creek Park. 6401 Shoal Line Blvd., Spring Hill; (352) 754-4027; hernandocounty.us. This small park features a small fishing pier, small boat and canoe launch, picnic tables, and restrooms. It also connects to Linda Pedersen Park. Open 24/7.

golf

Silverthorn Country Club. 4550 Golf Club Ln., Spring Hill; (352) 799-4653; silverthornclub.net. Eighteen holes, par 72, 132 slope, 96 bunkers, the regulation-length course, designed by Joseph Lee and open to the public, has earned the respect of area golfers. A fully stocked pro shop and affiliated PGA professionals help golfers master the nuances of the game. Afterwards, there's a full-service clubhouse in which to relax and enjoy a meal.

hiking & biking

Weekiwachee Preserve. 2345 Osowaw Blvd., Spring Hill; (800) 423-1476 (Florida only) or (352) 796-7211; swfwmd.state.fl.us/recreation/areas/weekiwachee.html. Owned by the Southwest Florida Water Management District (SWFWMD), locally known as "Swiftmud," the Weekiwachee Preserve comprises just over 11,000 acres of marsh, swamp, sandhills, and a number of small lakes and ponds. Hikers and bikers can enter from Osowaw Boulevard or from Shoal Line Boulevard, both at the southern end of the preserve, and there are about 7 miles of both paved and unpaved trails. Cars are admitted only on the second and fourth Saturdays of the month at the Osowaw Boulevard entrance. Canoes, kayaks, and boats with electric trolling motors only are allowed, but all must be hand-launched. Great Florida Birding Trail #69. Open sunrise to sunset.

scalloping

From the Hernando County line north to the Florida panhandle, scallop beds line the coast. All you need is a saltwater fishing license (unless you are with a licensed guide), snorkeling gear and a mesh bag. June through September is generally open to scalloping, but be sure to check the local regulations. Many area fishing guides offer scalloping runs. See the fishing section in Using This Guide.

scuba diving & snorkeling

Bendickson Tank Reef. 18 miles off the Hernando County coastline. (352) 754-4027. Serious divers will want to explore this artificial reef created in 1995. Consisting of 10 Vietnam-era Army tanks, concrete rubble, and other matter, the reef has attracted soft coral, sponges, and a variety of fish. The reef is part of the Hernando County Parks and Recreation system.

Weeki Wachee Springs State Park. More than a dozen dive shops from around Florida are registered to bring snorkelers and divers into Weeki Wachee Springs State Park. Check the park's website for approved guides. Watch for blackout dates—the park is still used to film underwater television and movie scenes.

where to eat

Bayport Inn Restaurant and Lounge. 4835 Cortez Blvd., Bayport; (352) 596-1088; bayportinnrestaurant.com. From U-peel shrimp to fried gator tail and prime rib, the Bayport Inn Restaurant and Lounge is known for good food, friendly service, and a scenic view overlooking the river and surrounding area. They have a full-service bar and a children's menu, and motorcycle riders have reserved parking on Sunday. Open for lunch and dinner. $$–$$$.

Brian's Place. 3430 Shoal Line Blvd., Hernando Beach; (352) 597-5101; briansonthebeach.com. Chef Brian Alvarez welcomes you to his place, which features Spanish, Italian, and Fusion cuisine. Creative tapas—think Habanero Honey Duck Wings or Eggplant Milanese with Goat Cheese—ah! entrees, and yummy desserts. The homemade sangria and guava cheesecake are well on their way to becoming local legends. Open for lunch and dinner and, on the weekends, for breakfast. $$–$$$.

Nellie's Restaurant. 6234 Commercial Way, Weeki Wachee; (352) 596-8321. Located diagonally across from Weeki Wachee Springs State Park in the Weeki Wachee Village

Shopping Center, Nellie's Restaurant has been serving up Mermaids and Eggs (real french-bread french toast and eggs), Angus beef burgers, homemade meatloaf, humongous homemade cinnamon rolls, and more for the past 25 years. They also have a small gift shop with handmade and whimsical craft items. Breakfast (served all day), lunch, and dinner. $–$$.

R Beach Restaurant. 4054 Shoal Line Blvd., Hernando Beach; (352) 592-5556; rbeachrestaurant.com. Somebody had fun with this menu—check out the Chickity-Do-Da wings or nuggets appetizers, the Baba Louper Grouper (with red peppers and mango salsa), and the Great Caesar's Ghost Steak Salad, all accompanied by karaoke, live jazz, or dance music. Full service tiki bar, and open for dinner only, except on Sunday when they open in time for a late lunch. $$.

Trader Bay Seafood Company. 4006 Shoal Line Blvd., Hernando Beach; (352) 597-5170; traderbayseafood.com. Bring a cooler and check out Today's Catch at Trader Bay Seafood Company for red snapper, grunt, and other just-caught Gulf of Mexico delicacies. Plus there's always something in the smoker. Don't want to cook? Pick up a platter of steamed or fried shrimp, scallops, or oysters with fries and slaw. Take it home or eat out on their deck. Life is good. $.

bayport: a confederate lifeline

Established in 1852, at the end of the Second Seminole Indian War, Bayport once was a thriving commercial port, with an official US customs house and post office, on Florida's West Coast. The Bay-Port House, established in 1855, was advertised as a health resort, and, for one year, Bayport was the Hernando County seat. Residents in the eastern part of the county said it was too far away, so in 1856, the county seat was moved to what is now Brooksville.

During the Third Seminole Indian War (1855–1858), Bayport likely was a place of refuge for soldiers. In 1861, however, Florida became the third state to secede from the Union. Supplies shipped from Bayport, and other Florida west coast ports, helped keep the Confederacy fed and clothed. Union forces responded by blockading the coast. One boat, which tried to sail from Bayport but was captured in 1863, was carrying almost 27,000 pounds of cotton.

There were several land-sea battles in the area. Finally, Union forces so completely destroyed Bayport that it was never rebuilt. To read more about the history of Bayport, go to fivay.org/bayport.html.

Traditions Restaurant at Silverthorn Country Club. 4550 Golf Club Lane, Spring Hill; (352) 799-4653; silverthornclub.net/restaurant.php. Serving breakfast, lunch, dinner, a weekly Twilight Grill menu, and occasional special event buffets, Traditions Restaurant is open to the public. Dinner entrees range from prime rib to lobster to Tamil Nadú, an Indian-style chicken with vegetables and penne pasta entree, and a full-service bar provides accompanying libations. $$–$$$.

where to stay

Bayport Inn Restaurant and Lounge. 4835 Cortez Blvd., Bayport; (352) 596-1088; bay portinnrestaurant.com. Think rustic. The inn part of the Bayport Inn is exactly 2 rooms. No phone, no pool, no pets. No cable, either. Who needs that when you're getting away from it all? But each room has a coffee pot, microwave, and small refrigerator—and a riverfront view. $.

Best Western Nature Coast. 9373 Cortez Blvd., Weeki Wachee. (352) 596-9000; best western.com. Located diagonally across from Weeki Wachee Springs State Park, this motel is pet-friendly and offers a complimentary continental breakfast along with the usual cable TV, pool, exercise facility, and other amenities. Some rooms allow smoking. $.

Hernando Beach Motel and Condos. 4291 Shoal Line Blvd., Spring Hill; (352) 596-2527); hernandobeachmotelcondos.com. Rocking chairs on the veranda, boat slips out back, fully furnished efficiencies in between. Fran Baird and Dwayne Adams welcome you to the Nature Coast and to your choice of a motel room, for short stays, or a condo for longer sojourns. Prices vary widely between motel and condos, so be sure to call for more information.

The Landings—River Point or Weeki Wachee. 6004 Cortez Blvd. or 7300 Shoal Line Blvd., Weeki Wachee; (352) 592-0097; nccsfl.com/coastline/rpl.htm. Chuck and Paula Morton welcome you to come and play in their backyard at one of their two small motels. They'll even provide the canoe; plus, there are laundry facilities and free TV and phone, and small pets are allowed on a case-by-case basis. Their 5 rooms (at each site) fill up fast, so definitely plan ahead. One unit is near Hospital Hole, a 112-foot dive site on the Weeki Wachee River. Two-night minimum. $.

Quality Inn Weeki Wachee. 6172 Commercial Way (US 19), Spring Hill; (352) 596-0667; qualityinn.com. Located just south of Weeki Wachee Springs State Park, this motel is pet-friendly and offers a complimentary hot breakfast, pool, exercise facility, and other amenities. Smoking is allowed in some rooms. $.

day trip 03

northwest

manatee country:
homosassa; crystal river

Coastal Citrus County abounds with rivers flowing into the Gulf of Mexico and with natural springs bubbling up from below. The comparatively warm waters attract a gentle giant, the West Indian manatee. Weighing as much as 3,000 pounds, and also known as sea cows, plant-eating manatees are so easygoing they allow humans to come into their home and swim with them. Homosassa and Crystal River both offer many opportunities to enjoy natural Florida at its best—and they both have some surprising historical sites that help us picture how people lived from before recorded history to less than a century ago.

homosassa

Homosassa, an unincorporated community on Florida's Nature Coast in western Citrus County, is home to one of Florida's most unusual citizens—a four-footed citizen, at that!—and to an underwater fishbowl view of Homosassa Springs. Ellie Schiller Homosassa Springs Wildlife State Park and the Yulee Sugar Mill Ruins State Park are within minutes of each other, and other preserves and parks offer countless opportunities to see natural Florida at its most relaxing best. The immediate area also offers scuba diving, snorkeling, canoeing and kayaking, scalloping, and fishing.

Citrus County Visitors and Convention Bureau. 9225 W. Fishbowl Dr., Homosassa; (352) 628-9305; visitcitrus.com. The Citrus County Visitors and Convention Bureau staff can help organize your visit. Or check their website for loads of information including a lodging

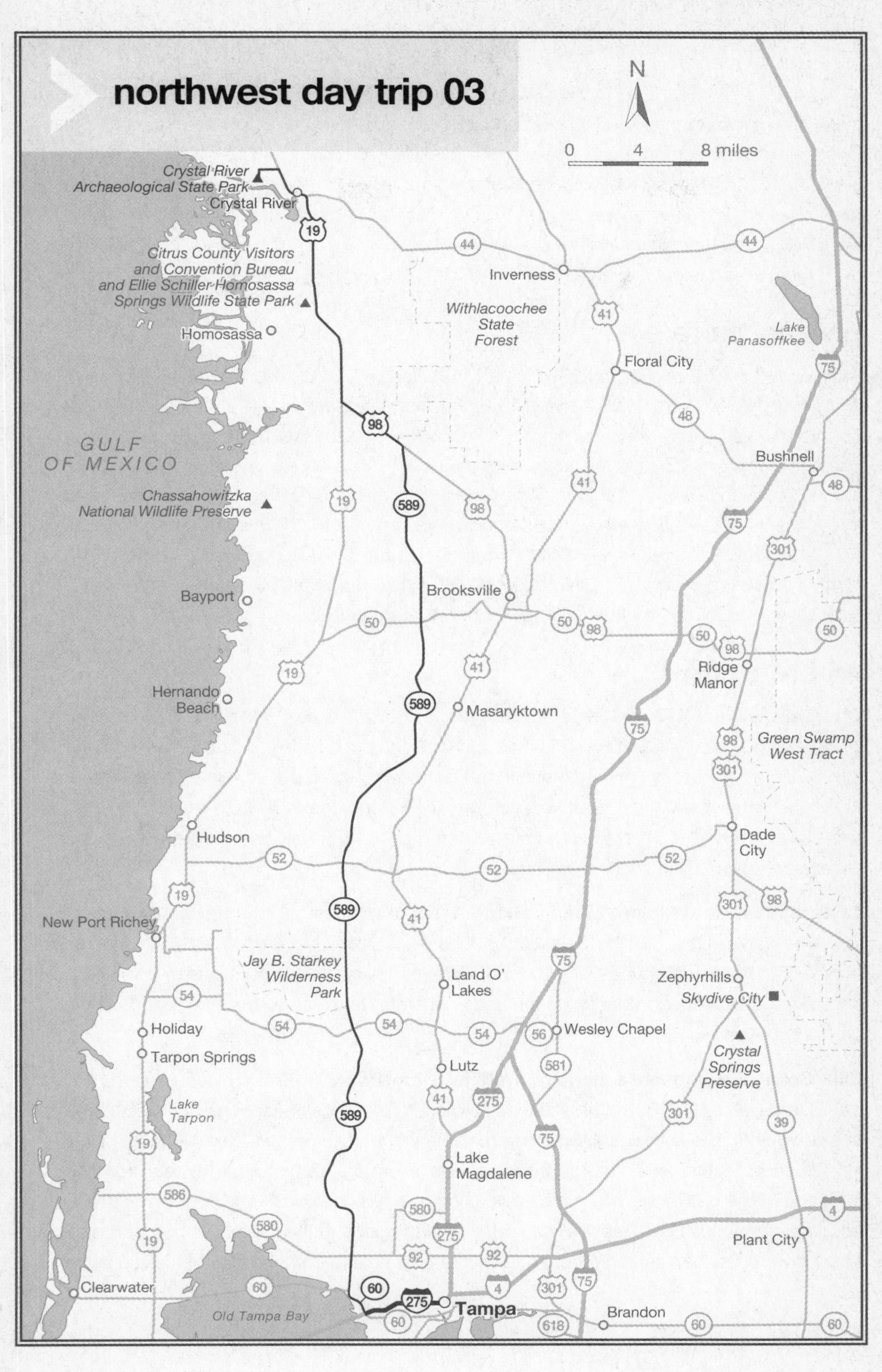

northwest day trip 03
N
0 4 8 miles
Crystal River Archaeological State Park
Crystal River
Citrus County Visitors and Convention Bureau and Ellie Schiller Homosassa Springs Wildlife State Park
Homosassa
GULF OF MEXICO
Chassahowitzka National Wildlife Preserve
Bayport
Hernando Beach
Hudson
New Port Richey
Holiday
Tarpon Springs
Lake Tarpon
Clearwater
Old Tampa Bay
Inverness
Withlacoochee State Forest
Floral City
Lake Panasoffkee
Bushnell
Brooksville
Ridge Manor
Masaryktown
Green Swamp West Tract
Dade City
Jay B. Starkey Wilderness Park
Land O' Lakes
Zephyrhills
Skydive City
Wesley Chapel
Crystal Springs Preserve
Lutz
Lake Magdalene
Plant City
Tampa
Brandon
19
44
41
75
48
98
589
301
50
52
54
56
581
275
39
586
580
92
4
60
618

map, lists of restaurants, fishing spots and guides, art galleries, and more—coupons, too! Of special note: Look on the website for the Eco-Heritage tab. You'll find a list of certified guides ready to give you the insider's scoop on the history of the area and on its ecosystems. The visitor center is open 8 a.m. to 5 p.m., Mon through Fri. They also maintain a kiosk with some information at the Ellie Schiller Homosassa Springs Wildlife State Park Visitor Center, which is open every day.

getting there

From downtown Tampa, take I-275 South to SR 60 West (also called Memorial Highway). Merge onto SR 60 via exit 39 (toward Tampa Airport/Clearwater) and continue to SR 589 Toll North; this becomes the Suncoast Parkway. Both stretches are toll roads, so be prepared to pay cash at several locations over the next 53 miles—unless you have purchased a Sun Pass (see driving tips in Using This Guide). Sun Pass holders can use the outer lanes to bypass the toll booths. Merge, via the exit on the left, onto US 98 North, also known as Ponce de Leon Boulevard and SR 700 North. Go about 5 miles and turn right onto US 98 North, which is now also US 19 North, aka S. Suncoast Boulevard. Go about 6 miles to W. Halls River Road. Turn left, then left again onto W. Fishbowl Drive.

where to go

Chassahowitzka National Wildlife Refuge. S. Mason Creek Road and S. Westview Drive; fws.gov/chassahowitzka or friendsofchazz.org/salt-marsh-trails.html. Most of the 31,000-acre estuarial salt marsh, home to thousands of birds, reptiles, manatees, and other wildlife, is accessible only by boat. But south of the Yulee Sugar Mill Ruins State Park you'll find access to a 10-acre area with trails, covered pavilion, kayak and canoe launch, and observation tower. Bring your own water.

Chassahowitzka Wildlife Management Area. myfwc.com/viewing/recreation/wmas/lead/Chassahowitzka. To the east of the Chassahowitzka National Wildlife Refuge lies another 33,000 acres of undeveloped land. Parts of this tract are accessible by car; hiking and biking trails abound. Management lands generally are open to hunters during certain parts of the year.

Ellie Schiller Homosassa Springs Wildlife State Park. 4150 S. Suncoast Blvd. (US 19), Homosassa; (352) 628-5343; floridastateparks.org/homosassasprings/default.cfm and citruscounty-fl.com/visitor.html. Spend some time in the visitor center, viewing the Winslow Homer art collection and area historical displays. From the visitor center, take a pontoon boat ride to the wildlife viewing area. Walk along a raised boardwalk and view black bears, cougars, numerous birds, reptiles, and other Florida wildlife in their spacious outdoor habitats. Or watch manatees and other aquatic creatures visiting from the Gulf of Mexico in the

florida's most unusual citizen

When our children were little, Homosassa Springs was a privately owned petting zoo with exotic and non-exotic animals. When the State of Florida purchased the park in 1989, they relocated most of the animals. But what do you do with a hippopotamus who has lived here most of his life? Born in 1960 at the San Diego Zoo, Lucifer the Hippo—Lu, to his friends—has lived at Homosassa Springs since he was 4 years old. It didn't seem right just to turn him out of house and home. Area residents didn't want Lu, a retired movie star, to leave; but, legally, he was an alien. In 1991, Governor Lawton Chiles made him an honorary Florida citizen, so he could stay here the rest of his life, a place he has called home now for almost half a century.

Fish Bowl, an underwater observatory. There is an on-site restaurant and 2 gift shops. Open every day from 9 a.m. to 5:30 p.m.

Homosassa Butterfly. 6991 W. Cardinal St.; (352) 628-6362; homosassabutterfly.com. From caterpillar to chrysalis to emergent butterfly, the butterfly gardens offer an up-close look at our fluttering friends. Open 10 a.m. to 5 p.m. every day except Easter Sunday, Christmas, and Thanksgiving.

Yulee Sugar Mill Ruins Historic State Park. CR 490/W. Yulee Drive, Homosassa; (352) 795-3817; floridastateparks.org/yuleesugarmill/default.cfm. This area once was a 5,000-acre sugar plantation owned by David Yulee. Union troops burned Yulee's home in 1864, but they couldn't find the sugar mill, now the only surviving sugar mill from pre–Civil War days in the United States. Interpretive panels provide information, or call ahead to request a 1-hour guided tour. The site is open daily from 8 a.m. to sundown. Admission is free. Pets on leashes are allowed, and there are picnic tables and restrooms in the park.

what to do

canoeing & kayaking

Most of the places listed under "where to stay" also rent canoes and kayaks. See canoeing and kayaking in Using This Guide for information about guides and blueway trails.

fishing

Fishing's good in western Citrus County, with plenty of places to cast a lure or drop a worm. See Using This Guide for information about charter captains and fishing guides.

scalloping

From the Hernando County line north to the Florida panhandle, scallop beds line the coast. All you need is a saltwater fishing license, snorkeling gear—and sometimes not even that—and a mesh bag. July through September 10 generally is open to scalloping, but be sure to check the local regulations. Many area fishing guides offer scalloping parties. See Using This Guide for information about finding guides.

swimming with manatees

Native Sun Tours. 5300 S. Cherokee Way, Homosassa; (352) 212-6142; nativesuntours.com. Swim with manatees in the Blue Springs of the Homosassa River. Rent snorkel gear or bring your own. Or rent a clear-bottom kayak and watch the manatees and other water creatures without getting wet.

where to shop

Gallery and Gift Shop at River Safaris. 10823 W. Yulee Dr., Homosassa; (800) 758-3474, (352) 628-5222; riversafaris.com/homosassa-art-gallery.html. The Gallery and Gift Shop feature the work of Florida artists—ceramic art, metal sculpture, fused and stained glass, paintings, and more. Also at this address, but in separate galleries, are the Glass Garage and Pepper Creek Pottery.

Howard's Flea Market. 6373 S. Suncoast Blvd., Homosassa; (800) 832-3532, (352) 628-3532; howardsfleamarket.com. Covering 55 acres and providing space for close to a thousand vendors, Howard's Flea Market is the place to shop for everything from antiques to produce and vacuum cleaners. Open Fri, Sat, and Sun from early morning to mid-afternoon.

where to eat

Fuji Asian Bistro. 4522 S. Suncoast Blvd., Homosassa; (352) 628-1888. We know. Delectable sushi rolls, Peking duck, and other Asian treats seem a bit out of character in Old Florida. But talk about a hidden treasure! Try a lunchtime bento box assortment. Vegan friendly, and open most days for lunch and dinner. $–$$.

Neon Leon's Zydeco Steak House. 10350 W. Yulee Dr., Homosassa; (352) 621-3663; neonleonszydecosteakhouse.com. Neon Leon is Leon Wilkeson of Lynyrd Skynyrd fame, and Wilkeson's family honors his memory with this steakhouse, which features American-style steaks and seafood, Cajun food—jambalaya, étouffée, gumbo, and more—and live zydeco music. The decor includes memorabilia from Wilkeson's career. Indoor or outdoor seating; children's menu. $–$$.

Olde Mill House Gallery and Printing Museum & Cafe. 10466 W. Yulee Dr., Homosassa; (352) 628-9411; oldemillhousegallery-printingmuseum.com. The website is under construction except for some photos in the gallery—but they will give you an idea of what to expect: cafe tables set amid antique letterpress print paraphernalia and other relics of times past. Owner Jim Anderson grew up in the printing business—call ahead to arrange a tour—and he also knows his way around a Cuban sandwich, deviled crab, and black beans and rice. Live blues music the third Saturday of each month. Open 10 a.m. to 3 p.m. Tues through Sat. $.

Riverside Crab House. 5297 S. Cherokee Way, Homosassa; (800) 442-2040, (352) 628-2474; riversideresorts.com. We're talking blue crabs here—caught locally and oh-so-sweet scrumptious! Plus steaks, prime rib, and an assortment of other entrees. Breakfast and lunch served most days. $$.

where to stay

Chassahowitzka Hotel. 8551 W. Miss Maggie Dr., Chassahowitzka; (877) 807-7783, (352) 382-2075; chazhotel.com. David and Kim Strickland, the fourth generation to operate the Chassahowitzka Hotel, welcome you to their recently renovated 8-unit hotel and the separate Miss Maggie's House on the Chassahowitzka River. A complimentary continental breakfast greets you in the morning; specially prepared dinners are available by reservation. Ask about their golf and fishing packages. No pets, no smoking. $.

Chassahowitzka River Campground. 8600 W. Miss Maggie Dr., Homosassa; (352) 382-2200; bocc.citrus.fl.us. This county-owned campground has spots for full-hookup RVs, tents, and primitive camping. You'll also find a nice bathhouse with laundry facility, shuffleboard court, covered pavilion, and community room. $.

Homosassa Riverside Resort. 5297 S. Cherokee Way, Homosassa; (800) 442-2040, (352) 628-2474; riversideresorts.com. Hotel rooms and suites, a pool, restaurant, lounge, and—oh, yes—a monkey island, home to five spider monkeys for several decades. The resort also offers lunch and dinner river cruises and can arrange for manatee swims, scalloping expeditions, fishing trips, and more. Rent a boat, kayak, or canoe from the marina. The bait and tackle/gift shop also has diving gear. $–$$.

MacRae's of Homosassa. 5300 S. Cherokee Way, Homosassa; (352) 628-2602; macraesofhomosassa.com. Riverfront motel rooms, the Shed—a bar featuring live entertainment—a bait house, and boat rentals—what more could anyone need? Check out the links to area guides and other doings. $–$$.

Nature's Resort RV Park. 10359 West Halls River Rd., Homosassa; (800) 301-7880, (352) 628-9544; naturesresortfla.com. Bring your own RV or tent or rent a cabin and stay for a day or a year on the Hall's River. Nature's Resort has a marina, bait and tackle shop, game room, store, swimming pool, horseshoes, volleyball, and a calendar full of activities. $–$$.

Upstairs Tree House. 10823 Yulee Dr., Homosassa; (800) 758-3474, (352) 628-5222; riversafaris.com/homosassa-vacation-rental.html. A cedar-lined upstairs home away from home, the tree house includes a full kitchen, fireplace, deck, use of canoes and kayaks, and more. Downstairs is the Glass Gallery, and out front is the working Pepper Creek Pottery studio. Two-night minimum. $.

crystal river

Remember graduating from the big, round, red pencils to the No. 2, hexagonal, yellow pencils? Ever wonder where the wood for those pencils came from? Beginning in the 1870s, the Dixon Mill processed cedar trees harvested from the area to produce the pencils used by hundreds of thousands—millions?—of people around the world. Before long, other people came, attracted to the natural beauty of the area, to the crystal waters that give Crystal River its name. But long ago, long before pencils were invented, other people lived here—people who have left only a few clues as to how they lived.

Citrus County Chamber of Commerce. 28 NW US 19, Crystal River; (352) 795-3149; citruscountychamber.com. For information about goings-on in Citrus County, visit the Chamber's website or stop in Mon through Fri from 9 a.m. to 5 p.m.

getting there

These directions take you to Crystal River Archaeological State Park and to Crystal River Preserve State Park. Get back on US 19 North and drive north about 7 miles to the city of Crystal River. As you head out of town, get in the left lane and watch for a brown information sign advising visitors to take the next left to get to Crystal River State Archaeological Park. The next left is in less than 500 feet, and there are no other markings. Make a diagonal left onto State Park Drive, which becomes W. State Park Street, and follow it to the next brown information sign. Turn left at N. Museum Point to go the Archaeological State Park; stay straight to go to the Preserve State Park.

where to go

Coastal Heritage Museum. 532 Citrus Ave., Crystal River; (352) 795-1755; cccourthouse .org/crystalriver.html. Built in 1939 by WPA workers using locally quarried limestone, the Coastal Heritage Museum was originally Crystal River's city hall. Today it provides a look back at Crystal River's history and at the way people lived in the not-too-distant past. Open Tues through Sat from 10 a.m. to 2 p.m. Donations are welcomed.

Crystal River Archaeological State Park. 3400 N. Museum Point, Crystal River; (352) 795-3817; floridastateparks.org/crystalriver. About the time of ancient Rome, Pre-Columbian people built a complex community here along the 6-mile-long, spring-fed Crystal

go from pre-columbian to post-einstein in less than a few miles

Along the Crystal River is the 4,700-acre Crystal River 3 Nuclear Power Plant, with four fossil fuel–generated plants and one nuclear-generated plant. Thick high-voltage lines extend out from the facility, held up by massive metal towers that, to me, look like a column of marching mechanical droids.

River. Follow the paved paths to different burial and other mounds, then climb stairs to the top of an almost 30-foot-high mound and imagine what life was like. A visitor center contains exhibits, pottery and other relics found at the site, and a short movie about the park. Pets on leashes are welcome (except in the visitor center). Open every day from 8 a.m. to sundown. The visitor center is open from 9 a.m. to 5 p.m. and is closed Tues and Wed. Great Florida Birding Trail #40.

Crystal River Preserve State Park. 3266 N. Sailboat Ave., Crystal River; (352) 563-0450; floridastateparks.org/crystalriverpreserve. Hike, bike, kayak, or canoe the land and water trails in the preserve. Two of the trailheads begin near the visitor center; other trails begin at other points in the Crystal River area. Eco-Heritage pontoon boat tours run 3 days a week; a sunset cruise is offered once a month. Great Florida Birding Trail: several sites.

what to do

Explore Kings Bay and surrounding waterways leading to the Gulf of Mexico, or opt for a freshwater experience, such as playing in natural springs. Many businesses rent canoes and kayaks, offer guided fishing or scalloping adventures, or provide manatee or dolphin encounters. We have listed a couple of places to get you started, but the Citrus County Visitor website (visitcitrus.com) lists dozens more.

canoeing & kayaking

Crystal River Kayak Company, Inc. 1420 SE US 19, Crystal River; (352) 795-2255; kayakcrystalriver.com. Canoe camping? No problem. Canoe wedding? Why not! Crystal River Kayak Company can put together just about any kind of canoeing or kayaking adventure you want. They open every day at 9 a.m. Most days they close at 5 p.m., but Sun and Wed they close at 2 p.m.

swimming with manatees

Snorkel with Manatees, Inc. 316 N. Hourglass Terrace, Crystal River; (352) 634-0435; snorkelwithmanatees.com. Swim or snorkel with manatees, take an airboat ride, or go scalloping or scuba diving. Snorkel With Manatees offers a number of options for people of all ages. Plus, they are a National Geographic Snorkeling Center. Call for the days and hours tours and swims are available.

where to shop

The Shoppes of Heritage Village. 657 N. Citrus Ave., Crystal River; (352) 564-1400; theshoppesofheritagevillage.com. More than a dozen shops, ranging from an antique treasure shop to a kayak center to a toy shop, fill what once were historic homes and cottages in Crystal River. Stop at the Heritage House Village Welcome Center and Gift Shop for a map, coupons, and maybe a sampling of something from the kitchen. Then wander from shop to shop, stop for a bite to eat, or enjoy the goings-on in the village. Check the Events section of the website. The shops are open Mon through Sat from 10 a.m. to 5 p.m. and on Sun between Thanksgiving and Christmas.

where to eat

Vintage on 5th. 114 NE 5th St., Crystal River; (352) 794-0004; vintageon5th.com. Dinner is an event at Vintage on 5th, located in a renovated 1940s-era church building. From rack of lamb to Gulf Coast oysters or shrimp and grits, nothing on the menu is ordinary. Their selection of wines has been recognized by *Wine Spectator* magazine, but every Wednesday is Go Corkless, meaning they invite guests to bring their own wine to enjoy with dinner. Open Tues through Sat, 5 to 9 p.m. (10 p.m. on Fri and Sat). $$–$$$.

where to stay

King's Bay Lodge. 506 NW 1st Ave., Crystal River; (866) 598-1581, (352) 795-2850; kingsbaylodgefla.com. Mitch and Tracy Wilson welcome guests to stay in one of their 18 efficiency units right on King's Bay, the start of the Crystal River. The hotel swimming pool, one of the very few remaining naturally spring-fed Old Florida pools, is cleaned by Mother Nature herself, as the pool is fed by spring water flowing through it. Drive in or boat in, as they have their own dock. No pets. Two-night minimum. $.

Plantation Golf Resort & Spa. 9301 W. Fort Island Trail, Crystal River; (800) 632-6262, (352) 795-4211; plantationgolfandspa.com. Set on 232 acres, Plantation Golf Resort & Spa has hosted guests for half a century. Play the course designed by Mark Mahannah, pamper yourself in the spa, swim with the manatees, or head out to catch a big one. The resort has 202 rooms and suites, a number of drink and dining options, and meeting rooms. Some rooms are pet-friendly. $$–$$$.

north

day trip 01

back in time:

brooksville; inverness; bushnell

Visualize a Florida without air-conditioning, paved roads, grocery stores, and telecommunication of any kind. Before the coming of the railroad in the 1880s, getting from one place to another within Florida's interior meant following game trails made by deer and other animals. There were no aerial maps or GPS systems to guide travelers around swampy areas or through massive palmetto thickets. People followed the animals; eventually the trails turned into paths, then roads.

This trip follows a loop just north of Tampa, through Florida's interior to the communities of Brooksville, Inverness, and Bushnell. Part of the route, more or less, follows one of those old trails. Today, the area attracts off-road ATV-ers, motorcyclists, and bicyclists. We will stop short of Ocala itself, and save that for another day. But we will visit museums, antique shops, battlefields, state parks, and—oh, yes—an Elvis-was-here site!

brooksville

Brooksville, the Hernando County seat, sits in a hilly area at the intersection of US 41 and SR 50 (Cortez Boulevard). Although it was not incorporated until 1880, white settlers began moving into the area at least as early as 1840, forming several small communities that eventually grew into each other. In 1924, during one of Florida's land booms, a Czechoslovakian group formed the town of Masaryktown just south. Nobleton is just north. The highway

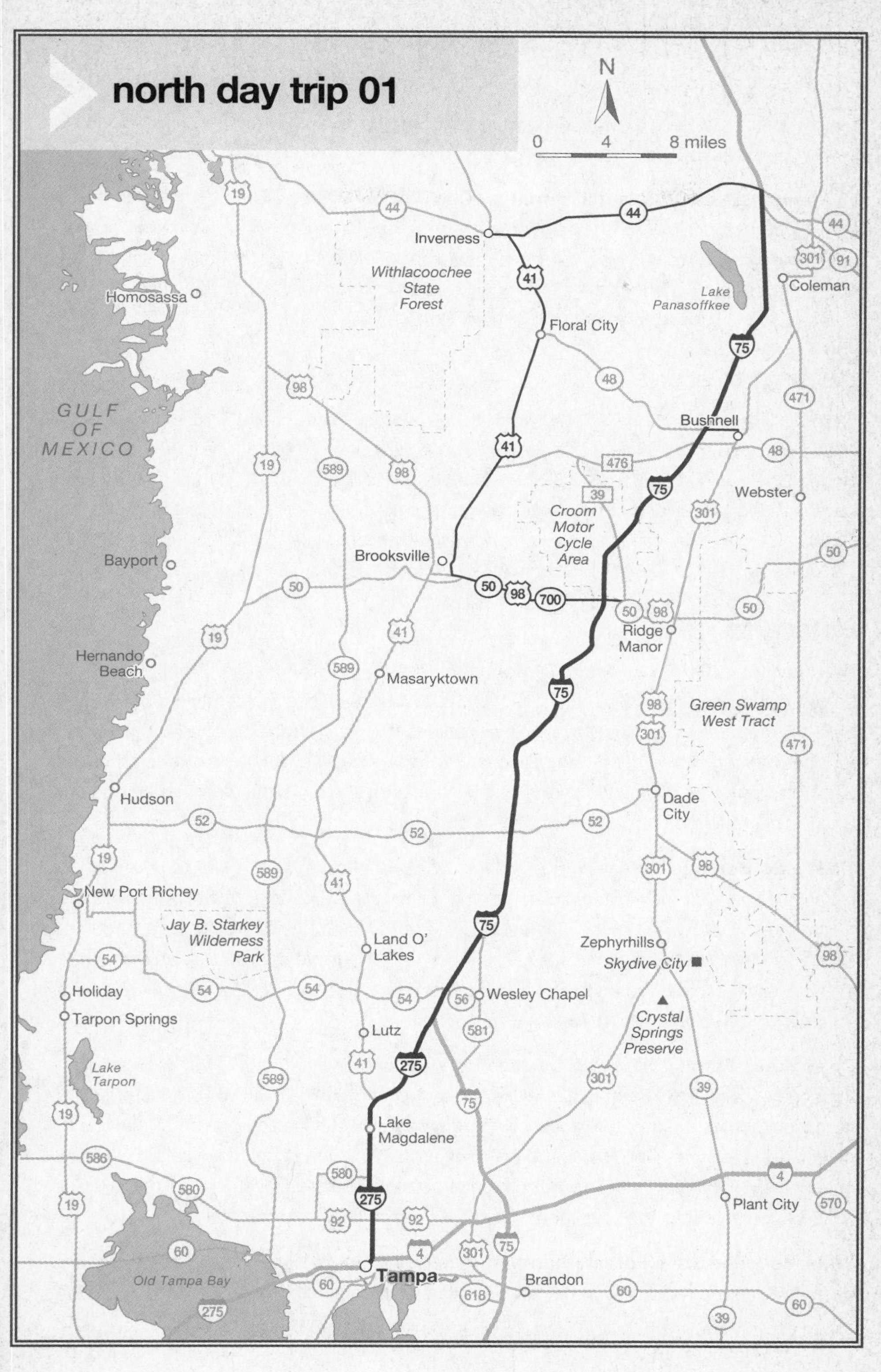
north day trip 01
N
0
4
8 miles
GULF OF MEXICO
Inverness
Withlacoochee State Forest
Homosassa
Floral City
Lake Panasoffkee
Coleman
Bushnell
Webster
Croom Motor Cycle Area
Bayport
Brooksville
Ridge Manor
Hernando Beach
Masaryktown
Green Swamp West Tract
Hudson
Dade City
New Port Richey
Jay B. Starkey Wilderness Park
Land O' Lakes
Zephyrhills
Skydive City
Holiday
Tarpon Springs
Wesley Chapel
Crystal Springs Preserve
Lutz
Lake Tarpon
Lake Magdalene
Plant City
Old Tampa Bay
Tampa
Brandon

system links Brooksville to several metropolitan communities; many people choose to work elsewhere but to live in Brooksville.

Hernando County Tourism Information Center. 31085 Cortez Blvd., Brooksville; (800) 601-4580, (352) 754-4405; naturallyhernando.org. The Hernando County Tourism Information Center's website contains a 4-page restaurant guide with a good map, a list of hotel and motel accommodations, bike trail maps, and lists of golf courses, antiques shops, and other places to go and things to do in Hernando County.

getting there

From downtown Tampa, take I-275 North toward Ocala. After about 15 miles, merge onto I-75 (ramp is on the left) toward Ocala, and continue another 28 miles to exit 301. Exit onto Cortez Boulevard, which is also SR 50 East, US 98 South, and SR 700 East. Head east toward Ridge Manor and Orlando; proceed less than a mile and watch for the Hernando County Tourism Information Center on your left. After stopping at the Information Center, backtrack on SR 50/US 98/SR 700 and follow it into the center of Brooksville (about 8 miles).

where to go

Brooksville's Historical Train Depot. #70 Russell St., Brooksville; (352) 799-0129; brooksvillehistoricaltraindepot.com. Back in 1885, four men invested a total of $20,000 to build 10 miles of railroad track and telegraph lines from Brooksville to an existing railway. Displays at the restored depot today document Brooksville's history; the depot also houses official records of various sorts, including burial records for area cemeteries. Open noon to 3 p.m. Tues through Fri.

Hernando Heritage Museum. 601 Museum Ct., Brooksville; (352) 799-0129; hernando historicalmuseumassoc.com. Housed in the historic May Stringer House, a restored Victorian-era 2-story home, the Hernando Heritage Museum has displays ranging from an extensive Mayan collection to an 1800s summer kitchen—more than 11,000 artifacts in all. You can even explore the attic. Open noon to 3 p.m. Tues through Sat—or call ahead to arrange for a weekend Ghost Tour.

Sweetfields Farm. 17250 Benes Roush Rd., Masaryktown; (352) 279-0977; sweetfields farm.com. Sweetfields Farm is a U-pick farm featuring organically grown produce ranging from blackberries to squash to zucchini. Bring a cooler, wear sneakers, and put the kids to work picking lettuce, sunflowers, and watermelon. Say hi to the cow, the goats, the chickens, and the pigs. And check out the natural mazes! Open seasonally, spring to fall. Call ahead to be sure they are open and to find out what's ready for harvesting.

Withlacoochee State Forest Recreation/Visitors Center. 15003 Broad St., Brooksville; (352) 754-6896; fl-dof.com/state_forests/withlacoochee.html. The Withlacoochee State

Forest, named one of the "10 Coolest Places in North America" by the World Wildlife Fund, is the third largest state forest in Florida. The Visitors Center is just north of Brooksville. The section of the Withlacoochee State Forest that lies in Hernando County is called the Croom Tract, and is located to the southeast of Brooksville (see What to Do, below). The Visitors Center is open Mon through Fri, 8 a.m. to noon and 1:30 to 4:30 p.m.

what to do

off-road atv & motorcycling

Croom Motorcycle Area. 15003 La Rose Rd., Brooksville; (352) 754-6896; fldof.com. Take exit 301-W (SR 50/US 98) off I-75. Look for the Best Western Motel on the north side of SR 50 and turn onto La Rose Road. Follow the road to the gatehouse. The Croom Motorcycle Area is 2,600 acres of off-road trails for ATVs and motorcycles. There are two day-use parking areas, a campground, and a young-rider area. No pets. The number listed above is for the gatehouse, which is open Thurs through Mon, 8 a.m. to 5 p.m. The area is closed Tues and Wed.

canoeing, kayaking & horseback riding

Hog Island Recreation Area. From the Withlacoochee State Forest Visitor Center on Broad Street, continue north to CR 476 and turn east toward Nobleton. Follow CR 476, crossing into Sumter County, to CR 635. Turn south. Follow the signs to Withlacoochee State Forest's Hog Island Recreation Area. There are hiking and equestrian trails, a campground (no electric), restrooms and showers, and a dump station. The canoe and boat launch puts you into the Withlacoochee River.

golfing

World Woods Golf Club. 17590 Ponce De Leon Blvd., Brooksville; (352) 796-5500; worldwoods.com. At World Woods Golf Club, it's not about the clubhouse or the restaurant or the spa—it's about the golf. The names of the courses—Pine Barrens and Rolling Oaks—describe both the courses and the two different ecosystems in which they sit. PGA.com's Advisory Board named the Tom Fazio–designed Pine Barrens one of the world's top 10 most beautiful courses. Plus there is a 23-acre practice park, a 2-acre putting course, and more. A restaurant on site is open 6:30 a.m. to 6:30 p.m. Open to the public.

mountain biking

Croom Off-Road Bicycle Trails. dep.state.fl.us. From the Withlacoochee State Forest Visitors Center on Broad Street, continue north to Croom Road. Turn east and follow Croom Road several miles to the Tucker Hill Fire Tower. This is the first of 3 parking areas leading to the bike trails. There are 3 bike trails with several "bailout points" on each. Primitive camping is allowed in one designated area. It's not exactly mountainous, but there are ravines and abandoned rock mines. Horse and hiking trails are also in the area.

where to shop

Downtown Brooksville has loads of antiques shops and boutique stores. Shop away!

where to eat

Coney Island Drive Inn. 1112 E. Jefferson St., Brooksville; (352) 796-9141; coneyislanddriveinn.com. Talk about iconic—this place has been dishing up the dogs since 1960. They do wings, ribs, burgers, and more, too, but it's the footlongs and fries that keep people coming back. It's rumored Elvis ate here. Open at 10 a.m. Mon through Sat; closing at 6 p.m. Mon through Tues, 9 p.m. Wed through Sat. Open 10:30 a.m. to 6 p.m. Sun. $.

Mallie Kyla's Cafe. 510 E. Liberty St., Brooksville; (352) 796-7174; malliekylas.com. Located in the historic Hawkins House, along with a florist and a gift shop, Mallie Kyla's serves soups, sandwiches, salads, and a heaping helping of delectable desserts. They're only open from 11 a.m. to 3 p.m. Mon through Sat, and reservations are accepted. People even call to reserve things like the crab bisque soup! Check the website for daily specials. $.

where to stay

There are a number of chain motels in the Brooksville area.

inverness

Inverness sits at the midpoint of a 20-mile-long chain of lakes called Lake Tsala Apopka (also called Tsala Apopka Lake), which begins near Floral City in the south. Inverness is the county seat for Citrus County and is also a destination spot for Elvis fans—the King of Rock 'n' Roll made a movie here in the 1960s.

Citrus County Chamber of Commerce (Inverness Office). 401 W. Tompkins St., Inverness; (352) 726-2801; citruscountychamber.com. You may already have picked up visitor information about Citrus County at the Welcome Center in Homosassa Springs. If not, stop in at the Chamber office in Inverness to get your bearings. They are open Mon through Fri from 8:30 a.m. to 4:30 p.m.

getting there

From Brooksville, travel north on US 41, which begins as Broad Street, about 21 miles to Inverness.

where to go

Fort Cooper State Park. 3100 S. Old Floral City Rd., Inverness; (352) 726-0315; floridastateparks.org/fortcooper. In 1836, this spot along Lake Holathlikaha became an area of refuge for sick and wounded soldiers of the First Georgia Battalion of Volunteers during the Second Seminole War. A replica stockade in the park helps visitors understand the era. The park has primitive campsites, picnicking, and hiking trails. Great Florida Birding Trail #55. Open 8 a.m. to sundown.

North Apopka Boat Ramp. 420 N. Apopka Ave., Inverness; inverness-fl.gov. The North Apopka Boat Ramp, a city park, serves small boats, canoes, and kayaks, providing access to Big Lake Henderson, Little Lake Henderson, and the Tsala Apopka Lake chain. There are picnic tables, grills, and a limited parking area; the park is within walking distance of the downtown area. Open sunrise to sunset.

Old Courthouse Heritage Museum. 1 Courthouse Square, Inverness; (352) 341-6429; cccourthouse.org/courthouse.html. Built in 1912 and listed on the National Register of Historic Places, the Old Courthouse Heritage Museum contains a number of interpretive exhibits and has information about other historic places within Citrus County. Open Mon through Fri, 10 a.m. to 4 p.m. Admission is free, but donations are gratefully accepted.

Wayside Park Boat Ramp. 1010 US 41 East, Inverness; inverness-fl.gov. Larger boats can access the Tsala Apopka Lake chain at the Wayside Park Boat Ramp. The park also has picnic tables and grills. Open sunrise to sunset.

Withlacoochee State Trail. 315 North Apopka Ave., Inverness; (352) 726-2251; dep.state.fl.us or railstotrailsonline.com. This 46-mile-long paved trail is Florida's longest rail trail. It runs from Citrus Springs in Citrus County to just north of Dade City, in Pasco County. There are several trailheads along the way, and the route is generally flat. Be sure to bring plenty of water, as there are stretches with no water. An unpaved equestrian trail runs next to

fun fact!

In 1961, portions of Elvis Presley's Follow That Dream *were filmed in the 1912 Citrus County Courthouse. Not long after, the courthouse was modernized to add air-conditioning, and the original beauty of the main second-floor historic courtroom was covered over and lost. When the Citrus County Historical Society wanted to restore the second-floor circuit courtroom, most of the reference photos used were stills taken from the MGM film.*

the bike trail for part of the route. The second website listed is hosted by the trail's Citizen Support Organization (CSO) and features photos, event listings, and other information. The trail's office is in Inverness—look for the little red caboose!

where to shop

Farmers' Market. 212 W. Main St., Inverness; (352) 726-2611; inverness-fl.gov. More than 30 vendors fill the Government Center Plaza each first and third Saturday of the month. Open 8 a.m. to 3 p.m.

where to eat

Frankie's Grill & Bar. 1674 US 41 North, Inverness; (352) 344-4545; frankiesgrill.com. Nothing fancy from the outside, but the steaks and burgers are on the grill—along with seafood, pasta, and chicken. Full bar. Check out their Sunday-After-Church Specials. Open every day at 11 a.m. Close at 9 p.m. Sun to Thurs, and at 10 p.m. Fri and Sat. $$.

Stumpknockers on the Square. 110 W. Main St., Inverness; (352) 726-2212; stumpknockers.net. Gator, frog legs, and catfish are on the menu here—along with the more usual steaks and chicken. Laid back and fun. $$.

where to stay

Central Motel. 721 US 41 South, Inverness; (800) 554-7241, (352) 726-4515; centralmotel.com. Central Motel sits right on the Withlacoochee State Trail, making it a stop for bikers and hikers. They offer secure storage for bikes, wireless access, and a swimming pool. No pets. $.

The Lake House Bed & Breakfast. 8604 E. Gospel Island Rd., Inverness; (352) 344-3586; thelakehouse.biz. Innkeeper Cathy Johnson invites guests to enjoy Southern hospitality at her restored 1930s-era hunting and fishing lodge on Big Lake Henderson. By reservation only. $.

Magnolia Glen Bed & Breakfast. 7702 E. Allen Dr., Inverness; (352) 726-1832; magnoliaglen.com. Old-world elegance, modern amenitites, and a view of the lake. Plus a hearty breakfast to start your day right. Innkeeper Bonnie Kuntz welcomes guests by reservation only. $.

bushnell

In 1823, two years after Spain gave up control of Florida and Oregon to the United States in exchange for control of the Texas territory, the US Army established Fort Brooke at what is today downtown Tampa. In 1827, Fort King was built at the site of today's Ocala. Bushnell sits on what was the trail between the two. Lake Panasoffkee is to the north; Webster is to the southeast.

getting there

Continuing the loop, take Lake Highway/SR 44E about 15 miles to I-75 South. Enter I-75 South toward Tampa and drive about 8 miles to exit 321 (CR 470) toward Sumterville. Keep left so you can take the ramp onto CR 470 South, which becomes CR 475 South. Stop at the Chamber office, or travel about 6 miles into Bushnell, where CR 475 South becomes N. Main Street (SR 48). After taking in the area, return to Tampa via I-75, thus completing the loop.

where to go

Sumter County Chamber of Commerce. 102 N. CR 470, Lake Panasoffkee; (352) 793-3099; sumterchamber.org. Located just off of I-75 between Sumterville and Bushnell, the Chamber office is open from 9 a.m. to 5 p.m. Check the "Visit Sumter" tab on their website for a list of agritourism venues in the county.

Dade Battlefield Historic State Park. 7200 CR 603, Bushnell; (352) 793-4781; floridastateparks.org/dadebattlefield/default.cfm. In late December 1835, 108 US Army soldiers under the command of Major Francis Langhorne Dade were ambushed at this spot by Seminole Indian warriors. Only three soldiers survived. The attack became the beginning of the Second Seminole War. The park's visitor center has a number of displays and a 12-minute video about the battle. Early each January, the park hosts a reenactment of the battle.

where to shop

Sumter County Farmers' Market/Webster Flea Market. 524 N. Market Blvd., Webster; (352) 793-2021; sumtercountyfarmersmarket.com. Webster, just south of Bushnell, boasts one of the state's largest flea markets, covering 40 acres and offering everything from produce to antiques to new and used odds and ends. Open Mon only from 6:30 a.m. to 4 p.m. Come back on Tues at noon to watch the cattle auction.

where to eat

The Speckled ButterBean. 522 Market Blvd., Webster; (352) 569-5333; speckledbutterbean.com. The Speckled ButterBean is a Southern-style country buffet—think grits, fried chicken, and fruit cobblers—serving breakfast, lunch, and dinner . . . oops, make that breakfast, dinner, and supper. Don't want the buffet? Order from their menu. The dinner menu includes salads, sandwiches, and burgers; supper features rib-eye steaks, prime rib, and grilled chicken. Open Mon through Sat from 6 a.m. to 9 p.m. $–$$.

where to stay

Pana Vista Lodge. 3417 CR 421, Lake Panasoffkee; (352) 793-2061; panavistalodge .com. Located on the outlet of the lake, Pana Vista Lodge has cottages, RV spaces (full hook-ups), and tent camping sites. They also rent boats, including pontoon boats. Two- and sometimes three-night stay minimum or there is an extra charge. $–$$.

Tracy's Point Fishing Lodge. 950 CR 437, Lake Panasoffkee; (352) 793-8060; tracyspoint.com. Bass and bluegill await the avid angler. Tracy's Point Fishing Lodge rents cabins and boats; they sell bait and tackle, too. Two-night stay minimum or there is an extra charge. $.

day trip 02

north

horse capital of the world:
ocala; dunnellon

The link between Tampa and Ocala goes back to the 1820s when, through a series of trades, treaties, and swaps, the US of A ended up in possession of La Florida. The US Army came to occupy the land before Spain, France, and England could rethink their loss of this peninsula to an upstart young country. Fort Brooke was established at what is now Tampa; Fort King was established at what is now Ocala. The road between the two was little more than a game trail. Today, Ocala officially bears the title of Horse Capital of the World, having more horses and ponies in residence than any other county in the United States in 1997. And we're not talking just any old four-footed equines, either. Ocala horse farms consistently have produced thoroughbred race winners, including the 1978 Triple Crown winner, Affirmed. Dunnellon, in the west of Marion County, is the second stop on the trip.

ocala

While Ocala may be a horse lover's dream come true, horses aren't the only things that get raced here. Motocross bike and stock car action offer a different kind of race experience for visitors. We'll also visit a motorsports museum, take a trip on a glass-bottomed boat, and stop off at an art museum or two. We have included in the Ocala area the smaller communities of Citra, Silver Springs, Reddick, and Weirsdale.

Ocala/Marion County Visitor Center. 112 N. Magnolia Ave., Ocala; (888) 356-2252, (352) 291-9169; ocalamarion.com. The Ocala/Marion County Visitor Center is well-stocked

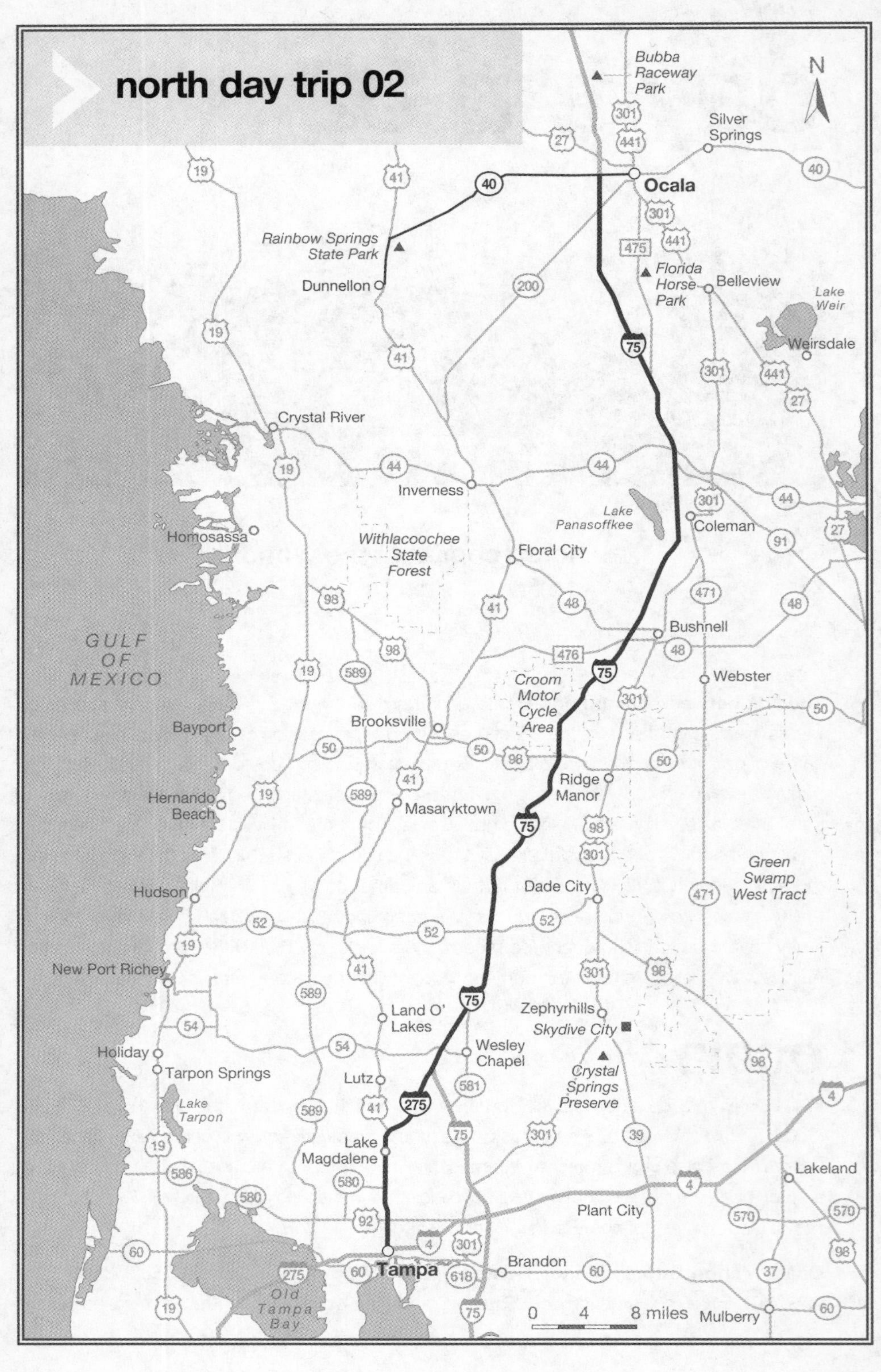
north day trip 02
N
Bubba Raceway Park
Silver Springs
Ocala
Rainbow Springs State Park
Dunnellon
Florida Horse Park
Belleview
Lake Weir
Weirsdale
Crystal River
Inverness
Homosassa
Withlacoochee State Forest
Lake Panasoffkee
Coleman
Floral City
Bushnell
Webster
GULF OF MEXICO
Croom Motor Cycle Area
Brooksville
Bayport
Ridge Manor
Hernando Beach
Masaryktown
Green Swamp West Tract
Hudson
Dade City
New Port Richey
Zephyrhills
Skydive City
Land O' Lakes
Wesley Chapel
Crystal Springs Preserve
Holiday
Tarpon Springs
Lutz
Lake Tarpon
Lake Magdalene
Lakeland
Plant City
Tampa
Brandon
Old Tampa Bay
Mulberry
0 4 8 miles

with information about the city, the county, and the surrounding area. Stop in and get your bearings. Pick up a local newspaper for even more current information, and ask about coupons and specials. The Visitor Center is open Mon through Fri from 9 a.m. to 5 p.m. Their website is open 24/7.

getting there

From downtown Tampa, head north on I-275 North for about 15 miles. Merge onto I-75 North and travel about 77 miles to the second Ocala exit (exit 352). From exit 352, merge onto W. Silver Springs Boulevard/SR 40 East, and travel east about 3 miles to US 27, aka US 301, US 441, SR 25, SR 500, and SR 200. Turn left onto US 27, et al., and turn right at the next street, NW 2nd Street. The next cross street is NW 1st Avenue; ahead and to your right is the back of the Visitor Center. If it looks like a bank building, that's because it used to be one. Parking is at the back or across the street. The front of the Visitor Center is located on N. Magnolia Avenue.

where to go

Appleton Museum of Art. 4333 E. Silver Springs Blvd., Ocala; (352) 291-4455; appleton museum.org. Built in the mid-1980s, the museum was a gift from Arthur I. Appleton, who owned a thoroughbred breeding and training facility, to display his extensive collection of art from Europe, Asia, Africa, and America. Today, the collection is considered one of the top in the Southeastern United States. Open Tues through Sat, 10 a.m. to 5 p.m. and Sun noon to 5 p.m.

Big Daddy Don Garlits Museum of Drag Racing. 13700 SW 16th Ave., Ocala; (352) 245-8661; garlits.com. In 1976, top drag racer Don Garlits founded the drag racing museum to preserve the history of a sport that began just after World War II. Today, his collection includes fuelers, stockers, "gassers," and funny cars from several eras and from around the world. Also on the property is the International Drag Racing Hall of Fame and a Museum of Classic Cars. Open every day except Christmas, 9 a.m. to 5 p.m.

swamp rats

Don Garlits, who began racing in 1950, dubbed his racers Swamp Rats, and he created more than 34 incarnations of Swamp Rat 1. In 2003, Garlits pulled Swamp Rat 34, built in the mid-1990s, out of the museum and ran it at Indy, clocking 310.81 mph.

Bubba Raceway Park. 9050 NW Gainesville Rd., Ocala; (352) 622-9400; ocalaspeedway.com. Operating since 1952, Bubba Raceway Park is the oldest short track course in Florida. Its ⅜-mile, D-shaped clay track hosts a number of championship races in various classes. Renovated in 2008, the park features grandstand bleachers, a no-smoking family section, new sound and light systems, and more. Check the website for the race schedule.

Florida Horse Park. 11008 S. US 475, Ocala; (352) 307-6699; flhorsepark.com. The Florida Horse Park is where most things equestrian take place, including World and Olympic level competitions. Check their calendar to find out when events ranging from dressage to jumping will be taking place. Dog events are also held here. Limited camping is available,

Historic Fort King Street. SE Fort King St., Ocala. Pick up a detailed booklet at the Visitor Center, then put on your walking shoes and prepare to be awed by 28 examples of beautifully restored late 19th- and early 20th-century homes. The well-researched booklet includes a glossary of architectural styles and terms as well as historical notes for each of the homes.

Motocross of Marion County. 2035 NW 146th Place, Citra; (352) 591-2377; mxmarioncounty.com. The address listed is the mailing address, so go to their website, look at the map (under Track Info), and follow the directions. Motocross of Marion County is Florida's oldest operator-owned track and has hosted motocross bike events for more than 25 years. Even if you don't ride, it's fun to watch. There are bleachers, restrooms, and concessions. No dogs unless muzzled and leashed.

Sholom Park. 6840 SW 80th Ave., Ocala; (352) 854-7435; hapi-info.org. Gardens and trees, a koi pond and streams, a labyrinth, and points of reflection, but most of all a tranquil walk amid natural surroundings. Open 8 a.m. to dusk. Donations welcomed. No pets, skates, skateboards, rollerblades, bicycles, or scooters. Quiet please.

Silver River State Park. 1425 NE 58th Ave., Ocala; (352) 236-7148; floridastateparks.org/silverriver/default.cfm. Rent a canoe, hike the trails, or take a horseback trail ride (in-park concession)—then rent a cabin, bring your RV, or pitch a tent, all at Silver River State Park. Learn about the area's history and ecology at the Silver River Museum and Environmental Education Center (open weekends and holidays, 9 a.m. to 5 p.m.) or come out for a stargazing session. Open 8 a.m. to sundown (except for special events) 365 days a year. Great Florida Bird Trail #30.

Silver Springs. 5656 E. Silver Springs Blvd., Silver Springs; (352) 236-2121; silversprings.com. Just around the corner from Silver River State Park, Silver Springs features glass-bottom boat views of its namesake artesian springs. Back in 1878, Hullam Jones figured out how to rig a dugout canoe with a glass viewing box—and the rest is history. Today, the park offers 3 different boat tours, a wildlife area featuring several shows, a Jeep tour, rides, and concessions. Concerts and special events are on the calendar, too. Wild Waters, a rides-and-slides water theme park, connects to Silver Springs and is open during the summer (wildwaterspark.com).

what to do

horse farm tours

Marion County is home to horse farms raising a variety of breeds. Some area horse farms offer guided tours or allow visitors to drive through and view the operations. Contact the Visitor Center for a list and be sure to call ahead. The Visitor Center also has a map of horse farms visible from the road, along a 14.7-mile circuit west of I-75 between exits 354 and 358, and information about horse-drawn carriage tours. Be mindful of traffic as you enjoy viewing the countryside.

horseback riding

Cactus Jack's. 11008 S. US 475, Ocala; (352) 266-9326; cactusjackstrailrides.com. Cactus Jack's is the designated horseback riding provider for the Florida Horse Park. They also offer rides in Silver River State Park and on the Ocala-area Greenway Trail System. Open every day, but reservations are required. Check the website for age and other limitations.

zipline ecotours

The Canyons Zip Line and Canopy Tours. 8045 NW Gainesville Rd. (CR 25A), Ocala; (352) 351-9477; zipthecanyons.com. Canyons? In Florida? Yup—old quarry mine canyons, that is. Check the website for age and weight limits.

where to shop

Gander Mtn. 3970 SW 3rd St. #101, Ocala; (352) 351-6186; gandermountain.com. In addition to all the sporting goods gear you'll need, the Ocala Gander Mtn. can give you the scoop on boat ramps, fishing hot spots, and guide services.

The Market of Marion. 12888 S. US 441, Belleview; (352) 245-6766; themarketofmarion.com. Market of Marion is Central Florida's biggest flea and farmers' market. Plus they host car shows, stamp camp, and other shows and events. Check the calendar to see what's happening when. Open Fri 8 a.m. to 2 p.m. Open Sat and Sun 8 a.m. to 4 p.m.

Ole Cracker House. 1734 NW Pine Ave., Ocala; (352) 732-8484. There are a number of antiques shops in Ocala and in the surrounding area—the visitor center has a list—but Ole Cracker House is definitely one of the largest. They are open Mon through Sat from 10 a.m. to 5 p.m. (sometimes later) and Sun from noon to 5 p.m.

Trés Chic. 416 SE Fort King St., Ocala; (352) 867-1199. Located in the John Dunn House in the historic district, Trés Chic features gifts and chic vintage items and other goodies. They are open 10:30 a.m. to 6 p.m. every day. The Muse Cafe is open 11 a.m. to 3 p.m.

western wear

RCC Western Stores. 2230 NW 10th Street, Ocala; (352) 629-7676; rccwesternstores .com. Clothing, toys, gifts, and items you won't see outside of horse country.

Russell's Western Wear. 890 NW Blitchton Rd., Ocala; (352) 304-6888; floridawestern wear.com/ocala-western-wear. Mostly clothing, hats, boots, and accessories, plus hunting and fishing wear.

Tack Shack of Ocala. 481 SW 60th Ave., Ocala; (352) 873-3599; tackshackocala.com. Don't have a horse? Visit this store anyway just to breathe in the scent of leather and all things horsey. Four times a year they host a Horsey Yard Sale.

where to eat

Aunt Fannie's. 1031 S. Pine Ave., Ocala; (352) 732-4497. Aunt Fannie's has been dishing up breakfast and burgers in Ocala for longer than some people can remember. Plus the menu is fun to read. Breakfast is served all day. Open 24/7. $.

Big Rascal BBQ & Grille. 3437 NW US 27, Ocala; (352) 732-0344; bigrascalbbq.com. Ribs, chicken, pork, and more—and bread pudding for dessert. Open 11 a.m. every day for lunch. Open for dinner Tues through Sat until 9 p.m. and until 8:30 p.m. on Sun. $$.

Harry's Seafood Bar & Grille of Ocala. 24 SE 1st Ave., Ocala; (352) 840-0900; hooked onharrys.com. With New Orleans–style food and atmosphere, Harry's features dishes like she-crab soup, jambalaya, and Parmesan-crusted tilapia étouffée—and chicken, pork, and burgers for non-seafood lovers. There's a kids' menu and a full bar. Take advantage of speed seating—call when you leave the house and put your name on the waiting list. Open every day at 11 a.m. Open until 10 p.m. Mon through Thurs, until 11 p.m. Fri and Sat, and until 9 p.m. Sun. $$.

Ipanema Brazilian Steakhouse. 2023 S. Pine Ave., Ocala; (352) 622-2172; ipanema ocala.com. Served Rodizio-style, the grilled meats make the rounds at Ipanema Brazilian Steakhouse and are accompanied by a well-stocked salad and vegetable bar. Open for lunch Tues through Fri, 11 a.m. to 2 p.m. Open for dinner Tues through Thurs, 5 to 9 p.m. and until 10 p.m. on Fri and Sat. Open 4 to 9 p.m. on Sun. $$$.

where to stay

Grand Oaks Resort. 3000 Marion County Rd., Weirsdale; (888) 750-1417, (352) 750-5500; thegrandoaks.com. Grand Oaks Resort welcomes guests, with or without their horses, to enjoy fly-fishing in the streams, trail riding its land, and relaxing in its Luxury Spa. Take driving lessons—carriage driving, that is. Grand Oaks Resort is the home of the Florida Carriage Museum. Accommodations include a lodge, chateaus, and cottages. $$–$$$.

Heritage Country Inn. 14343 W. US 40, Ocala; (352) 489-0023; heritagecountryinn.com. Innkeepers Christa and Gerhard Gross welcome guests to their 6-room inn. Each room is decorated to reflect a different period in Florida history. A full-course breakfast is part of the stay; dinner is available by reservation. $$–$$$.

Shamrock Thistle & Crown Bed & Breakfast. 12971 SE US 42, Weirsdale; (800) 425-2763, (352) 821-1887; shamrockbb.com. Stay in the Overcash family's 3-story Victorian historic home, enjoy a full breakfast and complimentary snacks, and then check out the things-to-do section on their website. Look especially at the Theater tab for listings of all the area little-theater company productions. $–$$$.

dunnellon

Dunnellon sits at the convergence of the Withlacoochee and Rainbow Rivers in the west part of Marion County. It is near Rainbow Springs State Park, known for its waterfalls and for nearby summertime tubing fun.

Dunnellon Chamber of Commerce. 20500 E. Pennsylvania Ave., Dunnellon; (352) 489-2320 or (800) 830-2087; dunnellonchamber.org. Want to know what's happening in Dunnellon? Stop at the Chamber office between 9 a.m. and 3 p.m. Mon through Fri or visit the Chamber website anytime.

getting there

From Ocala, head west on W. Silver Springs Boulevard (SR 40 West) about 20 miles. Bear left onto US 41 South, which becomes Williams Street, and travel about 5 miles into Dunnellon. Turn left on Pennsylvania Avenue to visit the Chamber of Commerce office.

where to go

Historic Dunnellon Depot. 12061 S. Williams St., Dunnellon; (352) 465-5005; dunnellon depot.com. The Greater Dunnellon Historical Society is housed in the Historic Dunnellon Depot; their museum is open on Tues from 3:30 to 7 p.m., but the Depot bustles with goings-on the rest of the week, too. For activities ranging from flea markets to a Sunday Cowboy Church to yoga classes and more, check their Events Calendar.

Rainbow Springs State Park. 19158 SW 81st Place Rd., Dunnellon; (352) 465-8555; floridastateparks.org/rainbowsprings. The park is a popular picnic spot with trails to walk, gardens to visit, and nature to enjoy. There is a canoe and kayak rental concession, with shuttle service in the park. The tubing area (10830 SW 180th Avenue Rd.) fills quickly, so be there early. The tubing run takes about 2 hours; tubes and shuttle service are provided through Nature Quest, Inc. The campground (entrance is also on 180th Avenue Road) is separate from the headsprings and the tubing area.

where to shop

The Historic Village Shops of Dunnellon. The area around City Hall has a number of antiques and specialty shops, cafes and other eateries, and more.

where to eat and stay

Blue Gator Tiki Bar and Restaurant/Angler's Resort Motel. 12189 S. Williams St., Dunnellon; (352) 465-1635, (352) 489-2397 (motel); blue-gator.com. Open every day for lunch and dinner and music and dancing, the Blue Gator is known for its seafood baskets and platters. The adjoining 9-unit Angler's Resort Motel offers singing pontoon boat river tours, boat rental, and more. Restaurant: $–$$. Lodging: $.

northeast

day trip 01

antiques, art & more:
groveland; howey-in-the-hills; leesburg; tavares; mount dora; clermont

Love to meander through the countryside? Love to discover out-of-the-way treasures? This trip, which winds through the Central Florida Highland's hills and between its lakes, is for you! Would you rather have a destination spot and leave the meandering to others? Okay. Put blinders on and don't enjoy the scenery—the destinations await.

This trip makes a circuit, stopping briefly in several small communities: Groveland, Howey-in-the-Hills, Leesburg, Tavares, Mount Dora, and Clermont. But each one of them invites more meandering, so feel free to stop at any point and explore further on your own. Plus, there are even smaller communities nearby. If we list a stop in one of these smaller communities, we'll note in parentheses which of the larger towns it is near.

groveland

Settled just after the Civil War—or War Between the States, depending on which side your ancestors fought—Groveland first was an agricultural community. In the late 1880s the Taylor brothers set up a turpentine company and built a company town called Taylorville. In 1910, a group of investors from Illinois bought land in the area, called it Groveland Farms, and sold tracts to "landseekers." The town officially became Groveland in 1912; today Groveland is home to Lake County's Welcome Center.

Lake County Welcome Center. 20763 US 27, Groveland; (352) 429-3673; lakecountyfl.gov/visitors. Stop in for brochures and tips on where to go and what to see in Lake County.

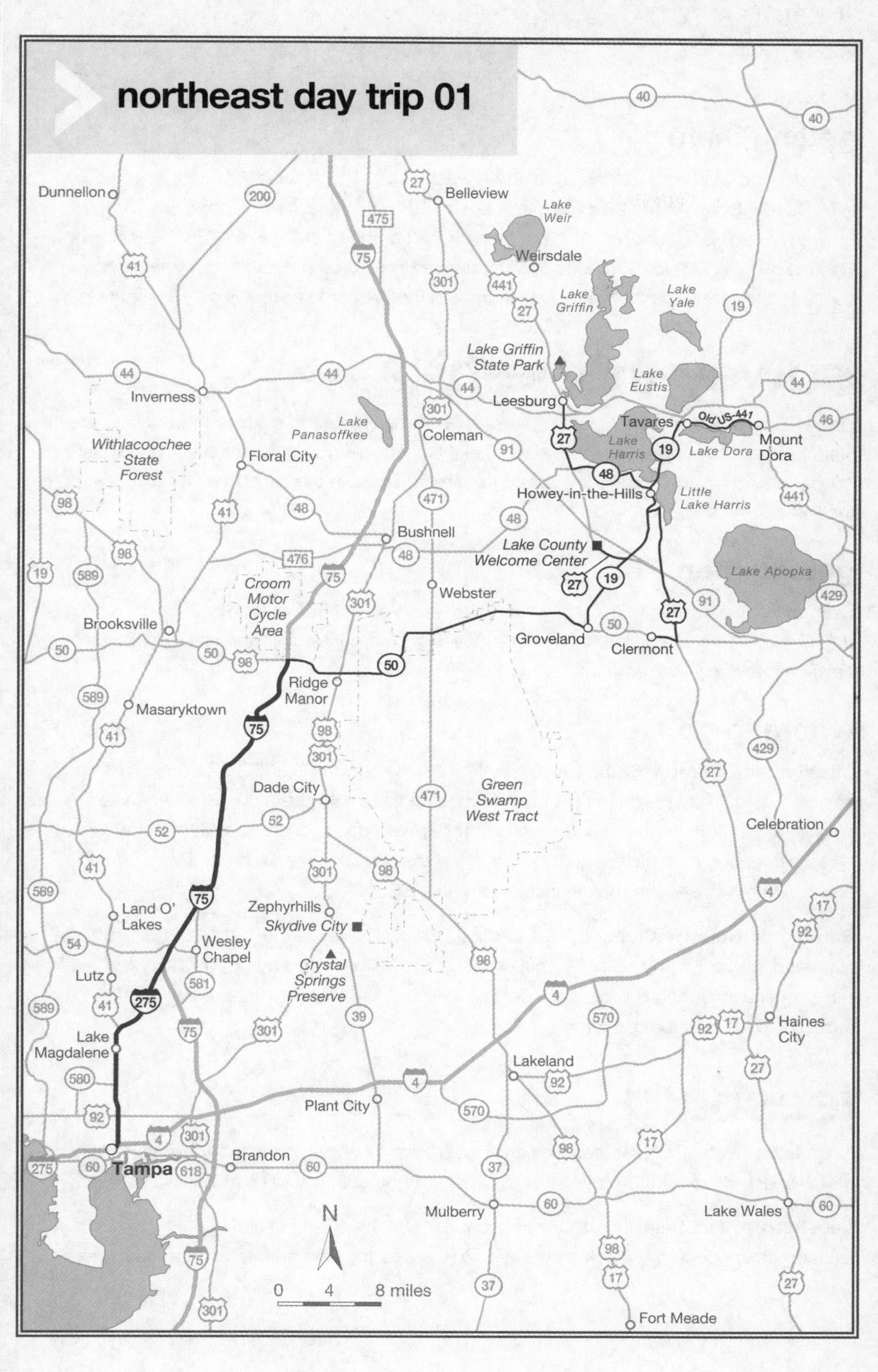

northeast day trip 01
Dunnellon
Belleview
Lake Weir
Weirsdale
Lake Griffin
Lake Yale
Lake Griffin State Park
Lake Eustis
Leesburg
Tavares
Old US-441
Mount Dora
Inverness
Lake Panasoffkee
Coleman
Lake Harris
Lake Dora
Withlacoochee State Forest
Floral City
Howey-in-the-Hills
Little Lake Harris
Bushnell
Lake County Welcome Center
Lake Apopka
Croom Motor Cycle Area
Webster
Brooksville
Groveland
Clermont
Ridge Manor
Masaryktown
Dade City
Green Swamp West Tract
Celebration
Land O' Lakes
Zephyrhills
Skydive City
Wesley Chapel
Crystal Springs Preserve
Lutz
Haines City
Lake Magdalene
Lakeland
Plant City
Tampa
Brandon
Mulberry
Lake Wales
N
0
4
8 miles
Fort Meade

getting there

From downtown Tampa, take I-275 North toward Ocala. Travel about 16 miles, then merge left onto I-75 North. Travel 28 miles to exit 301 for SR 50 East toward Ridge Manor/Orlando. Stay on SR 50 East for about 27 miles, then turn left onto S. Lake Avenue (SR 19 or Howey Road). Follow SR 19 for 6 miles to Independence Boulevard. Turn left and follow Independence Boulevard to US 27 South. Turn right and the Welcome Center is on your right.

howey-in-the-hills

Howey-in-the-Hills is Lake County's smallest community, but it is known throughout the state for its golf courses. Remember that Lake County has 1,000 lakes in its 1,200 square miles—water hazards here are as apt to include alligators in the sand traps as balls lost in the lakes.

getting there

From the Lake County Welcome Center, travel south on US 27 South (SR 25 South) about 0.5 mile to SR 19. Merge left onto SR 19, heading toward Howey-in-the-Hills and Tavares. Travel 6 miles and you're there!

where to go

Mission Inn Resort & Club. 10400 CR 48, Howey-in-the-Hills; (352) 324-3885; missioninnresort.com. The Mission Inn Resort & Club features two 4-star-rated 18-hole courses. A driving range, putting green, and practice bunker help golfers warm up for the challenge. Need pampering after all that golfing? Spa Marbella will soothe your stress away. Want to stay at the resort? Accommodations are available ($$).

Sarabande Country Club. 26945 Bella Vista Blvd., Howey-in-the-Hills; (352) 324-2511; sarabandegolf.com. The 18-hole regulation course was designed by Lloyd Clifton and features a beautiful rolling hills setting. Jackie's Grill on Lake Harris is open every day from 8 a.m. to 9 p.m., and there is a marina.

leesburg

Bounded by water on two sides—meaning you'll find lakeside parks and top-notch fishing here—Leesburg is Lake County's oldest city and is the gateway to Lake Griffin State Park.

Leesburg Area Chamber of Commerce. 103 S. 6th St., Leesburg; (352) 787-2131; leesburgchamber.com. Check the Chamber website for area events and to learn more

linked by lakes

The Harris Chain of Lakes isn't exactly a community, but it is what links these communities together. The lakes are (north to south) Lake Griffin, Lake Yale, Lake Eustis, Lake Harris, Little Lake Harris, Lake Dora, Lake Beauclair, Lake Carlton, and Lake Apopka. These nine lakes form the headwaters of the Ocklawaha River.

Before hard roads were built in this area—mostly after 1910—most people traveled by water from town to town. For information about fishing these lakes, including boat ramp information, go to lakecountybass.com/harris_chain_fishing.html.

about the community. Or stop in at the Chamber office—they're open Mon through Fri from 8:30 a.m. to 4:30 p.m.

getting there

From Howey-in-the-Hills, take CR 48 not quite 10 miles around the south side of Lake Harris to US 27. Turn north on US 27, which becomes S. 14th Street, and drive about 6 miles to Leesburg.

where to go & stay

Lake Griffin State Park. 3089 US 441/27, Fruitland Park (Leesburg); (352) 360-6760; floridastateparks.org/lakegriffin/default.cfm. Lake Griffin State Park connects via a canal with Lake Griffin itself. The full-facility campground includes pull-through sites for RVs up to 40 feet in length. Ask about the Bedtime Story Camper Lending Library full of picture books—for the young and young at heart. A canoe and kayak concession is on site and there are hiking and nature trails. Call ahead to find out the current water level; when the water level is low, larger boats can't launch here. $.

tavares

Tavares calls itself "America's Seaplane City," and the Seaplane Base & Marina makes for an interesting stop. Note that the route here is from Howey-in-the-Hills. You can get here from Leesburg, but the route to Tavares takes travelers across a bridge at the point where big Lake Harris connects with Little Lake Harris. The bridge itself, built in 1950, is listed on UglyBridges.com. The view? Anything but!

Tavares Chamber of Commerce. 912 N. Sinclair Ave., Tavares; (352) 343-2531; tavares chamber.com. Click on the Visitors tab of the Chamber website to bring up lists of restaurants, lodgings, shops, ecotours, and more. Or visit them in person Mon through Fri between 10 a.m. and 4 p.m.

getting there

From Leesburg, backtrack on US 27 to SR 48 into Howey-in-the-Hills. Then, from Howey-in-the-Hills, take SR 19 North not quite 7 miles (over the bridge) to W. Main Street. Turn right onto W. Main Street, go about 0.5 mile, then turn right again onto S. New Hampshire Avenue. Turn right onto S. New Hampshire Avenue, then left onto E. Ruby Street.

where to go

Seaplane Base & Marina in Wooton Park. 100 E. Ruby St., Tavares; (352) 742-6267; tavares.org. Watch the planes take off and land or go for a seaplane ride, take an eco-tour by boat of the Dora Canal, let the kids play in the extensive Splash Park (summer only), or rent a boat, kayak, or bike. Or just have a picnic—get take-out from nearby local restaurants or bring your own—and enjoy Lake Dora. The Seaplane Base is also a venue for community events.

Orange Blossom Cannonball. 301 E. Main St., Tavares; (352) 742-7200; orangeblossom cannonball.com. Take a 2-hour, 16-mile ride on the Orange Blossom Cannonball, pulled by a 1907 steam locomotive. Check the website for special runs. Runs Sat at 10 a.m. and 12:30 and 3 p.m. and on Sun at 12:30 and 3 p.m.

where to eat

AL's Landing. 111 W. Ruby St.; alslanding.com. AL's Landing gives you a choice of three restaurants in one location, right on Lake Dora. There's the Landing (352-742-1113), featuring sandwiches, burgers and salads, along with live entertainment and a full bar. The Landing opens every day at 11 a.m. $–$$. Then there's the Top Shelf (352-253-5237), offering upscale dining upstairs for a great view of the lake. $$–$$$. Finally, the Dockside (352-508-5841) dishes up barbecue on the deck from 11 a.m. to 8 p.m. $.

World's Worst Deli. 124 South Joanna Ave., Tavares; (352) 343-0745; worldsworstdeli .com. "Can't say you haven't been warned" is their claim; but argumentative types will love proving them wrong. Hmmm. WWD serves sandwiches, stacks, grillers, and salads. Open 11 a.m. to 3 p.m. Mon through Fri. $.

mount dora

Tucked away in peaceful central Florida, Mount Dora's historic downtown shopping area draws visitors from around the state—maybe farther. The town is home to the oldest inland yacht club in Florida, built in 1913, and the largest club in the United States Lawn Bowling Association. It has a lighthouse and more points of interest than probably can be fit into one day. But who says we can't come back?

Mount Dora Area Chamber of Commerce. 341 Alexander St., Mount Dora; (352) 383-2165; mountdora.com. Located inside the former Atlantic Coastline Train Depot, built in 1915, the Mount Dora Area Chamber of Commerce is stocked full of maps, brochures, and flyers. Ask about hot air balloon rides and Segway tours. Make this your first stop, and be sure to pick up a Visitor Map of Mount Dora itself. Then find a place to park your car, and put on your walking shoes so you can stroll Mount Dora's streets and browse the shops. Remember to look up—some shops and restaurants are on the second floor—and within-what looks like a door leading to just a corridor may be a foyer to an arcade area containing more shops.

getting there

From Tavares, take Old US 441 (E. Alfred Street) about 5 miles, at which point it will become W. 5th Avenue. Follow W. 5th Avenue about 0.5 mile to N. Alexander Street and turn right. The Chamber of Commerce is on your right.

where to go

Mount Dora History Museum and Old Jail. 450 Royellou Ln., Mount Dora; (352) 383-0006; mountdorahistoricalsociety.com. There is an authentic moonshine still in the museum, which is located in the alley between 4th and 5th Avenues and between Donnelly and Baker Streets. Open Tues through Sat from 1 to 4 p.m.

Mount Dora Trolley. 3rd Avenue and Alexander Street, Mount Dora; (352) 385-1023; florida-secrets.com/Florida_Tours/mount_dora_trolley_tour.htm. The trolley stops at the Chamber of Commerce building, so hop on for a 1-hour narrated tour of Mount Dora. The trolley generally runs Mon through Sat between 11 a.m. and 2 p.m., but call ahead to check.

where to shop

Artisans on 5th. 134 E. 5th Ave., Mount Dora; (352) 383-0880; artisansonfifth.com. Artisons on 5th is a cooperative featuring the work of almost 30 local artists. You'll find watercolors, wood art, fused glass, fiber art, and more. Open Mon through Sat from 10 a.m. to 5 p.m. and Sun from 1 to 5 p.m.

Renninger's Antique Center/Renninger's Farmers' and Flea Market. 20651 US 441, Mount Dora; (352) 383-8393; renningers.com/dora/dorahome.htm. Treasure hunt your way through 117 acres of vendors in this two-for-one location. The Antique Center is the largest in Florida, and the Farmers' and Flea Market isn't exactly small. Open Sat and Sun, 8 a.m. to 4 p.m. for the Farmers' and Flea Market, 9 a.m. to 5 p.m. for the Antique Center.

Village Antique Mall. 405 N. Highland St., Mount Dora; (352) 385-0257; villageantiquemall .com. More than 60 vendors under one roof. Check their events page, too, for festivals and other goings-on. Open every day from 10 a.m. to 6 p.m.

where to eat

One Flight Up. 440 Donnelly St., Mount Dora; (407) 758-9818; oneflightupmtdora.com. Located upstairs, One Flight Up serves coffee, desserts, wine, soups, salads, and sandwiches. Eat indoors or on a balcony overlooking Mount Dora's downtown area. Live music on the weekends; open mike on Monday. Open 9 a.m. to 11:30 p.m. $.

Saucy Spoon Downtown. 322 Alexander St., Mount Dora; (352) 383-1050; saucyspoon .com. Pork osso bucco with a port wine cherry sauce; hand-cut beef tenderloin with smokey bleu cheese, caramelized onion, and fig reduction; lobster truffle mac-n-cheese? Only at the Saucy Spoon Downtown. Open at 11 a.m. to midnight on Mon, Wed, and Thurs. Open 11 a.m. to 2 a.m. Fri and Sat. Open 11 a.m. to 9 p.m. Sun. Closed Tues. $$–$$$.

Windsor Rose English Tea Room & Restaurant. 142 W. 4th Avenue, Mount Dora. (352) 735-2551; windsorrose-tearoom.com. Enjoy a traditional English high tea or just come for breakfast (weekends), lunch, or an early dinner. Spirits, as in beer and wine, served, too. Open 11 a.m. to 5 p.m. Mon through Thurs. Open 9 a.m. to 5 p.m. Fri through Sun. $$.

where to stay

Heron Cay Lakeview Bed & Breakfast. 495 W. Old US 441, Mount Dora; (352) 383-7653; heroncay.com. Who doesn't love to pretend? It's easy to relive an earlier era at this Queen Anne–style Victorian mansion overlooking Lake Dora. Two of the rooms are pet-friendly. $$–$$$.

Lakeside Inn. 100 N. Alexander St., Mount Dora; (800) 556-5016, (352) 383-4101; lakeside-inn.com. The Lakeside Inn has been welcoming guests since 1883 and is a favorite spot for weddings and other events. Dine in the elegant Beauclaire Room—Sunday brunch is an event!—or enjoy rocking on the verandah. Boat tours of the lake depart from the Lakeside Inn's dock. $–$$.

clermont

The Florida Citrus Tower at Clermont is a landmark. This is the first stop on the trip, but we'll take in a winery, have our picture taken with the President of the United States, and learn to waterski, too.

South Lake Chamber of Commerce. 691 W. Montrose St., Clermont: (352) 394-4191; southlakechamber-fl.com. This Chamber covers several communites in south Lake County. Visit their website to learn more about this area, or stop in Mon through Fri from 8:30 a.m. to 4:30 p.m.

getting there

You can take the back roads from Mount Dora through Astatula down to Clermont, but the easier way is to go back to Tavares and take SR 19 South through Howey-in-the-Hills and all the way to US 27 North (almost 20 miles). Merge onto US 27 South toward Minneola/ Clermont, and travel about 6 miles. The Florida Citrus Tower is before you get to Minneola. It rises 226 feet in the air, so you should be able to see it.

where to go

Florida Citrus Tower. 141 N. US 27, Clermont; (352) 394-4061; citrustower.com. The Florida Citrus Tower rises more than 225 into the air, providing a panoramic view of Central Florida from its glassed-in observation deck. A gift shop is at the base of the tower. Open Mon through Sat from 9 a.m. to 5 p.m. Closed Thanksgiving and Christmas.

Lakeridge Winery & Vineyards. 19239 US 27 North, Clermont; (800) 768-9463, (352) 394-8627; lakeridgewinery.com. Take a tour and take a taste, then visit the gift shop. Check the website for festivals and other events. Open Mon through Sat from 10 a.m. to 5 p.m. and Sun from 11 a.m. to 5 p.m.

Presidents Hall of Fame. 123 N. US 27, Clermont; (352) 394-2836. Life-size wax figures of all US presidents and some first ladies, a larger than life-size-but-smaller-than-the-original replica of Mount Rushmore, and presidential china and other memorabilia fill the Presidents Hall of Fame. The National Presidents Hall of Fame also is home to a massive replica of the White House that has visited every presidential library and has toured overseas. There is an extra charge when the White House replica is at home and open for visitors. Open every day from 10 a.m. to 4 p.m.

what to do

Showcase of Citrus. 5010 US 27, Clermont; (352) 394-4377; showcaseofcitrus.com. The Arnold family invites visitors to see what goes on at a working citrus and cattle ranch. Sample some of the 25 varieties of just-picked citrus, then get a map and a bucket and go pick your own. Watch the fruit get processed, and visit the gift store. Or take a swamp buggy ride through the—what else?—swamps and fields to visit the cattle and other critters. Call ahead for reservations for the swamp buggy. Open every day, pretty much sunup to sundown. Summer hours are a bit shorter.

where to stay

Swiss Ski School. 13114 Skiing Paradise, Clermont; (352) 429-2178; swissskischool.com. Want to spend some time skiing or wakeboarding? Want to learn? And if your traveling partners aren't up to waterskiing, there's an 18-hole golf course, tennis courts, and more on site. $–$$$.

east by northeast

day trip 01

east by northeast

the disney domain:
magic kingdom park; epcot theme park; animal kingdom; hollywood studios; other disney experiences

Today we start with what used to be just the Magic Kingdom but has become an enchanted empire of interconnected theme parks, resorts, and entertainment complexes. Then we'll stop by each of the other worlds within Walt Disney World Resort. We'll hit the highlights within each park, but we'll also note some different ways to experience the Disney domain.

Please note: All directions to each of the theme parks originate in Tampa. Also, once you leave I-4 and enter the Disney domain it can be several miles to the nearest gas station. Do not assume your vehicle will run on fairy dust.

magic kingdom park

getting there

From downtown Tampa, take I-4 East toward Orlando. Travel about 58 miles to exit 62. Take exit 62 toward Disney World, cloverleaf around, and merge onto World Drive heading north. Follow N. World Drive about 6 miles toward Wilderness Lodge. Turn left onto Seven Seas Drive. Pay the fee, then follow the parking guides' directions to park. You are now in the Ticket and Transportation Center. Write down where you parked (!), walk to a designated tram stop, and wait for a tram to take you to the entrance. From here, take the monorail or the ferry to the Magic Kingdom.

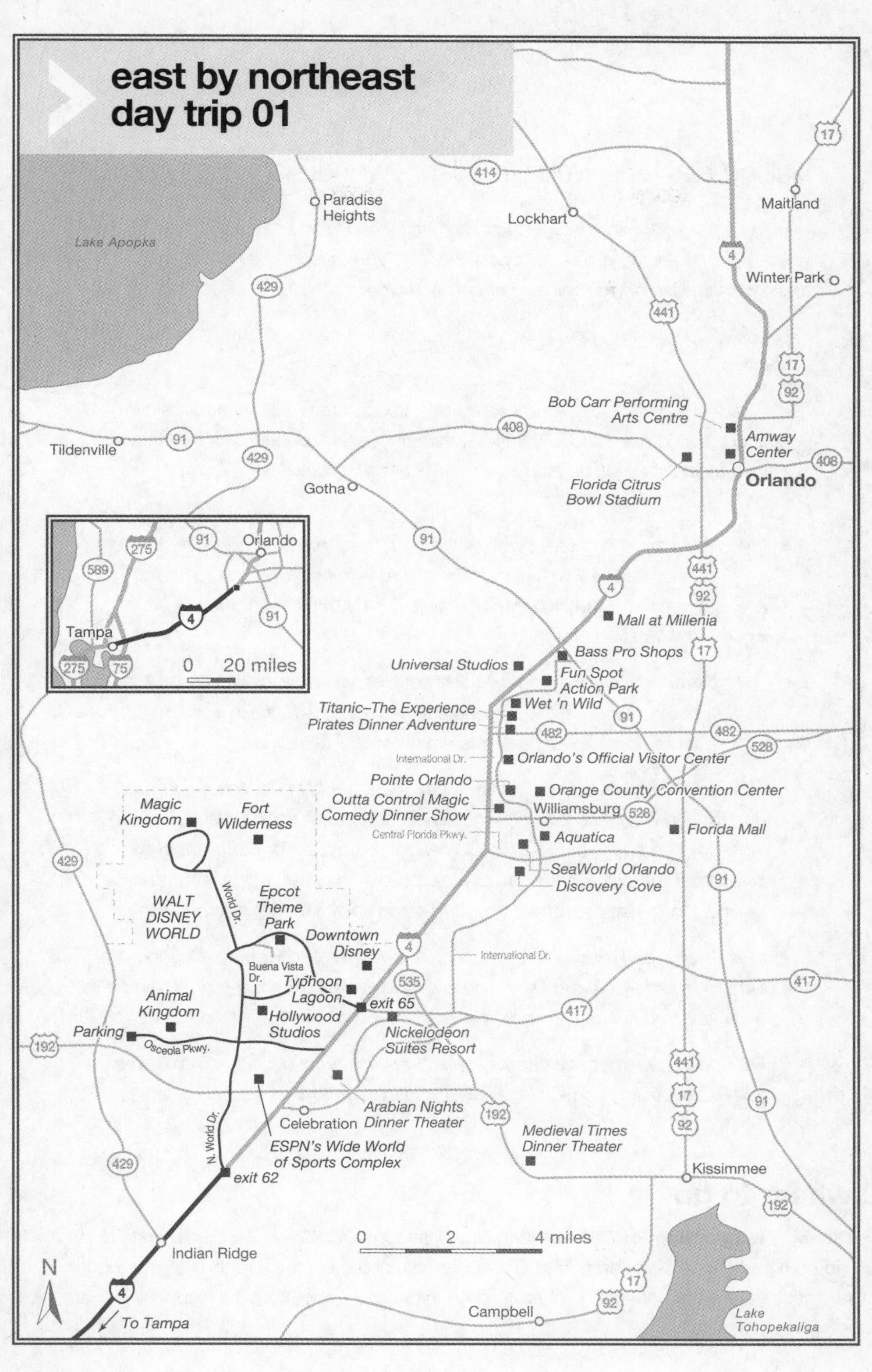

east by northeast
day trip 01
Lake Apopka
Paradise Heights
Lockhart
Maitland
Winter Park
Tildenville
Gotha
Bob Carr Performing Arts Centre
Amway Center
Orlando
Florida Citrus Bowl Stadium
Orlando
Tampa
0 20 miles
Mall at Millenia
Bass Pro Shops
Universal Studios
Fun Spot Action Park
Wet 'n Wild
Titanic–The Experience
Pirates Dinner Adventure
International Dr.
Orlando's Official Visitor Center
Pointe Orlando
Orange County Convention Center
Outta Control Magic Comedy Dinner Show
Williamsburg
Central Florida Pkwy.
Aquatica
Florida Mall
SeaWorld Orlando
Discovery Cove
Magic Kingdom
Fort Wilderness
WALT DISNEY WORLD
World Dr.
Epcot Theme Park
Downtown Disney
Buena Vista Dr.
Typhoon Lagoon
exit 65
International Dr.
Animal Kingdom
Hollywood Studios
Nickelodeon Suites Resort
Parking
Osceola Pkwy.
Celebration
Arabian Nights Dinner Theater
ESPN's Wide World of Sports Complex
Medieval Times Dinner Theater
N. World Dr.
exit 62
Kissimmee
0 2 4 miles
Indian Ridge
N
To Tampa
Campbell
Lake Tohopekaliga

visiting disney's website: disneyworld.disney.go.com

Window shop your way through the online Vacation Package Guide options; you'll find lots of information and tips specific to your needs. Just be aware that these guides assume you will stay at one of their resorts.

- *Look for Florida resident discounts, seasonal promotions, and other special offers.*
- *Check the Park Hours link for each day you plan to visit. Some hours change according to days and seasons. Sometimes resort guests' park tickets come with extra hours—Extended Magic Hours—at the beginning or end of the day.*
- *If you have small children, scroll to the bottom of the page and look for the Moms Panel Advice link, a discussion forum with helpful answers for parents. Also look for the In-Depth Planning Topics link. One of the guides is Traveling With Little Ones.*
- *Note the rider swap policy: While one adult stays with a child too small to go on a ride, the other adult enjoys the ride. As soon as that adult returns, the other gets to ride without having to wait in line all over again.*
- *The Guest Services link has information about pet kennels, the resort transportation system, and stroller, wheelchair, and electric convenience vehicle rentals. Read about the FASTPASS service, then look for the distribution areas near the entrances of most attractions at each park. It's like making a reservation to ride the attractions, and it can save a lot of waiting-in-line time.*
- *Most theme park tickets say they require adults to show photo ID when entering the park. At the least, you will need photo ID showing proof of age if you want to purchase alcoholic beverages.*
- *For additional information about Walt Disney World, wdwinfo.com bills itself as "The Internet's Largest Unofficial Online Guide to Walt Disney World."*

where to go

Disney's Magic Kingdom. 3111 World Dr., Orlando; (407) 824-4321; disneyworld.disney.go.com/parks/magic-kingdom. Visit Guest Services at the entrance to the Magic Kingdom for maps, event time sheets, and up-to-date information about what's happening in the parks. Within the Magic Kingdom lie 6 magical lands, arranged in a circle around the center of the kingdom. And in the very center of the kingdom? What else but a castle—Cinderella Castle to be exact. Cinderella Castle rises almost 200 feet in the air, and it makes a good meeting point. Just be sure to specify at which side of the castle you'll meet. We've waited on one side of the castle, checking our watches, while the rest of our party has been waiting on the other side, checking their watches. Cinderella Castle also is a quiet place to regroup. Enjoy the mosaic murals inside, which show scenes from the movie *Cinderella*. At the end of the day, Cinderella Castle is lit up by fireworks, bursting with color around the castle's turrets and spires.

Main Street, USA. The monorail or ferry from the Ticket and Transportation center unloads near the entrance to the Magic Kingdom. Straight ahead is the Walt Disney World Railroad Depot. Entrances to the Magic Kingdom are on either side of the depot. Once inside, you are in the Main Street, USA, area. To the left (as you face Cinderella Castle), is City Hall, where you will find Guest Services (lockers, stroller rental, etc.). At this point, you can either journey down Main Street—on foot or via horse-drawn trolley or one of those newfangled horseless carriage contraptions—or you can ride the Walt Disney World Railroad train around to Frontierland (the only other stop) and visit Main Street on the way out. Main Street, USA, features shops and restaurants.

Adventureland. Moving clockwise from the entrance, Adventureland is the first of the magical lands. To get there, either walk down Main Street and take the first left at the castle or take the train from Main Street, USA, get off at Frontierland, and walk back. Adventureland rides include the Jungle Cruise, Pirates of the Carribean, and the Magic Carpets of Aladdin. Or sing along with the birds in the Enchanted Tiki Room.

Frontierland. Continuing clockwise from Main Street, USA, Frontierland is the second of the magical lands. To get there, walk down Main Street and take the second left at the castle or take the train. Frontierland features Splash Mountain and the Big Thunder Mountain Railroad. Tom Sawyer Island, accessible only by raft, is a good place for kids to explore and burn off some energy.

Liberty Square. Tucked between Frontierland and Fantasy Land, Liberty Square offers a Riverboat excursion, the Hall of Presidents show, and the Haunted Mansion ride.

Fantasyland. Fantasyland is directly behind Cinderella Castle. To get there, either walk down Main Street, USA, cross the bridge, and walk through the castle or take the train to Frontierland and walk to Fantasyland. Here you will find the Prince Charming Regal Carousel, It's a Small World, Dumbo the Flying Elephant, Mad Hatter Tea Party, and more.

Tomorrowland. Tomorrowland is the last of the 6 lands and is located to the right of Cinderella Castle and next to Fantasyland. Here you can drive along the Tomorrowland Speedway, challenge Space Mountain, or pilot a spacecraft in the Astro Orbiter.

what to do

Behind-the-scenes tours. Especially if you have been to the parks several times before, a behind-the-scenes tour can be fun. Visit the train crew as they ready the steam engines to make their daily run, be part of an interactive adventure to save the Magic Kingdom from one of the Disney villains, or learn what it takes to make the magic happen. To make reservations, go to the main Disneyworld.disney.go.com website, click on the tab Things to Do, then click on the link Tours & Special Experiences.

Bibbidi Bobbidi Boutique. (407) 939-7895; disneyworld.disney.go.com/tours-and-experiences/bibbidi-bobbidi-boutique. It takes more than just a tap of the Fairy Godmother's wand, but in about an hour her assistants can transform youngsters into princesses or knights in this boutique located in Cinderella Castle.

Harmony Barbershop. (407) 934-7639. Need a trim? Call for an appointment to experience an old-fashioned barbershop. Baby's first haircut? Ask about their special package to commemorate the occasion.

The Pirates League. (407) 939-2739; disneyworld.disney.go.com/tours-and-experiences/pirates-league. Anyone can run away to sea and become a pirate, with the help of the Pirates League, that is. In less than an hour, guests of all ages become fearsome buccaneers. Call for reservations.

where to shop

Each of the 6 magical lands has bazaars, specialty shops, and vendors of all sorts.

The Emporium. disneyworld.disney.go.com/parks/magic-kingdom/shopping/emporium. Located on Main Street, USA, the Emporium takes up 1 full block, and it is the largest of the gift and souvenir shops in the Magic Kingdom.

where to eat

From ice-cream vendors to sit-down, fine-dining to family-friendly restaurants, and featuring foods from a number of cuisines, a feast for everyone is served in the Magic Kingdom.

Cinderella's Royal Table. disneyworld.disney.go.com/reservations/dining/cinderellas-royal-table. Dine with the Disney princesses at Cinderella Castle. Breakfast, lunch, and dinner served. Reservations must be made online. $$$.

The Crystal Palace. disneyworld.disney.go.com/reservations/dining/the-crystal-palace. Winnie-the-Pooh and friends join guests at this buffet and amazing sundae bar. Breakfast and lunch only. Reservations must be made online. $$$.

where to stay

Disney Resorts. disneyworld.disney.go.com/resorts. As if the themed attractions weren't enough, Disney operates a number of themed villas, resorts, hotels, and campgrounds. You can stay in a Pacific Northwest–themed lodge-style resort, an African lodge-style hotel in the middle of a game preserve, or a 1940s Atlantic City Boardwalk-themed resort. At peak season, all of the resorts are $$$-plus, except the Fort Wilderness Campground. However, if you purchase a package—room, park tickets, dining plan—during non-peak times, the prices drop significantly.

HotelOrlando.com. Disney-owned hotels aren't the only places to stay. This hotel-finder website lists more than 400 area hotels. Many are chain hotels and the Disney hotels and resorts are also listed.

Chain hotels. If you have a favorite chain, and maybe a rewards plan with one of them, check their website. Chances are, they have a hotel not far from the Disney World complex. Remember to add in parking fees at the Disney parks to the cost of your hotel room when comparing prices.

Rent a house. We kid you not. Especially if you have another family with whom to split the costs, this can be an inexpensive way to pay for a place to sleep at night and to help children de-theme, if needed. Most houses are fully furnished, including kitchen gear, so you can bring food and fix your own dinner and breakfast. Search online for "Vacation Home Rentals Orlando" or go to Orlando's Official Visitor Center's website (visitorlando.com) and look under Places to Stay/Vacation Home Rentals. Do your homework, and read the reviews.

epcot theme park

getting there

From downtown Tampa, take I-4 East toward Orlando. Travel about 58 miles to exit 67. Take exit 67 toward Epcot Theme Park, stay to the left on this long exit ramp and don't be fooled by the signs you pass—they are for vehicles in the right lane. Eventually the exit ramp splits. Take the left split toward Epcot and Downtown Disney and travel another almost 0.5 mile. Cloverleaf around onto SR 536 (Epcot Center Drive). Take the second exit to the right, and continue to the parking area. Pay the fee to park, write down where you parked, and follow the signs to the entrance.

where to go

Epcot Theme Park. (407) 824-4321; disneyworld.disney.go.com/parks/epcot. Built in 1982, the Exploratory Prototype Community of Tomorrow has grown to encompass a World Showcase area and a Future World area. Generally speaking, park hours are 9 a.m. to 9:30 p.m., but the World Showcase generally opens at 11 a.m. Closing each day is the *IllumiNations: Reflections of Earth* pyrotechnics display in and over the World Showcase Lagoon.

Future World. As you enter Epcot, you are in Future World, which is dominated by what looks like a giant golf ball sitting in the middle of the park. (Duck if you hear someone holler, "Fore!") Inside the futuristic sphere is Spaceship Earth, a gentle journey through time and space, which science fiction writer Ray Bradbury helped design and script. Other attractions in Future World include the Land Pavilion, where you can go *Soarin'* in a simulated hang-gliding adventure and view the *Circle of Life* show; The Seas with Nemo and Friends, which includes other underwater themed activities; and Innovations, Test Track, and Mission Space among others.

World Showcase. Eleven countries from around the world showcase their culture and their cuisine in pavilions rimming the World Showcase Lagoon. A few countries include rides in their exhibits—Donald Duck fans can spot him in Mexico's Gran Fiesta Tour, a boat ride featuring "The Three Caballeros"—and most offer shows of various types such as Off Kilter, the Celtic rock band performing in Epcot Canada and the Matsuriza Japanese Taiko drummers. Cast members in the stores come from the various countries; feel free to ask them about life "back home." Disney characters from each country's literature visit—see Pinocchio in Italy, for instance. Favorites, however, are the street performers—jugglers, mimes, living statues—you never know what you'll find. Look for the free KidCot fun stops at each country, where kids can create a craft.

what to do

Around the World at Epcot. (407) 939-8687; disneyworld.disney.go.com/tours-and-experiences/around-the-world-at-epcot. Take a Segway tour of the World Showcase area. Riders must be at least 16 years old and weigh between 100 and 250 pounds.

Behind the Seeds at Epcot. (407) 939-8687; disneyworld.disney.go.com/tours-and-experiences/behind-the-seeds. Want to know more about the plants and growing techniques you saw in the Living with the Land attraction? Take a 1-hour guided walking tour through the greenhouses. Open to all ages.

Seas Aqua Tour. (407) 939-8687; disneyworld.disney.go.com/tours-and-experiences/seas-aqua-tour. Go snorkeling with Nemo in the The Seas with Nemo and Friends Pavilion, a 5.7 million-gallon saltwater aquarium. Swimmers must be at least 8 years old; no special training is needed. Two other aquatic experiences also are offered: Certified scuba divers can explore the aquarium in Epcot DiveQuest, or spend some close-up time with dolphins in the Dolphins in Depth tour.

where to shop

Epcot has loads of unique shops featuring items from around the world. **Club Cool** in Future World offers samples of soft drinks from around the world in the Coca-Cola International Tasting Station. Yes, it's a gift shop, too. Jewelry, fashions, art work, wines, automobile accessories, holiday decorations, and more—plus the ubiquitous Disney souvenirs—all can be found at Epcot.

You've fallen in love with one of the handmade carpets at **Casablanca Carpets** in the Morocco Pavilion, but you can't quite picture yourself lugging it around from country to country. Never fear. Larger items can be shipped. Smaller items can be delivered to the Package Pick-Up and Shipping office in the Entrance Plaza. Stop by and claim your purchases on your way out of the park.

where to eat

Where *not* to eat is more the question! Epcot features a variety of dining styles and cuisines. Most countries offer both fine dining and fast-food-style experiences.

Coral Reef Restaurant. (407) 939-3463; disneyworld.disney.go.com/dining/coral-reef-restaurant. Dine on seafood while you watch bright marine life swim by in the Coral Reef Restaurant, located at The Seas with Nemo and Friends. Reservations can be made online or by phone. $$$.

Sunshine Season Food Fair. Located in the Land Pavillion, this food court has something for everyone at prices budget-conscious guests will appreciate. $–$$.

animal kingdom

getting there

From downtown Tampa, take I-4 East toward Orlando. Travel about 58 miles to exit 65. Take exit 65 toward Osceola Parkway and Animal Kingdom. Cloverleaf around, stay to the right to take the Disney World exit, and merge onto W. Osceola Parkway. From here, the road winds back and forth for a couple of miles. Follow the signs to Animal Kingdom (not Animal Kingdom Lodge). Keep right to arrive at the park. Pay the fee to park. Remember where you parked, then make your way to the entrance.

where to go

Animal Kingdom. (407) 824-4321; disneyworld.disney.go.com/parks/animal-kingdom/calendar. Animal Kingdom opened in 1998 as Disney's most "real-world" theme park based on the animals of the world. But, as with all Disney projects, the 1,700 animals from 250 different species are pretty much cast members in a larger imagined world of real and not-quite-real beasts. The park is divided into 7 areas, with Discovery Island and the Tree of Life at the center. Each area has its own story, attractions, and things to see. Enjoy the rides and shows. But do something else, too. Slow down. Watch closely. Let nature happen around you.

Oasis. As you enter the park, wander through the Oasis tropical gardens with babbling brooklets, waterfalls, and lush foliage. Look closely to see anteaters, sloths, deer, macaws and other animals and birds. The paths lead to the Discovery Island area.

Discovery Island area. Discovery Island is the hub from which visitors travel to each of the other lands. The Tree of Life is Animal Kingdom's iconic landmark on Discovery Island. Take time to view the animals sculpted into its trunk, but be mindful of people trying to get into the *It's Tough to be a Bug* 3-D feature show in the tree's base. Discovery Island has its own nature trails where you can see tortoises, otters, and more.

Camp Minnie-Mickey. Clockwise from the Oasis area, Camp Minnie-Mickey is the next area. Minnie and Mickey have gone fishing in the Adirondacks! Come, wander through their camp, and say hello to them and their friends; then view the 30-minute musical *Festival of the Lion King*.

Africa. Hike the Pangani Forest Exploration Trails and see gorillas. Ride the Kilimanjaro Safari open-air vehicle and see animals here, there, and everywhere. Then board the Wildlife Express Train to take a side trip to Rafiki's Planet Watch area, an area not connected directly to Discovery Island.

Rafiki's Planet Watch area. This is the Animal Kingdom's research and education center where visitors learn how the animals are cared for. There are wildlife shows and a petting area featuring unusual species of docile animals. Ride the train back to Africa to continue your journey.

Asia. Unlike in the real world, in the Animal Kingdom a short pathway takes you from the savannas of Africa to the bamboo forests of Asia. Want to see real Komodo dragons, tigers, and bats? Bats! Lots of them on the Maharajah Jungle Trek (as in walking). The bats are in a separate area—no one gets caught unawares. Then brave the Kali River Rapids—you will get wet, and we don't mean just a sprinkle—and experience Expedition Everest.

Dinoland, USA, area. A bridge at the base of Expedition Everest takes you into Dinoland, USA, with *Finding Nemo—The Musical*, the Primeval Whirl, TriceraTop Spin, a carnival-style arcade area, and more.

what to do

As with the other parks, there are several behind-the-scenes tours. The **Wild Africa Trek** views the animals from above; Wild by Design shows how Animal Kingdom was created. Call (407) 939-8687 for reservations.

where to eat

Most of the lands offer one or more places to eat, including the Yak & Yeti Restaurant in Asia and the Tusker House in Africa, but the signature restaurant lies just outside the entrance to the Animal Kingdom, which means you can eat here without buying a ticket to visit the park.

Rainforest Cafe. (407) 939-8687 (direct) or (407) 939-3463 (reservations); disneyworld.disney.go.com/dining/rainforest-cafe-animal-kingdom. This is a chain restaurant known for its ambiance—the interior simulates a rainforest and animatronic animals greet guests and recount the story of the rainforest accompanied by various sound effects. Selections range from burgers and pasta to salmon and steaks. Serves breakfast, lunch, and dinner. $–$$$.

hollywood studios

getting there

From downtown Tampa, take I-4 East toward Orlando. Travel about 58 miles to exit 62. Take exit 62 toward Disney World, cloverleaf around, and merge onto World Drive heading north. Follow N. World Drive about 2 miles, then take the exit toward Hollywood Studios/Wide World of Sports/Animal Kingdom. Stay to the left and take the ramp toward Hollywood Studios/Blizzard Beach Water Park/Animal Kingdom. Keep going straight onto S. Studio Drive South; Hollywood Studios is on your right. Pay the fee to park, remember where you parked, and make your way to the entrance.

where to go

Hollywood Studios. 351 S. Studio Dr. South, Orlando; (407) 824-4321; disneyworld.disney.go.com/parks/hollywood-studios. Walk through the Art Deco-y gates at Hollywood Studios and you find yourself on the backlot of a movie studio. Straight ahead is a gigantic sorcerer's hat reminiscent of the one Mickey wore in "The Sorcerer's Apprentice" segment of *Fantasia*, filmed in the late 1930s and released in 1940. Guests visit a number of shows—the *American Idol Experience*, two types of stunt shows, and the *Beauty and the Beast* stage show, among others—and rides—Star Tours (Star Wars ride), Rockin' Roller Coaster starring Aerosmith, Toy Story Mania, and the Twilight Zone Tower of Terror, among others.

what to do

Dine with an Imagineer. (407) 939-3463; disneyworld.disney.go.com/dining/dine-with-an-imagineer. Yup—an Imagineer. One of the people who makes the magic up for the rest of us to enjoy. Enjoy a 4-course prix fixe meal at the Hollywood Brown Derby and learn how the Imagineers make it all happen. Also available at the Flying Fish Cafe on the Disney Boardwalk.

where to eat

50's Prime Time Cafe. (407) 939-3463; disneyworld.disney.go.com/dining/50s-prime-time-cafe. TV forever changed our world, including our dining habits. At 50's Prime Time Cafe, home-cookin' style meals are accompanied by clips from 1950s-era sitcoms and "Mom's" reminders to sit up straight and eat your peas. All in good fun, of course. Serves lunch and dinner. $$–$$$.

other disney experiences

Blizzard Beach. 1500 W. Buena Vista Dr., Orlando; (407) 560-3400; disneyworld.disney.go.com/parks/blizzard-beach. Ride the chairlift to Mount Gushmore, then ride the toboggans down—wait. Chairlift? Toboggans? On a hot summer day? Cool! Blizzard Beach is one of two water parks at Walt Disney World Resort. Located near Animal Kingdom, the park includes an assortment of waterslides and rides and Tikes Peak, a play area for younger guests. A variety of food concessions keep energy levels up. Generally open 10 a.m. to 5 p.m., weather permitting, but check the calendar. Parking is free.

Disney's Boardwalk. 2101 Epcot Resorts Blvd., Lake Buena Vista; (407) 939-5100; disneyworld.disney.go.com/destinations/disneys-boardwalk. More shopping, dining, and entertainment options, this time with a turn-of-the-20th-century Atlantic City Boardwalk theme. Disney's Boardwalk rims Crescent Lake; Jellyrolls piano bar and the Atlantic Dance Hall, both for guests age 21 and older, are here. Parking is free.

Downtown Disney. 1780 Buena Vista Dr., Lake Buena Vista; disneyworld.disney.go.com/destinations/downtown-disney. Downtown Disney is divided into 3 areas: Pleasure Island, Downtown Disney Marketplace, and Downtown Disney Westside, which is the site of the Cirque du Soleil La Nouba live entertainment show (call 407-939-7600 or buy tickets online) and Disney Quest, an interactive gaming theme park. Design your own roller coaster, play virtual *Pirates of the Caribbean*, or learn to be a Disney animator—check the website for hours and height restrictions. All three areas in Downtown Disney have loads of shopping, dining, and entertainment options. Parking is free.

ESPN Wide World of Sports Complex. 700 Victory Way, Kissimmee; (407) 541-5600; espnwwos.disney.go.com/complex/welcome-center. We're talking real sports here, not the virtual kind—except for in the PlayStation Pavillion. Otherwise, it's all slide-in-at-home-plate real sports. The Atlanta Braves play spring training games here, and youth league competitions of all kinds are held here. Dining options include the ESPN Wide World of Sports Grill and other spots throughout the complex. Parking is free; valet parking is available.

Typhoon Lagoon. 1145 E. Buena Vista Blvd., Lake Buena Vista; (407) 560-4032; disney world.disney.go.com/parks/typhoon-lagoon. This tropically themed water park is located near Epcot and Downtown Disney. This one features sandy white beaches, a surf pool (with actual surfing lessons by reservation), and rafting falls and slides. You can even snorkel with sharks—for real! Look for the Shark Reef adventure. Food concessions are available. Generally open from 10 a.m. to 5 p.m., weather permitting, but check the calendar. Only one of the water parks is open from Oct to May each year so Disney can work new magic on the other one. Parking is free.

day trip 02

i-drive u crazy!
international drive

international drive

Where will you find the world's largest McDonald's—yes, as in Golden Arches? How about an indoor skydiving venue? An upside-down laboratory? All three sit on Orlando's International Drive, an eclectic mix of theme parks, world-class shopping centers, restaurants, and hotels near the Orange County Convention Center, the nation's second-largest convention facility. There are 5 mega mini-golf spots, too!

In this trip, we're focusing on everything but the theme parks and dinner theaters. Those get covered on other day trips.

Orlando's Official Visitor Center. 8723 International Dr., Suite 101, Orlando; (407) 363-5872; visitorlando.com. Even the Visitor Center is super-size—in terms of services, that is. Not only can you pick up maps and brochures here, you can also purchase discounted attraction tickets, take care of international currency exchange, and make hotel reservations. Ask for a free Orlando Magicard, which entitles you to savings throughout the area. Open 8:30 a.m. to 6:30 p.m. (last ticket sales at 6 p.m.) every day except Christmas Day.

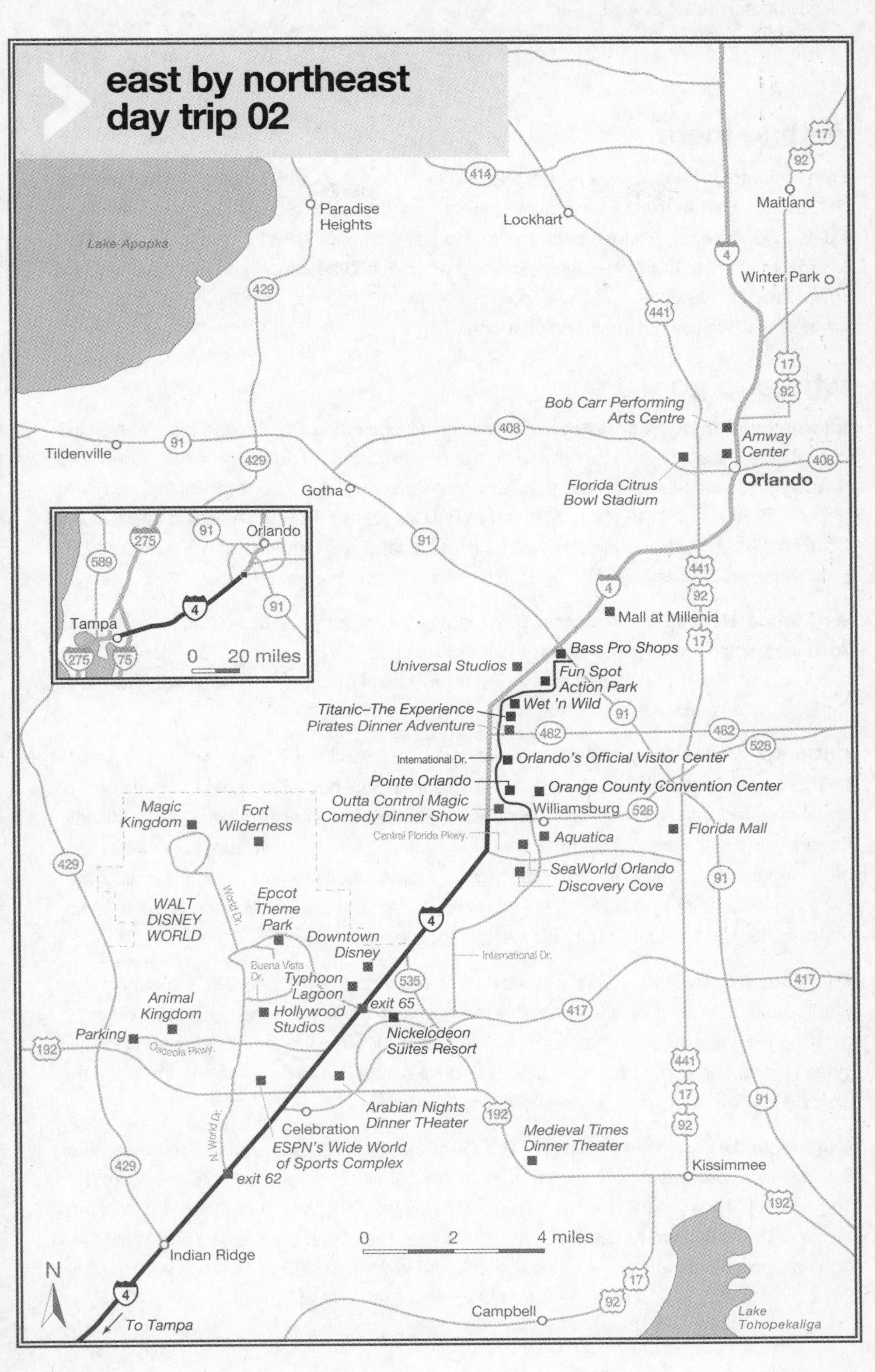

east by northeast
day trip 02
Lake Apopka
Paradise Heights
Lockhart
Maitland
Winter Park
Tildenville
Gotha
Orlando
Bob Carr Performing Arts Centre
Amway Center
Florida Citrus Bowl Stadium
Mall at Millenia
Bass Pro Shops
Universal Studios
Fun Spot Action Park
Wet 'n Wild
Titanic–The Experience
Pirates Dinner Adventure
International Dr.
Orlando's Official Visitor Center
Pointe Orlando
Orange County Convention Center
Outta Control Magic Comedy Dinner Show
Williamsburg
Central Florida Pkwy.
Aquatica
Florida Mall
SeaWorld Orlando
Discovery Cove
Magic Kingdom
Fort Wilderness
WALT DISNEY WORLD
World Dr.
Epcot Theme Park
Downtown Disney
Buena Vista Dr.
Typhoon Lagoon
exit 65
Animal Kingdom
Hollywood Studios
Nickelodeon Suites Resort
Parking
Osceola Pkwy.
Arabian Nights Dinner THeater
Celebration
ESPN's Wide World of Sports Complex
Medieval Times Dinner Theater
N. World Dr.
exit 62
Kissimmee
Indian Ridge
Campbell
Lake Tohopekaliga
To Tampa
N
0 2 4 miles
Tampa
0 20 miles

getting there

From downtown Tampa, take I-4 East toward Orlando for about 68 miles. Merge right onto SR 528 Toll East at exit 72 toward International Airport/Cape Canaveral. This is a toll road, but we won't be on it long enough to have to pay anything. Travel 1 mile to exit 1 toward International Drive. Exit to the right, cloverleaf around, and head north on International Drive toward the Convention Center/Wet 'n Wild. Merge onto International Drive; the Visitor Center is almost 2 miles down and on your right.

where to go

International Drive Resort Area. internationaldriveorlando.com. Explore the website and view the 28-page *I-Drive Visitor Guide* online, or ask for one to be mailed to you (allow 2 to 4 weeks). You can also purchase I-Trolley passes online, make hotel reservations, and learn about special events being held on International Drive. The I-Trolley runs along International Drive and Universal Boulevard, as well as some smaller side streets, from 8 a.m. to 10:30 p.m. Purchase a pass online, or be sure you have exact change with you.

Air Florida Helicopter Charters. 8990 International Dr., Orlando; (407) 354-1400; airfloridahelicopter.com. Take a short 8-mile hop around the area, or go for a longer aerial excursion of the region. Open every day from 9:30 a.m. to 7 p.m. Walk-ins welcome; 2-person minimum.

CoCo Key Water Resort. 7400 International Dr., Orlando; (877) 875-4681, (407) 351-2626; cocokeyorlando.com. Waterslides, a giant tipping bucket dumping 400 gallons of water, a water play area with water cannons, a video arcade, spots for teens, and a Minnow Lagoon for youngsters. What more could you want? Hmmm. How about a poolside bar area for parents? Okay, that, too. Plus hotel accommodations—it is a resort, after all. Water park admission is included in hotel guests' fees; day passes available for non-guests. Check the calendar for dates and hours the water park is open.

Fun Spot Action Park. 5551 Del Verde Way, Orlando; (407) 363-3867; funspot.tutengraphics.com. Multi-level and multi-skill-level go-kart tracks, bumper cars and boats, a ginormous Ferris wheel, and tamer slides and rides for the younger set. Plus two kinds of video arcade games and a snack bar. Sounds like a day's worth of fun to us. Check the website for days and times, especially during the holidays.

Magical Midway. 7001 International Dr., Orlando; (407) 370-5353; magicalmidway.com. Ever wonder what it feels like to be a human cannonball? Strap yourself into the Sling Shot and find out. The nice folks at the Magical Midway will shoot you more than 400 feet into the air—firmly attached to bungee cords, of course. There's also a Starflyer ride, multi-level go-karts, arcade games, and concessions. Open Mon and Tues 2 to 10 p.m.; Wed through Fri, 2 p.m. to midnight; and 10 a.m. to midnight on Sat and Sun.

Ripley's Believe It or Not. 8201 International Dr., Orlando; (407) 363-4418; ripleys.com/Orlando. It's called an odditorium, and even the outside fits that description. The building looks like one end is sinking into the ground; but never fear, it's only an illusion. Then again, you can believe it or not! Inside is a 16-gallery collection of oddities from around the world, based on the collection of Robert L. Ripley, a sports cartoonist who acquired strange facts and artifacts during the first half of the 20th century. ***Note:*** Some galleries may be disturbing to young children. Open 9:30 a.m. to midnight (last admission at 11 p.m.). Tickets purchased online cost less.

Titanic—The Experience. 7324 International Dr., Orlando; (877) 410-1912, (407) 248-1166; titanictheexperience.com. G. Michael Harris has made numerous dives to the R.M.S. *Titanic* wreck site and has salvaged almost 2,000 artifacts, many of which are displayed in this exhibit. His influence is evident in Titanic—The Experience. The 20,000-square-foot exhibit recreates several of the ship's areas, including the grand staircase. Costumed characters tell visitors about their lives and how they came to be on the *Titanic*. Open 9 a.m. to 9 p.m. every day; tours begin at 10 a.m. See the dinner theater section in Day Trip 04 (this section) for information about the evening event.

Wet 'n Wild. 6200 International Dr., Orlando; (407) 351-1800; wetnwildorlando.com. Wet 'n Wild is actually part of the Universal Studios Resorts complex, but we are listing it here because of its location, on International Drive but somewhat apart from the main Universal setting. However, look for combination ticket packages that include the other Universal attractions. Wet 'n Wild includes a higher percentage of multi-rider slides than most other water parks—which means smaller children can ride some of the larger slides if an adult is with them (other restrictions may apply—please check). The new Blastaway Beach kids' park–immediately to the left as you enter the park—offers more than an acre of watery fun. In addition to a wave pool, numerous slides and rides—some with sound and light enhancements—and regulation-size sand volleyball courts, Wet 'n Wild features 3 unique rides: Knee Ski uses a cable-operated ski tow to pull riders around a 0.5-mile course on a knee board; Wake Skating does pretty much the same thing only riders are upright on a skiboard; The Wild One features a personal watercraft pulling 2 people riding on large tubes. There are extra fees and extra restrictions and requirements for these 3 rides. Wet 'n Wild is open every day, but check the online schedule for hours, as they vary by season. Also, some rides close periodically for maintenance; call (800) 992-9453 to find out what is open or closed at any given time. There are a number of places to eat in the park, but Wet 'n Wild allows guests to bring coolers—no alcohol and no glass containers. Read the General Info page for other guidelines and information.

Wonder Works. 9067 International Dr., Orlando; (407) 351-8800; wonderworksonline.com/Orlando. No, you don't have to stand on your head to enter. But it is a bit disconcerting to walk into an upside-down building! Ah, but then you learn a tornado plunked this research laboratory smack dab in the middle of International Drive. Pass through the inverter, then explore all the interactive hands-and-feet-on exhibits. Make music by walking on a giant keyboard, take a ropes course, lie on a bed of nails, design your own roller coaster, play in the bubble lab—there's loads to do here. Open 9 a.m. to midnight.

where to shop

Bass Pro Shops Outdoor World. 5156 International Dr., Orlando; (407) 563-5200; basspro.com. All the camping, hunting, fishing, and outdoor gear you could ever need and then some. Look on their Events list for fly fishing clinics, boating classes, and conservation clinics. Open every day except Christmas Day. Mon through Sat open from 9 a.m. to 10 p.m.; Sun open 10 a.m. to 8 p.m.

Orlando Premium Outlets. 4951 International Dr., Orlando; (407) 352-9600; and 8200 Vineland Ave., Orlando; (407) 238-7787; premiumoutlets.com. That's right—not one but two outlet malls anchor International Drive. Look for Nieman Marcus and Saks Fifth Avenue Off Fifth at the International Drive store and stores like Barneys New York and Vera Bradley at the Vineland Avenue store. Shop 'til you drop, then shop some more. Check the website calendars for opening and closing times.

Outlet Marketplace. 5269 International Dr., Orlando; (407) 352-9600; premiumoutlets.com. And still more outlet stores. This one has shops like Calvin Klein, Coldwater Creek, Van Heusen, and Golf Passion. Does the shopping never end? Check the website calendar for opening and closing times.

Peter Glenn Ski & Sports. 5403 International Dr., Orlando; (407) 354-1234; peterglenn.com. So what if there's no snow in Florida? Use your imagination—that's what this area is all about, right? Snowboards and skis, plus skateboards, wakeboards, and all the appropriate attire one might need to indulge in such activities. Open Mon through Fri from 10 a.m. to 8 p.m.; Sat from 10 a.m. to 6 p.m.; and Sun from noon to 6 p.m.

Pointe Orlando. 9101 International Dr., Orlando; (407) 248-2838; pointeorlando.com. Specialty and boutique shops mix with upscale eateries and entertainment spots at Pointe Orlando. You'll find shops like Mindful Minerals, Armani Exchange, and Tommy Bahamas. Open every day at noon.

where to eat

The International Drive Resort Area website lists 11 pages of restaurants ranging from fast-food to gourmet cuisine. We're listing just a couple of unique spots here. Dinner theaters have their own separate day trip section.

BB King's Orlando. 9101 International Dr., Orlando; (407) 370-4550; bbkingclubs.com. Down-home Southern cooking, Memphis-style ribs, and live entertainment every night of the week. Plus a store to shop in. Let the good times roll, indeed. BB King's Orlando is located in the Pointe Orlando shopping area. Opens at 11 a.m. 7 days a week. Check the Live Music calendar on the website to see who is playing when. $$–$$$.

McDonald's. 6875 Sand Lake Rd., Orlando; (407) 351-2185; mcfun.com/restaurants/view/7. Yes, McDonald's. Only this one has the world's largest entertainment play space for the kids. We're talking a tree house play area with tubes to crawl around in and slides to take things down a level. Plus card-swipe arcade games with prizes and a toddler play area. This Mickey D's features the Bistro Gourmet menu with paninis, pasta, pizza, and more. Yes, you can still get a burger and fries. Open 24/7. $.

Ming Court Wok & Grille. 9188 International Dr., Orlando; (407) 351-9988; ming-court.com. A feast for all the senses, Ming Court offers elegance, artistry, and an extensive selection of Asian foods. Plus they have an imaginative menu for children (and any pet dragons they happen to bring along); live, traditional Oriental folk music nightly; and cooking classes (for groups of 20 or more). Lunch is served from 11 a.m. to 3 p.m. every day. Dinner is served from 4:30 to 11 p.m. every day. $$$.

where to stay

There truly is no lack of places to stay. The Visitor Center website lists them all with prices and amenities. However, not many include the chance to be slimed and not many look like a real castle.

Nickelodeon Suites Resort. 14500 Continental Gateway, Orlando; (407) 387-5437; nickhotel.com. For kids and kids at heart, Nickelodeon Suites Resort features themed suites; 2 pool areas with slides and flumes, interactive water towers, and poolside games and activities; Character Breakfasts with Nickelodeon characters; nightly shows; and, of course, lots of green SLIME! Want more? Okay—there's also mini-golf, a 4-D theater experience, food court, a teen hangout spot, a kids' spa, and seating at Studio Nick shows. Parents will find a business center, fitness facility, lounge area, and more. No pets. $$–$$$.

Holiday Inn Resort Orlando—The Castle. 8629 International Dr., Orlando; (877) 317-5753; thecastleorlando.com. The Castle offers all the amenities of a Holiday Inn and then some—a dive-in movie poolside each evening (weather permitting), an arcade room, specially furnished Kids Suites, business services, complimentary shuttle service to theme parks, laundry facilities, and royal decor inside and out. Small pets are welcomed. $–$$.

day trip 03

east by northeast

oh, orlando . . . more than theme parks!

orlando

orlando

Before Mickey, Harry, and Shamu moved in, Orange County was noted for its—surprise, surprise!—oranges. Acres and acres of orange groves filled the county. Devastating freezes moved growers further south, and theme parks moved in to take their places. Today, Orlando, the county seat, is home to businesses in the entertainment and technology industries and has one of the largest universities (in terms of enrollment) in the United States.

This day trip takes us to the greater Orlando area, which includes Maitland, Winter Park, and the most extensive collection of Louis Comfort Tiffany's works and of American pottery. We'll visit historical neighborhoods, art galleries and museums, sports venues, theaters, and more. First we'll stop at the Visitor Center, located on International Drive.

Orlando's Official Visitor Center. 8723 International Dr., Suite 101, Orlando; (407) 363-5872; visitorlando.com. Even though the Visitor Center is located on International Drive, it serves as the information gateway for the entire Orlando area. Pick up maps and brochures here, purchase discounted attraction tickets, take care of international currency exchange, and make hotel reservations. Ask for a free Orlando Magicard, which entitles you to savings throughout the area. Open 8:30 a.m. to 6:30 p.m. (last ticket sales at 6 p.m.) every day except Christmas Day.

east by northeast
day trip 03

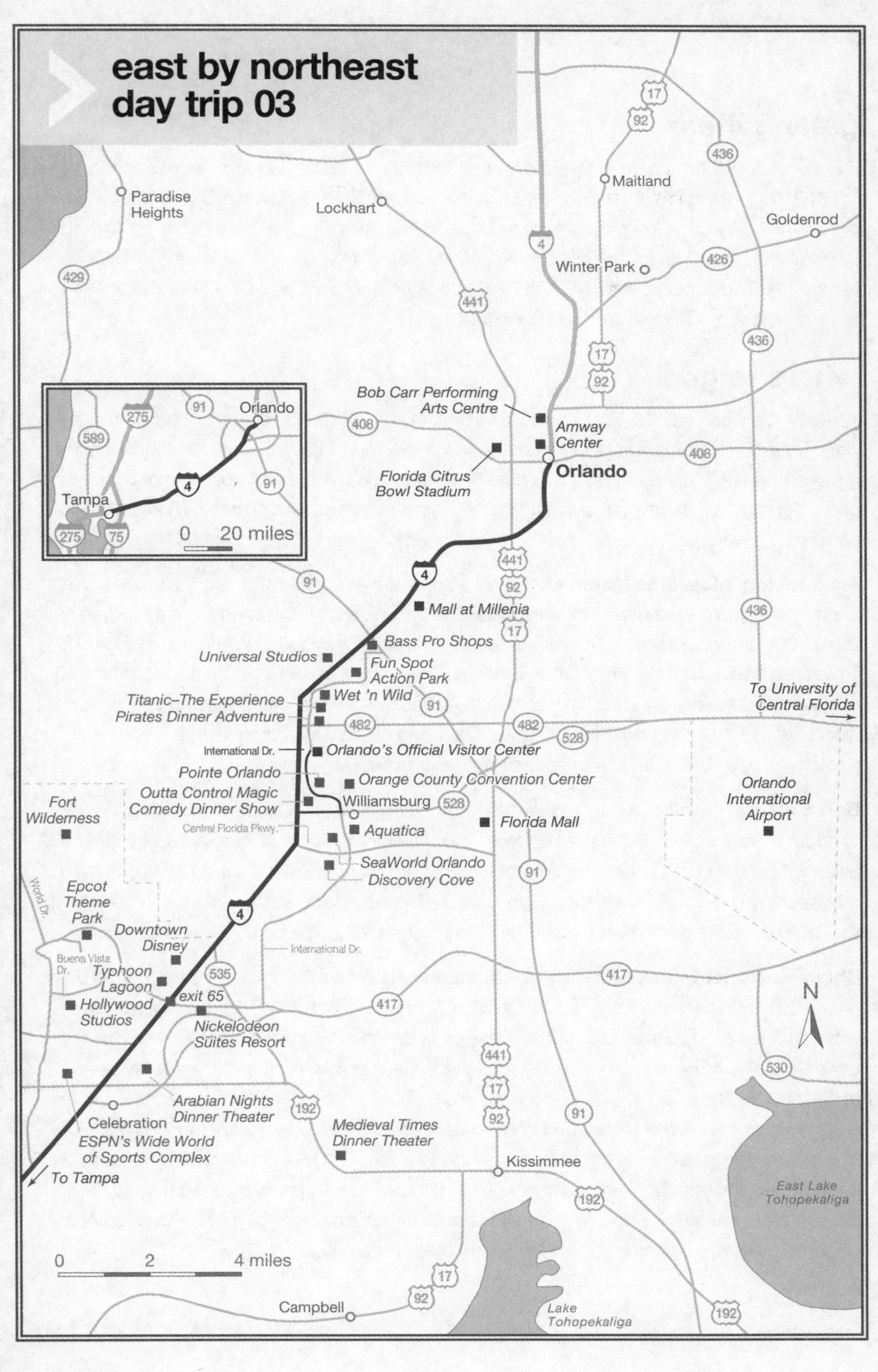

getting there

From downtown Tampa, take I-4 East toward Orlando for about 68 miles. Merge right onto SR 528 Toll East at exit 72 toward International Airport/Cape Canaveral. This is a toll road, but we won't be on it long enough to have to pay anything. Travel 1 mile to exit 1 toward International Drive. Exit to the right, cloverleaf around, and head north on International Drive toward the Convention Center/Wet 'n Wild. Merge onto International Drive; the Visitor Center is almost 2 miles down and on your right.

where to go

Amway Center. 400 W. Church St., Orlando; (407) 440-7000; amwaycenter.com. The Amway Center is where the NBA Orlando Magic work round-ball magic on the home court. It's also home to the Predators, a two-time AFL champion team, and it hosts major concerts and entertainment extravaganzas. The center has a play area for children, STUFF's Magic Castle, on Level 5.

Art & History Museums Maitland. 231 W. Packwood Ave., Maitland; (407) 539-2181; artandhistory.org. When the Maitland Historical Society and the Maitland Art Center merged in 2010, they brought together several collections of historical and artistic interest, including a Telephone Museum, Carpentry Shop Museum, the Waterhouse Residence Museum, and other art and history exhibits. The collection is housed on two campuses, one on Packwood Avenue, the other on Lake Lily Drive. Days and hours vary, but the office is open Mon through Fri from 9 a.m. to 5 p.m. except on major holidays.

Bob Carr Performing Arts Centre. 401 W. Livingston St., Orlando; (407) 426-1739; orlandovenues.net. The Bob Carr Performing Arts Centre features performances by the the Orlando Philharmonic Orchestra (orlandophil.org), the Orlando Ballet (orlandoballet.org), and other performing artists. ***Note:*** The Bob Carr PAC is scheduled to be replaced in 2014 by the Dr. Phillips Performing Art Center (drphillipscenter.org), currently under construction.

Charles Hosmer Morse Museum of American Art. 445 N. Park Ave., Winter Park; (407) 645-5311; morsemuseum.org. Louis Comfort Tiffany is most noted for his stained glass work, but he also designed furniture and jewelry and worked in other art forms. The Charles Hosmer Morse Museum collection includes pieces in every art form and from every period of Tiffany's life, making it the most comprehensive Tiffany collection. Also at the museum is an extensive collection of Rockwood pottery pieces and works by several American painters and artists. The museum is open Tues through Sat from 9:30 a.m. to 4 p.m. (open until 8 p.m. on Fri, Nov through Apr) and from 1 to 4 p.m. on Sun. A nominal fee is charged most days, but the museum is open free to all visitors on Fri from 4 to 8 p.m., Nov through Apr. Check the website calendar for lectures and other events.

Downtown Orlando Visitor Center. 201 S. Orange Ave., Orlando; (407) 246-2555; downtownorlando.com. Want to know what's happening just in the downtown area? This is the place to stop. Friendly volunteers can answer questions or you can use the interactive screens to learn more about Downtown Orlando. Ask about their guided Skyline Tour and other tours.

Florida Citrus Bowl Stadium. 1610 W. Church St., Orlando; (407) 849-2020; orlando venues.net. With a seating capacity of more than 70,000, the Florida Citrus Bowl Stadium hosts a number of major sporting and entertainment events, including the New Year's Day Capital One Bowl, Wrestlemania XXIV, Monster Jam, and a number of "Rock Superbowls."

Holocaust Memorial Resource & Education Center of Central Florida. 851 N. Maitland Ave., Maitland; (407) 628-0555; holocaustedu.org. One of the first Holocaust education centers founded in the nation, the Holocaust Memorial Resource & Education Center of Central Florida houses both permanent and temporary exhibits, as well as archives and a research library. The center is free and open to the public Mon through Thurs from 9 a.m. to 4 p.m., on Fri from 9 a.m. to 1 p.m., and on Sat from 1 to 4 p.m.

Leu Gardens. 1920 N. Forest Ave., Orlando; (407) 246-2620; leugardens.org. In the early part of the 20th century, Harry P. Leu built an industrial supply company and planted gardens. Not many people today remember the business, but people still come to see the gardens, located on Lake Rowena. Leu, who became known as the Johnny Appleseed of Central Florida, developed several strains of camellias. Today, the Harry P. Leu Gardens hold the third largest collection of camellias in the United States, the largest formal rose garden in Florida, and several acres of other types of gardens for visitors to enjoy and from which they can learn. The Leu House Museum is also open to visitors. The Gardens are open from 9 a.m. to 5 p.m. every day except Christmas Day; the Leu House Museum is open from 10 a.m. to 4 p.m. with tours every half hour. The Leu House Museum is closed Christmas day and the month of July. No pets. Admission is free on the first Monday of each month. Last admittance is at 4 p.m.

Mennello Museum of American Art. 900 E. Princeton St., Orlando; (407) 246-2478; mennellomuseum.com. From the Sculpture Gardens on the outside of the Mennello Museum to the brightly colored works of Earl Cunningham hung against equally colorful walls on the inside, the Mennello Museum of American Art offers an upbeat collection of works by contemporary American artists. The museum, located near Loch Haven Park, is open Tues through Sat from 10:30 a.m. to 4:30 p.m. and on Sun from noon to 4:30 p.m. Closed on major holidays.

Orange County Regional History Center. 65 East Central Blvd., Orlando; (800) 965-2030, (407) 836-8500; thehistorycenter.org. From pre-recorded history to the 21st century, the Orange County Regional History Center, located in the Old Courthouse building, covers it all. Visually rich and interactive, the exhibits are ranged on three floors of the center and include displays ranging from the influence of the cattle, citrus, and aviation industries to ones detailing the development of today's theme parks. A pioneer home shows how people lived in the 19th century, and a 1917 courtroom shows how the legal system operated. Traveling exhibits from the Smithsonian and other museums around the country rotate through the center's galleries. Open Mon through Sat from 10 a.m. to 5 p.m. and Sun from noon to 5 p.m.

Orlando International Airport. 1 Airport Blvd., Orlando; (407) 825-2001; orlandoairports .net. Located just south of the city (and south of the International Drive area), the Orlando International Airport is one of the busiest in the nation. We don't often think of airports as a place to do anything more than drop off and pick up travelers, but there are a number of shops and restaurants in the landside building, as well as a collection of art (go to orlando airports.net/art/collection.htm). Plus we've never outgrown the fun of watching planes take off and land.

Orlando Museum of Art. 2416 N. Mills Ave., Orlando; (407) 896-4231; omart.org. The OMA's collection includes exhibits on West African textiles, wood work, and masks; Art of the Ancient Americas, American Art Before 1945, American Art After 1945, and Contemporary American Graphics. The museum is open Tues through Fri from 10 a.m. to 4 p.m. and on Sat and Sun from noon to 4 p.m.

Orlando Science Center. 777 E. Princeton St., Orlando; (888) 672-4386, (407) 514-2000; osc.org. Permanent exhibits include NatureWorks, which focuses on reptiles; DinoDigs, which looks at prehistoric animals; and the Science Park, which explores the concepts of the physical sciences: electricity, magnetism, sound waves, and more. Look for the Severe Weather Center, which presents meteorology in the context of a weather channel, within the Our Planet, Our Universe exhibit. The KidsTown interactive gallery is especially for younger scientists. The pièce de résistance, however, is the Crosby Observatory, which houses Florida's largest publicly accessible refractor telescope. The Science Center also has an IWERKS domed theater and Digistar II Planetarium. Open Sun through Tues and Thurs through Sat from 10 a.m. to 5 p.m. Closed on Wed. Check their online calendar for astronomy events.

what to do

golf

There are more than 170 golf courses and at least 20 golf academies in the Orlando area. Many of those courses host top-level tournaments. No wonder the International Association of Golf Tour Operators chose Orlando as the "North American Golf Destination of the Year" in 2010. Look for the Orlando Golfer's Guide online at orlando.golfersguide.com for complete information about area courses and amenities. Visitorlando.com has information about golf packages under their Things to Do tab.

history

Historic Walking Tour. Go to the City of Orlando's website and download a four-page booklet with information about and photos of 28 different historical buildings in the downtown area. Want to take a guided tour with an expert? Call Downtown Orlando at (407) 254-4636 to make a reservation.

theater

Orlando Repertory Theater. 1001 E. Princeton St., Orlando; (407) 896-7365; orlandorep.com. The Orlando Repertory Theater produces plays for families and children. Past productions have included *Thoroughly Modern Millie*, *Seussical the Musical*, and *A Wrinkle in Time*. The Orlando Repertory Theater offers a number of education experiences for children and youth, and it partners with the University of Central Florida in offering an M.F.A. in Youth Theater.

Orlando Shakespeare Theater. 812 E. Rollins St., Orlando; (407) 447-1700; orlandoshakes.org. Yes, they perform the Bard's works here—and not just the tried-and-true but also some of the lesser-performed plays. They also produce more modern comedies, dramas, and revues, as well as plays for the young and young at heart. The Orlando Shakespeare Theater also offers a number of acting classes and performance opportunities for children and adults, and it partners with the University of Central Florida in offering an M.F.A. in Acting.

Theatre UCF. 4000 Central Florida Blvd., Orlando; (407) 823-1500; theatre.ucf.edu. Mainstage productions, black box productions, and dance concerts are held at the Theatre UCF. Student performers have a way of becoming tomorrow's award winners. Just sayin' . . .

where to shop

Florida Mall. 8001 S. Orange Blossom Trail, Orlando; (407) 851-7234; simon.com. With more than 260 stores and more than 30 restaurants, The Florida Mall is Central Florida's largest mall. There is an electric car charging station by the taxi stands near the Food Court entrance. Regular hours are 10 a.m. to 9 p.m. Mon through Sat and noon to 6 p.m. on Sun.

Mall at Millenia. 4200 Conroy Rd., Orlando; (407) 363-3555; mallatmillenia.com. A Forbes Company property, the Mall at Millenia features more than 150 shops and restaurants, a full-service US Post Office, foreign currency exchange, valet parking, and concierge services. The mall opens at 10 a.m. every day except Sat, when it opens at 9 a.m. The mall closes at 9 p.m. on Sun, at 9:30 p.m. Mon through Thurs, and at 10 p.m. on Fri and Sat. Restaurant hours may differ.

Park Avenue. 151 W. Lyman Ave., Winter Park; (407) 644-8281; parkave-winterpark.com. A brick-paved area with more than 140 boutique shops—including one of the only Dior outlets in the world—galleries, and restaurants. Schedule a consultation with "closetologist" Jackie Walker to make room for all your new treasures.

where to eat

Christo's Cafe. 1815 Edgewater Dr., Orlando; (407) 425-8136; christoscafe.com. Whether you want your basic bacon and eggs breakfast or something hearty for dinner—say country fried steak and gravy—Christo's serves the basic soups, sandwiches, and hot meals. Most breakfast items are served all day. Christo's Cafe is open Mon through Sat from 6:30 a.m. to 9 p.m. and on Sun from 7 a.m. to 3 p.m. $.

Funky Monkey Wine Company. 912 N. Mills Ave., Orlando; (407) 427-1447; funkymonkeywine.com. A wine bar and restaurant, the Funky Monkey Wine Company has two locations—this downtown one and another in Pointe Orlando on International Drive. The menu sounds typical, until you begin reading the descriptions—the duck breast, for instance, is seared and served with a spring berry reduction sauce, seasonal vegetables . . . and a goat cheese mash. The Funky Monkey Wine Company is open Mon through Thurs from 4:30 to 11 p.m., on Fri from 4:30 p.m. to 2 a.m., on Sat from 5 p.m. to 2 a.m., and on Sun from 5 to 11 p.m. $$$.

Hue Restaurant. 629 E. Central Blvd., Orlando; (407) 849-1800; huerestaurant.com. Located downtown in the business district, Hue Restaurant offers an upscale, simply classic dining experience. Small plates include tuna tartare, caprese pizza, and fried oysters. Main plates include duck breast, salmon, and steaks. Hue Restaurant opens every day at 11:30 a.m. and serves both lunch and dinner. On Sunday the restaurant opens at 11 a.m. for brunch. $$$.

McCormick & Schmick's Seafood Restaurants. 4200 Conroy Rd., Orlando; (407) 226-6515; mccormickandschmicks.com. Located in the Mall at Millenia, McCormick & Schmick's features fresh seafood, aged steaks, poultry, pasta, and more. The menu changes every day, depending on what seafood is available. Opens every day at 11 a.m. Closes at 11 p.m. Mon through Thurs, at midnight on Fri and Sat, and at 10 p.m. on Sun. $$$.

where to stay

Courtyard at Lake Lucerne. 211 N. Lucerne Circle East, Orlando; (407) 648-5188; orlandohistoricinn.com. The Courtyard at Lake Lucerne consists of four historic homes, in architectural styles ranging from Victorian to Art Deco, which have been turned into bed-and-breakfast establishments. Lovely gardens and courtyards add to the ambiance and are favorite places for weddings and other events. A complimentary expanded continental breakfast and a complimentary evening cocktail hour are included in the stay, as is high-speed Internet access. $$–$$$.

Grand Bohemian Hotel Orlando. 325 S. Orange Ave., Orlando; (866) 663-0024, (407) 313-9000; marriott.com/hotels/travel/mcoak-grand-bohemian-hotel-orlando-autograph-collection. The Grand Bohemian Hotel Orlando, a Marriott Autograph Collection hotel, might be an art and music lover's dream come true, a place where one can live for a few days in an art gallery surrounded by music. From the red Italian mosaic-tiled, barrel-vaulted ceiling in the lobby—to say nothing of the sumptuous red, black, and gold color scheme—to the gallery-quality artwork adorning the walls, the Grand Bohemian provides a feast for the eyes. Under the Klimtz Rotunda sits an Imperial Grand Bösendorfer piano, one of only two in the world, the music from which can be enjoyed in the Bösendorfer Lounge and in the Boheme restaurant, both of which serve breakfast, lunch, and dinner. Room amenities are what one might expect from an autograph collection hotel, and the business and fitness centers are always open. The pool is on the rooftop, and the Poseidon Spa (407-581-4838 for reservations) offers personalized services. Pets are welcomed. $$$.

day trip 04

east by northeast

other worlds to explore:
seaworld orlando group;
dinner theater worlds

This trip take us to the oceans of the world, to a medieval jousting tournament, and on board the *Titanic*—plus half a dozen other worlds within worlds. Never let it be said that central Florida is lacking in imagination! First we will visit the SeaWorld complex, which includes Aquatica and Discovery Cove. Then we'll look at what the Orlando area offers in the way of lunch and dinner shows.

seaworld orlando group

The SeaWorld Orlando group includes SeaWorld Orlando itself, a park themed around the world's oceans and the creatures inhabiting those oceans; Aquatica, SeaWorld's water park, which also features sea animal encounters; and Discovery Cove, SeaWorld's day resort with more water-animal adventures awaiting.

As with many attractions these days, it pays to review the websites before you go. As in pay $. Look for the online deals and packages that cover things like meals, parking, paddleboat rides, Skytower rides, stroller rental, and more. You can buy tickets at the gate, but you'll probably end up paying more than if you bought them online ahead of time. Don't want to wait in line for the rides? SeaWorld Orlando also offers Quick Queue options that allow you to pay for the privilege of going to the head of the line at many of the rides and attractions.

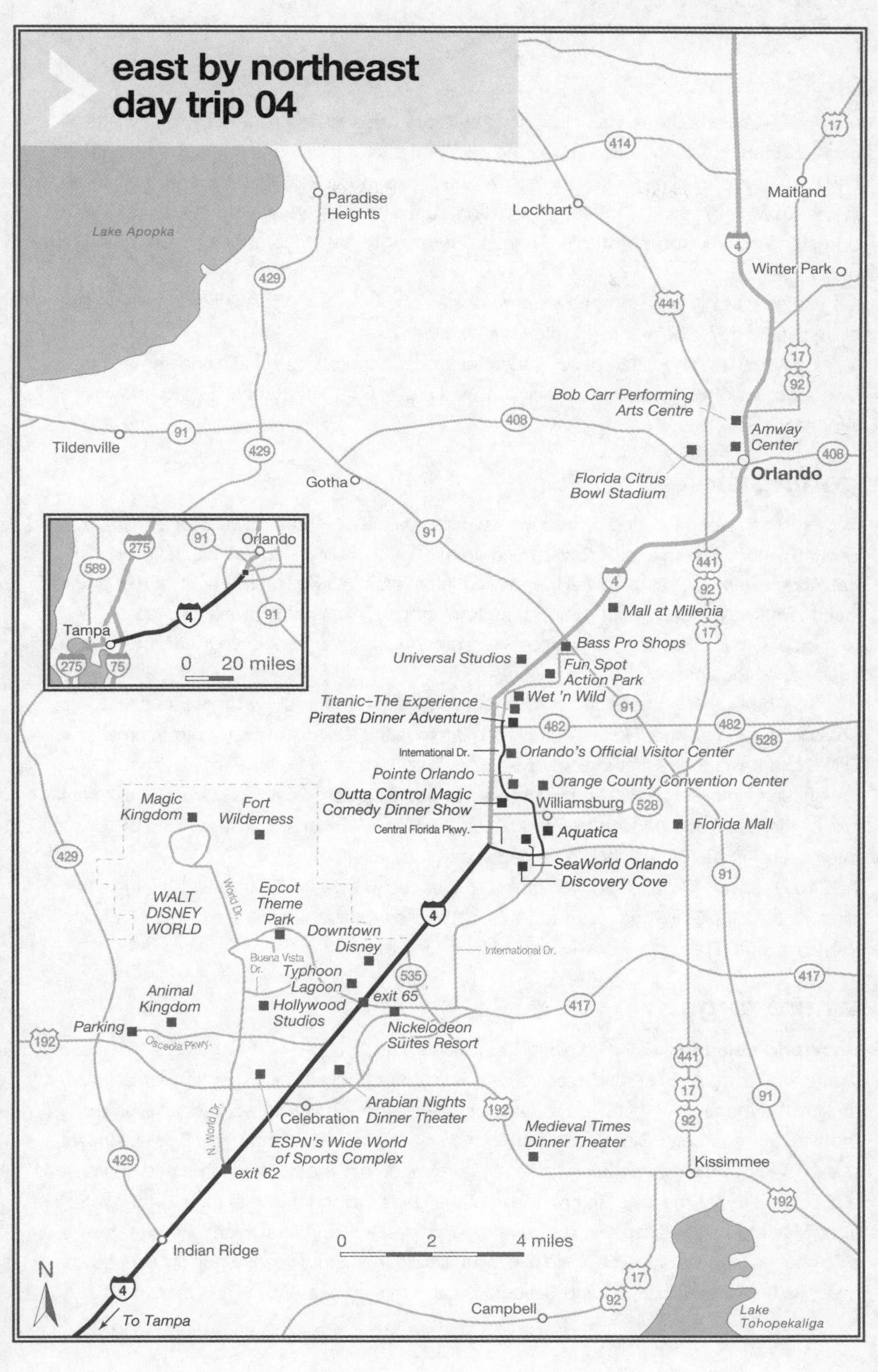
east by northeast
day trip 04
Lake Apopka
Paradise Heights
Lockhart
Maitland
Winter Park
Tildenville
Gotha
Orlando
Bob Carr Performing Arts Centre
Amway Center
Florida Citrus Bowl Stadium
Tampa
0 20 miles
Mall at Millenia
Bass Pro Shops
Universal Studios
Fun Spot Action Park
Wet 'n Wild
Titanic–The Experience
Pirates Dinner Adventure
International Dr.
Orlando's Official Visitor Center
Pointe Orlando
Orange County Convention Center
Outta Control Magic Comedy Dinner Show
Williamsburg
Central Florida Pkwy.
Aquatica
Florida Mall
SeaWorld Orlando
Discovery Cove
Magic Kingdom
Fort Wilderness
WALT DISNEY WORLD
World Dr.
Epcot Theme Park
Downtown Disney
Buena Vista Dr.
Typhoon Lagoon
Animal Kingdom
Hollywood Studios
exit 65
Nickelodeon Suites Resort
Parking
Osceola Pkwy.
Celebration
Arabian Nights Dinner Theater
ESPN's Wide World of Sports Complex
Medieval Times Dinner Theater
N. World Dr.
exit 62
Kissimmee
Indian Ridge
0 2 4 miles
N
To Tampa
Campbell
Lake Tohopekaliga

The SeaWorld, Aquatica, and Discovery Cove websites are fairly easy to navigate. A pop-up on the main page even gives the park hours for the day, the current temperature, and links to helpful spots within the site. At the top, click on Park Info; look for tabs called In the Know and Insider Tips for information about what to wear, where you might end up getting soaked (part of the fun, right?), and how to help little ones get the most out of their visit.

Some parking fees and passes are transferrable from SeaWorld Orlando to Aquatica on the same day. Check the website for restrictions.

SeaWorld Orlando has a pet kennel at the entrance. You must bring the animal's own food, proof of shots, etc. Check the web under Park Info/Kennel Services for more information.

getting there

To get to SeaWorld Orlando from downtown Tampa, take I-4 East toward Orlando. Travel about 67 miles east to exit 71 toward SeaWorld. Stay to the right so you can take the Central Florida Parkway ramp toward SeaWorld/International Drive. Merge right onto Central Florida Parkway, travel about a mile, then turn left onto SeaWorld Drive. Keep bearing left to the parking lot. Pay the parking fee, remember where you parked your car, then make your way to the entrance.

To Aquatica, if you are coming to Aquatica from Tampa, follow the same directions, but continue on Central Florida Parkway to International Drive. Turn left onto International Drive, and travel to the first major intersection. Turn right onto Water Play Way, and follow the entrance into the park. If you want to go to Aquatica from SeaWorld Orlando, exit right out of the SeaWorld parking lot, which puts you on Sea Harbor Drive. Once you cross International Drive, Sea Harbor Drive becomes Water Play Way.

To Discovery Cove, if you are coming to Discovery Cove from Tampa, follow the same directions as for SeaWorld Orlando, but continue on Central Florida Parkway, past SeaWorld Drive, to Discovery Cove Drive, the next road to your right.

where to go

SeaWorld Orlando. 7007 SeaWorld Dr., Orlando; (888) 800-5447, (407) 351-3600; seaworldparks.com. At SeaWorld, visitors can travel from tropical Key West to sub-zero Antarctica in a matter of minutes—and take a side trip to the mythical world of Atlantis along the way. As you enter SeaWorld Orlando, you'll see the 400-foot-tall Sky Tower straight ahead. The Sky Tower has been at SeaWorld Orlando since day one, and a ride up is still a good way to get the lay of the park and of the lands beyond. Near its base is the Waterfront Marketplace, with shops, restaurants, and street performers. From the entrance, a clockwise journey around SeaWorld takes you first to the Manta coaster ride (fly face down, head first!), Manta Aquarium, and Seaport Theater to see *Pets Ahoy*. Then stop in the Key

counter-clockwise to beat the crowds

You may have noticed that the tours take you through theme parks in clockwise fashion, starting to the left as you enter the parks and circling around to the right. That's how most people instinctively tour the parks.

To beat the crowds, then, consider going counter-clockwise. Move to your right and circle around that way. You'll generally find fewer lines at the rides on the right in the morning and at the rides on the left in the afternoon.

Or go all the way straight back and start from the point furthest from the entrance. Circle around either way—you'll usually still find yourself out of the thickest of the crowds.

West area and say hello to the turtles, more stingrays, and dolphins (find out when feeding times are scheduled) before heading to the Whale and Dolphin Theater where the *Blue Horizon* show is staged. Next up is Journey to Atlantis, a flume/coaster ride exploring the mythical lost city, followed by Kraken, a sea monster of a ride. Visit Clyde and Seamore at the Sea Lion & Otter Stadium (arrive early for the pre-show warmup), then wander over to the Nautilus Theater for *A'Lure, The Call of the Ocean* acrobatic show. By now, you are directly opposite the entrance. Shamu Stadium is next, with One Ocean, featuring some of the ocean's largest creatures. Then visit Shamu's Happy Harbor, where younger guests can climb nets, ride a carousel or a gentle coaster, play arcade games, and more. Then take a simulated helicopter ride to the Base Station Wild Arctic to see the real northern pole area. (At Christmas time, this becomes the Polar Express journey.) Finally, the Atlantic Bayside Stadium hosts concerts and shows—check the calendar to see what's coming up. Have we listed it all? What fun would that be?!

Aquatica. 5800 Water Play Way, Orlando; (888) 800-5447, (407) 351-3600; aquaticabyseaworld.com. Aquatica isn't just about slip-slidin' down screamer slides like Tassie's Twisters or playing on the beach at Cutback Cove. Aquatica is SeaWorld's waterpark, so you can expect animal encounters here, too. From the entrance, clockwise, you'll find Dolphin Plunge, which features a section of clear tubing running through the Commerson's Dolphin exhibit, giving the illusion you are actually swimming with—okay, zooming past—the dolphins. Keep going to your left and you reach Whanau Ride—make that four slide choices in one—and Omaka Rocks, with high-speed half-pipes. Next door is not one but two side-by-side wave pools at Cutback Cove and Big Surf Shores—and some beach area to lounge around on. Katie's Kookabura Cove features water fun for guests no taller than 48 inches. Speedsters can race each other at Taumata Racer, which has four side-by-side slides and timers at the end. Then comes the Walhalla Wave and the HooRoo Run—send the tube up the center lift so you don't have to lug it up yourself. Walkabout Waters lets kids do just that—climb on, walk around, splash in, and get splashed on. Roa's Rapids zips you around a swiftly flowing river. Finally, or anytime you need a break, Loggerhead Lane, a lazy tube ride, takes you inside an aquarium and is also the way to Tassie's Twisters.

Discovery Cove. 6000 Discovery Cove Way, Orlando; (877) 557-7404; discoverycove .com. Discovery Cove is a more laid-back day-resort experience offering unique animal encounters and water fun. Forget the animal shows. At Discovery Cove visitors have a 30-minute reserved time period to come face to face with dolphins. A walk-through aviary brings the birds close enough to feed from visitors' hands. Go snorkeling in the Grand Reef or take an underwater walk wearing diving helmets. Or just laze your way down the Wind-away River. Breakfast and lunch are included as are lockers, snorkel gear, specially formulated sunscreen, and admission to SeaWorld Orlando, Aquatica, or Busch Gardens Tampa Bay. Check out their Trainer for a Day program—or make arrangements for one of the dolphins to deliver a special-greetings message to someone else in your party. Check-in begins at 8 a.m.; resort hours are 9 a.m. to 5:30 p.m. daily.

what to do

Behind-the-Scenes at SeaWorld Orlando. Want to actually get in the water with the beluga whales? Or find out what it's like to work with the sea lions, dolphins, and beluga whales? Look for the Beluga Interaction Program, the Marine Mammal Keeper Experience, and other additional experiences online by clicking on the Attractions tab, then look for Exclusive Park Experiences. Reservations must be made in advance. Age and other restrictions may apply.

where to eat

Dining at SeaWorld Orlando. Dining options range from turkey legs and nacho platters at Captain Pete's Island Eats ($) to the Sharks Underwater Grille ($$–$$$), where the food is more on the order of filet mignon and pan-seared merluza. Look for information about the Makahiki Luau (admission $$$) under the Dinner Theater section.

Dining at Aquatica. No upscale dining here—there's something about swimsuits and steaks that don't quite go together. No worries, however; there are three spots keeping tummies full. The Banana Beach Cookout is a buffet with pizza, hot dogs, beef tips, chicken, sides, salads, and desserts. The WaterStone Grill has burgers, wraps, salads, and more. The Mango Market has sweet and salty snacks. You can pre-purchase a picnic or buy a dining pass. ***Note:*** Coolers under 16-quart size are allowed in the park, but they may contain only bottled water, baby food in plastic containers (no glass), and small snacks (individually wrapped, under 3 ounces).

where to stay

The Discovery Cove website lists a number of hotels and resorts in the area offering a number of perks to SeaWorld, Aquatica, and Discovery Cove guests.

dinner theater worlds

Whether your fantasies run to sitting in on the king's feast at a Medieval jousting tournament—yes, with real horses—or to laughing it up in a Prohibition-era speakeasy with Scarface Al himself, you'll find a dinner theater in the Orlando area to add to your fun. Some are musical theater style productions; with some the cast members mingle with the audience as part of the performance. Generally, guests arrive at an appointed time and place their meal orders. While they wait, pre-show entertainment and appetizers—with opportunities to purchase drinks, souvenirs, etc.—set the stage for what is to follow.

You'll find the reviews on these places are mixed. Most shows are serving hundreds of people at a seating, so menu choices may be limited. Dinner service may occur during brief lulls in the action of the show—and the show itself may capture your attention to the point you forget to eat! Many of these places also offer lunch service. Reservations are a must. Shop around for tickets—search online for ticket brokers looking to fill empty seats or offering package deals. Follow the venues on Facebook and Twitter for last-minute deals. Many shows offer discounts for online (as opposed to telephone) sales. All shows, with no discounts taken into consideration, are in the $$$ range.

This list does not include any of the Disney or Universal venue dinner theater shows. But it does include one spot that isn't quite a dinner theater and is more than a theme park. Old Town, in Kissimmee, has rides, games and shops—but it also features car cruises and concerts.

Note: Some shows, especially those involving the use of live animals, warn people with allergies and other conditions should attend at their own risk. Some shows also involve stroboscopic and pyrotechnic effects. Most shows can accommodate various dietary needs.

getting there

Most of the dinner shows are concentrated in one of two areas: the International Drive area or along W. Irlo Bronson Memorial Highway in Kissimmee. SeaWorld Orlando is at the southern end of International Drive, so you can find general directions from Tampa at the beginning of this chapter. For dinner theaters along W. Irlo Bronson Memorial Highway, take exit 64 toward US 192, which becomes W. Irlo Bronson Memorial Highway (also SR 530).

where to go

Arabian Nights. 3081 Arabian Nights Blvd., Kissimmee; (800) 553-6116, (407) 239-9223; arabian-nights.com. With more than 20-some equestrian and acrobatic acts featuring horsemanship traditions from around the world, the Arabian Nights dinner show is one of the largest and most exotic. They also offer one of the more varied menus. Extra experiences include before-show and after-show behind-the-scenes tours and the opportunity to perform in one of the shows.

Capone's Dinner & Show. 4740 W. Irlo Bronson Memorial Hwy., Kissimmee; (800) 220-8428, (407) 397-2378; alcapones.com. Mama Malone has prepared an all-you-can eat Italian dinner buffet, with some American specialties thrown in, too. Join in the fun—fedoras, boas, headpieces, and other costume accessories are available—and be prepared for interactive comedy and musical theater set in a Prohibition-era speakeasy. Mum's da woid!

Makahiki Luau. 7007 SeaWorld Dr., Orlando; (888) 800-5447; seaworld.com. Guests are greeted with flowered leis and a complimentary drink before settling in for a tropical-themed dinner and show. Fire dancers spin flaming torches, and hula lessons get everyone up and moving. Park admission is not required to attend the Makahiki Luau at the Sea Fire Inn.

Medieval Times Dinner & Tournament. 4510 W. Irlo Bronson Memorial Pkwy., Kissimmee; (866) 543-9637; medievaltimes.com. King Phillippe bids you welcome to his 11th-century castle, to a seat at his table, and to the Tournament of the Knights. Witness displays of falconry, see Andalusian stallions perform, and cheer for your favorite knight. Look for upgrade packages, which include a behind-the-scenes DVD and other amenities.

Old Town. 5770 W. Irlo Bronson Memorial Pkwy., Kissimmee; (407) 396-4888; myoldtown usa.com. Zip lines, roller coasters, a Ferris wheel, bumper cars, and go karts by day; classic car cruises, street parties with line dancing, and concerts by night. Plus a shopping mall and restaurants. Check the website for dates and times of concerts and cruises. Let's call this audience-participation mega-theater, yes?

Outta Control Magic Comedy Dinner Show. 9067 International Dr., Orlando; (407) 351-8800; wonderworksonline.com. The menu is pizza and salad, popcorn, dessert, and beverages; the show is a one-man, multi-personality magic and comedy act. No glitz, no glam—and one of the least expensive dinner shows in town. You do not have to purchase admission to Wonder Works to attend the show, but package deals are available.

Pirates Dinner Adventure. 6400 Carrier Dr., Orlando; (800) 866-2469, (407) 248-0590; piratesdinneradventure.com. The stage for this adventure is an 18th-century, fully rigged Spanish galleon anchored in a 300,000-gallon indoor lagoon. Guests are seated around the lagoon to cheer on the action. Look for upgrade packages, too.

Sleuths Mystery Dinner Show. 8267 International Dr., Orlando; (800) 393-1985, (407) 363-1985; sleuths.com. Three themed theaters, 13 mystery shows, and a nicely stocked gift shop, too. Guests help the cast figure out who dun it in these sometimes campy, always comedic productions.

Titanic Dinner Event. 7324 International Dr., Orlando; (877) 410-1912, (407) 248-1166; titanictheexperience.com. Guests are invited to Capt. Smith's retirement party, hosted by the Wideners, aboard the R.M.S. *Titanic* on her maiden voyage. Costumed characters involve guests in the 3-course dinner party, served in elegant style. The performance takes place throughout the 20,000-square-foot exhibit.

day trip 05

the universal experience:
universal studios florida;
islands of adventure; citywalk

The Universal Orlando Resort experience includes two theme parks—Universal Studios Florida and Islands of Adventure—Wet 'n Wild Waterpark (covered under Day Trip 02 of this section), and an entertainment megaplex called CityWalk. Oh, and did we mention there's also Harry's world—the Wizarding World of Harry Potter, that is—tucked within Islands of Adventure? A World within the Universe, one might say.

universal studios florida

This isn't just a theme park, it's a real, working movie and television production facility. Got an idea for a new program—and the investors to bankroll you? Scroll down to the bottom of Universal's website, look for the heading Support, and click on the Studio Production link. You'll find all the details you need to get the ball rolling on your project. Who knows? Maybe someday your blockbuster hit will be featured as one of the theme park attractions at Universal Orlando Resort!

In the meantime, Universal Studios Florida invites visitors to jump into the movie action on screen and behind the scenes.

getting there

From Tampa, take I-4 East toward Orlando. Travel about 78 miles, then take exit 75B, merging onto SR 435 North/S. Kirkman Road. Stay to the left to exit onto Kirkman Road.

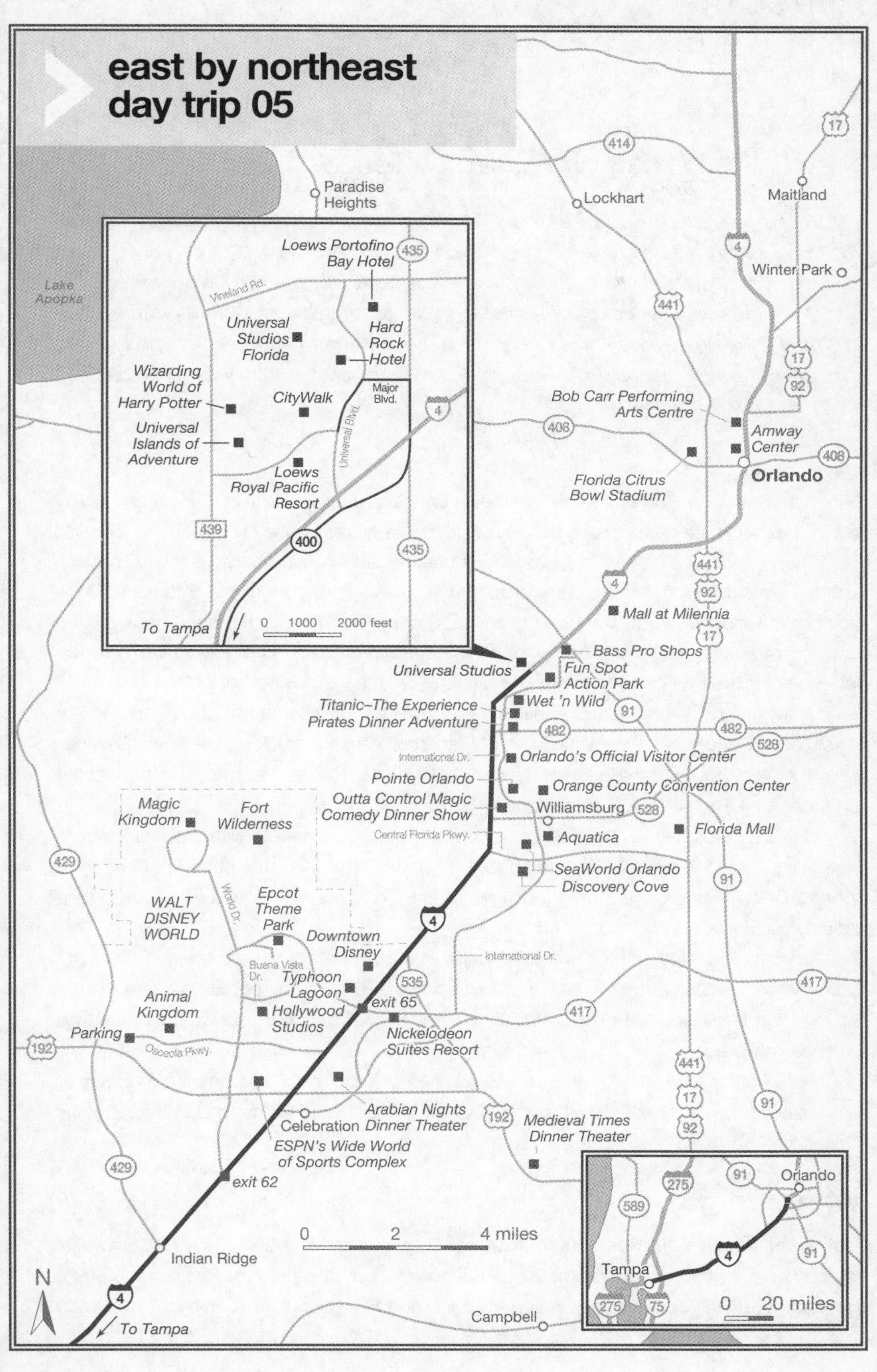

east by northeast
day trip 05
Paradise Heights
Lockhart
Maitland
Winter Park
Lake Apopka
Loews Portofino Bay Hotel
Vineland Rd.
Universal Studios Florida
Hard Rock Hotel
Wizarding World of Harry Potter
CityWalk
Major Blvd.
Universal Blvd.
Universal Islands of Adventure
Loews Royal Pacific Resort
To Tampa
0 1000 2000 feet
Bob Carr Performing Arts Centre
Amway Center
Orlando
Florida Citrus Bowl Stadium
Mall at Milennia
Bass Pro Shops
Universal Studios
Fun Spot Action Park
Titanic–The Experience
Wet 'n Wild
Pirates Dinner Adventure
International Dr.
Orlando's Official Visitor Center
Pointe Orlando
Orange County Convention Center
Outta Control Magic Comedy Dinner Show
Williamsburg
Florida Mall
Central Florida Pkwy.
Aquatica
SeaWorld Orlando
Discovery Cove
Magic Kingdom
Fort Wilderness
WALT DISNEY WORLD
World Dr.
Epcot Theme Park
Downtown Disney
Buena Vista Dr.
Typhoon Lagoon
exit 65
Hollywood Studios
Animal Kingdom
Parking
Osceola Pkwy.
Nickelodeon Suites Resort
Arabian Nights Dinner Theater
Celebration
ESPN's Wide World of Sports Complex
Medieval Times Dinner Theater
exit 62
0 2 4 miles
Indian Ridge
N
To Tampa
Campbell
Orlando
Tampa
0 20 miles

want to be part of a studio audience?

Stop by the Studio Audience Center, at the right of Universal Studios Florida's main entrance, to see what's in production and who needs people for a live studio audience. Or call (407) 363-8400 and select the Studio Audience extension when prompted. Or go to universalorlando.com/Shows/Impact-Wrestling.aspx. At this writing, Universal was looking for audiences age 14 and older for Impact Wrestling *tapings. You do not have to purchase theme park admission to be part of a studio audience.*

Turn left onto Major Boulevard, then left again onto Universal Boulevard. Park in one of the parking garages, pay the parking fee, and write down where you left your car.

Then make your way to the walkway connecting the parking garages with CityWalk. There are moving sidewalks to carry visitors along, or you can hike to the entrances. Once you are at CityWalk, the entrance to Universal Studios Florida is to the right—look for the arched entrance and the Universal globe. The entrance to Islands of Adventure is to the left—look for the Pharos Lighthouse—yes, it really works—at the port of entry.

A daytime pet kennel is available in the parking area. For information about this service, scroll to the bottom of the website, look for Plan Your Vacation, click on the Guest Services Link, then look for Theme Park Services on the right rail. Kennel information is toward the bottom of the Theme Park Services page.

Universal's parks also have a rider swap policy to allow people with small children to wait in line only one time. While one adult goes on the ride, the other stays with the child. When that adult returns, the other adult rides. Let the attendant know if you plan to take advantage of this option.

Most park tickets say they require adults to show photo ID when entering the park. Some visitors say yes, they've had to show photo ID. Others say no. Be prepared either way. At the least, you will need photo ID showing proof of age if you want to purchase alcoholic beverages.

For another look at the Universal Studios Resort complex, wdwinfo.com/universal/universal-studios-florida bills itself as the "DIS' Unofficial Online Guide to Universal Studios Orlando."

where to go

Universal Studios Florida. 6000 Universal Blvd., Orlando; (407) 363-8000; universalorlando.com. Enter through the massive Art Deco arched gates into the Plaza of the Stars. Beyond here lie Production Central on your left and Hollywood on your right. We'll start with Production Central and walk through each of the areas. Keep in mind that each of these areas has been recreated to look like the actual location. It's not just about the rides and shows—it's also about the illusion that we are actually in New York City or San Francisco. Some of these buildings have been used as settings in films, television shows, and commercials.

- **Production Central.** You can't help but notice the massive coaster—17 stories high— extending the full length of this side of the park. The entrance to Hollywood Rip Ride Rockit, where you choose your own soundtrack to accompany your ride, is about halfway down the long block, past the Shrek 4-D show on your right and past what, at this writing, is the home of the *Despicable Me* minions and the evil Gru. Look for characters from *Shrek* to make appearances nearby. The Universal Music Plaza Stage, a replica of the Hollywood Bowl in California, hosts live concerts for various events.
- **New York.** Twister . . . Ride It Out welcomes us to New York, where we'll also find Revenge of the Mummy, another coaster ride, and the Blues Brothers Show. Hmm . . . A "Chicago-style street party" in New York? Only in the movies, right? Although, it is located on the edge of New York that leads alongside a small lake to San Francisco, so technically it's in the middle of the country.
- **San Francisco.** Check out Beetlejuice's Graveyard Revue, and look for character meet-and-greet spots nearby, then ride Disaster! This area used to be called San Francisco/Amity, and the *Jaws* adventure would have been next. But it has closed, and the question of the moment is: What will take its place? In the meantime, we will move on.
- **World Expo.** Men in Black Alien Attack invites you to join the fight to save the galaxy from aliens. Once that's been accomplished, join the Simpsons on their ride through Krustyland.
- **Woody Woodpecker's KidZone.** Coming round the other side of the lake, we enter Woody's area where younger guests find activities more their size. Look for a water play area based on the Curious George Goes to Town Storybook, A Day in the Park with Barney sing-along show, Fievel's Playland playground, and another show, Animal Actors on Locations. Two more gentle rides are also in this area: Woody Woodpecker's Nuthouse Coaster and E.T. Adventure.
- **Hollywood.** Then we're back to Hollywood, the Hollywood of what some call its Golden Age—with replicas of Schwab's Pharmacy (where movie makers hung out and starlets waited to be discovered) and Mel's Drive-In. Hollywood is where we find out how aliens and monsters are created in Universal Orlando's Horror Make-Up Show. Terminator 2 3-D and Lucy—A Tribute round out the attractions here.

vip tours at universal

Anyone can be a VIP, right? For a price, that is. Guided VIP tours at Universal include valet parking, Universal Express skip-the-lines access to some rides and attractions, and discounts to some dining and shopping sites—but the price does not include the regular admission. For more information about small-group and large-group guided VIP tours, look under the Tickets tab on the website. To make reservations for a guided tour, call (407) 363-8295 or e-mail viptours@universalorlando.com. Allow several days for a response to emails. Even phone-in reservations should be made as far in advance as possible.

where to shop

Shops are scattered throughout Universal Studios Orlando, and they sell everything from character-related products to souvenirs to gifts and apparel. Have your purchases delivered for pick-up at the end of the day from the It's a Wrap souvenir shop, located near the exit.

where to eat

Street vendors take care of the need-it-now munchies, and there are fast-food and full-service restaurants of every type throughout the park. A couple of the more unusual ones are **Finnegan's Bar and Grille** (call 407-224-3613 for reservations; $$), a full-service Irish-American pub located in New York and featuring corned beef and cabbage, fish 'n' chips, and Guinness beef stew, among other items; **Mel's Drive-In** ($), a classic burger and fries place located in Hollywood; and the **Beverly Hills Boulangerie** ($), also located in Hollywood, and featuring breakfast croissants, soups, salads, and sandwiches.

islands of adventure

where to go

Universal Islands of Adventure. 6000 Universal Blvd., Orlando; (407) 363-8000; universalorlando.com. If Universal Studios Florida is set mostly in the real world, Islands of Adventure is planted firmly in the realms of the imaginary. Pass by the Pharos Lighthouse at the Port of Entry, then head to your right. We'll follow the most current map's traffic flow on this one and run counter-clockwise—which means you may encounter lighter traffic if you head in the opposite direction first. Each area really is pretty much an island connected by bridges to the other islands.

- **Seuss Landing.** Theme park rides based on books—what a novel idea! Choose your favorite Seuss character to ride upon at the Caro-Seuss-el; don't forget to look up and wave to Horton perched on top and guarding his Whoville friends. Then climb onto a couch for a story that suddenly becomes quite real as the Cat in the Hat takes charge. Go for a spin on One Fish, Two Fish, Red Fish, Blue Fish; then check out Gerald McGrew's interactive If I Ran the Zoo playground. Finally, fly on the High in the Sky Seuss Trolly Train Ride. Look for *Oh! The Stories You'll Hear*, a song-and-dance character show, and character appearances, too. ***Note:*** There are no maximum height restrictions in Seuss Landing. However, visitors with hearts three sizes too small may require additional assistance.

- **The Lost Continent.** Remember: Universal Studios Resort is a working movie production facility. So *Poseidon's Adventure* is a no-holds-barred, pull-out-all-the-stops special effects show, taking visitors under the sea to do battle with the forces of evil. If you win—and if you make it out alive—you'll be ready to cheer the stunt actors in *The Eighth Voyage of Sinbad*. Don't miss chatting with the Mystic Fountain.

- **The Wizarding World of Harry Potter.** universalorlando.com/harrypotter. Note that this attraction has its own website. Back in the "real" world, pass by the Hogwarts Express, newly arrived, and you find yourself in Hogsmeade Village. To the right, the Dragon Challenge presents two coasters, one dilemma: Which one to take? The Chinese Fireball or the Hungarian Horntail? Emerge victorious from either (or both!) and join in the Triwizard Spirit Rally Cheer or enjoy a presentation by Hogwarts students and their Frog Choir. Then visit Hagrid's hut and take off on the gentler Flight of the Hippogriff. Up ahead looms Hogwarts Castle; wind your way through various familiar scenes in Hogwarts Academy of Wizardry and Witchcraft before you encounter Harry Potter and the Forbidden Journey. This ride can be intense; but you can still go through the castle, even if you decide not to participate in the ride. ***Note:*** As of this writing, Universal Studios Resort has announced an expansion to the Wizarding World of Harry Potter. Details are under wizardly wraps.

- **Jurassic Park.** Stop at the Jurassic Park Discovery Center to see dinosaur skeletons and learn more about these creatures who roam—note the present tense—the "real" 21-acre Jurassic Park at Islands of Adventure. Explore Camp Jurassic playground with its water cannons, climbing nets, and secret mines; then strap yourself under one of the Pteranodon Flyers and take off for an eagle-eye . . . er, pteranodon-eye view of Jurassic Park. Co-existing with dinosaurs seems pretty cool, yes? You might change your mind after you experience the Jurassic Park River Adventure. Don't say we didn't warn you.

- **Toon Lagoon.** On to Toon Lagoon where Dudley Do-right's Ripsaw Falls flume ride awaits visitors with a penchant for watery fun. Across the way, Popeye & Bluto's Bilge Rat Barges run the river rapids with soaking results. A three-level playground awaits children at Me Ship—*The Olive*, where it turns out some of the soaking on the Bilge Rat Barges may have come from the water cannons on *The Olive*!

- **Marvel Super-Hero Island.** Never fear—Spiderman is here! And visitors can follow him through the concrete canyons of Gotham City in a 3-D adventure in the Amazing Adventures of Spider-Man. If you can swing with Spidey, you surely can face Dr. Doom's Fearfall and stand staunchly with the Fantastic Four, yes? It's only 150 feet straight up—and then down! The Incredible Hulk Coaster takes riders underground in its fury, and those who ride the Storm Force Accelatron help Storm defeat the malevolent Magneto. Whew! It's not easy being a superhero! Wind down by playing in Kingpin's Arcade—and be on the lookout for superheroes roaming the streets.

where to shop

Islands of Adventure has a number of shops in which to browse. The ones listed here are a few of the more unusual. **All the Books You Can Read,** located in Seuss Landing, carries a complete collection of Dr. Seuss books, DVDs, and more. Betty Boop fans go **Boop-Oop-A-Doop!** over the Betty Boop Store in Toon Lagoon. **The Comic Book Shop,** located in Marvel Super-Hero Island, sells official Marvel comic books, books, and memorabilia. The **Dinostore** in Jurassic Park sells dinosaur-related books, toys, and educational items. Choose your wand—rather, let your wand choose you—at **Ollivanders** in the Wizarding World of Harry Potter. At the **Pearl Factory,** in the Lost Continent, visitors can choose an oyster, have it opened, and set the pearl in a piece of jewelry.

where to eat

No matter how perilous the adventure, nobody goes hungry in the Islands of Adventure. Street vendors hawk their wares, and both fast-food and full-service establishments abound. A couple of places deserve special mention, however. **Circus McGurkus Cafe Stoo-pendous** ($), in Seuss Lagoon, offers kid-favorite foods along with circus-y acts. **Mythos Restaurant** ($$), located in the Lost Continent, has been consistently rated one of the top theme park restaurants for both its atmosphere and its cuisine. Call (407) 224-4012 for reservations. **Three Broomsticks** ($–$$) in the Wizarding World of Harry Potter serves British pub favorites like fish and chips, shepherd's pie, Cornish pasty, soup, salads, and more, buffet-style. Wash it all down with pumpkin juice or Butterbeer.

citywalk

where to go

CityWalk. 6000 Universal Blvd., Orlando; (407) 363-8000; universalorlando.com/Nightlife/Citywalk-Nightlife.aspx. Open 11 a.m. to 2 a.m. every day, CityWalk is full of restaurants, shows, and nightspots that are destinations in and of themselves. Visit the website for a complete listing and details. We list only a few places here. Some places require a cover charge for certain events. Some places are 21 and older only.

what to do

Blue Man Group. (888) 340-5476; universalorlando.com/Shows/Blue-Man-Group.aspx. Music, laughter, and lots of paint—sounds like anything but the blues. This 1 hour and 45 minute show is rated family-friendly. Check the calendar for performance times.

CityWalk's Rising Star. universalorlando.com/Nightlife/CityWalk/Rising-Star-Karoke .aspx. Karaoke with a live band. And backup singers. And a host. Full bar; appetizer menu. Open every night from 8 p.m. to 2 a.m. Live band Tues through Sat. Cover charge, but no charge to sing.

where to eat

Whether your tastes run to Emeril, Jimmy Buffet, Pastamore, or Bubba Gump Shrimp Company, there's a cuisine at CityWalk to fit the bill. You can even have your food served courtside—more or less—at NBA City. Plus there's a food court with numerous counter-service choices. Here are a couple of restaurants to whet your appetite.

Bob Marley—A Tribute to Freedom. (407) 224-3663; universalorlando.com/Restaurants/CityWalk/Bob-Marley-Tribute-Freedom.aspx. Jamaican food and reggae music served in a replica of Bob Marley's Jamaican home. Open Thurs through Sun at 4 p.m. Closes at 10 p.m. on Thurs and Sun; closes at 11 p.m. on Fri and Sat. $–$$.

Hard Rock Cafe Orlando. (407) 351-7625; hardrock.com. The Hard Rock Cafe Orlando is the world's largest Hard Rock Cafe and serves American cuisine in a rock concert atmosphere. Open 11 a.m. to midnight. $$–$$$.

Latin Quarter. (407) 224-3663; universalorlando.com/Restaurants/CityWalk/Latin-Quarter .aspx. Latin food from all 21 Latin American countries, including a Brazilian steakhouse, Churrascaria, served with live music each evening. And on Thurs through Sat nights, it becomes a dance club after 10 p.m. The restaurant is open 5 to 10 p.m. $$–$$$.

NASCAR Sports Grille. (407) 224-7223; nascarsportsgrilleorlando.com. Pulled pork, barbecue, burgers, and wings—plus a video arcade area. The shop opens at 9 a.m.; the restaurant is open 11 a.m. to midnight. $–$$.

where to stay

Universal Studios Resort has 3 on-site resort hotels. Guest perks at all 3 include Universal Express ride access, which allows guests to bypass the lines for rides and attractions, early park admission to the Wizarding World of Harry Potter, and more. All 3 resorts are pet-friendly, but read the individual hotels' policies for details. All 3 resorts offer supervised child care activities—again, read the information provided. Complimentary water taxis and shuttle buses convey guests to and from the parks. Complimentary Internet access may be available only in public areas—check to be sure. All three resorts are in the $$$ range at peak season and with no discounts. Check online for package deals and special offers.

Hard Rock Hotel. 5800 Universal Blvd., Orlando; (888) 273-1311, (407) 503-2000; universal orlando.com/Hotels/Hard-Rock-Hotel.aspx. Hard Rock Hotel is located on the Universal Studios Florida side of CityWalk. In addition to rooms and suites, a fitness center, a business services center, a game arcade, and several dining options, Hard Rock Hotel's public areas feature a vast collection of rock and roll memorabilia. The Graceland Suite comes with a baby grand piano, and all guests can borrow a Fender guitar—with amp and headphones—to wail away on for free and for the duration of their stay. Ask at the front desk when you check in, call (407) 503-2175 for more information, or look under the Hard Rock Hotel's Recreation/Hotel Activities link online. The Rock Shop sells Hard Rock Cafe memorabilia.

Loews Portofino Bay Hotel. 5601 Universal Blvd., Orlando; (888) 273-1311, (407) 503-1000; universalorlando.com/Hotels/Loews-Portofino-Bay-Hotel.aspx. Think Mediterranean elegance here—Loews Portofino Bay Hotel, located on the Universal Studios Florida side of CityWalk, is designed after the Italian resort town of the same name. In addition to rooms and suites, a business services center, a game arcade, and several dining options, Loews Portofino Bay offers 3 themed pool areas, a bocce ball court, and sunset serenades. The Mandara Spa and Fitness Center offers spa and salon services for adults and has a special selection of services for guests age 13 to 17. Call (407) 503-1244 for more information, or look under the Loews Portofino Bay Hotel Recreation/Activities link online. The Harbor Plaza area features fashion boutiques and gift item shops.

Loews Royal Pacific Resort. 6300 Hollywood Way, Orlando; (888) 273-1311, (407) 503-3000; universalorlando.com/Hotels/Loews-Royal-Pacific-Resort.aspx. Located on the Islands of Adventure side of CityWalk, Loews Royal Pacific Resort takes guests to the exotic South Pacific islands. In addition to rooms and suites, a business services center, a fitness center, and a game arcade, Loews Royal Pacific Resort offers a lagoon-style pool area with poolside activities including table tennis, volleyball, and more. Join in the Torch Lighting Ceremony, held on select evenings, and ask about golf packages to area courses. The resort offers several dining options, including a Wantilan Luau with dinner, traditional music, and hula dancing. Call (407) 503-3463 for reservations, or look under the Loews Royal Pacific Resort Recreation/Activities link online. Treasures of Bali, featuring island-wear, gifts, and more, is located across from the lagoon pool.

east

day trip 01

east

fly it high, drive it fast:
lakeland; auburndale; davenport; polk city

Now we turn more directly east to visit neighbors so close we sometimes take them for granted. Lakeland, Auburndale, Polk City, and Davenport have quiet charms waiting for us to enjoy. We'll visit speedways, fly-ways, and one-of-a-kind architecture.

The official visitor center for Polk County, Central Florida Visitor Information Center, is in Davenport, which is the spot furthest from Tampa. Take your pick. You can drive to Davenport and experience the amazing visitor center, pick up area information, and then work your way back to Lakeland. Or start in Lakeland, as we are, and work your way to Davenport. Either way, it's good. For folks who decide to start in Davenport, we're listing the pertinent information up front here.

Central Florida Visitor Information Center. 101 Adventure Ct., Davenport; (800) 828-7655, (863) 420-2586; visitcentralflorida.org. Located about 0.5 mile south of I-4 at exit 55 (US 27), the Central Florida Visitor Information Center is an attraction in itself. With a biplane protruding from the wall, a theater running a video about the area, interactive displays to help you make the most of your time here, and a putting green to whet your appetite for relaxation, this visitor center is a good place to start—or end . . . because there is always a next time, right? The visitor center is open 7 days a week from 9 a.m. to 6 p.m., and is closed on major holidays. The website is open 24/7.

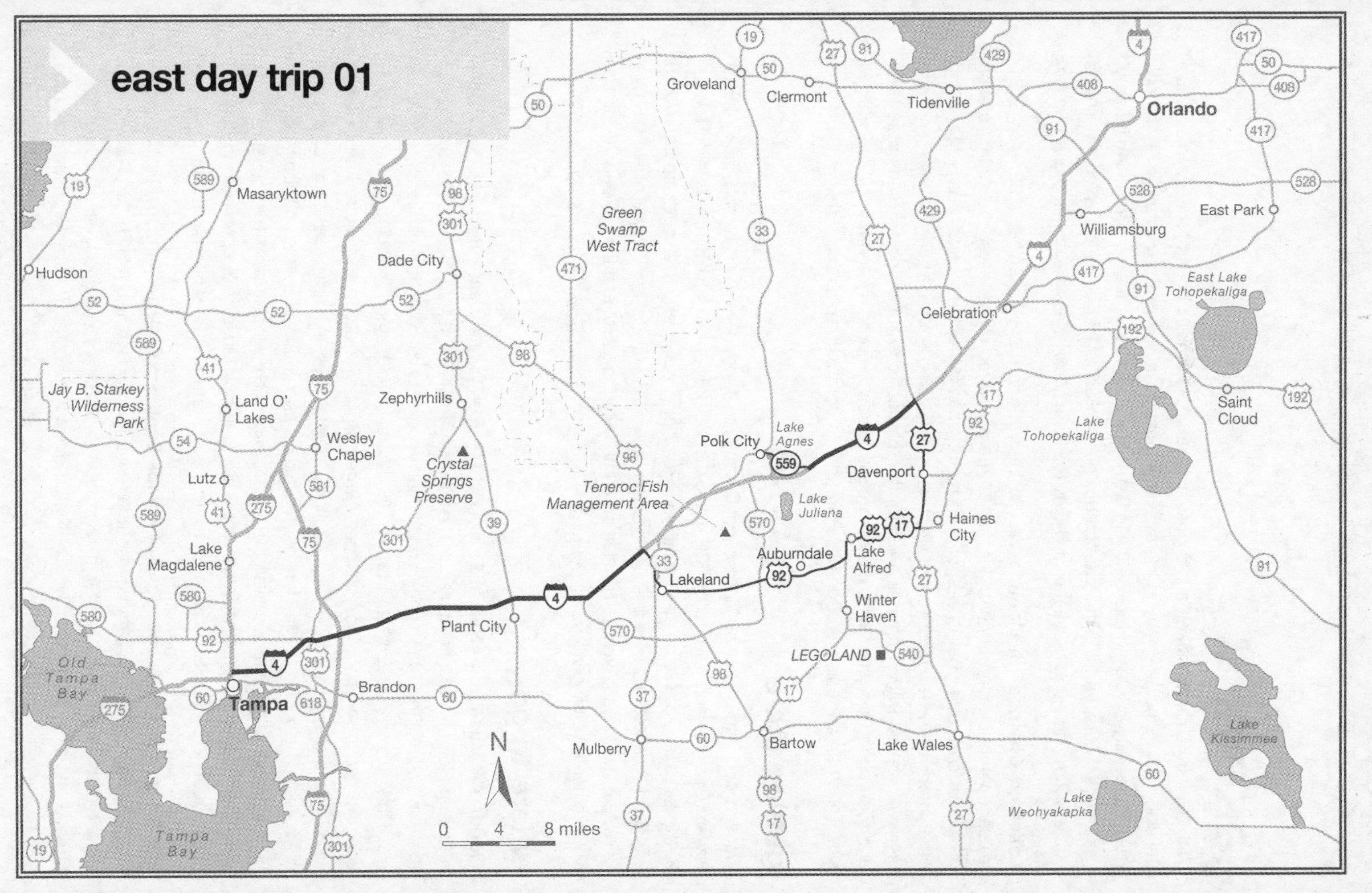
east day trip 01
Groveland
Clermont
Tidenville
Orlando
Masaryktown
Green Swamp West Tract
Williamsburg
East Park
Hudson
Dade City
East Lake Tohopekaliga
Celebration
Jay B. Starkey Wilderness Park
Land O' Lakes
Zephyrhills
Wesley Chapel
Crystal Springs Preserve
Polk City
Lake Agnes
Lake Tohopekaliga
Saint Cloud
Davenport
Lutz
Teneroc Fish Management Area
Lake Juliana
Haines City
Lake Magdalene
Auburndale
Lake Alfred
Lakeland
Winter Haven
Plant City
LEGOLAND
Old Tampa Bay
Tampa
Brandon
Mulberry
Bartow
Lake Wales
Lake Kissimmee
Lake Weohyakapka
Tampa Bay
N
0 4 8 miles

lakeland

With almost 40 named lakes and a host of smaller unnamed ponds, it's easy to see how Lakeland got its name. Many of the swans you see in the lakes are descendants of a pair given to the city by Queen Elizabeth II in the 1950s. Lakeland is the spring training home of the Detroit Tigers, and it is the site of the largest collection of Frank Lloyd Wright buildings in the world. Each October, Lakeland hosts the Lake Mirror Classic Auto Festival & Auction.

Lakeland Chamber of Commerce. 35 Lake Morton Dr., Lakeland; (863) 688-8551; lakelandchamber.com. Look under the Visit Lakeland tab on their website for information on where to go and what to see, or stop by the chamber office to pick up brochures and other information. The Chamber of Commerce is housed in what once was the library and is known as the Park Trammell building. It is one of several historic buildings preserved and repurposed by determined citizen groups. Enjoy the building and the lake on which it sits. The chamber office is open Mon through Fri from 8:30 a.m. to 5 p.m.

getting there

Our first stop is the Lakeland Chamber of Commerce: From downtown Tampa, take I-4 East toward Orlando, and travel about 32 miles. Get off of I-4 at exit 31/SR 539 South toward Kathleen/Lakeland. Merge onto Kathleen Road and travel about 2 miles south toward Lakeland. Turn left onto George Jenkins Boulevard/SR 548 East and travel about 0.5 mile to N. Massachusetts Avenue. Turn left onto Lake Morton Drive, and the Lakeland Chamber of Commerce building will be on your right.

where to go

Florida Air Museum at Sun 'n Fun. 4175 Medulla Rd., Lakeland; (863) 644-2431; sun-n-fun.org/Florida-Air-Museum.aspx. The Florida Air Museum, located on the grounds of the Sun 'n Fun Fly-In held each spring, has an extensive collection of vintage airplanes, ultralights, and more. Exhibits portray Florida's aviation history, including space exploration, Women in Aviation, the Tuskegee Airmen, flight simulators, and more. The museum also houses the Howard Hughes Aviation Collection, an extensive collection of aviation memorabilia belonging to Mr. Hughes. A gift shop and an extensive aviation library also are on the property; the library is available to researchers by appointment. The museum hosts a number of events throughout the year. The Florida Air Museum is open Mon through Fri from 9 a.m. to 5 p.m., Sat from 10 a.m. to 4 p.m., and Sun from noon to 4 p.m.

Frank Lloyd Wright Architecture at Florida Southern College. 111 Lake Hollingsworth Dr., Lakeland; (863) 680-4444; flsouthern.edu/fllwctr. Beginning in 1938, Frank Lloyd Wright, at the request of then FSC president Dr. Ludd Spivey, designed not just one building but an entire college campus. Nine of the buildings were completed by 1958; another nine were designed. Some of the buildings were constructed by the college's students themselves, in lieu of paying tuition. The "Child of the Sun" Visitor Center and gift shop is open Mon through Sat from 10 a.m. to 4 p.m. Self-guided walking tours are free; guided tours are offered by reservation. FSC is constructing another Wright-designed building, called a Usonian house, which will serve as an education center. To view a photo blog of the construction, go to buildingtheusonianhouse.com. The building is scheduled to open in late 2012.

Hollis Garden. 702 E. Orange St., Lakeland; (863) 834-2280; lakelandgov.net/parkrec/HollisGarden.aspx. Begin in the Grotto, and follow the history of Florida's interaction with humans through a historical tree section (including trees from Abraham Lincoln's home and Elvis's Graceland), an orchard, herb and vegetable gardens, and more. Plus there's a man-made garden of sorts, a sculpture garden—almost 20 areas in all. The gardens are free and open to the public from 10 a.m. to dusk, Tues through Sun. Call the number above for information about guided tours.

Lakeland Center. 701 W. Lime St., Lakeland; (863) 834-8100 (Administration), (863) 834-8111 (Box Office); thelakelandcenter.com. The Lakeland Center is a sports, convention, and entertainment complex that hosts everything from Broadway shows to rodeos. Jenkins Arena is home turf for the Lakeland Raiders indoor football team. Public ice skating is sometimes offered—look under Ticketing on the website.

Polk Museum of Art. 800 E. Palmetto St., Lakeland; (863) 688-7743; polkmuseumofart.org. The Polk Museum of Art contains 8 galleries of art. Permanent collections include Modern & Contemporary Art, Asian Art, African Art, Pre-Columbian Art, and Decorative Arts. Outside is a sculpture garden, which hosts the Florida Outdoor Sculpture Competition, a year-long, juried exhibition of sculptures created by artists from around the country. The Polk Museum of Art is open Tues through Sat from 10 a.m. to 5 p.m. and on Sun from 1 to 5 p.m. Summer hours are Tues through Sat from 10 a.m. to 4 p.m. only. The museum is open for free on Sat mornings from 10 a.m. to noon.

Tiger Town & Joker Marchant Stadium. 2301 Lakeland Hills Blvd., Lakeland; (866) 668-4437; lakelandflyingtigers.com. Since 1934, the Detroit Tigers have come to Lakeland for spring training, specifically to the facility known as Tiger Town. The Tiger's minor league team, the Lakeland Flying Tigers, also plays here, and a number of sports camps use the facilities, too.

what to do

fishing

Tenoroc Fish Management Area. Tenoroc Mine Road, Lakeland; myfwc.com/viewing/recreation/wmas/lead/tenoroc. Polk County has loads of lakes, rivers, and other waterways open for fishing. One area in particular near Lakeland is the Tenoroc Fish Management Area, which consists of reclaimed phosphate mining pits. Phosphate mining in the 1960s and

1970s left a number of pits that have been reclaimed as lakes and stocked with largemouth bass, bluegill, crappie, and other panfish. Hiking and horseback riding trails wind through the area. To keep the place from being overfished, all anglers are required to register and pay a nominal fee at the headquarters. One of the lakes is wheelchair accessible; there are 20 boat launching facilities with parking areas. Picnic and restroom facilities, educational kiosks, and fishing platforms and boardwalks make this place easy to fish. A separately managed sports shooting facility (trap/skeet; rifle, pistol, air guns; archery) also is on the property. The area is open Fri through Mon from 6 a.m. to 8 p.m. (closes at 7 p.m. when it's not Daylight Savings Time). Dogs must be on a leash. Call (863) 499-2422, Fri through Mon, between 8 a.m. and 5 p.m., for current fishing reports.

golf

There are a number of courses in the Lakeland area, ranging from professional-level country club courses to smaller municipal courses. The majority of the courses are open to the public, and all showcase central Florida's natural beauty. VisitFlorida.com/golfing and Visitcentralflorida.org have extensive listings of courses organized by city, but we're noting a couple of spots here to whet your golfing appetite.

Bramble Ridge. 2505 Bramble Ridge Dr. (or 2505 Winter Lake Extension Rd.), Lakeland; (863) 667-1988; brgolf.com. This 27-hole public course winds its way through the Florida wilds and offers both experienced golfers and beginners an enticing game. The course is part of the Sanlan RV Park property, which also includes a bird and wildlife sanctuary area with walking trails. The wildlife, of course, don't know they are supposed to stay in a particular area, so golfers sometimes share the course with various critters.

The Club at Eaglebrooke. 1300 Eaglebrooke Blvd., Lakeland; (863) 701-0101; eaglebrooke.com. Tee up—on one of six sets of tees—and take on this Ron Garl–designed, 18-hole course. Set in southern Polk County, the rolling fairways and multi-level greens both charm and challenge golfers of many skill levels. Eaglebrooke also offers swimming and tennis; lunch and dinner are served at the Clubhouse.

paintball, rock-climbing, & more

Off the Wall Adventures. 2055 Shepherd Rd., Lakeland; (863) 709-9253; offthewalladventures.com. Take on the rock-climbing wall, practice in the batting cages, and splat others on one of five paintball courses; or learn how to kayak, fish, or scuba dive, then take a charter trip to do just that.

where to shop

Downtown Farmers Curb Market. 200 N. Kentucky Ave., Lakeland; (863) 221-4633; ldda.org/Home/FarmersCurbMarket.aspx. This market isn't just about produce. Here you'll find a mix of arts, crafts, apparel, furniture, gift items, and more. Community entertainers often perform, too. Open Sept through June on Wed from 11 a.m. to 2 p.m. and Sat from 8 a.m. to 2 p.m.

where to eat

Abuelos. 3700 Lakeside Village Blvd., Lakeland; (863) 686-7500; abuelos.com. Yes, it's a chain; but there are only two Abuelos restaurants in Florida, and this is one of them. It's, as the menu says, the flavor of Mexico—but with some really interesting twists. The Enchiladas du Cozumel, for instance, are white wine–sauce covered guacamole-filled crepes served with shrimp, scallops, mushrooms, spinach, and roasted peppers. Notice the artwork in the restaurant, as well. Abuelos is open every day from 11 a.m. to 11 p.m. $–$$.

Red Door Wine Market. 850 S. Tennessee, Lakeland; (863) 937-9314; reddoorwinemarket.com. It's not a huge menu—Taco Tuesday might feature chicken tacos with caramelized onions, goat cheese, and spinach or maybe beef tacos with green salsa and sweet potato chips—and the atmosphere is casual funky. But there's live acoustic music Thurs through Sat, and the wines and micro-brews have garnered a fan base. Open Tues through Sat from 4 p.m to midnight. $–$$.

where to stay

Lake Morton Bed & Breakfast. 817 South Blvd., Lakeland; (863) 688-6788; lakemortonbandb.com. It's hard to believe this home began as a Sears, Roebuck and Co. catalog-ordered home; but, back in 1926, Sears offered what were essentially kit homes to be constructed using local labor. Over the years, the home grew. Today it features 4 small apartment-size suites, period furnishings, and a location in the historic district of Lakeland. $–$$.

The Terrace Hotel. 329 E. Main St., Lakeland; (888) 644-8400, (863) 688-0800; terracehotel.com. This historic boutique hotel began welcoming guests in 1924. Restored on the outside and refurbished on the inside, the Terrace Hotel reopened in 1998. Today it offers banquet rooms and meeting facilities and is a favorite wedding spot. The Terrace Grille serves breakfast, lunch, and dinner. The Terrace Hotel's rooms and suites feature double- or king-size beds, cable TV, free Internet access and phone service, coffeemaker, iron and ironing board, and other amenities. $$–$$$.

auburndale

Auburndale is a small community northeast of Lakeland. It has some lovely city parks, but is probably best known for the Auburndale Speedway, which, technically, is located in Winter Haven. Tough. We're listing it here.

getting there

These directions take you from Lakeland to the Auburndale Speedway. Take US 92 East/E. Memorial Boulevard east toward Auburndale. Travel about 4 miles, then turn right onto S. Coombee Road. Take the first left, which is E. Main Street, and travel about 6 miles. As you drive, E. Main Street becomes CR 542, which then becomes K-Ville Avenue. The road takes a couple of jogs during the transition from CR 542 to K-Ville Avenue, but stick with it. The Speedway is on your right.

where to go

Auburndale Speedway. 5640 K-Ville Ave., Winter Haven; (863) 551-1131; auburndale racing.com. The mailing address is Auburndale, the name of the track is Auburndale, and it's located just south of Auburndale. How it got a Winter Haven physical address is one of the mysteries of life. It's an oval, quarter-mile, semi-banked asphalt track running a variety of stock car races every Saturday evening. They also have a go-kart track running races during the day. Concessions are available.

where to eat

Peebles Bar-B-Q. 503 Dixie Hwy., Auburndale; (863) 967-3085. Real Southern barbecue and sweet tea are what bring folks to Peebles. They're only open Thurs through Sat from 11 a.m. to 9 p.m. and, last we checked, there was no AC inside. Still, there's always a pile of cars and trucks parked around it. $–$$.

where to stay

Lake Juliana Boating & Lodging. 600 Lundy Rd., Auburndale; (863) 984-1144; lundyville .com. Florida Craftsman-style cottages grace Lundyville, aka Lake Juliana Boating & Lodging, along with mobile homes and full hookup RV sites. Lake Juliana is an 895-acre freshwater lake, and Lundyville has boat slips available—paddleboats and row boats, too. Several nights a week, Lundyville turns into music-ville. One night it's acoustic favorites, another night it's karaoke. Sometimes there are special concerts. Nominal cover charges apply for the music events. The Polk County Chapter of the Nashville Songwriters Association International holds its meetings at Lundyville. $–$$.

Town Manor on the Lake. 585 SR 559, Auburndale; (863) 984-4008; townmanor.com. This 1930s-era estate-turned-B&B offers a multi-course breakfast and a choice of several suites furnished in period style. Guests are also welcome to use a common parlor area, library, and outdoors areas. No pets, although the owners' family includes a cat and a dog. $$–$$$.

davenport

Our next stop is the official Central Florida Visitor Information Center near Davenport. But . . . sometimes it's the journey and not the destination. The directions meander a bit from Auburndale to the Central Florida Visitor Information Center so we can mention a couple of lovely spots for lunch, a confectionary to satisfy your sweet tooth, and a couple of area golf courses to visit along the way.

Central Florida Visitor Information Center. 101 Adventure Ct., Davenport; (800) 828-7655, (863) 420-2586; visitcentralflorida.org. A more detailed description of the center—including putting green—is at the beginning of this chapter. The visitor center is open 7 days a week from 9 a.m. to 6 p.m., and is closed on major holidays. The website is open 24/7.

getting there

Take US 92 East/Magnolia Avenue toward Lake Alfred. Travel about 3 miles, at which point the road will turn to the left, so you'll be heading north on US 92 East/US 17 North. Continue about another mile to Lake Alfred. Stop and eat, if you like. If not, travel about 4 miles on US 92 East toward Haines City. When you reach US 27 South, turn left and travel north on US 27 South for almost 9 miles. The Central Florida Visitor Information Center will be on your right.

what to do

Highlands Reserve Golf Club. 500 Highlands Reserve Blvd., Davenport; (863) 420-1724; highlandsreserve-golf.com. Designed to recall the game's Scottish origins, this Mike Dasher course features open, spacious fairways set amidst what looks like highland moors—as well as sections lined with pine trees or citrus trees. A practice facility, pro-shop, and snack bar—even a roving beverage cart—ensure all golfing needs are met. ***Note:*** The website is worth a visit, even for non-golfers. Thoughtfully selected music accompanies beautiful photography and videography.

Southern Dunes Golf and Country Club. 2888 Southern Dunes Blvd., Haines City; (800) 632-6400 or (863) 421-4653; southerndunes.com. Some sections of this artistically sculpted and landscaped course, designed by Steve Smyers, belong in a gallery, but play through anyway. It's part of the ambience and challenge that's been bringing golfers here from around the world. An on-site restaurant serves breakfast and lunch.

where to eat & shop

Back Porch Restaurant. 115 Hwy. 557A, Lake Alfred; (863) 956-2227; thestablehome decor.com. The Back Porch Restaurant is actually the back porch area of the Stable, which sells home decor; the Barn, an antiques shop; and the Back Yard, a garden shop area.

Lunch comes served in a picnic basket, but you can eat indoors or outdoors. The shops are open 10 a.m. to 4 p.m., but the restaurant is open Tues through Sat, 11 a.m. to 3 p.m. $.

The Hotel Tea Room & Flower Corner. 301 W. Maple St., Davenport; (863) 421-0827; thehoteldavenportfla.com. Step back to a slower-paced, gentler time at The Hotel Tea Room where meals are served on china and the home-cookin' isn't hurried. Open Mon through Fri from 11:30 a.m. until "whenever the food runs out," The Hotel Davenport serves a southern-style lunch. Breakfast is served on Sat by reservation only. Dinner is served Tues (Southern table night) and Fri (steak night), both by reservation only. $$–$$$.

Lavender 'N' Lace Tea Room. 430 N. Lakeshore Way, Lake Alfred; (863) 956-3998; lavenderandlacetearoom.com. Lunch in style on quiche, crepes, or something equally exquisite; or just have tea—well, tea and Hummingbird Cake, or Trifle, or Tunnel of Fudge or one of the other irresistible desserts. There's also a garden and a gift shop to browse in this 1940s-era restored home. Reservations are recommended; last seating is around 2 p.m. or so. Open Mon through Sat, 11 a.m. to 3:30 p.m. $–$$.

Webb's Candy Shop. 38217 US 27 South, Davenport; (863) 422-1051; webbscandyshop.com. Stop in and watch them make old fashioned peanut brittle, goat's milk fudge, citrus candies, and hand-dipped chocolates. Try one of their many flavors of hand-scooped ice cream and browse the gift shop.They've been making sweet treats since 1932. Check out their stock of exotic wines, too. They're open every day except Christmas and Thanksgiving from 8 a.m. to 9 p.m.

polk city

Polk City's residents only number a couple of thousand people, but it is home to Fantasy of Flight, an attraction that draws many times that number of people each year to take a balloon ride, fly in a biplane, zip down a zip line, or try out a hang-glider simulator. Polk City is also the only city completely contained in the Green Swamp West Tract, a huge area in Central Florida that is ecologically diverse and crucial to maintaining the area's water supply. The directions take travelers from Davenport to Fantasy of Flight in Polk City.

getting there

From the Central Florida Visitor Information Center in Davenport, follow US 27 to I-4 West. Turn onto I-4 west and travel about 10 miles toward Lakeland. Take exit 44 toward Fantasy of Flight/Polk City and travel almost 1 mile north on SR 559 North. Turn left onto Broadway Boulevard. Fantasy of Flight is on your left.

where to go

Fantasy of Flight. 1400 Broadway Blvd. Southeast, Polk City; (863) 984-3500; fantasyofflight.com. Part museum, part hands-on try-it-out area, part wild-blue-yonder, Fantasy of Flight has a collection of vintage aircraft and a restoration workshop for visitors to explore. Fly a hot air balloon or try hang gliding—using simulators—take on the Wing Walkair ropes course, or zip down a 600-foot-long zip line. An interactive area helps visitors understand the principles of flight, and a tram tour explores some of the back areas of the property. Weather permitting, there may be aerial exhibitions. Make reservations for an actual balloon flight or a ride in a biplane. Fantasy of Flight and the aviation-themed gift shop are open 10 a.m. to 5 p.m. every day except Thanksgiving and Christmas Day. The Compass Rose Diner is open daily from 11 a.m. to 3 p.m.

Gen. James A. Van Fleet State Trail. (352) 516-7384; dep.state.fl.us. Running from Polk City to Mabel—29 miles of paved trail in all—this bike trail, formerly a railroad route, runs through the Green Swamp and is part of Florida's statewide system of greenways and trails. Pick up the trail in Polk City at the intersection of SR 33 and CR 665. The trail is open from 8 a.m. to dusk every day of the year. ***Note:*** This trail runs through a very isolated and rural part of Florida. Read the trail brochure and map carefully, take plenty of water, and be sure to let someone know where you will be and when you expect to return. Better yet, do all of that and ride with a friend.

day trip 02

build it big!

mulberry; winter haven; lake wales

Today we head east again, but not on I-4. We'll start with a fossil dig in Bone Valley near Mulberry, then visit Central Florida's newest attraction, LEGOLAND Florida, stop at a carillon bell tower, and end up at a cattle drive in Kissimmee State Park.

Before we start out, keep in mind the VisitCentralFlorida.org website, from Day Trip 01 in this section. Their website covers much of the area we will visit today, so it is a good resource for additional information.

mulberry

Remember the old saying about good things coming in small packages? The City of Mulberry has fewer than 5,000 residents, but it is the home to a major furniture company. And those foam cups we get at fast food restaurants? They may have been manufactured in Mulberry. But its first claim to fame was as the Phosphate Capital of the World. And, in mining the phosphate, hundreds of fossils and prehistoric skeletons have been found, earning the area the nickname of Bone Valley.

Note: Once we leave here, we're heading to Winter Haven and LEGOLAND Florida. But there's a fun barbecue restaurant halfway there, in Bartow, that I'm going to list here.

east day trip 02

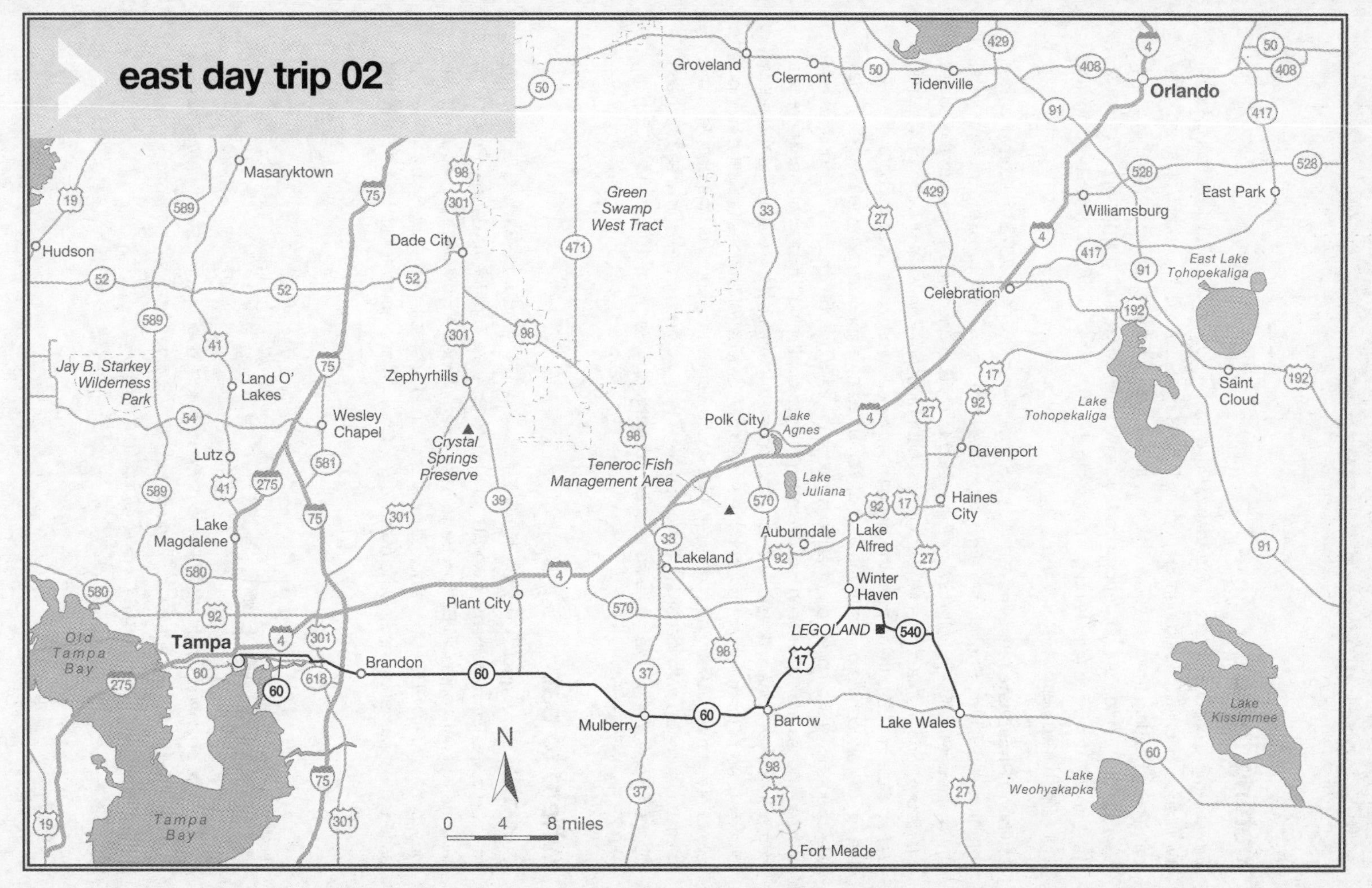

getting there

From Tampa, head east on SR 60/Adamo Drive East. Keep on SR 60, which has become W. Brandon Boulevard, through Brandon. SR 60 is now called E. Brandon Boulevard. Stay on SR 60, heading toward Willow Oak and then toward Mulberry. In all, you will have traveled about 30 miles. As you approach Mulberry, slow down and look for SR 37, aka SE 1st Street. Turn south (right) and go 1 block to the museum, which is a white building that looks like a train depot.

Mulberry Phosphate Museum. 101 SE 1st St., Mulberry; (863) 425-2823; mulberrychamber .org/attractions.htm. Phosphates are what make plants grow, what make our teeth white, and what put the fizz in soft drinks—folks used to order a cherry phosphate at the corner drugstore soda fountain. The Mulberry Phosphate Museum is in what used to be the train depot. Built in 1899, trains from the depot used to carry carloads of phosphate ore from the nearby phosphate mines to the Port of Tampa to be shipped around the world. Today the depot houses a collection of exhibits about the railroad, the phosphate industry, and dinosaur bones that have been discovered in the ore containing the phosphate. There is a complete baleen whale skeleton here, and a saber-tooth tiger skull. Outside is a dragline bucket used in the mining of phosphate. Allow time for kids (of all ages!) to sift through a pile of ore in the bucket. They can keep fossils and bones they find, and the people in the museum can help with identifying them. It's likely they will find some—this area has been dubbed Bone Valley. The museum is open Tues through Sat from 10 a.m. to 4:30 p.m., and admission is free.

where to eat

Curly Tails Barbeque. 330 Old Bartow Eagle Lake Rd., Bartow; (863) 533-5685; curly tailsbbq.com. (From Mulberry, take SR 60 East to Bartow. Turn left at Bartow Road, then take the first right onto Old Bartow Eagle Lake Road.) Whether you call it barbeque, bar-b-que, barbecue, or BBQ, slow-smoked meat garnished or smothered—take your pick—with assorted sauces beckons us wherever we go. Curly Tails is noted for its barbecue in this

wanna play earthcache?

The dragline bucket at the Mulberry Phosphate Museum is an official EarthCache site. Go to geocaching.com and search for "Digging Phosphate in Bone Valley EarthCache" to learn more about playing this game.

neck of the woods—and for a bit of the woods that somehow found its way indoors: There's what seems to be a tree growing right in the middle of the dining area, which adds a fun, outdoorsy touch to the meal. Open 11 a.m. to 9 p.m. Mon through Fri. $.

winter haven

Winter Haven is home to what was Florida's first theme park, Cypress Gardens, and what has become Florida's newest theme park, LEGOLAND. Cypress Gardens, a collection of beautiful botanical gardens, opened in 1936—coincidentally, just about the time that Ole Kirk Christiansen was becoming known for his toy workshop in Denmark. By the 1950s, Cypress Gardens had grown to include water-ski shows and other attractions, and Christiansen was beginning to refine what we know today as LEGO building blocks. Today, the Florida gardens are the setting for massive sculptures created out of LEGOs and for LEGO-themed rides. The coaster rides include one wooden coaster, a suspended-seat coaster, and other twisty-turny rides. Other rides are unique—many of them are interactive, meaning participants use their own brains and brawn to make things happen. The park is being marketed especially to families with children ages 2 to 12, but who says imagination has an age limit?

getting there

From Mulberry, continue east on SR 60 toward Bartow/Winter Haven. Travel almost 9 miles, then bear left, then right to go around Bartow on US 98 South/E. Van Fleet Drive/SR 700 South/SR 35 South. In less than 0.5 mile, turn left onto US 17 North and follow it about 9 miles to SR 540 East/Cypress Gardens Boulevard. Turn right onto SR 540 East/Cypress Gardens Boulevard and travel not quite 4 miles to Kehoe Way. Turn right onto Kehoe Way, then right again on Helena Road, then left onto LEGOLAND Way. (***Note:*** Not all GPS and maps have caught up with the changes. If yours does not recognize 1 LEGOLAND Way as an address, enter 6000 Cypress Gardens Boulevard.) Pay the parking fee, remember where you parked, and then make your way to the entrance. Pets are not allowed inside, but there is a kennel near the entrance. Call ahead for information about pet care.

where to go

LEGOLAND Florida. 1 LEGOLAND Way, Winter Haven; (877) 350-5346; florida.legoland.com. LEGOLAND Florida, set on Lake Roy, features 150 acres of amazing creations made out of LEGOs of all sizes, coaster rides and other attractions, and the still truly magnificent gardens. As with other theme parks we have visited in these pages, we'll walk through in clockwise order. If you want to hit the coaster rides first, then go the other way. Food concessions and shops are located throughout the park. Check the calendar for days and times the park is open.

- **The Beginning & Fun Town.** As you enter, Island in the Sky, part of the original Cypress Gardens, lifts visitors 150 feet into the air for a panoramic view of LEGOLAND and the surrounding area. Also at The Beginning is The Big Shop, one of the world's largest LEGO stores. Stop at the Factory to see how LEGOs are made, then go for a ride on the double-decker LEGO carousel. The Fun Town Theater features 4-D movies throughout the day.

- **Miniland USA.** Walk around this incredible display of what it is possible to create with LEGOs. Several themed areas—Florida, California, Las Vegas, Washington, D.C., New York City, and an imaginary pirate-themed section—are recreated, some with animation and some with interactive areas.

- **Pirates' Cove.** Where else will you see waterskiing pirates but in the Pirates' Cove Live Water Ski Show? Swashbuckling stunt skiers invade the cove and someone must save the day. . . .

- **Cypress Gardens.** The entrance to the gardens is next to the water-ski stadium area. Even if you pass this up for now, make a point of returning. At the very least, walk to the center where there is a massive banyan tree—a tree that sends down roots from its branches, which become new trees over time—that takes our breath away no matter how many times we've seen it.

- **Imagination Zone.** Build your own car and run it on a digitally timed track. Or build and program your own LEGO Mindstorms robot (sign up for a time slot at the beginning of the day). The Hero Factory is an interactive play area. Kid Power Towers require kids (and kids at heart) to power themselves to the top of a tower, while seated, then "freefall" back to the bottom.

- **LEGO Technic.** Ride the Test Track coaster in a life-size LEGO Technic vehicle, take on the Aquazone Wave Racers, and then experience pedal power on the Technicycle, which flies riders into the air.

- **LEGO City.** Compete in the Rescue Academy—shoot water cannons to see who will put the fire out first. Earn your LEGOLAND Drivers' License at the Ford Driving School (ages 6 to 13) or at the Ford Jr. Driving School (ages 3 to 5). Boating School lets visitors pilot their own boats. Think you're ready for Flying School? Maybe. But this is a suspended-seat, steel coaster that swoops and soars around the track. Don't say we didn't warn you. This area also has a live acrobatics and comedy show called the Big Test, featuring the Fun Town Fire Crew, who are trying to pass their test to become official firefighters.

- **LEGO Kingdoms & Land of Adventure.** Accept Merlin's Challenge and you're on a wooden coaster ride. Gentler rides include Safari Trek and Coastersaurus. Then do the

Beetle Bounce from the top of an obelisk. Next door is a dark ride, the Lost Kingdom Adventure, where riders zap targets with laser blasters and try to find the lost treasure. At Pharoah's Revenge, launch foam balls at targets and match wits with a maze. The Forestman's Hideout multi-level playground lets kids climb rope nets and more; the Royal Joust takes younger riders aboard LEGO horses through a medieval jousting tournament. Ride the Dragon through the castle, then fly with him on a coaster ride.

- **DUPLO Village.** Especially for the youngest visitors, DUPLO Village features a DUPLO farm-themed playground, Granny's Jalopies ride, the Big Rig Rally Ride, and a Junior Fire Academy activity.

- **LEGOLAND Waterpark.** There's plenty of watery fun here during the summer months, including a build-your-own river raft area, the Joker Soaker watery playground, a wave pool, and loads of slippery slides. The Waterpark requires an extra admission fee.

lake wales

Lake Wales sits on Florida's ridge, making it one of the highest spots in the state. Its downtown area contains a number of historic buildings, and the area also features the Bok Tower Gardens and carillon, Spook Hill, and Chalet Suzanne, an internationally known bed-and-breakfast. Also nearby is Lake Kissimmee State Park.

getting there

From Winter Haven, head east about 3 miles on SR 540 East toward Waverly. When you reach US 27 South (before you get to Waverly), turn right onto US 27 South and travel about 6 miles to Lake Wales. Turn left onto W. Central Avenue and the Chamber of Commerce is on your left.

Lake Wales Area Chamber of Commerce. 340 W. Central Ave., Lake Wales; (863) 676-3445; lakewaleschamber.com. Stop in and pick up visitor information here. The chamber office is in the middle of the historic district; take a walking tour while you are here. The office is open Mon through Fri from 8 a.m. to 4 p.m., except on holidays.

where to go

Bok Tower Gardens. 1151 Tower Blvd., Lake Wales; (863) 676-1408; boktowergardens.org. This National Historic Landmark was built on Iron Mountain, 298 feet above sea level, in the mid-1920s by Edward William Bok, who had retired in 1919 after 30 years as editor of the *Ladies' Home Journal*. Bok Tower Gardens consists of gardens and bird sanctuary areas designed by Frederick Law Olmsted, Jr., who also helped design New York's Central

lake wales on youtube

For a really unique and upbeat look at the area, look for the music video link "A Tribute to Lake Wales" on the Lake Wales Area Chamber of Commerce's website. Or go to YouTube.com and search for "Bok State of Mind." The City of Lake Wales's website also has a helpful page for visitors: cityoflakewales.com/city/visitor.htm.

Park. In the garden is a 205-foot-tall carillon Singing Tower, designed by Milton B. Medery and with sculptural decoration by Lee Lawrie. The Pine Ridge Nature Preserve and Trail is also on the property. Carillon concerts are at 1 and 3 p.m. each afternoon, with shorter bell sounds every half hour. The 60-bell carillon housed in the Singing Tower is not open to the public, but take time to see the Great Brass Door and the wrought iron gates on the north side of the tower. Various concerts, art programs, and other events take place at the gardens throughout the year. The Bok Tower Gardens is open every day of the year from 8 a.m. to 6 p.m. (last admission is at 5 p.m.). The Visitor Center and Blue Palmetto Cafe are open from 9 a.m. to 5 p.m. Picnic areas are off the main parking lot. Bok Tower Gardens has an unattended "pet pen" where pets can stay, for a fee, while their owners tour the gardens. Ask at the Visitor Center about a Discovery Back Pack to help children enjoy their visit to Bok Tower Gardens. Also on the property is the 1930s-era Pinewood Estate, the winter home of C. Austin Buck, vice-president of Bethlehem Steel at the time. This estate was acquired by Bok Tower Gardens in the 1970s. The estate is open Mon through Sat from noon to 4 p.m. and on Sun from 1 to 4 p.m. There is a separate admission charge for the estate.

Davidson of Dundee. 28421 US 27 South, Dundee; (800) 294-2266; dundeegroves.com. Stop in and watch them make marmalade, jelly, and citrus candy the way they have for almost 50 years. Tours and samples vary, depending on the season, so each trip is a new experience. During citrus season, you can order all sorts of citrus and other fruit. Open every day from 9 a.m. to 6 p.m.

Lake Kissimmee State Park & Cow Camp. 14248 Camp Mack Rd., Lake Wales; (863) 696-1112; floridastateparks.org/lakekissimmee. Just a short jog to the east of Bok Tower Gardens on SR 60 is Lake Kissimmee State Park, one of our favorite places to enjoy Florida au naturel. Lake Kissimmee State Park is surrounded by three lakes—Florida's third largest lake, Lake Kissimmee, Lake Rosalie, and Tiger Lake—so there are boat ramps and plenty of places to fish. There are also 6 miles of horse trails and a 13-mile hiking trail with primitive camp areas. Weekends between Oct 1 and May 1, one spot of the park undergoes a time warp and visitors are apt to find themselves back in 1876 surrounded by a herd of scrub cattle tended by a "cow hunter" at the Cow Camp. He's had no one to talk to but the recalcitrant cows he's been rounding up to bring to Port Tampa so they can be shipped to Cuba, so stay and chat a while. Lake Kissimmee State Park is open from 7 a.m. to sundown every day. Cow Camp hours are 9:30 a.m. to 4:30 p.m. on holidays year-round and on weekends from Oct 1 to May 1. Groups of 15 or more can request the Cow Camp living history program at other times during the year. A camp store is open on weekends; boat rentals are available, as are guided overnight backpacking tours and other events.

Spook Hill. N. Wales Drive (5th Street) between E. North Avenue and Burns Avenue, Lake Wales. Aw, c'mon. You know you want to try it. Whether it's hokey or a hoax or really haunted, cars do appear to roll uphill at a certain spot on a road in Lake Wales. The local legend involves a Native American tribal chief who battled a gargantuan 'gator to save his village. But we'll let you read the rest for yourself. You'll see the sign as you drive north on 5th Street/N. Wales Drive. Stop and read it. Then drive ahead—downhill—to the white line, put your car in neutral, and take your foot off the brake. See what happens! Caution: This is a public road, so use your flashers and be alert.

where to eat

Cherry Pocket Steak and Seafood Shak. 3100 Canal Rd., Lake Wales; (863) 439-2031; cherrypocket.com. Cherry Pocket Steak and Seafood Shak—they also have cabins and RV spots—sits on Lake Pierce near Lake Wales. Seating is indoors or out on the deck; live music and karaoke liven weekend evenings. Steaks, seafood, chicken, and various fettucini dishes fill the substantial menu, plus they have a raw bar. They serve lunch every day from 11 a.m. to 4 p.m. Dinner is served Sun through Thurs from 4 to 9 p.m. and on Fri and Sat from 4 to 10 p.m. $$–$$$.

Norby's Steak & Seafood. 2425 Hwy. 60 East, Lake Wales; (863) 604-1456; norbysgreat steaks.com. Steak and seafood pretty much says it all. From filet mignon to rib eyes, Maine lobster to shrimp—with some chicken and pasta dishes for good measure—Norby's is pretty much an institution in Lake Wales. Look for early-bird and other specials on the website, and look for the link to Al's Place, selling burgers and chili dogs not far away. Norby's is open Mon through Thurs from 4:30 to 8:30 p.m., Fri and Sat from 4:30 to 8:45 p.m., and on Sun from 3:30 to 8 p.m. $$–$$$.

where to eat & stay

Chalet Suzanne Restaurant and Country Inn. 3800 Chalet Suzanne Dr., Lake Wales; (800) 433-6011, (863) 676-6011; chaletsuzanne.com. The Hinshaw family has opened their home, dubbed Chalet Suzanne, to travelers since 1931. The home is an eclectic "house that grew," so each room is different. Guests come for breakfast, lunch, or dinner or to stay a while in one of the 26 rooms. The estate has its own airstrip, and the Courtyard Spa's services are available by appointment. Some RV sites are also available. Chalet Suzanne's food quite literally is legendary, from the broiled grapefruit—a Chalet Suzanne original—to the Soup Romaine, which is canned on site and has been specially requested by astronauts for several space missions. Visit the soup cannery while you are at the chalet. Accommodations: $$–$$$; Dinner: $$$.

southeast

day trip 01

start your engines!

sebring; avon park; lake placid

South Central Florida, which is where we are headed for the next two day trips, shows up on the map as a lot of white space, crisscrossed by a few black lines and a few red lines. Don't let that fool you—there's a lot to see and do in that supposedly empty space. This trip takes us to the oldest permanent road-racing track in North America, Sebring International Raceway, which today hosts part of the American Le Mans Series.

With Sebring as our center point, we'll explore the surrounding area, which includes Avon Park, to the north—home of the first lawnmower racing complex in the United States—and Lake Placid, the Town of Murals, to the south. Each of these towns is no more than 20 miles from Sebring and all three are fairly new towns, in comparison with the larger course of history. Trains, more than the automobile, provided a means of transporting people in and citrus and cattle out, so each of our three stops has a train depot to visit. And all that white space? Turns out it really is green and brown and blue, and it is populated with critters. Their habitat is crisscrossed with hiking and horseback trails that don't show up on regular maps.

Note: Speaking of maps, not long ago Highlands County renumbered many of the addresses along US 27. But not all websites and other marketing tools have been changed to reflect the new numbers. Nor have all the mapping systems caught up with the changes. If you run into difficulties finding a place, call and ask if they had a different address a couple of years ago.

southeast day trip 01

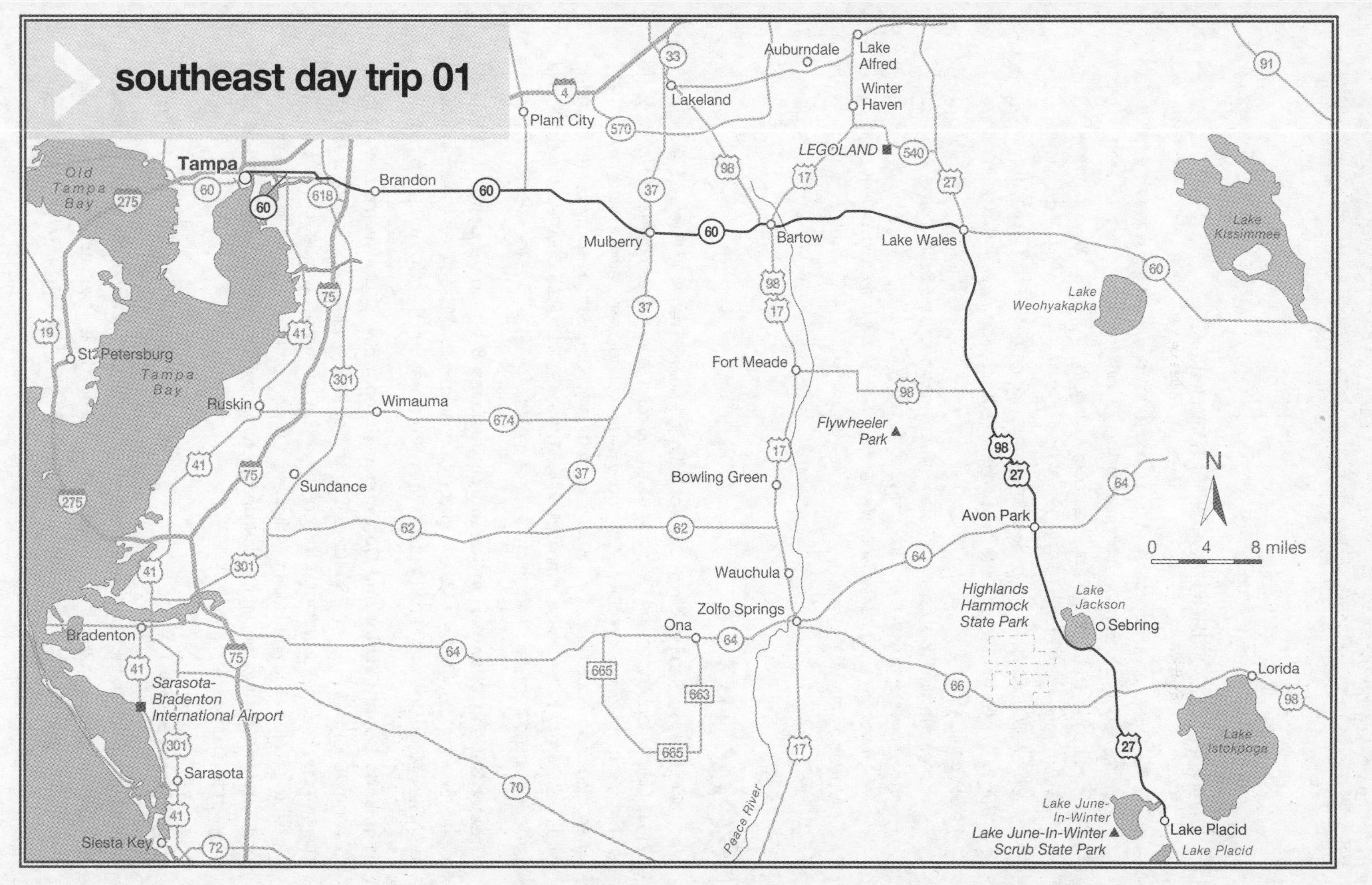

florida's heartland: feeding the nation

The 1909 Enlarged Homestead Act opened much of the central Florida area that includes Highlands County to homesteading. Before then, the area had been designated in 1842 for the Seminole people, who originally had lived in northern Florida. By the end of the Third Seminole War (1856–1858), most of the Seminole people had been forcibly removed to Arkansas or further west. The few remaining Seminole people retreated into the Everglades where they lived in hiding into the 20th century.

Once the land was opened to homesteading, settlers began to come. Citrus groves and cattle ranches grew, and today Florida is the third largest beef-producing state east of the Mississippi River and is the tenth largest beef-producing state in the nation.

sebring

Yes, there is also a Sebring, Ohio, home of Sebring Pottery. The same George Sebring who, with his family, developed the Ohio community and pottery business came to Florida to do some fishing one winter. He loved the countryside around Lake Jackson and, about 1911 or so, decided to build a second Sebring community here. Sebring's city center is on the southeast side of Lake Jackson and is, literally, a street—Circle Park Drive—in the shape of a circle. Radiating from the circle, the main streets of the town look like the spokes of a wheel.

Greater Sebring Chamber of Commerce Business & Welcome Center. 227 US 27 North, Sebring; (863) 385-8448; sebring.org. Located in the Village Plaza shopping center on US 27 North, the Welcome Center is open Mon through Fri from 8 a.m. to 5 p.m.

Highlands County Visitor and Convention Bureau. 501 S. Commerce Ave., Suite 3, Sebring; (800) 545-6021, (863) 402-6909; visithighlandscounty.com. Look for the Commerce Avenue Annex building at the corner of S. Commerce Avenue and S. Eucalyptus Street to find the Highland County Visitor and Convention Bureau. Stop in between 8 a.m. and 5 p.m. Mon through Fri to pick up maps, brochures, and other information about Highlands County.

getting there

While it is possible to take back roads and meander our way to Sebring in strictly southeasterly fashion, we're going to stick to main roads and head east, then turn south. This means we will retrace part of our route from a previous day trip (East Day Trip 02).

From Tampa take Adamo Drive East/SR 60 east. Travel through Brandon, Valrico, Mulberry, Bartow, and Lake Wales—about 50 miles, in all. Merge onto US 27 South toward Avon Park and Sebring. Drive through Avon Park for now and continue to Sebring.

where to go

Amtrak Station & Historic Sebring Depot. 601 E. Center Ave., Sebring; amtrak.com. Amtrak's Silver Star runs from Miami to New York with stops along the Eastern Seaboard, including at Sebring. The depot is also called the Old Sebring Seaboard Airline Depot, the name of the line that ran during Sebring's earlier years and which built the station in 1924. You don't have to go all the way to New York—ride the train to Winter Haven, have lunch, and return the same day. The station is open every day from 9:30 a.m. to 5 p.m.

Children's Museum of the Highlands. 219 N. Ridgewood Dr., Sebring; (863) 385-5437; childrensmuseumhighlands.com. Kids ages 1 to 12 will find activities here to challenge their brains and their muscles. They can make music on unusual instruments, try boulder climbing (like rock climbing only sideways), or build a dam on a river. Open Tues through Sat from 10 a.m. to 5 p.m. Thurs the museum stays open until 8 p.m., and the admission fee is half price after 5 p.m.

Highlands County Fair Convention Center. 781 Magnolia Ave., Sebring; (863) 382-2255; hcfcc.net. It's not just the Highlands County Fair that is held here; throughout the year concerts, sports competitions, and exhibitions of various types fill the stages and arenas here.

Highlands Hammock State Park. 5931 Hammock Rd., Sebring; (863) 386-6094; floridastateparks.org/highlandshammock. Highlands Hammock State Park was one of the first parks to make up the Florida State Park system, established in 1935. The park itself opened in 1931, after local citizens bought the property, made improvements, and tried to have it admitted into the national park system. Between 1934 and 1940, a Civilian Conservation Corps team worked to develop a botanical garden nearby. With World War II looming, the CCC camp was shut down in 1941, and the gardens were absorbed into the park. Today, visitors can explore the park's 9,000 acres of natural beauty and visit the Civilian Conservation Corps (CCC) Museum to learn about 1930s-era history. A 1-hour tram ride orients visitors to the park; the tram runs Tues through Fri at 1 p.m. and on Sat at 1 and 2:30 p.m. Hiking, biking, and equestrian trails wind through the park; one bike trail links to a county trail beginning at Lake Jackson in Sebring. Check the Events calendar for periodic music concerts held in the park. Campsites—full facility, group, equestrian, and primitive—and picnic areas are available. Great Florida Birding Trail #122. Campsites $.

Sebring International Raceway. 113 Midway Dr., Sebring; (800) 626-7223, (863) 655-1442; sebringraceway.com. Most car races are about speed. But 12 Hours at Sebring, held here since 1952 on the third Saturday in March, is about endurance. Speed, too, but mostly endurance—12 hours of racing around 3.7 miles of track that is partly concrete landing strips dating back to the days when the area was a World War II Army air-training base and partly newer asphalt paving. Twelve hours of negotiating 17 different curves and enduring bone-jarring, undercarriage-scraping bumps from hitting the seams joining the concrete sections leave cars and drivers battered. Upwards of 160,000 or so people attend the event. The rest of the year, Sebring International Raceway hosts other motor-sports events. Put together a group of 10 people or more and you can take a tour of Sebring (Jan through Apr only, except for race week; call for reservations). And people come throughout the year just to pay homage to this part of racing history. The raceway adjoins Sebring Regional Airport, so many fans fly in. Trackside accommodations include the Château Élan Hotel & Conference Center (see Where to Stay), RV parking, and tent camping. There is a midway full of vendors and exhibits; spectators have access to the paddock area and can walk the track before the race. No pets. Read the FAQs on the website for a listing of other guidelines.

where to eat

Don José Mexican Restaurant. 4731 Lakeview Dr., Sebring; (863) 385-9326; donjose mexican.com/florida. Sit outdoors overlooking the lake, or sit indoors and enjoy the hacienda decor. Either way, take time to read the extensive menu, then try to decide between the Chicken Guadalajara, the Steak a la Tampiquena, and the Red Snapper Serrano. They have a full bar, vegetarian dishes, and a children's menu. Don José is owned by the Arceo family, whose other restaurant is in New Jersey. Open Mon through Fri from 11 a.m. to 10 p.m. Open Sat from noon to 10 p.m. and Sun from noon to 9 p.m. $–$$.

Sebring Diner. 4040 US 27 South, Sebring; (863) 385-3434; sebringdiner.com. If you miss spotting this place, it's because somebody wasn't paying attention! The big DINER sign over the front door is your first clue, and the polished-chrome-and-glass look is the second clue that this diner—open 24/7—is a burger-and-fries-with-a-milkshake kind of place. But that's not all they serve. Prime rib, rosemary chicken, Reuben sandwiches, fried green tomatoes, pasta, and seafood also are on the menu. Breakfast is served anytime. All this and free wireless Internet access, too. $–$$.

where to stay

Château Élan Hotel & Conference Center. 150 Midway Dr., Sebring; (863) 655-7200; cesebring.com. Château Élan Hotel & Conference Center sits right at Turn 7, aka Hairpin Turn, which makes for a great view on race days. The hotel offers guests a pool, free Internet access, in-room video games, a 24/7 fitness center, and an on-site spa offering various personal care treatments and services. Esperante Restaurant serves breakfast, lunch, and dinner; the HairPin Lounge is a full-service bar. $$–$$$.

Inn on the Lakes Hotel. 3101 Golfview Rd., Sebring; (800) 531-5253, (863) 471-9400; innonthelakes.com. The Inn on the Lakes Hotel, located on the south side of Lake Jackson, offers both rooms and suites—some overlook Lake Jackson; others, especially those in the main tower, offer a more panoramic view of the area. In-room Internet access is provided, as is access to an on-site fitness center. Ask about golf packages, as there are a number of courses in the area offering various challenges. Close by is Back In Touch Wellness Spa & Apothecary, which offers guests discounted services. Guests enjoy a complimentary full breakfast at Chicanes, an on-site restaurant and bar serving breakfast, lunch, and dinner. Pets are welcomed. $–$$$.

Kenilworth Lodge. 1610 Lakeview Dr., Sebring; (800) 423-5939, (863) 385-0111; kenilworthlodge.com. George Sebring built this Mediterranean Revival grand hotel in 1916 to entice wealthy northerners to winter in Florida—and then to invest in land here. Today Kenilworth Lodge, listed on the National Register of Historic Places, has such modern amenities as high-speed Internet access in all rooms, but it has retained its original grace and charm. Accommodations range from villas to rooms, cottages, apartments, and suites, and all guests enjoy a complimentary expanded Continental breakfast each morning. In addition to an Olympic-size pool and a fitness room, guests can also play table tennis, horseshoes, billiards, and more—or maybe add a few pieces to a communal jigsaw puzzle someone has begun on the verandah. Kenilworth Lodge is noted for its golf packages. The Lakeview Restaurant at Kenilworth serves breakfast, lunch, and dinner; and the Cusworth Arms Pub & Wine Bar—open "4ish to 9ish"—offers a selection of beers and wines and a place to chat. Some minimum-stay requirements may apply. $–$$.

avon park

Avon Park, just a few miles north of Sebring, is the area's oldest city, as it was established in the mid-1880s. One resident was convinced the spot reminded her of Stratford-upon-Avon, and so the town acquired its name. Home cooks everywhere should pay homage to Avon Park, as this is where Brown 'N' Serve rolls were invented in 1949. Avon Park once was the site of the largest military bombing and gunnery range, and was a major World War II training site. Today, the range is still used for training and is called Avon Park Air Force Range.

Avon Park Chamber of Commerce. 28 E. Main St., Avon Park; (863) 453-3350; apfla.com. Stop in Mon through Fri from 9 a.m. to 4 p.m. to learn more about the area.

getting there

From Sebring, travel north on US 27 about 10 miles. When you reach CR 64, which is also Main Street in Avon Park, turn right to go to the city center.

where to go

Avon Park Air Force Range. 29 South Blvd., Avon Park; (863) 452-4254; avonparkafr .com. Military bases often include land that is open for public use, and Avon Park Air Force Range, located 11 miles northeast of Avon Park on SR 64, is one such base. There are miles of trails to hike, lakes and ponds to fish (including some stocked ponds especially helpful to the youngest anglers), and 3 campgrounds to stay in. Be aware that the land is also open to hunting at various times of the year, and plan accordingly.

Avon Park Mower-Plex. 2155 Herrick Rd., Avon Park; floridalawnracing.net. Sebring may have the oldest permanent road-racing track in North America, but Avon Park, home of the Florida Lawn Mower Racing Association, has the first dedicated lawnmower racing facility in the United States. Racers ages 10 and up can race various classes of riding mowers. Racers earn points and compete in a national circuit—some have even been featured on ESPN. Races are held about once a month—check the Web event calendar for details and spectator admission fees.

Depot Museum & Historical Society of Avon Park. 3 N. Museum Ave., Avon Park; (863) 453-3525; hsaponline.org. The train no longer stops in Avon Park, but the 1926-era depot has been preserved as the city's museum. The Historical Society even purchased one of the old Zephyr Line's dining cars; today, area groups often reserve the car for special luncheon events. The museum is open Tues through Fri from 10 a.m. to 3 p.m.

Flywheeler Park. 7000 Avon Park Cutoff Rd., Fort Meade; (863) 285-9121; floridaflywheelers.org. Antique steam engines, tractors, autos, and other machines are the focus of the Florida Flywheelers Antique Engine Club. Members exhibit at events around the state, but a few times a year they hold tractor pulls and other events to which the public is invited. Visitors will see a steam engine–powered sawmill, antique construction and farm equipment, flivvers, and more on the 240-acre grounds. Check the website calendar to see when events are scheduled. The park is located about 10 miles northwest of Avon Park.

South Florida Community College Museum of Florida Art & Culture. 600 W. College Dr., Avon Park; (863) 784-7240 or (863) 453-6661; mofac.org. Permanent collections include works of the Florida Highwaymen, Florida Masters (Christopher Still, Clyde Butcher, and others), and historical collections. The museum is open Wed through Fri from 12:30 to 4:30 p.m. and by appointment for group tours. The museum is closed June through Aug.

where to shop

Mile Long Mall. Think of "mall" in the old-fashioned sense of being a shaded walkway as well as in the newer sense of being a series of connected shops. The Mile Long Mall in Avon Park is a bit of both. There is a walkway area with trees and a bandstand, and there are shops and restaurants of various sorts located in downtown Avon Park. Some of the buildings date back to the 1920s.

where to stay & eat

The Jacaranda Hotel. 19 E. Main St., Avon Park; (863) 453-2211; hoteljac.com. The Jacaranda Hotel has been welcoming guests since 1926. Back then, guests included baseball players and movie stars like Babe Ruth and Clark Gable. Since 1988, the hotel has been owned by South Florida Community College Foundation, Inc., and the north side of the facility is used as student housing. Rooms and suites are available to the public. The hotel has an outdoor swimming pool and Internet service, and the original elevator is still in service. A buffet lunch is served Mon through Fri from 11 a.m. to 2 p.m. A Grand Buffet is served Sun from 11 a.m. to 2 p.m. A dinner buffet is served Jan through Mar from 4:30 to 7:30 p.m. The restaurant is closed on Sat. Accommodations: $–$$$. Dinner: $$.

lake placid

Lake Placid is the youngest of the three cities. Chartered in 1925 as the Town of Lake Stearns, its name was changed in 1927 to Lake Placid when Dr. Melvil Dewey—of the Dewey Decimal System of cataloging library books fame—arrived with plans to establish a second Lake Placid Resort. Dewey had established Lake Placid Resort in New York as a health resort for educators, and he wanted to do something similar in Florida. Today the town is known as the Town of Murals, because of the outdoor paintings covering many buildings' walls, and as the Caladium Capital of the World, because 98 percent of the world's caladium bulbs come from here. The very tall tower in town once was the tallest in the area, but it is no longer open to the public.

Greater Lake Placid Chamber of Commerce & Mural Gallery. 18 N. Oak Ave., Lake Placid; (863) 465-4331; lpfla.com. Stop in and pick up brochures and other information about the town and the surrounding area. See below for information about the Mural Gallery, also located at the chamber office. The chamber office is open Mon through Fri from 9 a.m. to 4 p.m. and on Sat from 10 a.m. to 1 p.m.

getting there

From Sebring, take US 27 South about 15 miles to Lake Placid. Turn right on E. Interlake Boulevard, then take the third right on N. Oak Avenue.

where to go

Archbold Biological Station. 123 Main Dr., Venus; (863) 465-2571; archbold-station.org. Since 1941, scientists have conducted long-term ecological research at the Archbold Biological Station, the primary division of an independent, not-for-profit, research institution called Archbold Expeditions. Located just south of Lake Placid off SR 70 West, Archbold is listed on the National Register of Historic Places and as a National Natural Landmark. The Station is open to day visitors. Day visitors can view a video about the biodiversity of the area and pictorial exhibits about the station. A 0.5-mile, self-guided nature trail is located at the south end of the grounds; picnic tables are at the north end. Groups of 10 or more people can make reservations for a guided tour. ***Note:*** A 7-panel mural in Lake Placid depicts the life of Richard Archbold and his contributions to the scientific world and to the Lake Placid community. Look for the mural at 19 West Interlake Blvd., Lake Placid (a Miller's Central Air building).

Henscratch Farms Vineyard & Winery. 980 Henscratch Rd., Lake Placid; (863) 699-2060; henscratchfarms.com. Drive on out and enjoy the Florida countryside. Pick some strawberries, grapes, or blueberries—depending on the season, of course—and taste some of the wine made at Henscratch Farms Winery. The chickens don't just provide entertainment; they also supply the country store with fresh eggs. The store also sells wines and jams and sauces and syrups. Want to stomp some grapes? Ask about the Grape Stomp, held each August! Henscratch Farms is open Tuesday through Saturday at 10 a.m. and on Sunday at noon. Most of the year, the Farms closes at 4 p.m.; December through April it stays open until 5 p.m. Tuesday through Saturday. June and July the Farms is open only on the weekends. Call ahead to confirm what fruit is in season.

Lake June-in-Winter Scrub State Park. Daffodil Rd., Lake Placid; (863) 386-6099; floridastateparks.org/lakejuneinwinter/default.cfm. Cactus? In Florida? Yup. In the ecosystems called scrub, many desert-like plants—including prickly pear cactus—and animals thrive. Lake June-in-Winter Scrub State Park is one of those areas, and it is home to a number of rare plant and animal species. Visitors can hike or fish, and there is a picnic area with restroom facilities (composting toilet). But there is no drinking water available, so bring plenty. The gate fee is $2 per vehicle; leave it in the box as you enter. Great Florida Birding Trail #125.

Lake Placid Depot Museum. 12 W. Park St., Lake Placid; (863) 465-1771; lphsdepotmuseum.org. Built in the late 1920s for use by the Atlantic Coast Line Railroad, the depot stopped serving passenger lines in the 1950s and closed for good in the 1970s. Today, the restored depot's exhibit areas include a 1929 sawmill steam engine, a proverbial red caboose, a 1920s-era jail cell, and many photos, furnishings, and equipment from the surrounding area. Learn more about Melville Dewey, creator of the Dewey Decimal System of organizing library books and the person who convinced the railroad to build a depot in Lake Placid. Dewey also pushed for a simplified phonetic spelling system, going so far as to change the spelling of his own name to Melvil Dui. The museum is open Mon through Fri, Oct through May, from 10 a.m. to 1 p.m., but call ahead, especially during the holiday season.

Mural Gallery. 18 N. Oak Ave., Lake Placid; (863) 465-4331; htn.net/lplacid/murals/murals.htm. The nickname "Town of Murals" doesn't even begin to describe it. Lake Placid literally has become a canvas on which noted artists depict the town's history. Almost 50 murals adorn the walls of buildings around town. Some include sound effects. All have an item hidden or left out for sharp eyes to spot. Even trash containers get into the spirit. To get the most enjoyment from the murals, visit the Mural Gallery, located at the Chamber of Commerce office, before exploring. In the gallery, visitors can watch a 10-minute video about the murals and can see the artists' original renderings—miniatures compared to the murals themselves. Buy a guidebook or view the information on the website about each of the murals. Group tours can also be arranged.

Toby the Clown Foundation & American Clown Museum. 109 W. Interlake Blvd., Lake Placid; (863) 465-2920; tobysclownfoundation.org. Keith "Toby" Stokes began clowning in what was then Lake Placid Clinic, bringing smiles to people who had reasons not to. The clinic grew into a hospital, and the demand for Toby's merry heart grew as other hospitals expressed interest. In 1991, Toby began teaching other people to be clowns. Today, more than 1,500 clowns around the United States and Canada are graduates of Toby's Clown School. The American Clown Museum is the only one known to be in the United States. Call ahead for hours and days.

what to do

Fishing. With almost 30 lakes in the immediate area, Lake Placid is a fisherman's paradise. The Chamber's website has a page (lpfla.com/lakes.htm) listing the lakes, depth of each, and availability of public boat ramps. Stop in or call the chamber office for information about fishing guides, or see p. xiv in Using This Guide for a list of guides.

where to eat

Jaxson's Bar and Grill. 443 Lake June Rd., Lake Placid; (863) 465-4674; lprestaurants.com/jaxsons. Jaxson's Bar and Grill really means it when they say "Grill." Grilled steaks, seafood, and chicken—or even alligator!—keep people coming back. Throw in lakeside dining, and it doesn't get much better. They are open from 11 a.m. to 10 p.m. every day. $-$$.

Main Street America Eatery. 15 S. Main St., Lake Placid; (863) 465-7733. This is the place for breakfast. Lunch, too, during the week, but mostly breakfast. Main Street America Eatery is open Tues through Fri from 7 a.m. to 2 p.m., on Sat from 7 a.m. to noon, and on Sun from 7 a.m. to 1 p.m. No credit cards. $.

where to stay

Trail's End Fishing Resort. 4232 Trails End, Lorida; (888) 603-9209, (863) 655-0134; trailsendfishingresort.com. Trail's End Fishing Resort sits on the east side of Lake Istokpoga, the area's largest lake, about halfway between Sebring and Lake Placid. Accommodations include furnished cabins, furnished double-wide mobile homes, and RV spots. They have a double boat ramp, bait and tackle store, and boat rentals—plus laundry facilities and boat rentals. Pets are welcomed. $-$$.

day trip 02

southeast

one man's castle:
wauchula; zolfo springs; ona

Hardee County, to Tampa's southeast, is another rural county with some hidden treasures. The county is part of the Bone Valley area we first met when we traveled east (Day Trip 02). People still find fossilized bones and other matter here, especially along the Peace River, which runs through Hardee County. We'll make our first stop in Wauchula, the county seat, visit an historic state park, then venture south to where one man has quite literally built himself a castle complete with a boat in a moat.

wauchula

Wauchula is another community with roots to the US Army's occupation of Florida. Fort Hartstuff was established here in 1856 during the Third Seminole War. The community grew into a town when the Florida Southern Railway built a depot here in 1886 and named it Wauchula, a Miccosoukee-derived word meaning "call of the sand hill crane." Today, the town consists of about 5,000 people.

Hardee County Chamber of Commerce. 107 E. Main St., Wauchula; (863) 773-6967; hardeecc.com. Stop in for information about the area, especially about the historic railroad depot and other buildings downtown. The chamber office is open Mon through Fri from 8 a.m. to 4:30 p.m.

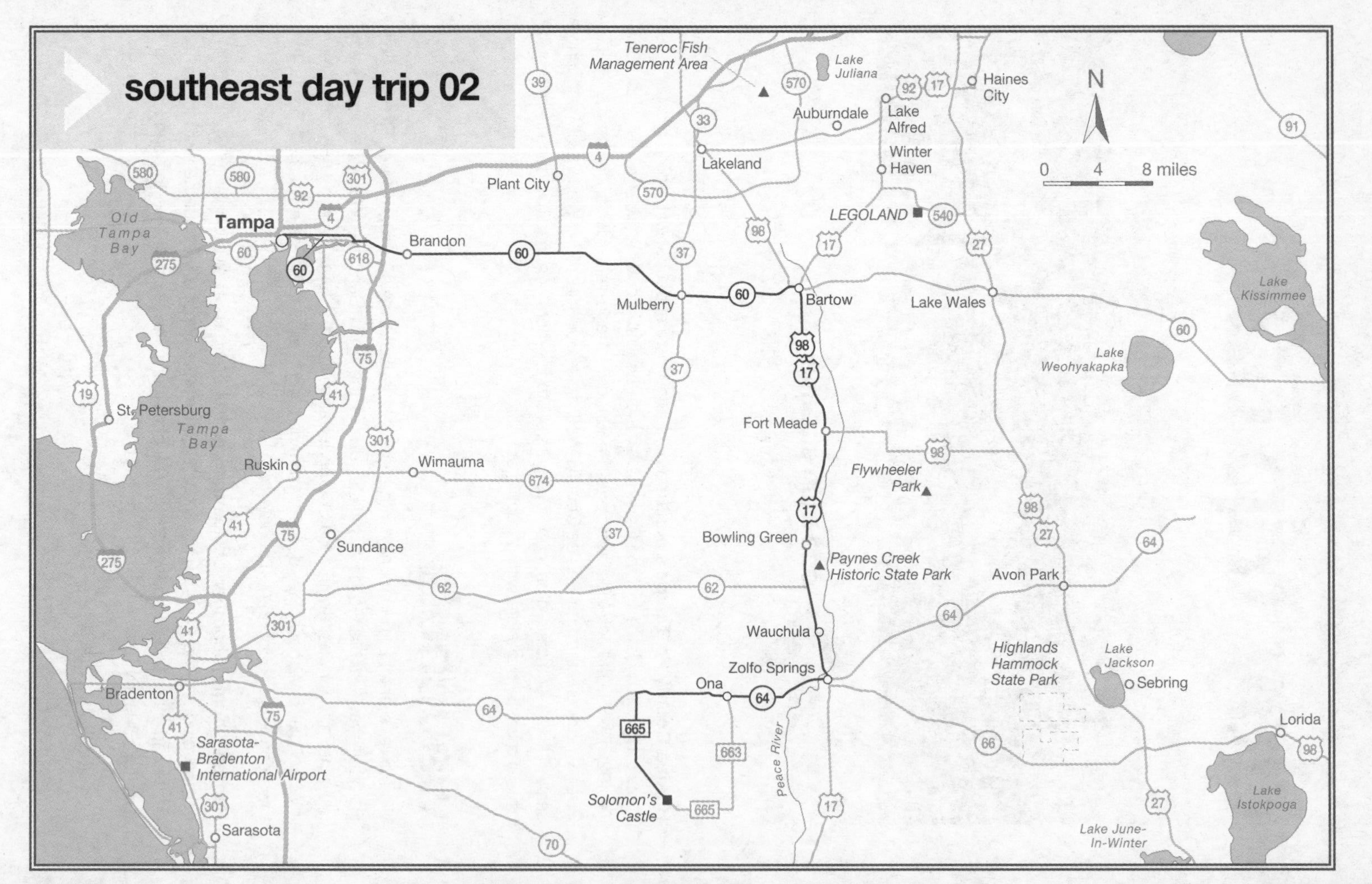
southeast day trip 02
Teneroc Fish Management Area
Lake Juliana
Haines City
Auburndale
Lake Alfred
Winter Haven
Lakeland
Plant City
LEGOLAND
N
0 4 8 miles
Old Tampa Bay
Tampa
Brandon
Mulberry
Bartow
Lake Wales
Lake Kissimmee
Lake Weohyakapka
St. Petersburg
Tampa Bay
Fort Meade
Ruskin
Wimauma
Flywheeler Park
Sundance
Bowling Green
Paynes Creek Historic State Park
Avon Park
Wauchula
Highlands Hammock State Park
Lake Jackson
Sebring
Zolfo Springs
Ona
Bradenton
Lorida
Sarasota-Bradenton International Airport
Peace River
Solomon's Castle
Sarasota
Lake Istokpoga
Lake June-In-Winter

getting there

From Tampa, take Adamo Drive East/SR 60 east through Brandon and Mulberry toward Bartow—about 35 miles in all. At Bartow, stay straight to go onto US 98 South/E. Van Fleet Drive/SR 700 South/SR 35 South, then turn slightly right on US 17 South/US 98 South/SR 700 South/SR 35 South/SR 555 South. Follow US 17 South through Fort Meade and Bowling Green toward Wauchula, about 25 miles. Look for E. Main Street, and turn left.

where to go

Paynes Creek Historic State Park. 888 Lake Branch Rd., Bowling Green; (863) 375-4717; floridastateparks.org/paynescreek/default.cfm. Backtrack up US 17 to Bowling Green and turn right at Main St. East; follow the signs to the park. Paynes Creek Historic State Park sits along the Peace River; Paynes Creek, a tributary of the river, flows through the park. The creek and the park are named after Captain George S. Payne, who, in 1849, was killed by renegade Seminoles at the Kennedy-Darling Trading Post along with a clerk. The US Army responded by building Fort Chokonikla nearby. Less than a year later, however, the fort was abandoned as so many soldiers were dying of mosquito-borne diseases. Today the park's visitor center contains exhibits about the history of the area. Video programs about the Seminole Wars are shown on weekends and holidays. There are picnic tables and a playground, but the only camping available is the youth (group) camping area. The park has several hiking trails, and a canoe and kayak launch site provides paddlers with access to the Peace River and to Paynes Creek. In March of each year, reenactors bring the Fort Chokonikla Encampment to life with black powder rifle and cannon exhibitions, archery demonstrations, and historic interpreters. The park is open 8 a.m. until sunset every day; the visitor center is open 9 a.m. to 5 p.m. daily.

what to do

Fossil Hunting. The Peace River area is part of Bone Valley, an area full of fossilized bones and shells. It also is one of the few areas in Florida where it is legal to search for fossils—provided you purchase a permit and follow the guidelines. To apply for a fossil-hunting permit online, go to the Florida Museum of Natural History's website (flmnh.ufl.edu/vertpaleo/vppermit.htm) and follow the links. More information about what kind of fossil-hunting activities are allowed can be found at the Florida Department of Environmental Protection's website (dep.state.fl.us/geology/geologictopics/fossil.htm). Paleo Discoveries (772-539-7005; paleodiscoveries.com) offers fossil-hunting expeditions in the Wauchula and other areas. Serious fossil hunters will want to explore the FossilHunters.com website. And ask at the chamber office for local fossil enthusiasts who might be willing to share information with you.

where to eat

Java Cafe. 202 W. Main St., Wauchula; (863) 767-9004; java-cafe-wauchula.com. Java Cafe serves breakfast Mon through Fri from 7 to 10:30 a.m. and lunch until 3 p.m. On Friday nights they reopen at 5:30 and serve steaks, seafood, and other entrees until 9 p.m. Sun they serve lunch from 11 a.m. to 2 p.m. They are closed on Sat. They offer a wide selection of coffees and teas—and save room for dessert. Just sayin' . . . $$.

where to stay

Quilter's Inn Bed & Breakfast. 106 S. 4th Ave., Wauchula; (863) 767-8989; thequiltersinn .com. Hardwood floors, period furnishings, a fire ring on the patio, and whimsical touches throughout greet guests to the Quilter's Inn Bed & Breakfast, a 1920s-era Craftsman-style home. A country breakfast is included in the rates, as is cable TV and Internet access. A minimum stay may be required during some events. $–$$.

Thousand Trails: Peace River. 2555 US 17 South, Wauchula; (863) 735-8888; thousand trails.com/getaways/florida/peaceriver.asp. Part of the Thousand Trails network of RV resorts and campgrounds, the Peace River site offers RV and tent spots and a few cabins. There is a small store and cafe, a swimming pool, meeting house with game room, miniature golf, hiking trails, and scheduled activities. Members have priority when making reservations, but unfilled spots are open to the public. $.

zolfo springs

Zolfo Springs is a small town of fewer than 2,000 people. When a crew of Spanish-speaking 19th-century phosphate miners worked their way down the Peace River to this spot, they smelled *zolfo*, or sulphur, in the river's springs. Ironically, in 1913, the 250 or so residents of Zolfo Springs invested $1,600 in drilling for water. At about 465 feet, drillers struck a flow of fresh water so forceful it shot 12 feet into the air. Today, Zolfo Springs is an agricultural community and is home to the Mancini brand of roasted pepper products.

getting there

From Wauchula, head south down US 17 South about 4 miles. You're there.

where to go

Cracker Trail Museum & Village. 2822 Museum Dr., Zolfo Springs; (863) 735-0119; hardeecounty.net/crackertrailmuseum/index.html. See how people have lived in various times in this corner of Florida. Displays are both inside and outside, and a slide show of old photographs plays daily in the museum. The museum is a stop on the Florida Cracker Trail Association's annual cross-state trail ride, held each February. The museum, located on the

Pioneer Park grounds, is open Tues through Sat from 9 a.m. to 5 p.m. Call ahead for holiday hours and to schedule group tours.

Peace River Refuge & Ranch. 2545 Stoner Ln., Zolfo Springs; (863) 735-0804; peace riverrefuge.org. Peace River Refuge & Ranch is a nonprofit organization that accepts exotic and other wild animals that have been abandoned or confiscated. Guided educational tours are available twice a month by advance reservation only, and there are internship opportunities available to college students.

Wildlife Refuge. 650 Animal Way, Zolfo Springs; (863) 735-9531; hardeecounty.net. Located on the grounds of Pioneer Park, the Wildlife Refuge houses Florida wild animals that cannot be released back into the wild for various reasons. A boardwalk allows visitors to see the animals in a natural habitat. The refuge is closed on Mon and Wed. Other days, the refuge is open from 10 a.m. to 4 p.m. Combo tickets are available for the refuge and the Cracker Museum.

where to eat

Acapulco Cafe. 410 US 17 South, Zolfo Springs; (863) 735-0677. Mexican food taquerias predominate in this small town, which puts it just this side of heaven to some of us—but they tend to come and go. Acapulco Cafe is open Sun and Mon from 9 a.m. to 3 p.m., Wed and Thurs from 9 a.m. to 8 p.m., and Fri and Sat from 9 a.m. to 9 p.m. Closed Tues; no credit cards. $–$$.

Pioneer Restaurant. 2902 US 17 South, Zolfo Springs; (863) 735-0726. Open 7 days a week, Pioneer Restaurant serves breakfast, lunch, and dinner, including prime rib. Mon through Sat they're open from 6 a.m. to 8 p.m. Sun they're open from 7 a.m. to 2 p.m. No credit cards. $–$$.

where to stay

Pioneer Park. 231 Wilbur C. King Blvd., Zolfo Springs; (863) 735-0330; hardeecounty.net. This Hardee County park has sites for tents and RVs. There are restrooms with showers, a playground and picnic area, and a boat ramp to the Peace River. Bank fishing on nearby lakes is allowed (with license, etc.). Pets on leashes are allowed. Also on the premises are the Cracker Museum and the Wildlife Refuge (separate fees apply). $.

ona

We're not actually going to Ona, which is pretty much just a rural crossroads with a post office. But Ona is the mailing address for our next adventure, located southwest of Ona. So pack a hefty suitcase full of punny-bone groans, make sure your gas tank is well above empty, and let's head to Solomon's Castle.

getting there

From Zolfo Springs, take CR 64/Florida Cracker Trail west through Ona to CR 665, not quite 15 miles. At CR 665, turn left. Travel about 9 miles on CR 665. The first 6 or so miles will be a straight stretch, then you'll bend to the left. Keep going—enjoy the cattle and horses and trees—to Solomon Road. Turn left and follow the road to Solomon's Castle.

where to go, eat & stay

Solomon's Castle. 4585 Solomon Rd., Ona; (863) 494-6077; solomonscastle.org. Howard Solomon marches to the beat of a different drummer. How many other artists can you think of who would buy a cow pasture in the middle of nowhere, fill it with one-of-a-kind largely immovable works of art, and wait for people to show up so he could regale them with his decidedly tongue-in-cheek commentary? Howard Solomon's home quite literally is his castle, the materials for which have been reclaimed from unlikely sources—try printing press plates for the castle siding. The castle contains galleries with more than 300 of Solomon's sculptures, some of them mechanized, created from recycled materials ranging from auto parts to garden tools. More items are outside. If you're lucky, it will be Solomon himself who takes you on a tour—be sure to bring a full supply of "I can't believe I fell for that one" groans. Have lunch or dinner on the Boat in the Moat restaurant (sandwiches, salads, hot meals). You can even stay overnight in the castle tower's Blue Moon Room, and other facilities are under construction. Solomon's Castle is a popular spot for weddings and parties. Solomon's Castle is open from 11 a.m. to 4 p.m. every day except Mon from Oct 1 through June 30. The Boat in the Moat restaurant stays open until 9 p.m. on Fri and Sat (and for groups by special arrangement on other evenings) and offers a special evening menu. Solomon's Castle does not accept credit or debit cards. Accommodations: $. Dinner: $–$$.

south

day trip 01

a light goes on:

fort myers/cape coral; sanibel/captiva/pine islands

The Caloosahatchee River flows west from Lake Okeechobee, enters Lee County, and widens as it passes Fort Myers. It becomes a broad waterway, then empties into the Gulf of Mexico. On the south side and upriver from the Gulf is Fort Myers, winter home of Henry Ford and Thomas Edison a century ago and home today to spring training for the Boston Red Sox and the Minnesota Twins. On the north side of the Caloosahatchee is North Fort Myers and, closer to the Gulf, Cape Coral. Captiva and Sanibel—two barrier islands known for the seashells that wash ashore here—along with Pine Island, another barrier island, face Cape Coral.

Thousands of years ago, this area was home to the Calusa people. Later, the waters off this area were winter fishing grounds for Cuban fishermen; still later, it became a port for shipping goods to and from Cuba and elsewhere. Today, the area's businesses and industries include a number of healthcare-related companies, electronics firms, and retail headquarters.

Fort Myers/Cape Coral and Sanibel/Captiva/Pine Islands are the two areas we visit during this day trip from Tampa—and these are the southernmost points this book covers.

fort myers/cape coral

Drive down the McGregor Boulevard and it's easy to see why Fort Myers is called the City of Palms. Those palms were the idea of Thomas Edison, who planted many of them in the 1920s.

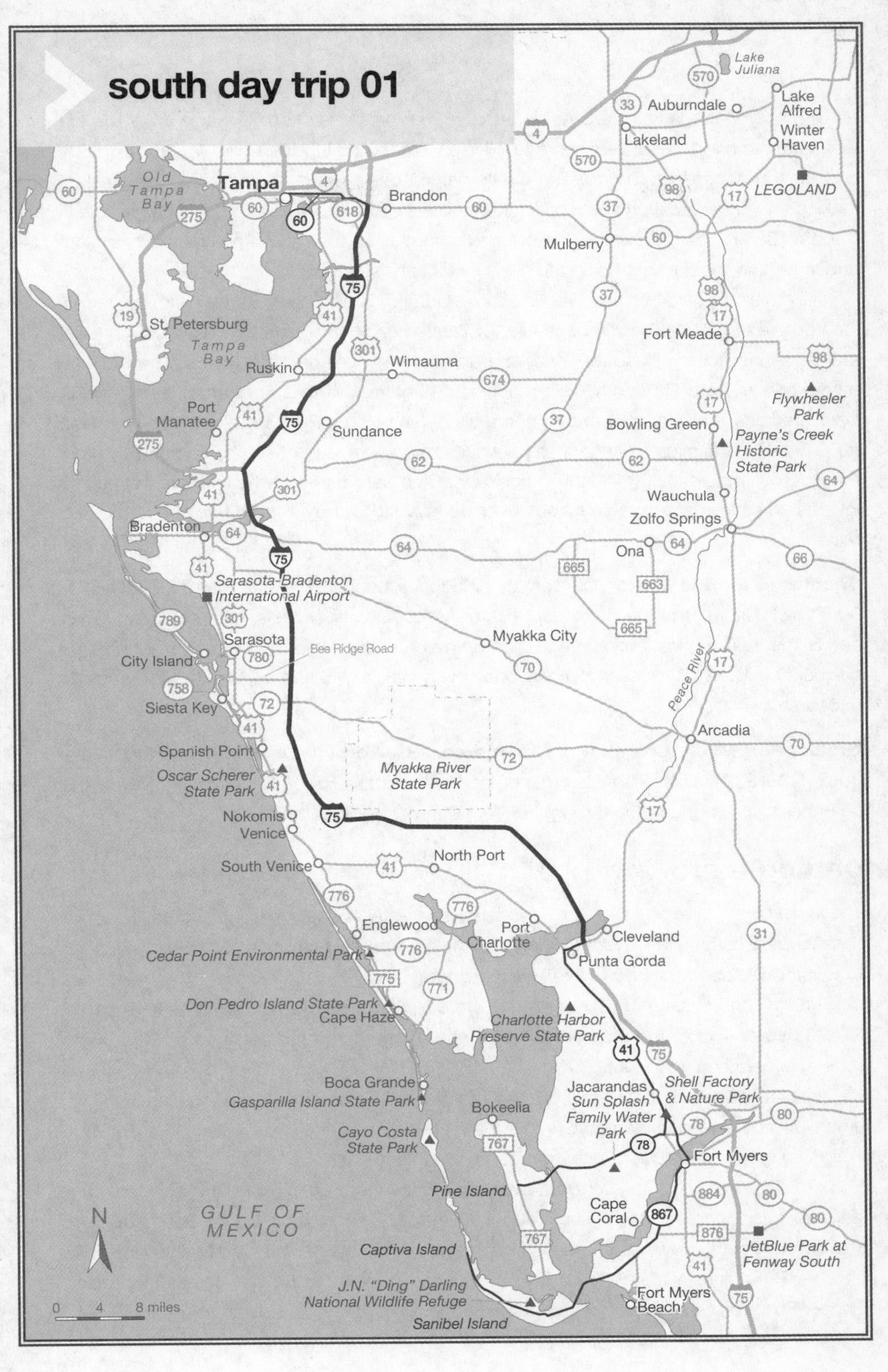
south day trip 01
Lake Juliana
Auburndale
Lake Alfred
Lakeland
Winter Haven
LEGOLAND
Old Tampa Bay
Tampa
Brandon
Mulberry
St. Petersburg
Tampa Bay
Fort Meade
Ruskin
Wimauma
Flywheeler Park
Port Manatee
Sundance
Bowling Green
Payne's Creek Historic State Park
Wauchula
Zolfo Springs
Bradenton
Ona
Sarasota-Bradenton International Airport
Sarasota
Bee Ridge Road
Myakka City
City Island
Peace River
Siesta Key
Arcadia
Spanish Point
Oscar Scherer State Park
Myakka River State Park
Nokomis
Venice
North Port
South Venice
Englewood
Port Charlotte
Cleveland
Punta Gorda
Cedar Point Environmental Park
Don Pedro Island State Park
Cape Haze
Charlotte Harbor Preserve State Park
Boca Grande
Gasparilla Island State Park
Shell Factory & Nature Park
Jacarandas Sun Splash Family Water Park
Bokeelia
Cayo Costa State Park
Fort Myers
Pine Island
GULF OF MEXICO
Cape Coral
Captiva Island
JetBlue Park at Fenway South
J.N. "Ding" Darling National Wildlife Refuge
Fort Myers Beach
Sanibel Island
N
0 4 8 miles

Fort Myers began as a US Army fort in 1850, during the Third Seminole War. The fort was abandoned in 1858, reoccupied by Union Troops during the Civil War (1863–1865), and then abandoned for good. The area's natural beauty attracted northern industrialists looking for winter vacation spots other than those in Europe. Thomas Edison came here in the late 1880s and built a home. He invested money in the area, installing an electric system and importing the palms gracing the city's historical district.

On the north side of the river lies Cape Coral, a brand new city by historical terms. Incorporated in 1970, the city began in 1957 when Jack and Leonard Rosen bought several thousand acres of undeveloped land across the river from Fort Myers. The Rosens, entrepreneurs from Baltimore, built roads and hundreds of miles of canals, using the fill from dredging the canals to create home sites. Like Henry Plant in the 1880s, who built huge hotels in the middle of nowhere to entice northerners to invest in the Tampa Bay area, the Rosen brothers built the Cape Coral Yacht Club before they had sold more than a few lots, as an enticement to buyers from around the world. Today the city has about 150,000 residents.

Southwest Florida Visitor Center. 26600 Jones Loop Rd., Punta Gorda; (941) 639-0007; swflvisitor.com. The Southwest Florida Visitor Center serves Charlotte, Lee, Collier, and Sarasota Counties. Stop here to load up on brochures, information, and maybe some discount coupons. The visitor center is open every day from 6 a.m. to 11 p.m. The website, of course, is open 24/7.

Greater Fort Myers Chamber of Commerce. 2310 Edwards Dr., Fort Myers; (800) 366-3622; (239) 332-3624; fortmyers.org. Located just over the Edison Bridge in Fort Myers, the chamber office is open Mon through Fri from 9 a.m. to 4:30 p.m.

getting there

These directions take us first to the regional visitor center, located in Punta Gorda. The second set of directions continues to the Greater Fort Myers Chamber of Commerce. Places to visit include spots on Fort Myers Beach, as well.

From Tampa, take I-75 South south toward Naples. Travel about 95 miles to exit 161/CR 768 West. Exit to the right on exit 161, and merge right onto Jones Loop Road. The Visitor Center is on your right.

Instead of getting back on I-75, we'll take the Tamiami Trail—pronounced Tammy-ammy and otherwise known as US 41—the rest of the way into Fort Myers. The Tamiami Trail is so named because it runs from Tampa to Miami.

From the Visitor Center, continue west on CR 768/Jones Loop Road to Tyler Road. Turn left onto Tyler Road and travel south about 1.5 miles. Turn left onto US 41 South/Tamiami Trail/SR 45 South. Travel south about 13 miles, then take a slight left onto N. Tamiami Trail/US 41-BR (Business Route) South/SR 739 South. Travel about 5 miles across the Edison Bridge. Edwards Street is at the end of the bridge. Turn right onto Edwards Street.

where to go

Barbara B. Mann Performing Arts Hall at Edison State College. 8099 College Pkwy., Fort Myers; (800) 440-7469, (239) 481-4849; bbmannpah.com. The Barbara B. Mann Performing Arts Hall hosts Broadway series shows and concerts of various musical genres. The box office is open 10 a.m. to 5 p.m. Mon through Fri, 10 a.m. to 2 p.m. on Sat, and until curtain on the day of any show.

Burroughs Home & Gardens. 2505 1st St., Fort Myers; (239) 337-0706; burroughshome.com. One of Fort Myers's oldest homes, built in 1901 by John T. Murphy, who in 1879 had formed the Montana Cattle Company, this Georgian Colonial Revival–style mansion eventually became the home of Mr. and Mrs. Nelson Burroughs and their children. On Fri at 11 a.m., visitors can tour the home and gardens; a catered lunch also is available.

Edison & Ford Winter Estates. 2350 McGregor Blvd., Fort Myers; (239) 334-7419; edisonfordwinterestates.org. Thomas Edison discovered the Fort Myers area in the late 1880s, bought land here—reportedly within 24 hours of arriving—and built a vacation home. Edison's mind rarely took a vacation, however, so he built a laboratory and a botanical garden—he tried to find a domestic source of rubber and tested bamboo for use as filaments in his lightbulbs—so he could continue working when he was in Florida. In 1916, Henry Ford bought the house next door so the families could vacation together. Today, the estates are open to the public. Various tours are offered, including a couple of boat tours and one especially for families with children. The botanical garden includes one of the largest banyan trees in the United States. The museum is open from 9 a.m. to 5 p.m. every day except Thanksgiving and Christmas.

Hammond Stadium. 14100 Six Mile Cypress Pkwy., Fort Myers; (239) 533-7275; minnesota.twins.mlb.com. The Twins, part of the American League Central Division, has been training in Fort Myers since 1991. Hammond Stadium is part of the Lee County Sports Complex, which also includes several other ball fields, a softball complex, batting cages, and other facilities. The Fort Myers Miracle, a Twins minor league affiliate team, also plays at Hammond Stadium. Twins games tend to sell out early—home team side tickets (third base side) are in the 108–115 (box/stadium seats) and 209–217 (bleachers/reserved) sections.

Imaginarium Hands-On Museum & Aquarium. 2000 Cranford Ave., Fort Myers; (239) 321-7420; imaginariumfortmyers.com. Talk about an aptly named facility! When the City of Fort Myers outgrew their water treatment facility, they used their imaginations and turned it into a hands-on museum. The water holding tanks became a 180,000-gallon lagoon system harboring freshwater fish, turtles, and several species of waterfowl. The still-working water tower is the site for an outdoor pavilion area. Children of all ages can experiment with Science in Motion as they create roller ball tracks, become meteorologists and create a video broadcast of themselves giving the weather report, and touch stingrays and other marine life in the Sea-to-See Touch Tanks. All this and a 3-D movie, live demonstrations, and loads of interactive exhibits. The Imaginarium is open Mon through Sat from 10 a.m. to 5 p.m. and on Sun from noon to 5 p.m.

JetBlue Park at Fenway South. 11581 Daniels Pkwy., Fort Myers; (888) 733-7696.; boston.redsox.mlb.com. The Boston Red Sox, part of the American League's Eastern Division, has been coming to Fort Myers for spring training since 1993. For most of that time, they played at the City of Palms Park. Beginning in 2012, however, the Sox took the field at JetBlue Park at Fenway South, so nicknamed because its design replicates to a large degree Boston's Fenway Park. Word is the field will have two scoreboards—a modern, digital one and a manual one that was used at Fenway Park until 2001 and has been in storage since then. The Red Sox dugout is on the third base side where the even-numbered sections are.

Manatee Park. 10901 SR 80/Palm Beach Blvd., Fort Myers; (239) 533-7275; leeparks.org. One side of Manatee Park sits on the Orange River. The other side is on a Florida Power and Light warm-water discharge canal. When the temperatures drop during the winter months—yes, even in Florida it can get a tad chilly—the warm water attracts manatees. Visitors to the park have a good view of the manatees from walkways. Also in the park are a butterfly garden, an ethnobotany trail, a fishing pier, children's activities, and more. Volunteers are on hand to answer questions about the manatees and about the park every day, Dec through Mar, at 2 p.m. There is also a canoe and kayak concession in the park (Calusa Blueway Outfitters & Gift Shop, 239-481-4600).

Southwest Florida Museum of History. 2031 Jackson St., Fort Myers; (239) 321-7430; swflmuseumofhistory.com. What once was the Atlantic Coastline Railroad depot is now the Southwest Florida Museum of History. Where passengers once waited to board trains, visitors now view exhibits of artifacts and photographs of the area as it once was. One display includes more than 1,200 pieces of Depression and carnival glass. Also on the property is a 1926 La France fire pumper and a 1929 private Pullman rail car. The museum also hosts walking tours of the downtown area and a number of historical presentations. The museum is open Tues through Sat from 10 a.m. to 5 p.m.

what to do

Castle Golf. 7400 Gladiolus Dr., Fort Myers; (239) 489-1999; castle-golf.com. We don't often include miniature golf courses in our lists of things to do. But Castle Golf is one of a kind. It's locally owned, not a chain, it has been rated among the top miniature golf spots in the state, and it is a favorite of locals. From the knight in not-quite-shining armor and a dragon or two to the castle itself, Castle Golf invites players to putt-putt their way through Once-Upon-a-Time tropical gardens. Nighttime lighting and other effects create a different atmosphere. A picnic area is open to guests.

Murder Mystery Dinner Train. 2805 Colonial Blvd., Fort Myers; (800) 736-4853, (239) 275-8487; semgulf.com. Ride the Seminole Gulf Railway, a real working train system hauling freight throughout southwest Florida since 1987. At night, passengers on the train enjoy a 5-course dinner while watching a murder mystery unfold. Reservations are a must.

Sun Splash Family Water Park. 400 Santa Barbara Blvd., Cape Coral; (239) 574-0558; Open between mid-Mar and mid-Sept, the Sun Splash Family Water Park has 14 acres of rides and slides. The park, owned by the City of Cape Coral, is also used for swim lessons, lifeguard camps, and other aquatic education adventures. In the off-season, the grounds are used for other festivals and events.

where to shop

Bell Tower Shops. Daniels Parkway/CR 876 and US 41 South, Fort Myers; (239) 489-1221; thebelltowershops.com. Forty boutique shops and trendy retailers, including Saks Fifth Avenue, Fresh Market, and Williams-Sonoma, join several restaurants ranging from Mimi's Cafe to DaRuMa Japanese Steakhouse & Sushi Lounge at the Bell Tower Shops open-air mall. Check the website for special events. The mall is open 10 a.m. to 9 p.m. Mon through Sat and from noon to 5 p.m. on Sun.

Cape Coral Farmers Market. Club Square (SE 47th Terrace and SE 10th Place), Cape Coral; (239) 549-6900; capecoralfarmersmarket.com. Every Saturday morning (mid-Oct to early May), produce and seafood vendors, artists and craftspeople, plant and garden vendors, and others gather on Club Square from 8 a.m. to 1 p.m. Sometimes there is live music and other entertainment.

Fleamasters Fleamarket. 4135 Dr. Martin Luther King Jr. Blvd., Fort Myers; (239) 334-7001; fleamall.com. More than 400,000 square feet of vendors, the Music Hall entertainment pavilion featuring live music, and 20 restaurants and snack bars are at the Fleamasters Fleamarket, which is open Fri, Sat, and Sun from 9 a.m. to 5 p.m.

Shell Factory & Nature Park. 2787 N. Tamiami Trail, North Fort Myers; (800) 282-5805, (239) 995-2141; shellfactory.com. Shells, shell jewelry, shell lamps, shell just-about-anything-you-can-imagine—plus several lines of collectible items including Department 56, Fontanini, and John Perry Studio items—are what shoppers find at the Shell Factory. There is also a Nature Park & Botanical Gardens with a 7,000-square-foot rainforest aviary (admission fee); a full-service restaurant and other eateries; a Fun Park & Video Arcade with bumper boats, miniature golf, water wars, and video arcade games; and a Holiday House where every day is Christmas. Every Wednesday evening there's a Singles Mingle with live music, and there are other events throughout the year. The Shell Factory and the Fun Park are open every day from 10 a.m. to 6 p.m.; the Nature Park is open every day from 10 a.m. to 5 p.m.

where to eat

Annie's. 814 SE 47th St., Cape Coral; (239) 945-3133. Sometimes you just want breakfast or a simpler meal. Annie's has been around almost forever and serves breakfast—the mini omelet and the pancakes are must-tries—and lunch—daily hot meal specials and an assortment of burgers and sandwiches. Annie's is open every day from 7 a.m. to 1:30 p.m. $.

Bistro 41. 13499 S. Cleveland Ave., Fort Myers; (239) 466-4141; bistro41.com. Located at Bell Tower Shops, Bistro 41 serves lunch and dinner every day and holds a Wine University course plus other special events. Select from such entrees as their Pork Pot Roast braised in port wine or their Flat Iron Steak Chimichurri—or opt for their prix fixe 41 Special. They open every day at 11:30 a.m. and close at 9:30 p.m. Mon through Thurs, at 10:30 p.m. Fri and Sat, and at 8 p.m. on Sun. $$–$$$.

Cheeseburger in Paradise Bar & Grill. 5050 Daniels Pkwy., Fort Myers; (239) 481-4386; cheeseburgerinparadise.com. How can we not list a place like this in a place like this? Sports on the screens; burgers on the grill—and did we mention the chocolate nachos? Open 11 a.m. to 1 a.m. every day. $–$$.

Nervous Nellie's. 1131 First St., Fort Myers Beach; (239) 463-8077; nervousnellies.net. Whether you arrive by boat (dock at the Snug Harbor Marina) or by car or on foot, Nervous Nellie's welcomes you to its "crazy waterfront eatery." Live music, a menu that doesn't quit (7 different kinds of Reubens!), and Ugly's Waterside Bar upstairs make for a memorable mealtime experience. Nervous Nellies is open 11 a.m. to 10:30 p.m. every day; Ugly's is open until midnight. $–$$.

Yabo. 16681 McGregor Blvd., Fort Myers; (239) 225-9226; yaborestaurant.com. Located in Kingston Plaza, Yabo features Italian food and live, eclectic, and somewhat avant-garde music. Check their Facebook page for current specials and gigs. Yabo's is open Tues through Sat from 6 to 9 p.m. $$.

where to stay

Casa Playa Resort. 510 Estero Blvd., Fort Myers Beach; (800) 569-4876, (239) 765-0510; casaplayaresort.com. A private beach, heated pool, laundry facilities, and an all-suite motel describes Casa Playa Resort. Two floors are pet-friendly (read the guidelines); and the exterior painting gives guests the sense they are living inside a work of art. $$$.

Fort Myers Beach RV Resort. 16299 San Carlos Blvd., Fort Myers Beach; (877) 570-2267; rvonthego.com/Fort-Myers-Beach-RV-Resort.html. The Fort Myers Beach RV Resort offers a heated pool with spa, a fitness room, scheduled activities, and more. Pets are welcomed. $.

Hideaway Waterfront Resort and Hotel. 4601 SE 5th Ave., Cape Coral; (239) 542-5812; hideawayflorida.com. Lounge in a hammock, lie by the pool, or take a paddleboat out and tour Cape Coral by canal. The Hideaway Waterfront Resort and Hotel offers a quiet place from which to explore the surrounding area. $–$$.

Mango Street Inn. 126 Mango St., Fort Myers Beach; (239) 233-8542; mangostreetinn.com. Colorful rooms with kitchens, bicycles to ride, and beach chairs with umbrellas—plus the more usual amenities—make this a beachy kind of place to stay. A 3-day minimum stay is required; small pets are okay (read the guidelines). Dan and Tree Andre serve a breakfast buffet to guests and can provide a list of activities and restaurants. $$.

sanibel/captiva/pine islands

Pine Island, the largest of the three islands, lies facing Cape Coral and runs from the mouth of Charlotte Harbor in the north to the outlet of the Caloosahatchee River in the south. Pine Island connects to Cape Coral by a bridge that includes the smaller island of Matlacha (Mat-luh-chay), which lies between Pine Island and Cape Coral. Several small communities are on the island from Bokeelia in the north to St. James City in the south.

Sanibel Island curves around the southern end of Pine Island; its eastern end faces Fort Myers Beach. Captiva Island is a small island off the northwest end of Sanibel Island.

All three islands have attracted artists—even the telephone poles don't escape creative touches—so be on the lookout for galleries here and there.

Greater Pine Island Chamber of Commerce Welcome Center. 4120 Pine Island Rd., Matlacha; (239) 283-0888; pineislandchamber.org. Stop in Mon through Fri from 9 a.m. to 5 p.m. and Sat or Sun from 10 a.m. to 1 p.m. for information about the Matlacha and Pine Island areas. Ask about trolley tours. ***Note:*** The address above is a temporary location—probably through the summer of 2013—while their original location at 3460 Pine Island Rd. undergoes reconstruction.

Sanibel Island Chamber of Commerce Visitor Center. 1159 Causeway Rd., Sanibel Island; (239) 472-1080; sanibel-captiva.org. The Visitor Center—it's the multi-colored re-purposed house on the left—is located just as you come over the causeway from Fort Myers. Here you'll find everything you need to know about Sanibel and Captiva Islands. They are open every day from 9 a.m. to 5 p.m.

getting there

To reach Sanibel Island from Fort Myers, follow CR 867 to the Sanibel Causeway. The Causeway will take you directly to the island. Sanibel Island is about 23 miles from Fort Myers.

bicycling on sanibel island

Because parking is at a premium on Sanibel and Captiva Islands, many people like to bicycle around. Bike racks are often available for use free of charge, whereas cars pay to park. And some beach access points are only accessible on foot or on foot after locking up one's bike.

For a good description of the bike paths and beach access points on Sanibel and Captiva Islands—along with a listing of the rental places on Sanibel, on Captiva, and in Fort Myers—go to SanibelTrails.com. The site also lists island hotels offering bikes to their guests; some are complimentary, and some are rented for a fee. Florida law requires bike riders under age 16 to wear a helmet. From personal experience, we say helmets are a good idea at any age.

To travel to Captiva Island from Fort Myers (about 31 miles), follow the directions above to Sanibel Island. Then, the Causeway becomes Periwinkle Way. Turn right onto Palm Ridge Road, which becomes Sanibel-Captiva Road. Follow it to Captiva Island.

To get to Pine Island, take SR 78 West/Pine Island Road from Cape Coral across the causeway to Pine Island. The Welcome Center at 3460 Pine Island Rd. is in Matlacha, before you get to Pine Island itself.

Note: Some of the causeways are toll roads. Be prepared with more than just change—it's a hefty charge.

where to go

Bailey-Matthews Shell Museum. 3075 Sanibel-Captiva Rd.; (888) 679-6450, (239) 395-2233; shellmuseum.org. The Bailey-Matthews Shell Museum is more than just a collection of shells—it is devoted to the study of mollusks, particularly those with shells. The museum contains more than 30 exhibits, some of which are interactive, about the critters that live in the shells, how shells have been used throughout history, and more. The website also has a photographic shell guide (look for the SWFL Shells tab) to help beachcombers identify their finds. The museum is open every day from 10 a.m. to 5 p.m.

J.N. "Ding" Darling National Wildlife Refuge. 1 Wildlife Dr., Sanibel; (239) 472-1100; fws.gov/dingdarling. There are five different National Wildlife Refuges in the Lee County area, but the J.N. "Ding" Darling NWR is the largest and includes much of the north side of Sanibel Island. The refuge consists of acres and acres of mangroves that make it attractive to migratory bird populations. Stop at the Visitor Center for information about navigating any of the 3 trails or about canoeing or kayaking the waters. The Visitor Center also has interactive exhibits and a hands-on area for children. Tarpon Bay Explorers (239-472-8900; tarponbayexplorers.com) operates the concessions at the refuge. They have tram tours, boat tours, guided fishing and paddling trips, equipment rental, and more. The refuge is open Sat through Thurs from 9 a.m. to 5 p.m. Jan through Apr and from 9 a.m. to 4 p.m. May through Dec. The refuge is closed every Fri. Tarpon Bay Explorers is not located on the refuge property itself; it is open every day at 8 a.m.

Museum of the Islands. 5728 Sesame Dr., Pine Island; (239) 283-1525; museumoftheislands.com. Housed in the island's first library, this small museum contains a number of displays of donated artifacts depicting various eras in the islands' histories. The museum is open Nov through Apr, Tues through Sat from 11 a.m. to 3 p.m. and on Sun from 1 to 4 p.m. May through Oct, the museum is open Tues, Thurs, and Sat from 11 a.m. to 3 p.m.

Randell Research Center at Pine Island. 13810 Waterfront Dr., Pineland; (239) 283-2062; flmnh.ufl.edu/rrc. The Randell Research Center is a program of the University of Florida's Florida Museum of Natural History. Visitors can walk the self-guided Calusa Heritage Trail to learn more about the area's earliest peoples. Guided tours are available Wed and Sat at 10 a.m. The area is open from dawn to dusk, but the Visitor Center—with its bookstore and gift shop—is open Mon through Sat from 10 a.m. to 4 p.m.

what to do

Fishing. The Pine Island Sound area is considered the Tarpon Capital of the World, and sport fishing enthusiasts migrate here when the tarpon do. Whether you want to fish from a bridge, boat, kayak, or pier, you'll find long lists of fishing guides ready to give you advice on how to land the big one. Start with the resources listed in the Using This Guide, p. xiv, but also ask the local visitor center or chamber of commerce for a list. Ask, too, at the front desk of your hotel or inn. And keep your ears open in coffee shops and bars—wherever anglers congregate to swap tales.

Great Calusa Blueway Kayak and Canoe Paddling Trail. calusablueway.com. Paddle the waters of Lee County as people before you have done for thousands of years. Explore bays, islands, and rivers on your own or with a guide/outfitter. The website has maps, lists of outfitters, spots to launch your canoe or kayak, fishing information, and more.

Shelling. Because Sanibel and Captiva are situated east-west instead of north-south like most barrier islands, the ocean currents deposit more shells here than on other islands. Storms tend to churn the waters and pull shells from the sea floor, so after a storm has gone through is a good time to look for shells—during low tide is even better. Sand dollars and other critters that are alive must be returned to the ocean. If the little "hairs" on the bottom of a sand dollar move, it is alive. If it is not alive, you can keep it. So find a bucket and a scoop (easier on your back), slather on some sunscreen and wear a hat, and see what treasures you can find. Pets on leashes are okay on Sanibel Island beaches, but pets are not allowed at all on Captiva Island beaches. Here is a site that will give you more information about each of the beaches: sanibel-captiva.org/play/beaches.asp. And here is a site that tells you how to clean the shells once you have found them: captivaisland.com/shelling.html. ***Caution:*** Uncleaned shells left in a warm car or packed in a suitcase result in a—shall we say—memorable aroma.

where to shop

Captiva Island. A number of shops can be found on Andy Rosse Lane in Captiva—also at the north end of Captiva Drive.

Pine Island Center. Although each of the other towns on Pine Island has some shops, Pine Island Center is considered the island's commercial area. Stroll through several shopping areas.

ShopsOnSanibel.com. This website features 4 different shopping centers within a short distance of each other on Periwinkle Way and Tarpon Bay Road. Each has a different flavor and different types of shops and places to eat.

The Tower Gallery. 751 Tarpon Bay Rd., Sanibel Island; (239) 472-4557; towergallery-sanibel.com. The Tower Gallery is a cooperative gallery where several area artists sell their work. As such, there's almost always something going on—visiting artists exhibit here, receptions highlight featured artists, etc. The gallery is open every day from 10 a.m. to 9 p.m.

where to eat

The Bubble Room. 15001 Captiva Dr., Captiva Island; (239) 472-5558; bubbleroomrestaurant.com. This is one of those you've-gotta-see-it-to-believe-it places. Decorated—and we mean decorated—in early- to mid-20th-century kitsch and staffed by Bubble Scouts, the Bubble Room serves ribs, chicken, seafood, steaks, and more—all with a basket of their bubble bread and sticky buns. Lunch is served from 11:30 a.m. to 3 p.m. every day. Dinner is served from 4:30 to 9 p.m. Sun through Thurs and until 9:30 p.m. on Fri and Sat. $$–$$$.

Doc Ford's Rum Bar & Grille. 975 Rabbit Rd., Sanibel Island; (239) 472-8311; docfordssanibel.com. Fans of Randy Wayne White's series of mysteries set on Sanibel and featuring marine biologist Dr. Marion Ford will recognize settings from the novels as they wander the area. At Doc Ford's, it's easy to imagine the grizzled guy next to you is Doc Ford himself—who knows? In any case, have an Island Mojito and enjoy the South American spices and touches such as jicama, plantains, quinoa, and Panama-style chorizo sausage enhancing chicken, pork chops, salmon, grouper, and rib eye steaks. Doc Ford acquired a taste for these flavors as he traveled the tropics—coincidentally, so did White. Guests are the richer for it. Doc Ford's is open every day from 11 a.m. to whenever. It's island time, remember? $$–$$$.

The Mucky Duck. 11546 Andy Rosse Ln., Captiva Island; (239) 472-3434; muckyduck.com. Located on the northernmost part of Captiva Island, the Mucky Duck is British-pub cozy on the inside and island-friendly on the outside. Offering nightly sunsets—check the calendar on the website for times—along with steaks, seafood, and—what else!—roasted duck, the Mucky Duck is accessible by beach or by car. The Mucky Duck is open every day (except Thanksgiving and Christmas) from 11:30 a.m. to 3 p.m. for lunch and from 5 to 9:30 p.m. for dinner. $–$$.

where to stay

Bokeelia Tarpon Inn. 8241 Main St., Bokeelia; (239) 283-8961; tarponinn.com/contact.html. Located at the northernmost end of Pine Island, the Bokeelia Tarpon Inn is a gracious 1914-era home with its own fishing pier, boat ramp, and docks. Kayaks, bicycles, and golf carts are good ways to explore the area—after a lovely breakfast, of course. Evening hors d'oeuvres and wine round out the day. No pets, and no children under age 10 (some exceptions). $$$.

Cabbage Key Inn & Restaurant. (239) 283-2278; cabbagekey.com. If you really, really want to get away from it all, Cabbage Key is the spot. You can't drive to it. It's accessible only by boat. And once the last water taxi bringing day tourists departs? Then it's just island residents and inn guests. No cars, no paved roads. The inn, built in 1929, once was the home of mystery novelist Mary Roberts Rinehart's son and his family. Accommodations include rooms in the inn and cottages created from outlying buildings, including what once was the Rinehart children's playhouse. The inn is the only restaurant on the island, and it serves breakfast, lunch, and dinner every day of the year. They'll even cook whatever fish you have caught that day. No pets, and there is a 2-night minimum stay. $$–$$$.

Captiva Island Inn. 11508 Andy Rosse Ln., Captiva Island; (800) 454-9898, (239) 395-0882; captivaislandinn.com. Rent a room, rent a cottage, or rent a 5-bedroom house. Located right in Captiva Village, the Captiva Island Inn offers a tropical base from which to explore Captiva's beaches (360 steps away) and the village. The inn has a pool and breakfast at a local restaurant is included in the fee. Rates fluctuate widely depending on whether it is a low, mid, or high volume season. $$$.

Palm View Inn & Sandpiper Inn. 706 and 720 Donax St., Sanibel Island; Palm View: (877) 472-1606 or (239) 472-1606; Sandpiper: (877) 227-4737 or (941) 472-1529; palmviewsanibel.com. Cozy and colorful—and within walking distance of the beach—which, after all, is the point, yes? All units have flat-screen TVs, kitchens, and access to outdoor grills. Adult bikes and beach equipment are available to guests. A 2- to 4-day minimum stay may be required. $$–$$$.

South Seas Island Resort. 5400 Plantation Rd., Captiva Island; (866) 565-5089; southseas.com. Once, legend says, it was a pirate's hideaway where they held captives for ransom and once—really and truly—it was a key lime plantation. Today, the north end of Captiva Island is home to the South Seas Island Resort, and it's a wildlife preserve, too. Accommodations for humans include rooms, suites, villas, and even private homes. Accommodations for critters can be observed from a kayak or by taking a nature walk. Amenities include one of the top 9-hole executive golf courses in the world; the Kay Casperson Lifestyle Spa & Boutique; resident fishing experts and an on-site sailing school; watersports including parasailing, jet skis, and hydrobikes; and special activities for children and teens. In fact, the South Seas Island Resort was named one of *Parents* magazine's Top 10 Beach Resorts for Families. $$$.

day trip 02

south

muscle car mania:
port charlotte/punta gorda; englewood/boca grande

Slick your hair back for this adventure. We're headed south to Charlotte County to one of the largest collections of GM Muscle Cars in the nation. Oh—and pack some old sneakers or water shoes, too. We'll also be getting really up close to some marine life.

Charlotte County, named after Queen Charlotte, wife of King George III—yes, the one Thomas Jefferson accuses of tyranny in the Declaration of Independence—encompasses the outlets to two rivers. The Peace River, flowing from the Polk County area, picks up phosphorus as it passes through the Bone Valley area. It carries that phosphorous with it as it flows south. When the Peace River empties into Charlotte Harbor, the phosphorous acts like fertilizer, feeding the mangroves and making the estuary area the most productive in Florida. Punta Gorda, on the south side, and Port Charlotte, on the north side, face each other across Charlotte Harbor.

Note: There is a body of water called Charlotte Harbor, and there is also a town just south of Port Charlotte called Charlotte Harbor. So far, we've referred only to the body of water. You may see an address or two listing Charlotte Harbor—rest easy, we're not sending you in the middle of the bay to go shopping!

The second river emptying into the area is the Myakka River, which originates just north of Charlotte County. The Myakka flows along Port Charlotte's west side; the Peace River flows along Port Charlotte's east side.

There are lots of beaches and parks in the area. We'll take a guided wading tour of the estuary—you did remember to pack the water shoes, yes?—do some shopping, then

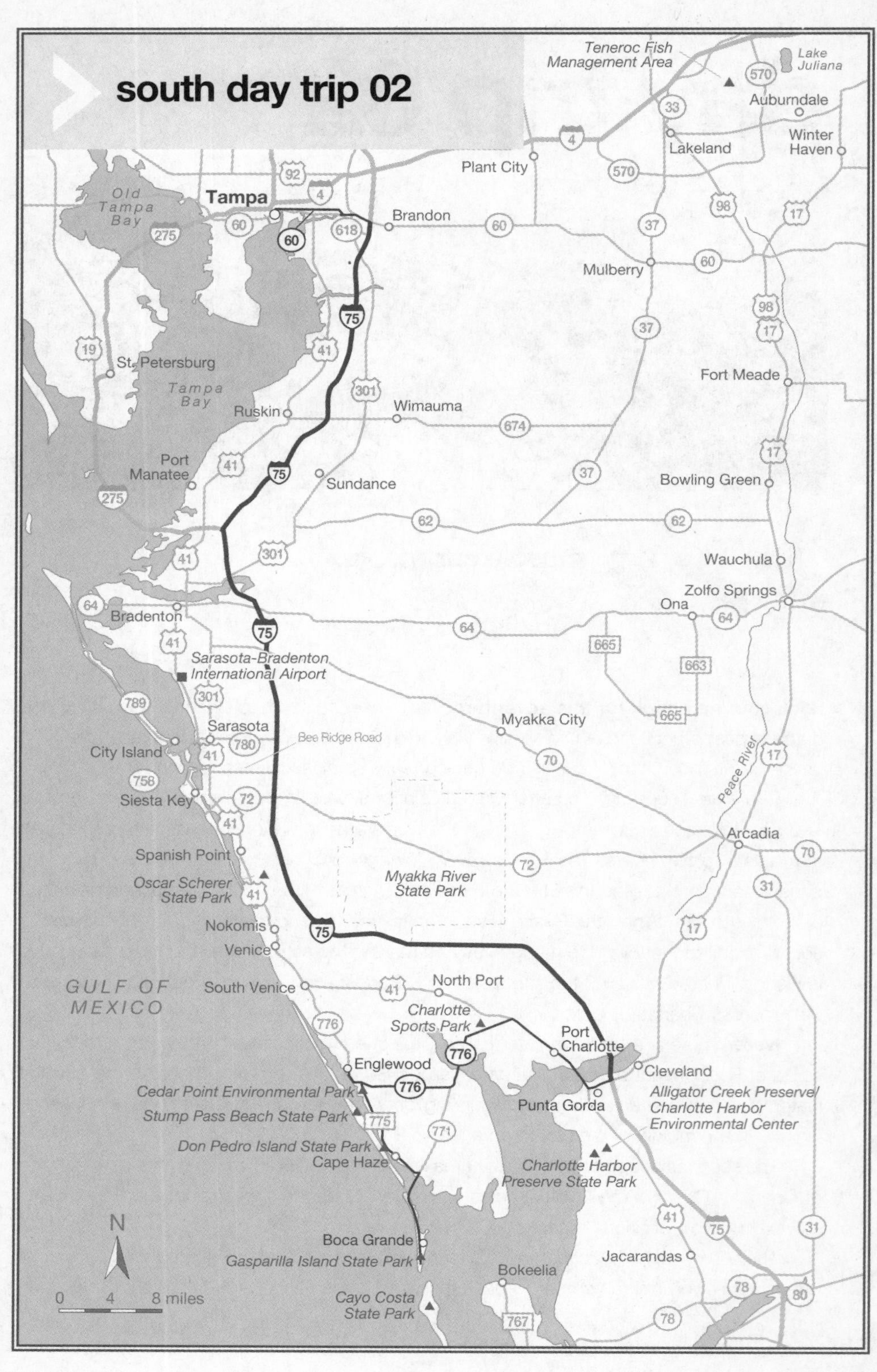
south day trip 02
Tampa
Old Tampa Bay
Brandon
Plant City
Lakeland
Auburndale
Winter Haven
Teneroc Fish Management Area
Lake Juliana
Mulberry
St. Petersburg
Tampa Bay
Ruskin
Wimauma
Fort Meade
Port Manatee
Sundance
Bowling Green
Wauchula
Zolfo Springs
Ona
Bradenton
Sarasota-Bradenton International Airport
Sarasota
City Island
Bee Ridge Road
Myakka City
Siesta Key
Peace River
Arcadia
Spanish Point
Oscar Scherer State Park
Myakka River State Park
Nokomis
Venice
GULF OF MEXICO
South Venice
North Port
Charlotte Sports Park
Port Charlotte
Englewood
Cleveland
Cedar Point Environmental Park
Punta Gorda
Alligator Creek Preserve/ Charlotte Harbor Environmental Center
Stump Pass Beach State Park
Don Pedro Island State Park
Cape Haze
Charlotte Harbor Preserve State Park
N
Boca Grande
Gasparilla Island State Park
Jacarandas
Bokeelia
0 4 8 miles
Cayo Costa State Park

check out that collection of more than 200 classic cars. If it's spring training time, we can even take in a Tampa Bay Rays game.

port charlotte/punta gorda

In Spanish, Punta Gorda means "fat point." That's an apt description for this rounded piece of land jutting into Charlotte Harbor, and it may have been what Juan Ponce de Léon termed it so later explorers—in those days before maps—would recognize it. Ponce de Léon was looking for the fountain of youth, so they say. What a shame he didn't recognize that the keys to a youthful outlook were right there in Punta Gorda—plenty of sun, sand, and surf.

In the 1880s, however, Punta Gorda was called Trabue after Colonel Isaac Trabue of Kentucky who bought the land that would become Punta Gorda. Trabue also cultivated pineapples, which he sold to pay for the prizes he gave in his annual chess tournament. Punta Gorda gained a reputation for being the Pineapple Capital of the nation.

Southwest Florida Visitor Center. 26600 Jones Loop Rd., Punta Gorda; (941) 639-0007; swflvisitor.com. The Southwest Florida Visitor Center serves Charlotte, Lee, Collier, and Sarasota Counties. Stop here to load up on brochures, information, and maybe some discount coupons. The visitor center, tucked in a corner of a gas station and convenience store, is open every day from 6 a.m. to 11 p.m. The website, of course, is open 24/7.

getting there

From Tampa, take I-75 South south toward Naples. Travel about 95 miles to exit 161/CR 768 West. Exit to the right on exit 161, and merge right onto Jones Loop Road. The Visitor Center is on your right.

where to go

Alligator Creek Preserve. 10941 Burnt Store Rd., South Punta Gorda; (941) 575-5435; checflorida.org/Alligator_Creek.html. Part of the Charlotte Harbor Environmental Center, Alligator Creek Preserve has 4 miles of nature trails to explore. Check the calendar for guided hikes and other events. The Caniff Visitor Center is open Mon through Sat from 9 a.m. to 3 p.m. and on Sun from 11 a.m. to 3 p.m., but the park itself is open for hiking every day during daylight hours (you may need to park outside the gate and walk in). Dogs on leashes of no more than 6 feet in length are okay—as the guidelines put it, "You may have a well-trained dog; but we have untrained, unleashed wild animals." The other center operated by the CHEC is the Cedar Point Environmental Park in Englewood. Great Florida Birding Trail Site #21S.

Charlotte County Historical Center. 22959 Bayshore Rd., Charlotte Harbor; (941) 629-7278; charlottecountyfl.com/Historical/events.asp. This repository for historical artifacts and records from Charlotte County is open Tues through Fri from 10 a.m. to 5 p.m. and on Sat from 10 a.m. to 3 p.m. Some of their collection is available online, too.

Charlotte Sports Park. 2300 El Jobean Rd., Port Charlotte; (941) 235-5010; charlotte countyfl.com/CommunityServices/ParkPages/SportsPark. Charlotte Sports Park is the spring training home of our very own Tampa Bay Rays. Where else would a Florida team go during the winter but to a Florida town just a little further south? When the Rays aren't at the Charlotte Sports Park, the Charlotte Stone Crabs (stonecrabsbaseball.com), a Cal Ripken–owned Minor League Baseball team, plays here. For tickets to Rays spring training games, go to tampabay.rays.mlb.com and look for the Spring Training link.

Military Heritage Museum. 1200 W. Retta Esplanade, Unit 48, Punta Gorda; (941) 575-9002; freedomisntfree.org. With memorabilia, photographs, and displays tracing our country's military heritage from the Civil War to the conflicts in the 21st century, the Military Heritage Museum makes the point that "Freedom isn't free." Most of the items were donated by area veterans who served around the world; many veterans serve as volunteer docents to answer questions and share their personal experiences with visitors. The museum is open Mon through Sat from 10 a.m. to 8 p.m. and Sun from noon to 6 p.m. The museum is closed Easter, Thanksgiving, and Christmas. Admission is free; donations are gratefully accepted.

Punta Gorda Speedway. 8655 Piper Rd., Punta Gorda; (941) 575-7223; puntagorda speedway.com. Until recently, this was the Charlotte County Motorsport Park. The name may have changed, but the stock car racing action still goes on most Saturday nights. The track is a ⅜-mile banked asphalt that also hosts sprint cars and karts.

Rick Treworgy's Muscle Car City. 3811 Tamiami Trail, Punta Gorda; (941) 575-5959; musclecarcity.net. They're lined up and spiffed up, and Rick Treworgy's collection of more than 200 cars from the 1920s to the early 1970s waits to take visitors on a trip down Memory Lane. The collection, located north of the visitor center, includes one of the largest GM Muscle Car displays in the nation. Can't bear to leave the cars there? Check out the Car Corral where you just might find your dream car for sale. There's a good-size gift shop, too, and a diner (see below). Check the calendar for car shows and other events. They are open 9 a.m. to 5 p.m. Tues through Sun.

what to do

Babcock Wilderness Adventures. 8000 SR 31, Punta Gorda; (800) 500-5583; babcock wilderness.com. Looking for something really out of the ordinary? How about a swamp buggy tour through the wilder areas of the Babcock Ranch, a real working cattle ranch, and Telegraph Cypress Swamp? You'll see a small museum, and there's a gift shop, picnic facilities, and the Gator Shack Restaurant. Reservations are required.

where to shop

Fishermen's Village. 1200 W. Retta Esplanade, Punta Gorda; (800) 639-0020, (941) 639-8721; fishville.com. With a resort (2-bedroom furnished villas), a day spa, a host of boutique and specialty shops, and several eateries—all on an award winning yacht basin marina—Fishermen's Village is a destination in itself. This waterfront shopping mall lets visitors browse for apparel, gifts, and other items while still enjoying the beautiful Florida blue skies and ocean waves. Check the calendar for live entertainment and other activities scheduled throughout the year.

where to eat

Muscle Car City Diner. 3811 Tamiami Trail, Punta Gorda; (941) 575-5959; musclecarcity.net/diner.html. Serving breakfast (omelets, biscuits and gravy, bagels), lunch (burgers and fries, salads, sandwiches), and dessert (root beer floats!) in a 1960s-era diner, Muscle Car City Diner is open Tues through Sun from 8 a.m. to 4 p.m. $.

Torch Bistro. 2113 Tamiami Trail, Punta Gorda; (941) 575-3505; torchbistro.com. Urban chic in Punta Gorda? You got it. Torch Bistro, Steaks and Rumtini Bar adds extraordinary touches to ordinary ingredients—like salmon broiled in champagne—and turns pork osso bucco into "wow." The range of dishes extends from Thai coconut curry chicken to Grandma's Meatloaf (topped with tomato marmalade). They also are one of very few restaurants to offer Nyotaimori—by reservation only—a Japanese art form of sushi service using live models. Torch Bistro serves lunch from 11:30 a.m. to 2 p.m. Mon through Fri. Dinner is served Mon through Sat from 4:30 to 9 p.m. $$–$$$.

Visani featuring The Comedy Zone. 2400 Kings Hwy., Port Charlotte; (941) 629-9191; visani.net. Not quite dinner theater but more than just a restaurant, Visani offers a full—really full!—menu of mostly Italian entrees and specialty pizzas. After dinner, Visani presents stand-up comedy and live music acts from around the country. Check the calendar for the entertainment schedule and ticket prices. Reservations are a must. Visani is open Tues through Fri from 3:30 to 9 p.m. and on Sat from 4 to 11 p.m. They are also open some Mondays—check the calendar for special events. $$–$$$.

where to stay

Banana Bay Waterfront Motel. 23285 Bayshore Rd., Charlotte Harbor; (941) 743-4441; bananabaymotel.com. If you're looking for laid-back and homey instead of fancy-schmancy, Banana Bay Waterfront Motel might be the place for you. Efficiencies and motel rooms are linked by welcoming walkways, an on-site dock lets you tie up your boat, Wednesday nights (in season) are movie nights, and Saturday nights means karaoke, music, and dancing. Plus they have a whole list full of ideas people can do during their stay—including an airplane ride! High-speed Internet, a pool, and laundry facilities, too. Pets are welcome. $$.

The Wyvern Hotel. 101 E. Retta Esplanade, Punta Gorda; (941) 639-7700; thewyvern hotel.com. Part of the Luxe network of boutique hotels, the Wyvern Hotel offers sleek, sophisticated surroundings including a rooftop pool and bar/lounge, a guest fitness center, and in-room amenities that whisper luxury. Lulu, an on-site Latin fusion restaurant, serves breakfast, lunch, and dinner—lobster mac and cheese or coffee mustard pork tenderloin? Oh, my! $$$.

englewood/boca grande

West of Port Charlotte and across the Myakka River, a peninsula of land forms the west side of Charlotte Harbor. Englewood is about halfway down the peninsula and most directly across from Port Charlotte. Boca Grande is at the southern end of Gasparilla Island, a barrier island between the Gulf of Mexico and the mainland. The area between Englewood and just past Boca Grande—not even 20 miles—contains four state parks.

Englewood–Cape Haze Chamber of Commerce & Visitor Center. 601 S. Indiana Ave. (SR 776 and Hosmer), Englewood; (941) 474-5511; englewoodchamber.com. Most of us will follow the directions below and arrive by car. Alternatively, you can fly in and land at Buchan's Air Field, a grass landing strip located about 2.5 miles north of the Visitor Center. But then you'd have to hike or take a taxi. In any case, stop in for information about the area. They're open 8 a.m. to 5 p.m. Mon through Fri.

getting there

From Punta Gorda, take the Tamiami Trail/US 41 north about 8 miles to El Jobean Road/SR 776 West. Turn left onto El Jobean Road/SR 776 West and travel about 17 miles, crossing over the bridge from El Jobean to Charlotte Beach. Stay on SR 776, which means you will bear right after you cross the bridge. Follow SR 776 to S. Indiana Avenue and turn right. The Visitor Center is on your right.

To get to Boca Grande from Englewood, take Placido Road south along the main peninsula. Travel about 10 miles through Grove City, Rotonda, and Cape Haze to Placido. Cross the Boca Grande Causeway. Once you cross the causeway, you are on Gasparilla Road. Follow it south about 7 miles to Boca Grande.

where to go

Cayo Costa State Park. 880 Belcher Rd., Boca Grande; (941) 964-0375; floridastate parks.org/cayocosta/default.cfm. The southernmost of the state parks in this area, Cayo Costa State Park is accessible only by boat or by ferry (call Tropic Star at 239-283-0015 for times and for information about canoe or kayak rental) from Boca Grande. The docks (no electric or water hookups) are on the east side of the island, and a free tram takes visitors to the western gulf side of the island. Rustic cabins and tent campsites are available on the island. Bikes can be rented at the ranger station. Snorkeling, fishing, and shelling are the main activities, but there's certainly nothing wrong with building a sand castle or two along any of the 9 miles or so of white sand beaches. The park is open from 8 a.m. to sunset every day. Great Florida Birding Trail Site #S27.

Cedar Point Environmental Park. 2300 Placida Rd., Englewood; (941) 475-0769; checflorida.org/Cedar_Point.html. You'll need your old sneakers or wading shoes for this place, as the Cedar Point Environmental Park—not a state park—offers guided wading tours of Lemon Bay. Some pontoon boat tours and other adventures are also available—check the calendar to see when these are scheduled. The visitor center is open Mon through Fri from 8:30 a.m. to 4:30 p.m. and there are trails to explore. No pets are allowed in the park. This is the second location for the Charlotte Harbor Environmental Center; the other is the Alligator Creek location in Punta Gorda. Great Florida Birding Trail Site #S18.

Don Pedro Island State Park. 880 Belcher Rd., Boca Grande; (941) 964-0375; floridastateparks.org/donpedroisland/default.cfm. The mailing address is Boca Grande, but Don Pedro Island State Park lies just north of Cape Haze. Rather, part of the park lies north of Cape Haze—the Cape Haze side of the park includes a boat dock from which boaters launch to cross Lemon Bay to the other, larger, part of the park. The barrier island part of the park is accessible only by private boat or by ferry (941-697-8825). Within this relatively small area—the park is only 230 acres and encompasses non-contiguous areas on Lemon Bay—are 10 distinct natural eco-communities, ranging from dunes to a hardwood hammock. Picnic areas and hiking trails are on both sides of the bay. The park is open from 8 a.m. to sunset every day.

Gasparilla Island State Park. 880 Belcher Rd., Boca Grande; (941) 964-0375; floridastateparks.org/gasparillaisland/default.cfm. So was this or was this not the island where the dastardly José Gaspar and his motley crew of buccaneers buried treasure? Was nearby Captiva Island where they held lovely maidens and not-so-lovely-but-wealthy other people captive until they were ransomed or tired of and killed? Well, it's a nice story, but it's probably one propagated by early advertisers trying to attract tourists to the area. Up in Tampa, we went along with it and created a whole festival around it. Today, however, the island is the setting for the city of Boca Grande. At the southernmost tip of the island lies Gasparilla Island State Park, which consists of a stretch of beach area ending at the Boca Grande Lighthouse, now a museum and visitor center. The ranger offices for Cayo Costa and Don Pedro Island State Parks are also housed here. The park is open from 8 a.m. to sunset every day.

Stump Pass Beach State Park. 700 Gulf Blvd., Englewood; (941) 964-0375; floridastateparks.org/stumppass/default.cfm. Located at the south end of Mansota Key and including the two islands directly to the east in Lemon Bay—Peterson Island and Whidden Key—Stump Pass Beach State Park offers beachy activities on the west and excellent kayaking, sailing, and water-skiing conditions on the east. During the summertime, the ranger leads turtle and other nature walks. The park is open from 8 a.m. to sunset every day.

where to shop

Olde Englewood Village. W. Dearborn Street, Englewood; oldeenglewood.com. Shops, galleries, and restaurants line W. Dearborn Street, and every Thursday there's a farmer's market from 9 a.m. to 2 p.m. (englewoodfarmersmarket.org). Check the calendar for special events.

where to eat

Farlow's on the Water. 2080 S. McCall Rd., Englewood; (941) 474-5343; farlowsonthe water.com. Wander through their herb garden to pique your appetite with the pungent scent of herbs, then enjoy Caribbean cuisine with a hint of a southern accent. The Trunk Bay Red Snapper, for instance, is served on a banana leaf and is topped with sliced tomatoes and coconut-encrusted sliced bananas in a banana-rum sauce—and the menu includes fried green tomatoes as an appetizer. They have a full bar, and there is live music Wed through Sat. Farlow's is open from 11 a.m. to 9 p.m. Mon through Thurs and 11 a.m. to 11 p.m. Fri and Sat. $–$$.

The Loose Caboose. 433 W. 4th St., Boca Grande; (941) 964-0440; loosecaboose.biz. The Loose Caboose is known for its homemade—as in made on the premises—ice cream, and that's certainly a good reason to drop in. But they also serve lunch every day and dinner every day except Wed. And the dinners aren't just burgers and fries. Lamb tenderloin is on the menu as is crispy duck, chicken pot pie, and a slew of salads. Family-owned and operated, the Loose Caboose serves lunch every day from 11 a.m. to 4 p.m. and serves dinner every day except Wed from 5:30 to 9 p.m. $$–$$$.

where to stay

Englewood Bay Motel & Apartments. 69 W. Bay St., Englewood; (941) 475-1769; englewoodbaymotel.com. On the east side of Lemon Bay, this small motel has 13 units—mostly 1- and 2-bedroom efficiencies plus some cottages and condos. There's a quiet courtyard with a barbecue area, laundry facilities, and free wireless Internet. $$.

Gasparilla Inn & Club. 500 Palm Ave., Boca Grande; (877) 403-0599; (941) 964-4500; the-gasparilla-inn.com. Take on the Pete Dye Signature 18-Hole Championship Golf Course, situated on its own private island, where the water hazards are mostly located in the Gulf of Mexico. Don your crispest whites and play croquet on the lawn. Take a seaplane tour or a sunset cruise. Go tarpon fishing or play on the beach. Visit the spa for some pampering. The Gasparilla Inn & Club offers rooms and suites, cottages and villas—all with Tempur-Pedic temperature-controlled beds for the ultimate in sleep comfort. The Gasparilla Inn & Club has been welcoming guests since 1913. $$$.

day trip 03

south

venetian sunsets & my, oh my, myakka:
siesta key; venice; arcadia

Like a string of petite pearls, a number of smaller communities lie south of Sarasota, each with its own charm and each built on the dreams of previous generations. This day trip takes us to some of those communities, from Siesta Key in the north to Venice in the south. We'll also venture directly east from Siesta Key to touch the treetops on an elevated canopy walkway in Myakka River State Park and visit the town of Arcadia, which boasts more than 20 antiques shops in a 4-block section of downtown and hosts the All-Florida Championship Rodeo.

So get ready for a busy day—or maybe just plan on sinking into the sand and toasting a Venetian sunset!

siesta key

Three cheers to Siesta Key, whose beach received the top award from Dr. Beach for 2011. Dr. Who? Dr. Beach. Dr. Beach is really Dr. Stephen P. Leatherman, a professor of environmental studies at Florida International University in Miami. As director of FIU's Laboratory for Coastal Research, Dr. Leatherman, who has studied beach and coastal issues around the world, got into the beach-rating business kind of by accident. Back in 1989, a reporter asked him about the country's best beaches. Suddenly, he found himself with a new sideline and a new nickname. Every Memorial Day weekend since then, Dr. Beach has issued a Top 10 Best Beaches list (drbeach.org).

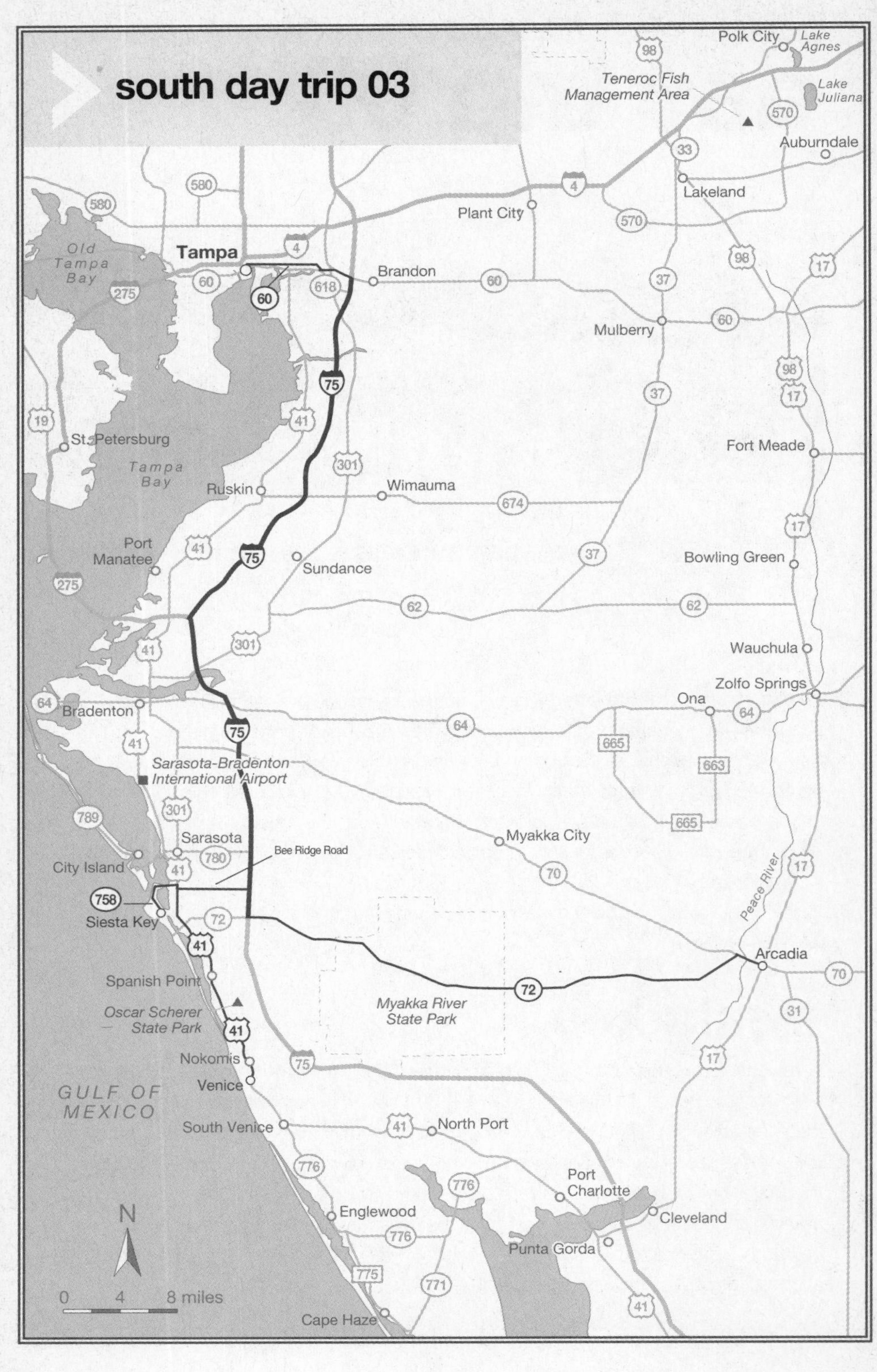
south day trip 03
Polk City
Lake Agnes
Teneroc Fish Management Area
Lake Juliana
Auburndale
Lakeland
Plant City
Tampa
Old Tampa Bay
Brandon
Mulberry
St. Petersburg
Tampa Bay
Fort Meade
Ruskin
Wimauma
Port Manatee
Sundance
Bowling Green
Wauchula
Zolfo Springs
Ona
Bradenton
Sarasota-Bradenton International Airport
Sarasota
Bee Ridge Road
Myakka City
City Island
Siesta Key
Peace River
Arcadia
Spanish Point
Oscar Scherer State Park
Myakka River State Park
Nokomis
Venice
GULF OF MEXICO
South Venice
North Port
Port Charlotte
Englewood
Cleveland
Punta Gorda
Cape Haze
N
0 4 8 miles

But Siesta Key is more than just sugary-white sandy beaches and ocean waves. You'll find funky shops and restaurants, day spas, and water sports. Want to go parasailing? You got it! Let's go!

Siesta Key Chamber of Commerce. 5118 Ocean Blvd., Siesta Key; (866) 831-7778, (941) 349-3800; siestakeychamber.com. Drop in, and let the friendly folks at the Siesta Key Chamber of Commerce help you get oriented to the island. Pick up some maps and brochures—and maybe a coupon or two. They are located in Davidson's Plaza, and they are open Mon through Fri from 9 a.m. to 5 p.m.

getting there

From Tampa, take I-75 S toward Naples. Travel not quite 50 miles to exit 207. Take exit 207 and merge onto Bee Ridge Road/SR 758 West. Travel west on Bee Ridge Road about 5 miles to US 41/S. Tamiami Trail. Turn right onto US 41, then turn left onto Siesta Drive. Travel west on Siesta Drive about 1.5 miles to Higel Avenue/SR 758. Turn left onto Higel Avenue and follow it about 1 mile to Ocean Boulevard. Turn right onto Ocean Boulevard and travel about 1 mile. The chamber offices are in Davidson Plaza, which should be on your right.

what to do

Beaches. Siesta Key has 3 beaches from which to choose: Turtle Beach, the farthest from Siesta Village, has a playground, picnic area, horseshoe and volleyball areas, a boat launch, and good shelling. Crescent Beach has only one access point, so it tends to be a bit quieter. The coral rock formations at Point of Rocks, at the southern end of Crescent Beach, are known for their snorkeling and diving opportunities. Siesta Beach is located north of Siesta Village and has tennis and volleyball courts, a shaded picnic area and playground, and concessions. Beach wheelchairs are available to help everyone enjoy the beach.

Fishing. See p. xiv in Using This Guide for a list of guides or ask at the Chamber of Commerce for a list of outfitters, guides, and charter captains. Ask at the bait and tackle shops for information about surf fishing.

Watersports. Parasailing, jet skiing, and charter sailing opportunities abound. Quieter fun is to be had, too. How about taking a Segway tour or pedaling a surrey bike that seats 4 or more passengers? Many feet make light work, yes? Plus there are paddleboards, kayaks, and windsurfing boards to rent. Check the chamber's website or call and ask for a list of providers.

where to shop

Siesta Village. Whether you need a bathing suit or evening attire, a beach ball or a manicure, there are lots of little shops, salons, galleries, and restaurants in the village. However, the village is a bit bigger than just a village. If you plan on walking, wear comfy shoes. Enjoy!

where to eat

Anna's Restaurant & Deli. 217 Avenida Madera, Siesta Key; (941) 349-7790; or 6535 Midnight Pass Rd., Siesta Key; (941) 349-4888; surfersandwich.com. Anna's is pretty much an institution on Siesta Key—they've been dishing up deli-style sandwiches and salads since 1971. Anna's is open 10:30 a.m. to 4 p.m. every day. $.

Capt. Curt's Crab & Oyster Bar. 1200 Old Stickney Point Rd., Siesta Key; (941) 349-3885; captaincurts.com. Seafood, seafood, and more seafood—with some baby back ribs, prime rib, burgers, and dogs. In fact, Captain Curt won top prize in the International Chowder Championships in Newport, Rhode Island! The kids will love how their food is served—let's just say it will get thrown away but not trashed. Hmmm . . . The Sniki Tiki Bar serves tapas-style appetizers and small plates, sandwiches, and more. The restaurant and the tiki bar open at 11 a.m. Mon through Sat and at noon on Sun. Lots of live music and karaoke. The restaurant closes at midnight Sun through Wed and at 2 a.m. Thurs through Fri. The tiki bar closes at 2 a.m. every night. $–$$.

SKOB. 5238 Ocean Blvd., Sarasota; (941) 346-5443; skob.com. Really—it's Siesta Key, even though the USPS says otherwise. SKOB, aka Siesta Key Oyster Bar, is a one-of-a-kind experience. For one thing the walls are made of money. Literally. Feel free to add some with your own message attached. There's lots of live music and football on the screens. Oh, yes. And oysters. And other food, too. But mostly seafood with fajitas, steak, and a pasta dish for good measure. They're open every day from 11 a.m. to 2 a.m. $$–$$$.

where to stay

Hyatt Siesta Key Beach. 915 Seaside Dr., Siesta Key; (941) 346-5900; siestakeybeach.hyatt.com. This Hyatt Residence's suites range from 1,800 to 3,000 square feet in size—no worrying about tripping over each other's luggage here. Hand-rubbed mahogany furniture complements the neutral tones with touches of cobalt and citrus of the rooms. There's a flat-screen TV in the master bath, which also has a Kohler WaterTile rain shower and massage soaking tub. If you can tear yourself away from the suite, the pool has private cabanas, and the beach is just steps away. The concierge gladly will arrange activities and make reservations—and will also provide referrals for babysitters, if needed. $$$.

venice

Venice is one of the few Gulf Coast cities in Florida to sit directly on the Gulf of Mexico—no barrier islands lie off her shores. As a result, the ocean currents wash shells and sharks' teeth onto the sand for beachcombers to find. On the northeast side, Roberts Bay separates Venice from the mainland. An Intracoastal Waterway canal cut around the east and south sides of Venice in 1960 effectively turned the town into an island.

New York physician Dr. Fred Albee came here in 1916 and purchased land where Nokomis is—actually, he pretty much bought the small town located across Roberts and Dona Bays—and commissioned a city planner from Boston to lay the foundation for a larger community. Beginning in the late 1920s, Cleveland, Ohio, railroad engineers came here to retire, after their union purchased land in Venice. In 1960, Venice became the winter home for the Ringling Brothers Barnum & Bailey Circus. Today, the town attracts visitors from around the world who come to enjoy its natural beauty.

In this section, we'll be listing spots of interest along the mainland from Osprey to Venice.

Venice Chamber of Commerce. 597 Tamiami Trail South, Venice; (941) 488-2236; venicechamber.com. The Venice Chamber of Commerce building sits at the corner of Tamiami Trail and Golf Drive—a big, white, can't-miss-it kind of building. Inside, you'll find friendly folk ready to share information and tales about their community. They're open Mon through Fri 9 a.m. to 5 p.m.

getting there

From Siesta Key, take Tamiami Trail/US 41 South south not quite 17 miles. You'll pass through Osprey and Nokomis. Stay on Tamiami Trail/US 41 South after you cross Dona and Roberts Bays. Continue past W. Venice Drive. The Venice Chamber of Commerce offices are on your left on Tamiami Trail/US 41 South just past Palermo Place.

where to go

Historic Spanish Point. 337 N. Tamiami Trail (US 41), Osprey; (941) 966-5214; historicspanishpoint.org. This 30-acre site once belonged to Mrs. Potter (Bertha) Palmer, a cattle rancher who, in 1917, was elected vice-president of the Florida State Livestock Association. At the same time Mrs. Palmer was overseeing a 15,000-acre cattle ranch, she also was building beautiful gardens and helping to build the Sarasota area. Visitors to Historic Spanish Point can wander the point on a little over a mile of paved and shell paths. Mrs. Palmer also preserved the homestead of the people from whom she purchased the land; the Webb homestead can be seen along with a chapel, a pioneer boatyard, and midden mounds from an even older culture. The visitor center is open from 9 a.m. to 5 p.m. Mon through Sat and from noon to 5 p.m. on Sun.

Oscar Scherer State Park. 1843 S. Tamiami Trail, Osprey; (941) 483-5956; floridastateparks.org/OscarScherer. Squirrels aren't the only critters that bury acorns for later retrieval. Florida scrub jays, a species of bird found only in Florida, do, too. Oscar Scherer State Park is one place to see these birds and a host of other animals, too. Hiking and biking trails—including the Legacy Trail (see below) run through the park. Canoes and kayaks can be rented and the waters explored—but no motors are allowed on boats. Both freshwater and brackish-water fishing spots lure anglers. Check the calendar for ranger-led paddles (night ones, too!), walks, and other activities. Campsites are available, and a nature center is open most days from 10 a.m. to 3 p.m.

Venice Area Audubon Society Rookery. 4200 S. Tamiami Trail, Venice; veniceaudubon .org. The Venice Area Audubon Society's office and Welcome Center is tucked behind the Sarasota County administration building. To get to the Welcome Center and rookery, turn south onto Annex Road, which is just south of the county administration building. The Welcome Center is a small, white building on the right; the rookery area is located on the small lake to the south of the Welcome Center. Nature photographers travel here during the winter months, when most nesting activity takes place, but the birds are here year-round. Ask about field trips, bird walks, and other activities.

Venice Train Depot. 303 E. Venice Ave., Venice; (941) 861-5000; venicehistory.com/ activities.php. Most of the time the Venice Train Depot is meeting room space rented by the county. Parties and gatherings are held in the Freight Room or in the Caboose. But the property is also a trailhead on the Legacy Trail (see listing) and tours of the depot are scheduled year-round on Sat from 10 a.m. to 12:30 p.m. Nov through Apr, tours are also available on Mon, Wed, and Fri from 10 a.m. to 2:30 p.m.

what to do

Legacy Trail. (941) 861-5000; co.sarasota.fl.us/LegacyTrail/default.asp. Challenge yourself to a 10-mile bike ride on the Legacy Trail, a rails-to-trails project. Ride from the Venice Train Depot (see above) to Bay Street Park, just south of Sarasota. Because the trail runs along a former railroad corridor, it's a straight shot. But the trail passes through several parks, including Oscar Scherer State Park, and through a variety of other environments. There are rest areas each mile. Download a map and other information from the website.

where to shop

Venice Farmers' Market. Corner of Nokomis and Tampa Avenue, Venice; thevenice farmersmarket.com. You never know what you'll find at the Venice Farmers' Market—handmade quilts, fresh strawberries and cabbage, homemade pickles and pies. Every Saturday morning from 8 a.m. to noon, this outdoor market comes to life.

where to eat

Sharky's on the Pier. 1600 Harbor Dr. South, Venice; (941) 488-1456; sharkysonthepier .com. Talk about convenient—step off the sand and into Sharky's, which really is on a fishing pier. They serve salads, sandwiches, and wraps with a beachy flair—shrimp nachos? Hmmm!—and heartier seafood, steak, and pasta entrees, as well. Most nights there's live music to liven things up a bit. Sharky's is open Wed, Thurs, and Sun from 6 to 10 p.m. and Fri and Sat from 8 p.m. to midnight. $$–$$$.

Venice Wine & Coffee Company. 201 W. Venice Ave., Venice; (941) 484-3667 (gourmet foods side), (941) 484-1668 (coffee and wine bar side); venicewineandcoffeecompany.com. This is one of those "Is it a shop or is it a restaurant?" places. Browse through the gourmet foods shop or let them create a gift basket—they're open from 10 a.m. to 5 p.m. Mon through Fri and from noon to 4 p.m. on Sun during the winter months. On the other side, you can get your morning fix of caffeine, along with baked goodies, beginning at 8 a.m. Simple lunches and desserts are served Mon through Sat from 11:30 a.m. to 2:30 p.m. Evenings there's almost always some kind of wine tasting or wine social event going on, and they stay open at least until 8 p.m. Check their newsletter (online) for current events. Lunch: $.

where to stay

A Beach Retreat. 105 Casey Key Rd., Nokomis; (866) 232-2480, (941) 485-8771; abeachretreat.com. Nokomis is the mailing address, but the physical location is smack-dab on Casey Key, mostly a narrow strip of land with one road running its length. Units range from efficiencies to 3-bedroom condos. There is a heated swimming pool, bayside docks, a laundry room, and wireless Internet access. A Beach Retreat is also close to the causeway for easy mainland access. $$$.

Inn at the Beach. 725 W. Venice Ave., Venice; (800) 255-8471, (941) 484-8471; innatthebeach.com. Less than a block from the beach, Inn at the Beach offers both single rooms and up to 2-bedroom suites with kitchen. A complimentary Continental breakfast is included. The inn's rooms surround a courtyard with pool, and did we mention the beach is less than a block away? $$$.

arcadia

Resilient might be the best word to describe Arcadia, the present-day De Soto County seat. Before 1921, however, Arcadia was the county seat for a De Soto County that included what now are four other counties (Charlotte, Hardee, Glades, and Highlands). Much of the town was destroyed in a 1905 fire and, almost a century later, the town took a severe hit from Hurricane Charley in 2004. Arcadia today is known for its antiques shops and for the rodeos they host.

De Soto County Chamber of Commerce. 16 S. Volusia Ave., Arcadia; (863) 494-4033; desotochamberfl.com. The chamber office is small, but friendly. They have limited visitor information, but they'll help you all they can. The office is open Mon through Fri from 8 a.m. to 4 p.m. except when they are closed for lunch or are out on chamber business.

getting there

From Siesta Key, take SR 72 East/Stickney Point Road (which soon becomes Clark Road) east about 42 miles. When you come to the T in the road, turn right onto SR 70 East. Travel about 2 miles on SR 70 East toward Arcadia. As you enter Arcadia, the road splits twice. Stay to the right both times—one time you must stay right, the other time it is easier to do so. When you reach US 17/S. Brevard Avenue, turn left to Oak Street. This is the heart of the downtown area.

where to go

Arcadia All-Florida Championship Rodeo. 124 Heard St., Arcadia; (800) 749-7633, (863) 494-2014; arcadiarodeo.com. Back in 1929, the local American Legion post wanted to build a new building and thought a rodeo might bring in the needed funds. Since then, the Arcadia rodeo has helped fund a number of charitable organizations in the area. The Arcadia All-Florida Championship Rodeo hosts the Professional Rodeo Cowboys Association–sanctioned Arcadia All-Florida Championship Rodeo each March. They also have a July 4 event and other professional events throughout the year. Order early—tickets for these events go on sale months in advance. Gates open at 11 a.m. and performances begin at 2 p.m., but there's much to see beforehand—concessions, too. Youth rodeo events are held monthly Sept through Apr and are free; these begin around 10 a.m. and often last until evening. Concessions are available during the youth events, too. Rodeos are rain-or-shine events. The rodeo office is open Mon through Fri from 9 a.m. to 4 p.m.

Herrmann's Royal Lipizzan Stallions. 32755 Singletary Rd., Myakka City; (941) 322-1501; hlipizzans.com. The Lipizzan breed of horses has had a remarkable history, most recently being rescued from war-torn Europe by General George S. Patton during World War II. Just west of Arcadia, visitors can watch Herrmann's Royal Lipizzan Stallions train during the winter months (generally, Nov through May) for their touring schedule the rest of the year. There is some bleacher seating, but bring a lawn chair just in case. They ask a nominal donation from visitors.

Myakka River State Park. 13208 SR 72, Sarasota; (941) 361-6511; floridastateparks.org/myakkariver. Covering 58 square miles, Myakka River State Park is one of Florida's largest and oldest state parks. Its southernmost lands reach below Venice; to the north, Myakka River State Park extends almost parallel with Sarasota. Access to the park is off SR 72, between Siesta Key and Arcadia. A visitor center near the entrance to the park helps orient newcomers to the park and is well worth a stop. In addition to the more usual activities of hiking, biking, horseback riding, and fishing, visitors to Myakka River State Park can take an airboat tour of the Upper Myakka Lake or a tram ride into the wilds, can climb a 74-foot-high tower for a panoramic view of the area, and can walk long an elevated (as in 25 feet above the ground) boardwalk—including an 85-foot-long suspension bridge—to experience the woods in a different way. Bicycles, canoes, and kayaks can be rented. Campsites include tent and RV sites, but there are also 5 historic log cabins built in the 1930s and since modernized—a bit, that is. No TV and no phones mean you can enjoy real peace and quiet. Many ranger-led and other activities are on the calendar—sometimes there are music concerts and other events. Myakka River State Park has a very strong Citizens Support Organization; their website has much additional information (myakkariver.org).

Turner Agri-Civic Center. 2250 NE Roan St., Arcadia; (863) 993-4807; turnercenter.com. The Turner Agri-Civic Center hosts concerts, craft shows, and events including barrel racing. Check the calendar to see what is scheduled during your visit.

what to do

Canoe Outpost–Peace River. 2816 NW CR 661, Arcadia; (800) 268-0083, (863) 494-1215; canoeoutpost.com/peace/default.asp. The Canoe Outpost rents canoes and kayaks for day runs or for overnight camping trips, and they'll drop you off upriver and let you paddle your way back to your vehicle. Look for information online or ask about fossil hunting, camping, and picnicking spots.

Fossil Expeditions. (239) 368-3252; fossilexpeditions.com. Fossil hunting expert Mark Renz will meet you at one of several Arcadia-area public boat ramps to take you fossil hunting along the Peace River. He'll provide everything you need for the fossil digging part, but read the website first so you understand that you will be wading and sifting and will dress accordingly.

where to shop

Antique District. There are more than 20 antiques shops within 4 blocks of each other in downtown Arcadia. Plus, there's an antiques fair the fourth Saturday of each month. Here are two shops to whet your appetites.

Cherry Hill Antiques. 120 W. Oak St.; (863) 993-2344; cherryhillantiques.com. Check their calendar for speakers and other events. The shop is open Wed through Sat from 11 a.m. to 4 p.m. or by appointment.

Miss Pearl's Place. 8 W. Oak St., Arcadia; (863) 494-0232; misspearlsplace.com. Miss Pearl's Place carries vintage and antique furnishings and smaller collectible items. They also house a picture framing shop and a second antique dealer's wares. Open Tues through Sun from 10 a.m. to 4:30 p.m.

where to eat

Last Chapter Coffee House and Cafe. 15 W. Oak St., Arcadia; (863) 494-0506. Last Chapter serves breakfast sandwiches, bagels and muffins, and soups, salads, sandwiches (fried bologna aficionados, take note), and wraps for lunch. They are open Mon through Fri from 7:30 a.m. to 5 p.m., Sat from 9:30 a.m. to 5 p.m., and Sun from 11 a.m. to 5 p.m. $.

Mary Margaret's Tea & Biscuit. 10 South Polk Ave., Arcadia; (863) 494-0615; marymargaretsteaandbiscuit.com. Don your hat and gloves—and don't forget your parasol—then sashay on over to Mary Margaret's Tea & Biscuit. Dine in a Victorian setting on such dainties as lobster bisque, quiche, and soups, sandwiches, and wraps. Scones? Of course! For those desiring a drop of something stronger, beer and wine are also available. They are open every day from 11 a.m. to 4 p.m. $.

where to stay

Oak Park Inn. 2 Oak St., Arcadia; (863) 494-9500; oakparkinnarcadia.com. You can stay in the Bunkhouse or go Art Deco—each of the 12 rooms is furnished in a different style in the Oak Park Inn—one of only three buildings in Arcadia to survive a 1905 fire that wiped out the entire town. Breakfast at a local restaurant is included in the stay. Rooms have wireless Internet access and large flat-screen TVs with DVD player. $$.

day trip 04

the greatest show on earth!
sarasota

sarasota

Got a great idea for a new product? One spot we'll visit today is an inventions incubator where anyone with vision can build a better mousetrap—or create the next world-changing device. Seriously. All the technical and mechanical equipment is there for you to create a prototype of your idea. You provide the vision. Which is pretty much the story of how Sarasota came to be.

Driving through modern-day Sarasota—with its museums, performing arts venues, and upscale everything—it's hard to believe that, just over a hundred years ago, it was a tiny town. Twenty-five years before it reached tiny town status, Sarasota was just a settlement with a couple of houses and not much else around it.

What made the difference? Vision—the ability to see beyond what is to what might be. Just the act of building a house bespeaks that kind of vision. But a few people who came to Sarasota envisioned something even more. John Hamilton Gillespie made good on an overzealous land promoter's promises in the mid-1880s and turned the settlement into a town. Owen Barr turned the town into a city. Bertha Palmer and John and Mable Ringling brought art and culture—and more. Palmer, the widow of a Chicago developer, became a major cattle rancher and was elected vice-president of the Florida State Livestock Association—two years before women received the right to vote in national elections. John and Mable Ringling brought the circus to town, built an incredible estate and

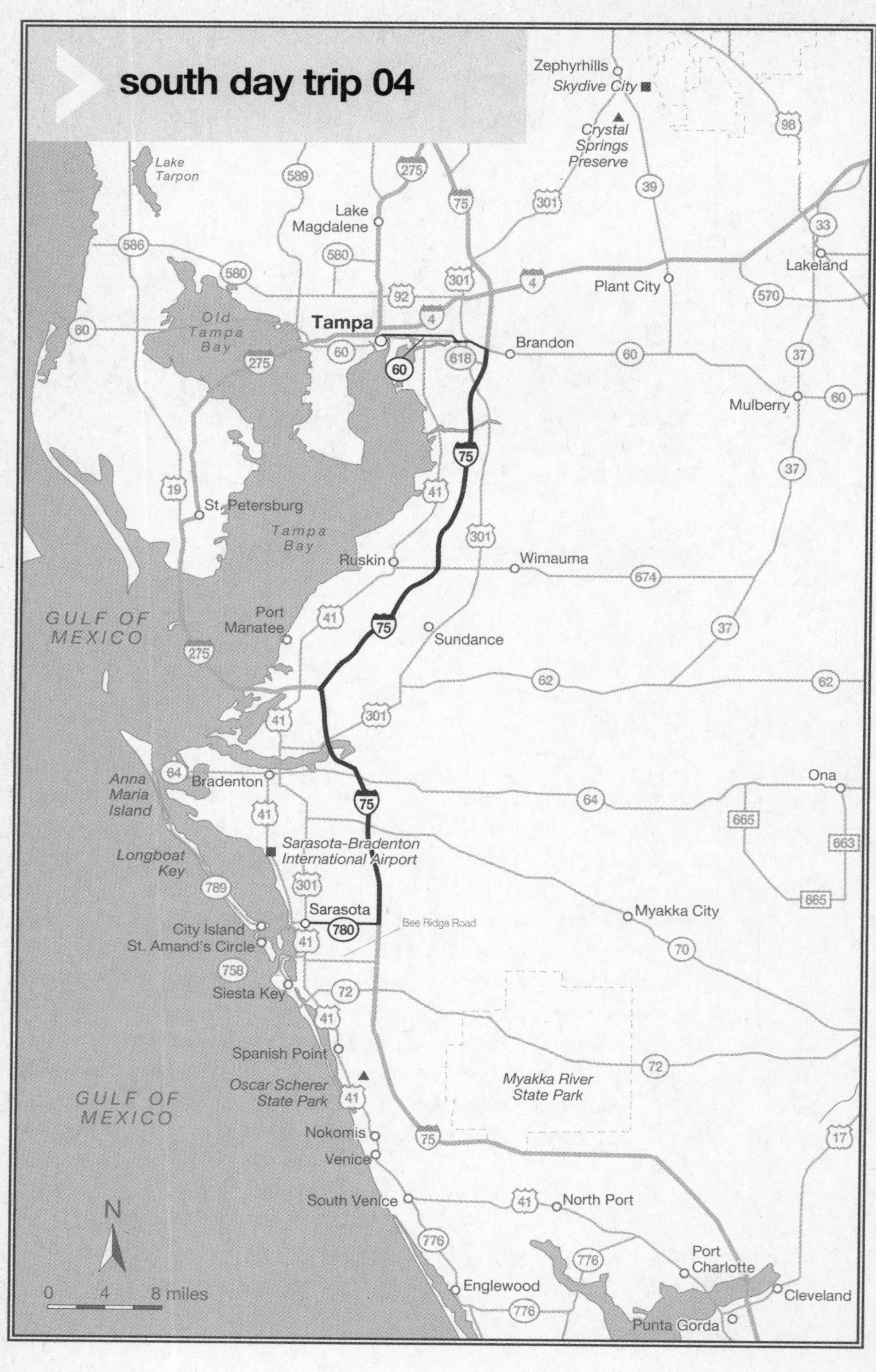
south day trip 04
Zephyrhills
Skydive City
Crystal Springs Preserve
Lake Tarpon
Lake Magdalene
Lakeland
Plant City
Old Tampa Bay
Tampa
Brandon
Mulberry
St. Petersburg
Tampa Bay
Ruskin
Wimauma
GULF OF MEXICO
Port Manatee
Sundance
Anna Maria Island
Bradenton
Ona
Longboat Key
Sarasota-Bradenton International Airport
Sarasota
Bee Ridge Road
Myakka City
City Island
St. Amand's Circle
Siesta Key
Spanish Point
Oscar Scherer State Park
Myakka River State Park
GULF OF MEXICO
Nokomis
Venice
South Venice
North Port
Port Charlotte
Englewood
Cleveland
Punta Gorda
N
0 4 8 miles

art collection, and even had a theater in Italy dismantled and rebuilt on their Sarasota property.

Maybe it's not just the circus that is the greatest show on earth. Sarasota seems to have been putting on quite a show throughout all of its years—all it has taken is vision.

Sarasota County Visitor Information Center and History Center Museum. 701 N. Tamiami Trail, Sarasota; (800) 800-3906, (941) 957-1877; sarasotafl.org. This visitor center isn't just about handing out brochures and information. Exhibits about Sarasota County's history help visitors see their stay in the larger context of being part of a parade of people who have walked the same beaches and marveled at the same kinds of sunsets. Brochures abound, and there is a gift shop, too. The center is open Mon through Sat from 10 a.m. to 5 p.m. From mid-Jan through Easter, the center is also open on Sun from 11 a.m. to 2 p.m. The Van Wezel Performing Art Center and G. Wiz are within walking distance; the Art Center Sarasota is next door.

getting there

From Tampa, take Adamo Drive East/SR 60 East to I-75, about 9 miles. Alternatively, you can avoid stoplights and surface traffic by taking the Selmon Expressway east to I-75; the Selmon Expressway is a toll road and portions of it may be electronic collection only, meaning you must have a pass or can expect a bill in the mail. The Selmon Expressway also has very few exits. Once you are on it, you are on it.

Either way, once you get to I-75, merge onto I-75 heading south toward Naples. Travel south on I-75 about 46 miles to the SR 780 West exit toward Sarasota/St. Armand at exit 210. SR 780 West is also called Fruitville Road. Travel west on Fruitville Road/SR 780 West about 6 miles to US 41. Turn right on US 41/N. Tamiami Trail and travel about 0.5 mile to 10th Street. Make a U-turn on 10th Street and immediately turn left into the parking area for the Municipal Auditorium, which is next door to the visitor center. Parking spaces are angled into the curb on both sides of the area, and there are also parallel parking spaces in the middle. It's an odd configuration—keep your eyes open for through traffic as you walk from your car to the Sarasota County Visitor Information Center and History Center Museum or other buildings.

where to go

Ed Smith Stadium. 2700 12th St., Sarasota; (800) 745-3000; (941) 954-4101; baltimore.orioles.mlb.com. This is the Orioles' second time in Sarasota for spring training. They were also here from 1989 to 1991, but they definitely are not strangers to Florida. Since 1901, the Orioles have spent some of their spring training time in St. Petersburg (1914 and 1992–1995), Tarpon Springs (1925–1927), West Palm Beach (1928–1936), Deland (1942), Miami (1947 and 1959–1990), Daytona Beach (1955), Sarasota (1989–1991), and Fort Lauderdale (1996–2009). The newly renovated stadium seats upwards of 7,500 people and is known for its ballpark cuisine—bison burgers and crab cake sandwiches being right up there with the Esskay hot dogs.

G.WIZ—The Science Museum. 1001 Boulevard of the Arts, Sarasota; (941) 309-4949; gwiz.org. Located near the Van Wezel Performing Arts Center, G.WIZ—The Science Museum offers creative ways to experience different scientific concepts. Play a laser harp and learn about light and sound waves. Make an animated video complete with sound. More intriguing is the Fab Lab (fabrication laboratory) with real technical and manufacturing equipment anyone can use to create a prototype anything! G.WIZ (Gulfcoast Wonder & Imagination Zone) is not just for kids—it's for anyone interested in learning more about how things work and why. Mar through Aug, G.WIZ is open Mon through Sat from 10 a.m. to 5 p.m. and on Sun from noon to 5 p.m. Sept through Feb, the museum is closed Mon. They are also closed some holidays.

Marie Selby Botanical Gardens. 811 S. Palm Ave., Sarasota; (941) 366-5731; selby.org. More than just a pretty spot with plants, the Marie Selby Botanical Gardens offers a beautiful backdrop for watercolor and other art classes, photography classes, yoga, and tea tastings. With 14 acres of different types of gardens—bamboo, palms, bonsai, orchids, and a Tropical Conservatory of rainforest plants—the gardens are studied by researchers, depicted by artists, and enjoyed by people of all ages and walks of life. An on-site cafe offers soups, sandwiches, and desserts (10 a.m. to 4 p.m.), or visitors can bring their own lunches (no grills or coolers). Cell phones should be silenced, but there is wireless Internet in several spots. A gift shop is available. Check the events calendar for classes and special gatherings. The gardens are open from 10 a.m. to 5 p.m. every day except Christmas Day. The gardens close at 3 p.m. on Thanksgiving, Christmas Eve, and New Year's Eve.

Mote Marine Laboratory & Aquarium. 1600 Ken Thompson Pkwy., Sarasota; (800) 691-6683, (941) 388-4441. Mote Marine Laboratory conducts a number of marine research projects. The aquarium lets visitors sit in on narrated shark training sessions, touch stingrays and other marine animals, and view a number of aquatic settings where different types of plants and animals live. General admission includes access to Mote Aquarium, the Ann and Alfred E. Goldstein Marine Mammal Research and Rehabilitation Center, and Immersion Cinema. Other experiences are available separately and range from tours through the Seahorse Conservation Lab to EcoTours by boat. The aquarium is open every day of the year from 10 a.m. to 5 p.m.

Ringling Grounds. 5401 Bay Shore Rd., Sarasota; (941) 359-5700; ringling.org. John Ringling was from Iowa, Armilda "Mable" Burton was from Ohio—neither was from a wealthy family. Yet they became one of the richest couples in the United States because of the circus empire he and his brothers built. They moved to Sarasota in the 1920s and soon the area was also the winter home of the Greatest Show on Earth. Several attractions are on the grounds of the Ringling property. A cafe is on site, and picnic tables are available outdoors. Ask for information about how to help children enjoy and learn from the artwork. The John & Mable Ringling Museum of Art complex is open every day except Thanksgiving, Christmas, and New Year's from 10 a.m. to 5 p.m. On Thurs, they remain open until 8 p.m. and there is discounted admission from 5 to 8 p.m.

- **The John and Mable Ringling Museum of Art.** The Ringlings collected original European masterworks, and the Ringling Museum of Art contains paintings by Rubens, van Dyck, Tintoretto, El Greco, and many other artists—as well as an extensive Asian art collection. The building is a work of art in itself, and the garden contains full-size casts of such sculptures as Michelangelo's *David*.
- **Cà d'Zan ("House of John").** This 56-room mansion was built in 1925 and is patterned after the Doge of Venice's palace. Filled with furnishings and artwork, this is the second museum in the Ringling complex.
- **Circus Museums.** This museum celebrates Ringling's most famous legacy—the Ringling Family Circus. The Circus Museums contain parade wagons, costumes, posters, and the private rail car of John and Mable Ringling.
- **Historic Asolo Theater.** Built in 1798 in Asolo, Italy, the theater was dismantled in the 1940s, brought to Sarasota, and reconstructed on the grounds of Cà d'Zan. Today it hosts opera, theater, and dance performances.

Sarasota Classic Car Museum. 5500 N. Tamiami Trail, Sarasota; (941) 355-6228; sarasota carmuseum.org. Car lovers and sociologists will appreciate the collection of antique, vintage, and classic cars and the ways they have transformed our cultures. Included in the collection are cars owned by John Lennon and Paul McCartney. The Sarasota Classic Car Museum is open from 9 a.m. to 6 p.m. every day of the year except Christmas Day.

Sarasota Jungle Gardens. 3701 Bay Shore Rd., Sarasota; (941) 355-1112; sarasota junglegardens.com. On the grounds of what once was a private home and gardens grew Sarasota Jungle Gardens. Open to the public since 1940, the gardens is one of Florida's oldest continuously operating attractions. Visitors walk through 10 acres of gardens, watch various animal shows, and feed the roaming flamingos. A playground lets kids work off some energy and the Flamingo Cafe offers sandwiches and snacks. Sarasota Jungle Gardens is open from 10 a.m. to 5 p.m. every day except Thanksgiving and Christmas Day.

Van Wezel Performing Arts Center. 777 N. Tamiami Trail, Sarasota; (800) 826-9303, (941) 953-3368; vanwezel.org. Local wags have dubbed it the "purple people seater," but no one ever forgets the Van Wezel once they've been there. Built in 1968–1969, this performing arts center, reminiscent of seashells and overlooking Sarasota Bay, was designed by William Wesley Peters, who worked with Frank Lloyd Wright; the lavender and purple colors were selected by Frank Lloyd Wright's widow. Renovated in 2000, the Van Wezel today hosts classical concerts, Broadway shows, and other music and performing arts events.

what to do

Beaches. Beaches in the Sarasota area include Longboat Key, Lido Key, and Bird Key. Public beaches are mostly found on Lido Key, just across a small bridge from St. Armand Circle. Parking is limited.

Circus History Tour. sarasotacircushistory.com/tour. Go to the website and download the Sarasota's Circus Heritage Guide. The flyer and map give directions to several places with historical circus connections between Sarasota and Venice.

Circus Sarasota. (941) 355-9335; circussarasota.org. Founded in 1997 by husband and wife circus veterans Pedro Reis and Dolly Jacobs, Circus Sarasota performs most often under the big top near Ed Smith Stadium. Acts include aerialists, acrobats, clowns, equestrian teams, and more.

Sailor Circus. 2075 Bahia Vista St., Sarasota; (941) 361-6350; sailorcircus.org. Sailor Circus is known as "the greatest little show on earth," as performers are all in elementary, middle, or high school. The Sailor Circus began in 1949 as part of Sarasota High School's gymnastics program—over the years they have performed around the world. Today, the Sailor Circus presents a number of shows at their complex during the winter months. Circus Sarasota recently acquired Sailor Circus.

where to shop

St. Armands Circle. starmandscircleassoc.com. Just over the causeway from the Ringling complex, on St. Armand's Key, is an upscale shopping and dining area. With more than 140 shops and restaurants, set around a neatly designed circle, St. Armands Circle is a shopping destination for Gulf Coast Floridians. The St. Armands Winter Art Festival, held each January, is one of the top in the country.

Palm Avenue District. palmavenue.org. Two blocks west of Bayfront Drive and running for about a block either side of Main Street, Palm Avenue was the place to see and be seen back in the day. Today its exclusive shops and galleries and salons still attract discerning shoppers. First Friday Gallery Walks from 6 to 9 p.m. on the first Friday of the month include live music and and other performances. Gallery openings often are scheduled to coincide with the First Friday Gallery Walks.

where to eat

Cafe L'Europe. 431 St. Armand's Circle, Sarasota; (941) 388-4415; cafeleurope.net. The building once was John Ringling's real estate office, but for the past almost 40 years it has been Cafe L'Europe. Guests can dine indoors or outdoors on Continental cuisine such as Shrimp a la Greque, rack of lamb, filet mignon, and Chicken Breast Kavalla. Even the side dishes are beyond ordinary—macaroni and cheese is one thing, but White Truffle Macaroni and Cheese? *Bon appétit!* Cafe L'Europe serves lunch from 11:30 a.m. to 3 p.m. every day and serves dinner from 5 to 9 p.m. every day. During the winter, they sometimes stay open later. Call for reservations. $$$.

Goodfellas Cafe and Winery. 4571 Clark Rd., Sarasota; (941) 538-6535; winemaking pantry.com. New York–style thin-crust pizza baked in a wood-fired brick oven? Mmmm. Plus they make their own wine. Can it get much better? How about locally made gelato? Plus grilled paninis, bruschetta, cannoli. Double mmmm. Ask about winemaking and wine-tasting events. Goodfellas is open Mon through Sat from 9 a.m. to 9 p.m. $.

New Pass Grill & Bait Shop. 1505 Ken Thompson Pkwy., Sarasota; (941) 388-3050; newpassgrill.com. You can't miss this place. Located just before you go over the bridge to Longboat Key, it's the collection of somewhat ramshackle buildings with the bicycles on the roof. And it really is a tackle and bait shop, too—probably as many of their customers tie up at the dock out back as drive up. They serve breakfast sandwiches and Danish and whatnot from 7 a.m. to 10:30 a.m. After that, its burgers and (really good) fries, sandwiches, fish and chips, and more until 5 p.m. Order at the window, then take a table outside and watch the boat traffic and the birds. Open every day. $.

Yoder's Amish Village. 3434 Bahia Vista St., Sarasota; (941) 955-7771; yodersrestaurant .com. Sarasota has a sizeable Amish and Mennonite community, and several restaurants in the area serve Amish or Amish-style cooking. Basically, that means serving the kind of hearty meals hardworking farmers come home to—fried chicken and mashed potatoes, pot roast and veggies, pot pies, and more. Yoder's has been cooking for the Sarasota community since 1975. Desserts? Pies—more than 20 different kinds, including their most famous, Peanut Butter Cream Pie—and other goodies, too. They also have a produce market, a deli/

locally owned restaurants

For a listing of independently owned restaurants in the Sarasota/Manatee area, go to freshoriginals.com. You'll find online coupons and event listings, too.

market, and a gift shop. Breakfast is served Mon through Sat from 6 to 11 a.m. Lunch and dinner are served from 11 a.m. to 8 p.m. Mon through Sat. $–$$.

where to stay

Hotel Ranola. 118 Indian Place, #6, Sarasota; (866) 951-0111; hotelranola.com. Polished hardwood floors, bold tiles and other touches of color, and sleek furnishings—this boutique hotel, built in 1926, has yesteryear charm with modern amenities such as free wireless Internet access, a rooftop sundeck, and access to a nearby fitness facility. $$$.

The Cypress. 621 Gulfstream Ave. South, Sarasota; (941) 955-4683; cypressbb.com. Overlooking Sarasota Bay, The Cypress Bed & Breakfast Inn offers guests well-appointed rooms, a sumptuous breakfast, and a relaxing veranda and gardens. For those who find relaxation in remaining connected, the rooms and suites all feature cable TV and wireless Internet, too. Look for their Procrastinator's Special! $$$.

day trip 05

orange you glad you asked?!

bradenton/palmetto; anna maria island; ellenton

Manatee County, the third county rimming Tampa Bay, lies directly south of Hillsborough County and is home to one of Florida's other largest ports, Port Manatee. In fact, Port Manatee is the closest US deepwater seaport to the Panama Canal. Manatee County is also home to the nation's largest orange juice processing plant—that glass of orange juice you drank this morning? There's about a 40 percent chance it came from the Bradenton area.

We'll be visiting the port and taking an Orange Blossom Tram Tour, along with seeing a theater production staged in a 1929 estate and having dinner on a pier sticking off the tip of Anna Maria Island—about as close to "on the water" dining as you can get without actually getting in the water. In Ellenton, we'll go shopping—yes!—and visit the Historic Gamble Mansion.

bradenton/palmetto

Facing each other across the Manatee River, Bradenton on the south side and Palmetto on the north side form a sizeable community that people sometimes just pass through on their way farther south. But one of the nation's largest artists' colonies is here as is half of the world's longest fishing pier.

Bradenton Area Convention and Visitors Bureau. (941) 729-9177; annamariaisland-longboatkey.com. Go online to order a visitor's guide, to find accommodations and restaurants, and to learn about upcoming events. If you want to stop in and speak to someone face to

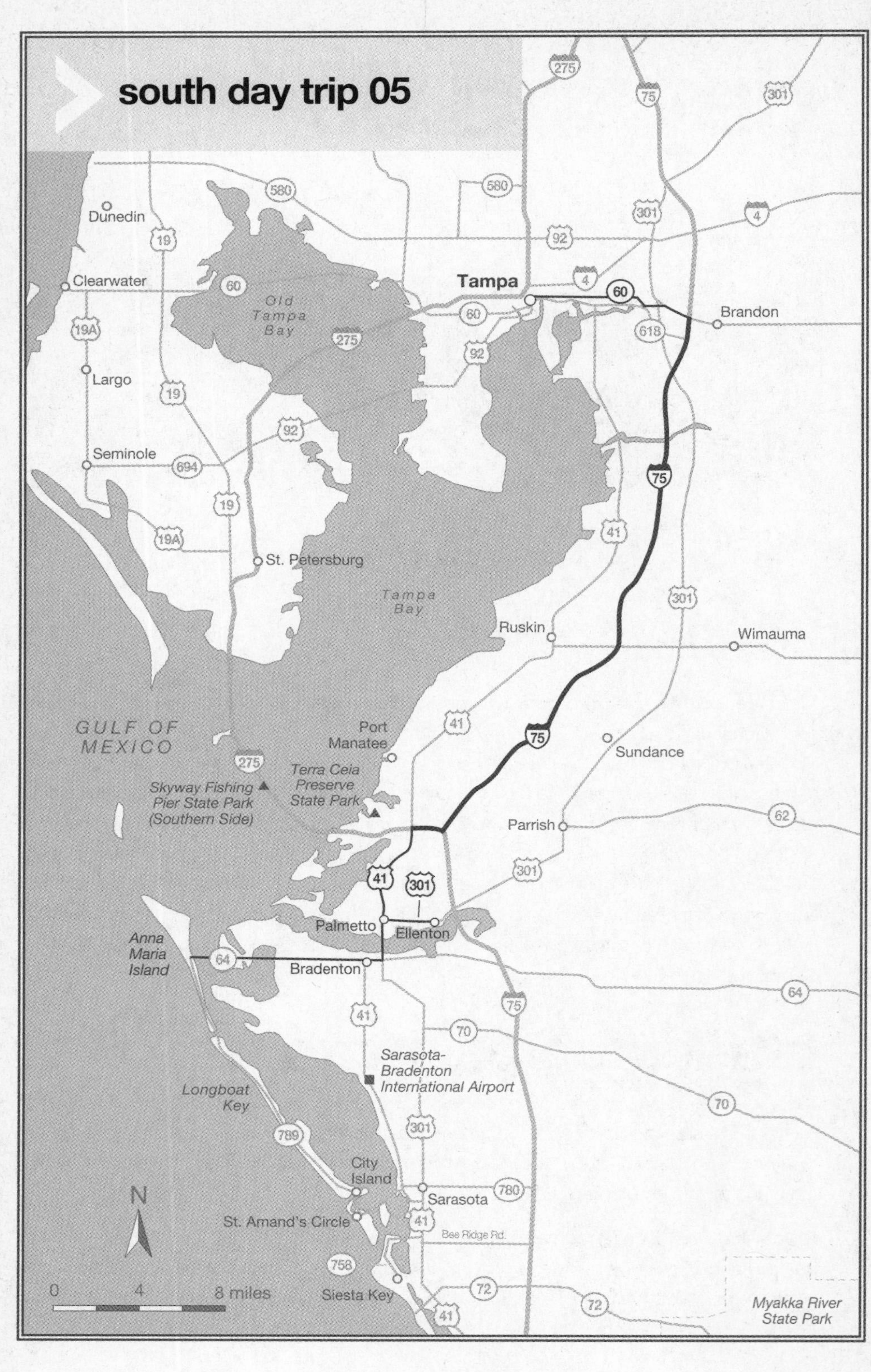
south day trip 05
Dunedin
Clearwater
Largo
Seminole
St. Petersburg
Old Tampa Bay
Tampa
Brandon
Tampa Bay
Ruskin
Wimauma
GULF OF MEXICO
Port Manatee
Sundance
Skyway Fishing Pier State Park (Southern Side)
Terra Ceia Preserve State Park
Parrish
Palmetto
Ellenton
Anna Maria Island
Bradenton
Sarasota-Bradenton International Airport
Longboat Key
City Island
Sarasota
St. Amand's Circle
Bee Ridge Rd.
Siesta Key
Myakka River State Park
N
0
4
8 miles

face, go to the office at the Manatee County Convention Center, aka Manatee Civic Center (listed below). They have brochures and other information.

getting there

From Tampa, take Adamo Drive East/SR 60 East to I-75, about 9 miles. Alternatively, you can avoid stoplights and surface traffic by taking the Selmon Expressway east to I-75; the Selmon Expressway is a toll road.

Either way, once you get to I-75, merge onto I-75 heading south toward Naples. Travel south on I-75 about 27 miles to I-275 North via exit 228 toward St. Petersburg. Travel not quite 2 miles on I-275 North, then take exit 2—exit to the right—then turn left, and merge onto US 41 South toward Palmetto/Bradenton. Travel about 6 miles south to Haben Boulevard. You will see the large sign for the Manatee Convention Center on the corner of US 41 South and Haben Boulevard. Turn left onto Haben Boulevard and travel to Riviera Dunes Way, where you can make a U-turn and turn into the Manatee Convention Center.

where to go

Manatee County Convention Center. 1 Haben Blvd., Palmetto; (941) 729-9177; annamariaisland-longboatkey.com. Signs directing visitors to this facility still read MANATEE CIVIC CENTER; follow them, and you'll get to the right place. All sorts of events are held here—gymnastics competitions, craft shows, conventions, and other events. The offices, located on the south side, also have tourist information.

McKechnie Field. 1611 9th St. West, Bradenton; (941) 747-3031; bradenton.marauders.milb.com and pittsburgh.pirates.mlb.com. The Pittsburgh Pirates, part of the National League's Central Division, have been playing spring-training games at McKechnie Field since 1969. Their training facility, called Pirate City, is located nearby. McKechnie Field opened in 1923 and has hosted a number of major league teams. When the Pirates return to Pittsburgh, one of their minor league affiliates, the Bradenton Marauders, takes the field.

Mixon Fruit Farms. 2525 27th St. East, Bradenton; (800) 608-2525, (941) 748-5829; mixon.com. Take the Orange Blossom Tram Tour through the groves and see what it takes to produce your morning OJ waker-upper. The 1-hour tour includes a stop at the Wildlife Refuge. Also on the property are a gift shop, butterfly garden, koi pond, and a maze especially for children. The Groveside Cafe serves breakfast and lunch—and those luscious vanilla-orange swirl cones. The cafe is open from 8:30 a.m. to 5 p.m., Mon through Sat, and the shop opens at 10 a.m. Tram tours are at 11 a.m. and at 1 and 3 p.m., weather permitting. Concerts and other special events are often held on the grounds.

South Florida Museum, Bishop Planetarium, and Parker Manatee Aquarium. 201 10th St. West, Bradenton; (941) 746-4131; southfloridamuseum.org. It's a three-fer at the South Florida Museum! Admission to the museum also includes admission to the planetarium and to the aquarium, where visitors can greet Snooty, a West Indies manatee. The Museum's core collection is the Montague Tallant Collection of Florida's First People's Artifacts. Check the calendar for planetarium shows and other events. Jan through Apr and the month of July, the complex is open Mon through Sat from 10 a.m. to 5 p.m. and on Sun from noon to 5 p.m. The complex is closed on Mon during the months of May, June, and Aug through Dec. They are also closed the first Sat in Nov, Thanksgiving, Christmas, and New Year's Day, and the second Mon in March.

what to do

Emerson Point Preserve. 5801 17th St. West, Palmetto; (941) 721-6885; mymanatee.org/home/government/departments/natural-resources/resource-management/preserves/emerson-point.html. With walking trails, boardwalk and observation tower, a canoe and kayak launch, and picnic areas, Emerson Point Preserve allows visitors to explore Manatee County's natural habitat. The preserve also is the site of southwest Florida's largest Native American Temple Mound. A welcome/ranger station is open Fri and Sat from 9 a.m. to 4 p.m. Great Florida Birding Trail Site #113.

Port Manatee. 300 Tampa Bay Way, Palmetto; (941) 722-6621; portmanatee.com. We take so much for granted about how the things we buy in stores get there and about how manufacturers ship their products across this country and around the world. Take a free open-air tram tour at Port Manatee to learn what happens behind the scenes to keep our supply chain moving smoothly. Marvel at really big ships and at the equipment used to load and unload products and materials. Tours are scheduled at 10 a.m. on Mon and Wed from late Oct to early May, weather permitting. You must make reservations and, for security purposes, will be required to produce a government-issued photo ID when you arrive. Look for the Public Tours link on their website for other information about the tours. Call (941) 722-6621 for reservations.

Powel Crosley Theater. 8374 N. Tamiami Trail, Sarasota; (941) 722-3244; annamariaisland-longboatkey.com/powel-crosley. Located at the southern end of Manatee County and next to the University of South Florida, Sarasota-Manatee campus, the Powel Crosley estate is operated by Manatee County as a wedding and events venue. Built in 1929 as a winter home, the estate also hosts intimate theater productions. Join Mrs. Crosley and her guests, including Ernest Hemingway, for an evening of literary hilarity or experience *A Victorian Christmas at the Crosley*. Check the calendar for other productions throughout the year. Seatings are by reservation only.

Sarasota Polo Club. 8201 Polo Club Ln., Sarasota; (941) 907-0000; sarasotapolo.com. Pack a picnic and head to the Sarasota Polo Club to watch a match or two. Matches played on Sunday are open to the public. There is an admission fee for adults; children under 12 are free. You can either tailgate—bring an umbrella or small pop-up for shade; coolers and alcohol are okay, too—or sit in the bleachers. Some concessions are available, as well.

Tailgate spots are first-come, first-served and they tend to fill quickly. Check the website for matches and other special events. Groups of 30 to 75 or so can arrange for special seating and even a pre-match demonstration.

Skyway Fishing Pier State Park. 7901 US 19 South, Palmetto; (941) 729-0117; skyway piers.com. Half of the world's longest fishing pier juts into Tampa Bay from near where the Sunshine Skyway Bridge begins its journey across the mouth of the bay. The other half is on the St. Petersburg side, the result of a tragic accident in 1980 when a freighter hit the old bridge during a violent thunderstorm, causing the center span to collapse. After the new bridge was built in 1987, the surviving approaches became drive-on fishing piers. The piers are open 24/7 and are lighted at night. The bait shops rent fishing rods, have restrooms, and sell snacks, too. No alcohol and no pets. The telephone number and website listed above are for the state-contracted bait shop on the pier. To contact Florida park rangers about the Skyway Fishing Pier State Park, call (727) 865-0668 or go to floridastateparks .org/skyway/default.cfm.

Terra Ceia Preserve State Park. 130 Terra Ceia Rd., Terra Ceia; (941) 721-2068; swf wmd.state.fl.us/recreation/areas/terraceia.html. There's not much in the way of facilities or amenities here—that means no restrooms and no water—but there is some prime paddling to be found at the Terra Ceia Preserve State Park. Launch a canoe, kayak, or small boat at the launch on the north side of Bishop Harbor Road.

where to shop

Red Barn Flea Market and Plaza. 1707 1st Street East, Bradenton; (800) 274-3532, (941) 747-3794; redbarnfleamarket.com. For more than 25 years, Red Barn Flea Market and Plaza has been a small business incubator in the Bradenton area. True, some of the 600-plus vendors are just there for the weekend, having moved their home garage sale to a more public venue. But many of the vendors are start-ups exploring what it means to be in business for themselves. A few have expanded to more full-time status—these businesses occupy the Plaza part of the Red Barn area and are open Tues through Sun from 10 a.m. to 4 p.m. The rest of the Red Barn Flea Market is open Fri through Sun from 8 a.m. to 4 p.m. Treasure hunters will find everything from perfumes to popcorn, antiques to appliances, and more.

Village of the Arts. (941) 747-8056 (Artists' Guild of Manatee); villageofthearts.com. Just east off US 41 and between 9th Avenue West and 17th Avenue West is an area covering several blocks that has become home to more than 30 working artists—one of the largest artist colonies in the country—and related businesses and restaurants. In addition to regular working and business hours, Village of the Arts hosts monthly First Weekend Art Walks from 6 to 9:30 p.m. on the first Friday and from 11 a.m. to 4 p.m. on the first Saturday of each month. Workshops, lectures, gallery openings and other events occur throughout the month—check the website for dates and times. ***Note:*** There is a parking garage on the corner of 8th Avenue West and 12th Street West. Evenings and weekends, the parking garage is free.

where to eat

Ezra Cafe. 5629 Manatee Ave. West, Bradenton; (941) 792-0990; ezrafinefoods.com. Located in the west side of Bradenton, Ezra Cafe creatively combines ingredients to produce intriguing plates to tempt the palate. Consider, for instance, the mango ponzu-glazed duck served with butternut squash risotto, buttered snow peas, and tempura green onions. Lunch is served Mon through Fri from 11 a.m. to 2 p.m. Dinner is served Mon through Sat from 5 to 9:30 p.m. $$–$$$.

Ortygia Restaurant. 1418 13th St. West, Village of the Arts, Bradenton; (941) 741-8646; ortygiarestaurant.com. The decor is colorfully artsy; the food is equally artistic. Dine inside or outside on the patio where the entertainment might be an opera singer or a blues musician. Either way, the offerings from the kitchen are Sicilian through and through. With such dishes as Farasumagru—red-wine-and-tomato-braised sirloin stuffed with prosciutto, provolone, sweet sausage, egg, asparagus, and pancetta—on the menu, it's a sure bet dinner won't be run of the mill. Ortygia Restaurant is open from 11:30 a.m. to 8:30 p.m. Tues through Sat. $$.

Popi's Place Too. 815 8th Ave. West, Palmetto; (941) 721-9525; popisplace.com. Popi has five different places throughout Manatee County, but the first one is Popi's Place Too, and the last one is Popi's Place VI in West Bradenton. The food is plentiful—breakfast ranges from oatmeal to crab cakes Benedict; dinners include prime rib and Mediterranean chicken. All of Popi's Places are open every day, but each has slightly different hours. This one is open from 6 a.m. to 8:30 p.m. $$.

where to stay

Palmetto Riverside Bed and Breakfast. 1102 Riverside Dr., Palmetto; (941) 981-5331; palmettoriverside.com. Located on the north side of the Manatee River, the Palmetto Riverside Bed and Breakfast, owned by the Lippens family, offers European-style hospitality in an historic home built in 1913 and listed on the National Register of Historic Places. All rooms are exquisitely furnished, but the octagonal Riverview Room is especially lovely. A 200-foot pier allows guests to boat in, as well. Breakfast is complimentary; dinner is available by reservation. No pets; well-behaved children ages 8 and above are welcome. $$$.

anna maria island

Three cities on a 7-mile strip of island? Plus white, sandy beaches? That's Anna Maria Island, which is connected to the mainland by two bridges, one at the city of Bradenton

Beach and the other at the city of Holmes Beach. The third city is Anna Maria, in the north part of the island.

Anna Maria Island Chamber of Commerce. 5313 Gulf Dr. North, Holmes Beach; (941) 778-1541; annamariaislandchamber.org. The chamber is located a few blocks north of the bridge and is open Mon through Fri from 9 a.m. to 5 p.m. and on Sat from 9 a.m. to 1 p.m.

getting there

From Bradenton, take Manatee Avenue West across Palma Sola Bay and Perico Island to Holmes Beach on Anna Maria Island. Turn left down East Bay Drive to head to the city of Bradenton Beach. Or wind your way to the right and follow Gulf Drive North to reach Anna Maria further north.

what to do

Anna Maria Island Trolley. (941) 749-7116; annamariaislandchamber.org/VisitUs/SavetheTrolley.aspx. Ride the trolley—free!—from the Anna Maria City Pier to Coquina Beach (in the city of Bradenton Beach). The trolley runs from 6 a.m. to 10:30 p.m. every day; for 75 cents, you can connect to the Longboat Key trolley and ride all the way to St. Armand's Circle and even into downtown Sarasota. The trolleys have bike racks on the front.

where to shop

Historic Bridge Street. bridgestreetmerchants.com. Look for shops, galleries, ice-cream shops, miniature golf, and restaurants along Historic Bridge Street in Bradenton Beach. Bridge Street stretches from Gulf Drive North right to the Bradenton Beach City Pier, where Rotten Ralph's Restaurant welcomes diners. You will also find parasailing opportunities, dive guides, jet ski rentals, and other water sport businesses, too. Sundays, Nov through Apr, the area is also an open-air market featuring fresh produce, artwork, crafts, and more.

where to eat

Rod and Reel Pier. 875 N. Shore Dr., Anna Maria; (941) 778-1885. Built in 1947, the Rod and Reel Pier is one of three public piers on the Island. At the end is a casual restaurant serving breakfast, lunch, and dinner. The bar and pier are downstairs; the restaurant is upstairs (no ramp), and the view is magnificent. Hang out and watch people fish, or bring your gear and catch some yourself. Breakfast is served from 8 to 11 a.m. every day; lunch and dinner are served until 8:30 p.m. ***Note:*** Some older GPS systems show this address as being in Holmes Beach. $–$$$.

The Waterfront Restaurant. 111 S. Bay Blvd., Anna Maria; (941) 778-1515; thewaterfront restaurant.net. Eat outside (first-come, first served) or dine inside (reservations accepted); the food is imaginative either way. From the Carnitas Michoacan—orange juice–braised pork served on tortillas with all the trimmings—to the Grouper Oscar, the Waterfront's menu is extensive and enticing. Ask about their wine-tasting events. The Waterfront Restaurant is located near the City Pier and has a lovely view of the Sunshine Skyway Bridge. Lunch is served from 11:30 a.m. to 4:00 p.m. and dinner is served 4:30 to 9 p.m. Sun through Thurs and from 4:30 to 10 p.m. Fri and Sat. $$$.

where to stay

Anna Maria Beach Cottages. 112 Oak Ave., Anna Maria; (800) 778-2030, (941) 778-1503; annamariabeachcottages.com. Located on the Gulf side of the island, Anna Maria Beach Cottages consist of 2- to 4-bedroom homes and smaller apartment cottages. A pool, patio grill area, and laundry facilities offer home-away-from-home comforts, and the beach is just steps away. Borrow some bicycles and explore the island or take the trolley around. The cottages have several pricing tiers; the highest "peak" season requires a 7-night minimum stay. No pets. $$$.

***Dream Lover* Boat & Breakfast.** Bradenton Beach Marina; (941) 724-0699; bedand.breakfast.com/fl-bradenton-beach-anna-maria-is-dreamloverboatandbreakfast.html. Looking for something a bit different? Join Kay and Jonathon Cook aboard their 56-foot Nautical ketch. Several different cabin options include twin bunks or queen-size bed. Start with a cocktail hour and orientation on the deck or in the cockpit, and learn about life aboard a boat. Breakfast is included, so pack light (soft-sided luggage) and put on your boatin' shoes. $$$.

Sunrise Garden Resort. 512 Spring Ave., Anna Maria; (855) 742-7336, (941) 778-2000; sunrisegardenresort.com. Located closer to the bay side of the island, Sunrise Garden Resort has studio units and 1- and 2-bedroom suites that open onto either the pool area or the garden area. The resort has a laundry facility, barbecue area, and free wireless Internet. The bay-side beach is about half a block away. Pets are welcomed. Some seasons require a 2-night minimum stay. $$–$$$.

ellenton

Located upriver from Palmetto, on the northern side of the Manatee River, Ellenton is a small community with a big mall. An outlet mall, to be precise, and it's one that attracts shoppers from Pinellas and Hillsborough Counties as well as its own Manatee County. The Gamble Mansion Historic State Park also is located in Ellenton.

getting there

From Palmetto, travel east on US 301 North about 2 miles. If you reach I-75, you've gone too far.

where to go

Gamble Plantation Historic State Park. 3708 Patten Ave., Ellenton; (941) 723-4536; floridastateparks.org/gambleplantation. The Gamble Plantation Historic State Park contains South Florida's only surviving pre–Civil War era plantation house. Major Robert Gamble homesteaded 160 acres beginning in 1843. By 1849, his property included 3,500 acres of sugarcane—but the sugar market didn't cooperate, and he had to sell it all in 1859 to pay debts. The visitor center is open Thurs through Mon from 8 to 11:45 a.m. and 12:45 to 4:30 p.m. and is closed Thanksgiving, Christmas, and New Year's Days. Guided tours of the house and the grounds are available 6 times a day on days when the visitor center is open. There are picnic tables and restrooms on the grounds, and the park itself is open from 8 a.m. to sunset every day of the year.

what to do

Florida Railroad Museum. 12210 83rd St. East, Parrish; (877) 869-0800, (941) 776-0906; frrm.org. Located northeast of Ellenton, the Florida Railroad Museum is a labor of love. Volunteers have worked to preserve a section of railroad track and a selection of engines, cars, and cabooses. Today, visitors relive the way people used to travel in the days before paved roads connected towns in Florida. The Florida Railroad Museum is open every Sat and Sun from 10 a.m. to 4 p.m. and the train leaves at 11 a.m. and 2 p.m. The property also includes a small gift shop, but the primary attraction is the train itself. They also have special runs throughout the year, including a dinner theater mystery train and the Pumpkin Patch Special. Check the website for the dates and times of special events. Want to try your hand at driving a train? You can do that, too—look for the Locomotive Rental link on the website.

where to shop

Ellenton Premium Outlets. 5461 Factory Shops Blvd., Ellenton; (941) 723-1150; premiumoutlets.com. Located just east of I-75 (exit 224) on US 301, Ellenton Premium Outlets has outlet stores from places like Saks Fifth Avenue Off 5th, Polo Ralph Lauren Factory Store, and other name-brand outlet stores—130 of them, to be exact. Take note: Ellenton Premium Outlets is about serious shopping—there is a not-huge food court, but there are no big restaurants taking up valuable shopping space. Ellenton Premium Outlets is open Mon through Sat from 10 a.m. to 9 p.m. and Sun from 10 a.m. to 7 p.m. They are closed Easter, Thanksgiving Day, and Christmas Day.

where to eat & stay

Dayspring. 8411 25th St. East, Parrish; (941) 776-1018; dayspring.dioswfl.org. Conference centers and retreats often have rooms left over that are available to people willing to respect the center's purpose. They can also make great places for inexpensive family reunions. Dayspring is part of the Episcopal Diocese of Southwest Florida and is used for everything from choir and youth group retreats to quilting weekends and good-friends getaways. Accommodations range from dorms to cabins—many of which are nicely furnished and all of which are air-conditioned. A dining hall offers meals, by arrangement, at specified times. Located on the Manatee River, the center has paths to walk and canoes and kayaks to paddle. $–$$.

west

day trip 01

west

artin' around:
st. petersburg; gulfport

From its somewhat sleepy 'burg beginnings in the 20th century, the City of St. Petersburg has become a major player in the art world. When nobody else seemed to want the most comprehensive collection of original Salvador Dalí works—being offered for free to anyone willing to properly house and display it—St. Petersburg got its act together in a hurry and snagged the collection. After Dale Chihuly's stunning glass creations filled the St. Petersburg Fine Arts Museum in 2004, city art lovers built a home for a permanent collection.

Next door to the west, Gulfport also has a reputation as an artists' community. Art Walks held twice each month bring artists and art lovers together, drawing attention to the galleries and shops in the area.

Other types of arts thrive here, too, and the area's natural beauty can be enjoyed in parks and preserves. Plus—St. Petersburg is home to the Tampa Bay Rays and the other half of the world's longest fishing pier. So much to do, so little time.

Virtual Visitor Site: VisitStPeteClearwater.com. Order a free print copy of the visitor guide to the county or view it page by page online. You will also find links to various attractions, restaurants, and hotels—and some ads for discounts, too.

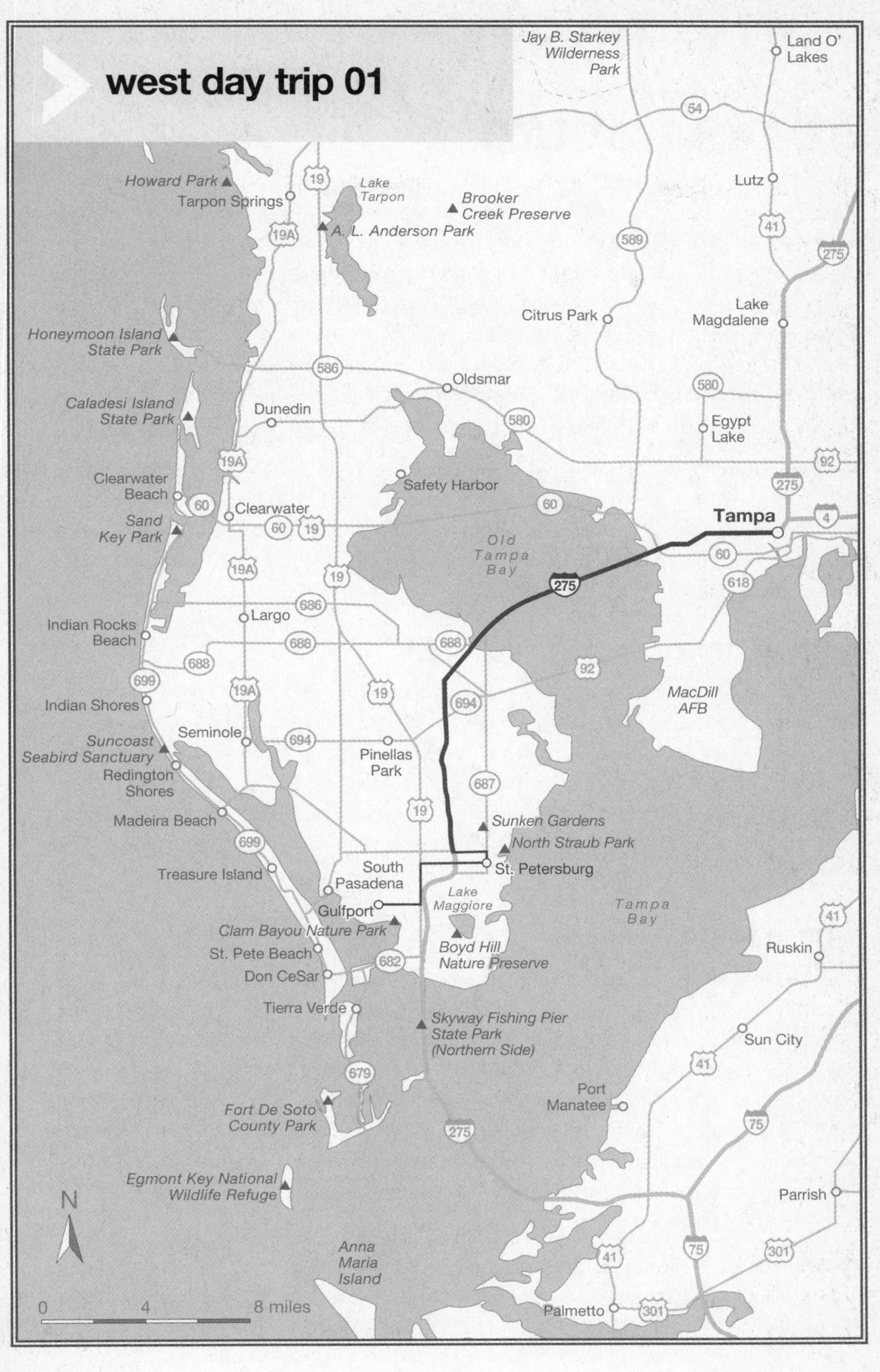
west day trip 01
Jay B. Starkey Wilderness Park
Land O' Lakes
54
19
Lake Tarpon
Howard Park
Tarpon Springs
Brooker Creek Preserve
Lutz
19A
A. L. Anderson Park
41
589
275
Citrus Park
Lake Magdalene
Honeymoon Island State Park
586
Oldsmar
580
Caladesi Island State Park
Dunedin
580
Egypt Lake
19A
92
Clearwater Beach
Safety Harbor
275
60
Clearwater
60
Tampa
4
Sand Key Park
60
19
Old Tampa Bay
60
19A
19
275
618
686
Largo
Indian Rocks Beach
688
688
688
92
699
19A
19
694
MacDill AFB
Indian Shores
Seminole
694
Pinellas Park
Suncoast Seabird Sanctuary
Redington Shores
687
19
Madeira Beach
Sunken Gardens
699
North Straub Park
South Pasadena
St. Petersburg
Treasure Island
Lake Maggiore
Tampa Bay
Gulfport
41
Clam Bayou Nature Park
Boyd Hill Nature Preserve
St. Pete Beach
Ruskin
682
Don CeSar
Tierra Verde
Skyway Fishing Pier State Park (Northern Side)
Sun City
679
41
Port Manatee
Fort De Soto County Park
275
75
Egmont Key National Wildlife Refuge
Parrish
N
Anna Maria Island
41
75
301
0
4
8 miles
Palmetto
301

st. petersburg

Named after the birthplace of the Russian immigrant who, in 1889, built a railroad from north Florida to a wharf in a town with fewer than 300 residents, St. Petersburg today is Florida's fourth largest city and has the largest municipal marina in the southeast. St. Petersburg is the site of the world's first regularly scheduled commercial aviation—in 1914—and of the nation's first, and still one of the world's largest, reclaimed water systems. Major League Baseball's Grapefruit League—spring training—began in St. Petersburg, also in 1914.

We'll focus on St. Petersburg's remarkable collection of art museums and centers, but we'll also visit some parks, take in a game at the Trop, and note some other attractions. Nor will we neglect the creature comforts—great restaurants and iconic hotels await.

St. Petersburg Area Chamber of Commerce. 100 2nd Ave. North, St. Petersburg; (727) 821-4069; stpete.com. Stop in to ask questions or to load up on brochures and other information about the area. Be sure to pick up a map and information about Central Avenue Shuttle and the Looper Trolley. The chamber office is open Mon through Fri from 9 a.m. to 5 p.m. and on Sat from 9 a.m. to 4 p.m.

getting there

From Tampa, take I-275 South over the Howard Frankland Bridge and continue to follow I-275 South toward St. Petersburg, about 22 miles. At exit 23A, which exits to the left, merge onto I-375 toward St. Petersburg/The Pier, and travel just over 1 mile. As I-375 ends, it deposits drivers onto 4th Avenue North right past the Old Coliseum building, a site of many arts-related events. Continue heading east on 4th Avenue North about 2 blocks to 4th Street North, and turn right. Continue 2 blocks to 2nd Avenue North, and turn left. The St. Petersburg Area Chamber of Commerce building is on the right.

where to go

Chihuly Collection. 400 Beach Dr. Northeast, St. Petersburg; (727) 822-7872; moreanartscenter.org. Unbelievable. That's a word often heard from people seeing, for the first time, Dale Chihuly's massive, colorful, wildly imaginative art-glass installations. The Chihuly Collection, presented by the Morean Arts Center, is housed in the first building especially constructed to showcase Chihuly's works. In addition to the Chihuly Collection, the Morean has a hot shop at their gallery just a few blocks away (719 Central Ave.). Visitors can watch glass-blowing demonstrations and even try their hand at working with glass. The Chihuly Collection is open Mon through Sat from 10 a.m. to 6 p.m.—on Thurs it is open until 8 p.m.—and on Sun from noon to 6 p.m.

Dalí Museum. 1 Dali Blvd., St. Petersburg; (800) 442-3254, (727) 823-3767; thedali.org. In January 1980, a private collector was trying to give—as in for free—the most

getting around town

- ***Street-wise:*** *Because downtown St. Petersburg has many one-way streets, it's easy to miss a turn and become confused. Streets run north and south, while avenues run east and west. Central Avenue, which runs east-west, is the dividing line, and it allows two-way traffic: 1st Avenue North is 1 block north of Central Avenue and runs parallel to it, 1st Avenue South also runs parallel to Central Avenue but is 1 block south. North of Central Avenue, 1st Street is 1st Street North; south of Central Avenue, it is 1st Street South. The street numbers get larger the farther west you travel. US 19 is also 34th Street in St. Petersburg.*
- ***Parking Meters:*** *Many of the city's parking meters can be paid using your cell phone. Go to parkmobile.com to set up an account. Or carry quarters.*
- ***Trolley:*** *The St. Petersburg Trolley Downtown Looper route can save parking aggravation. Call (727) 821-5166 or go to loopertrolley.com for information about the Looper.*

comprehensive collection, outside of Spain, of original Dalí artwork to any group who would preserve the body of work intact. Established museums weren't interested. Within a couple of months, a group of far-sighted area leaders put together a foundation, secured funding, and did everything necessary to receive and manage the collections. Today the works are housed in a brand new, somewhat surrealistic building at the Progress Energy Center for the Arts. The works—oils, watercolors, sketches, sculptures, and other works completed from 1917 to 1970—include massive paintings as high as 14 feet tall. Look under the Visit tab online for the Tips link for ways to share the museum with children. The museum is open Mon through Sat from 10 a.m. to 5:30 p.m.—staying open until 8 p.m. on Thurs—and from noon to 5:30 p.m. on Sun. Cafe Gala serves Spanish-style foods and is open during museum hours.

Mahaffey Theater. 400 1st St. South, St. Petersburg; (727) 892-5767; themahaffey.com. Also part of the Progress Energy Center for the Arts, the newly renovated Mahaffey Theater hosts concerts, shows, and events. The Mahaffey is one of the three main performance centers for the highly acclaimed Florida Orchestra (floridaorchestra.org), whose offices are just a few blocks away.

Museum of Fine Arts. 255 Beach Dr. Northeast, St. Petersburg; (727) 896-2667; fine-arts.org. The MFA's permanent holdings include almost 5,000 works representing both the ancient and modern worlds, including works by Claude Monet, Robert Henri, Georgia

O'Keeffe, and Aaron Siskind. Our favorite spot is a black-box room, the Helen Harper Brown Gallery, where crystalline creations by Tiffany, Galle, and other artists are lit from below and behind. The MFA Cafe is open from 11 a.m. to 3 p.m. for lunch Tues through Sat and for brunch on Sun to museum visitors and non-visitors alike. The MFA is open Mon through Sat from 10 a.m. to 5 p.m.—on Thurs, the MFA stays open until 8 p.m.—and on Sun from noon to 5 p.m.

St. Petersburg Clay Company. 420 22nd St. South, St. Petersburg; (727) 896-2529; stpeteclay.com. Located in the 1920s-era Historic Seaboard Train Station, St. Petersburg Clay Company rents studio space to clay artists, hosts workshops by clay artists from around the world, and presents ceramics exhibits. The Morean Arts Center's Center for Clay offers classes and workshops. The SPCC's kiln collection ranges from gas kilns to soda and salt kilns to wood-fired, raku, and pit kilns, including a huge Japanese-style 16th-century anagama kiln. St. Petersburg Clay Company is open Tues through Sat from 10 a.m. to 5 p.m. Call ahead for information about demonstrations.

what to do

Al Lang Stadium. 230 1st St. South, St. Petersburg; (727) 551-3000; stpeteinternational baseball.com. The World Series may soon be a real world series—if the St. Pete Baseball Commission has anything to say about it, that is. Beginning in 2012, St. Petersburg International Baseball comes to Al Lang Stadium with teams from Canada and the Netherlands playing spring squads from several NL and AL teams. This could get interesting . . .

American Stage Theatre Company. 163 3rd St. North, St. Petersburg; (727) 823-7529; americanstage.org. American Stage Theatre Company, the first Tampa Bay–area nonprofit theater company to operate under a full contract with Actors' Equity Association, helped pioneer the Small Professional Theatre contract with Actors' Equity. They produce 6 mainstage productions each year in the Raymond James Theater in St. Petersburg, an outdoor production called American Stage in the Park, cabaret, improv, and other programs.

Boyd Hill Nature Preserve. 1101 Country Club Way South, St. Petersburg; (727) 893-7326; stpete.org/boyd. Within this 245-acre preserve in the middle of residential St. Petersburg are 5 distinct ecosystems, a bird of prey aviary, and overnight camping facilities. Tram tours run every day at 1 p.m. and also at 10 a.m. on Sat. Boyd Hill Nature Preserve is open from 9 a.m. to 7 p.m. Tues through Fri, from 7 a.m. to 7 p.m. on Sat, and from 9 a.m. to 7 p.m. on Sun. The preserve is closed on Mon and Thanksgiving, Christmas, and New Year's Day. Check the Friends of Boyd Hill's website (friendsofboydhill.org) for additional information about activities and events. No pets.

Florida Holocaust Museum. 55 5th St. South, St. Petersburg; (727) 820-0100; flholocaust museum.org. The Florida Holocaust Museum, now one of the largest Holocaust museums in the United States, has as its centerpiece exhibit an original boxcar used during World

War II to transport Jews and other victims of the Nazi regime to the concentration camps. Visitors view scenes from pre-war Jewish life, learn about the history of anti-Semitism, see a scale model of Birkenau, and learn about "righteous Gentiles" who risked their lives to save others. Some of the museum's previous exhibits and speakers have included other victims of discrimination such as Jackie Robinson, who helped integrate baseball, and Carl Wilkins, the only American who stayed in Rwanda in 1994 rather than be evacuated. The Florida Holocaust Museum is open from 10 a.m. to 5 p.m. every day except Rosh Hashana, Yom Kippur, Thanksgiving, Christmas, and New Year's Day. The last admission is at 3:30 p.m.

The Pier/Waterfront Parks. 800 2nd Ave. Northeast, St. Petersburg; (727) 821-6164; stpetepier.com. St. Petersburg's early town leaders wisely set aside the waterfront areas as parks. From the North Shore area, by the Vinoy and North Straub Park, near the Museum of Fine Arts to South Straub Park, is about a 6-block stretch of grass and trees. The approach to the Pier—including the St. Petersburg Museum of History and a beach area—runs between North and South Straub Parks. Plans are in the works to replace the inverted pyramid building at the end of the Pier; for now there are shops, restaurants, and an aquarium. Farther south, Pioneer Park and Demens Landing provide more park area. Then come Al Lang Stadium; the Progress Energy Center for the Arts, which includes the Mahaffey Theatre, the Center Plaza Waterfront Park, and the Dalí Museum; and Albert Whitted Park, a small park with a great view of the planes landing and taking off from the Albert Whitted Airport next door. Many events and festivals are held in these parks. The rest of the time people enjoy them for what they are—green space looking out onto blue space.

Sunken Gardens. 1825 4th St. North, St. Petersburg; (727) 551-3102; stpete.org/sunken/index.asp. Walk down into the gardens, what used to be a small lake at the bottom of a sinkhole. In 1902, George Turner Sr., a plumber who loved to garden, bought the lake and the 6 acres of land it was on. He drained the lake and turned the mucky bottom into a garden. Today Sunken Gardens, owned by the City of St. Petersburg, is filled with more than 50,000 flowering and ornamental plants and trees and is the site of yoga and other classes. Sunken Gardens is open from 10 a.m. to 4:30 p.m. Mon through Sat and from noon to 4:30 p.m. on Sun. No pets. Children must be accompanied by an adult at all times.

Skyway Fishing Pier State Park. 11101 34th St. South, St. Petersburg; (727) 865-0668; skywaypiers.com. Half of the world's longest fishing pier juts into Tampa Bay from near where the Sunshine Skyway Bridge begins its journey across the mouth of the bay. The other half is on the Manatee County side near Bradenton. The piers are open 24/7 and are lighted at night. The bait shops rent fishing rods, have restrooms, and sell snacks, too. No alcohol and no pets. The telephone number and website listed above are for the state-contracted bait shop on the drive-on pier. To contact Florida park rangers, call (727) 865-0668 or go to floridastateparks.org/skyway/default.cfm.

Tropicana Field. 1 Tropicana Dr., St Petersburg; (888) 326-7297, (727) 825-3250; tampabay.rays.mlb.com. Home of the Tampa Bay Rays, the Trop is one fun spot—even before you get to the game. Visit the Ted Williams Museum and Hitters Hall of Fame in Centerfield Street, get splashed by a cownose ray, and play carnival games in Right Field Street. Tropicana Field is MLB's only field with artificial turf and all-dirt base paths (not just sliding areas around the bases). And the roof glows orange when the Rays win a home game. Two good things to know about game-day parking: 1) If your car has 4 or more people in it, parking in some lots on some game days is free. 2) The website has a map of parking areas—park in the city parking garage on 1st Avenue South just east of 2nd Street South, then take a free shuttle to Gate 4. Wanna go behind-the-scenes? Take a 90-minute tour and see what it's like to sit in the dugout or up in the press box. Check the website for days and times the tour is offered. Call (727) 825-3162 or email ballparktours@raysbaseball.com at least 48 hours in advance to reserve your spot. Group rates are available for groups of 20 or more; check the website for parking and other information. Wear your walking shoes!

where to shop

Art Galleries. In addition to gift shops in the museum and art centers listed, many artists make St. Petersburg their home. Look for upscale galleries along Beach Drive near the Museum of Fine Arts and working artists' studio/galleries along Central Avenue. The Downtown Arts Association's website (stpetearts.org) lists more than 20 galleries and museums.

Antiques. St. Petersburg also has a number of antiques shops. Some are strung along Central Avenue, others are on Dr. Martin Luther King Jr. Street North (9th Street North), and still others are scattered throughout the city. The Discover Downtown Guide & Map lists several antiques shops. Pick up a map—they are widely available—or go to discoverdowntown.com and click on the interactive map link.

Haslam's Book Store. 2025 Central Ave., St. Petersburg; (727) 822-8616; haslams.com. A St. Petersburg institution since 1933, this 30,000-square-foot building holds more than 300,000 bestsellers, technical and trade books, religious books, and children's books, making it Florida's largest new and used independent book store. Check their website for author visits and book signings. They are open Mon through Sat from 10 a.m. to 6:30 p.m. and on Sun from noon to 5 p.m. Note to classic video gamers: Check out the Doom link on their website—chase monsters and hunt for treasure throughout a virtual Haslam's.

Mazzaro Italian Market. 2909 22nd Ave. North, St. Petersburg; (727) 321-2400; mazzarosmarket.com. Mazzaro is not your intimate Italian table for two with violin serenade. It's loud, packed with people, and heady with the heavenly smells of bread baking in a real brick oven, coffee roasting, and oniony/garlicky food cooking. You'll find a real butcher shop, a cheese department, a take-out-or-eat-on-the-patio deli, homemade pasta, and gelato. Fri and Sat, Mazzaro's certified sommelier conducts wine tastings. Mazarro is open 9 a.m. to

6 p.m. Mon through Fri and 9 a.m. to 2:30 p.m. on Sat. Mazzaro is closed on Sun—and they close the whole store for a couple of weeks' vacation during the summer. You can order online, too.

Saturday Morning Market. 230 1st St. South, St. Petersburg; saturdaymorningmarket.com. Fresh produce, fresh-baked breads and pastries, orchids and herbs, art work and craft wares, plus live music and other entertainers and loads of food concessions, too—you never know exactly what you'll find at the Saturday Morning Market. But you know there will be a variety of vendors, many who have been selling their wares at the Saturday Morning Market for a decade now. Located on the waterfront in the parking lot of Al Lang Stadium, the market is open every Sat, weather permitting, from 9 a.m. to 2 p.m.

where to eat

Ferg's Sports Bar & Grill. 1320 Central Ave., St. Petersburg; (727) 822-4562; fergssportsbar.com. Long before the Rays came to town, Mark Ferguson bought an old mechanic's shop and turned it into a sports bar in the hopes that Major League Baseball would see the light and plant a team in St. Petersburg. Today, Ferg's stretches through almost 2 city blocks and helps Rays—and other sports team fans—celebrate the spirit of sports. Serving bunches of burgers, wings, soups, salads, sandwiches, and a smoked fish spread with crackers and hot sauce, Ferg's opens every day at 11 a.m. Mon through Sat, they close at 2 a.m. On Sun, they close at 10 p.m. $.

Marchand's Bar & Grill. 501 5th Ave. Northeast, St. Petersburg; (727) 824-8072; marchandsbarandgrill.com. Located in the Renaissance Vinoy Resort & Golf Club, Marchand's serves breakfast, lunch, Afternoon Tea, and dinner—all exquisitely presented. Lemon soufflé pancakes sprinkled with fresh raspberries and toasted pine nuts for breakfast are a must try, as is the sweet potato ravioli with braised short ribs, roasted fig, and goat cheese for dinner. Afternoon Tea, including a Toddle Tea for younger guests, is served by reservation only at Marchand's on Wed and Sat afternoons. Several items on their menus are gluten-free. Marchand's serves breakfast every day from 6:30 to 11:30 a.m., lunch on Mon through Sat from 11:30 a.m. to 2:30 p.m., and dinner every day from 5 to 10 p.m. Sunday brunch is served from 10 a.m. to 2 p.m. and reservations are strongly recommended. $$–$$$.

Red Mesa. 4912 4th St. North, St. Petersburg; (727) 527-8728; redmesarestaurant.com. Red Mesa offers upscale Mexican/Caribbean food, with an emphasis on seafood and served with an occasional twist of the Far East. Go for the crab and shrimp enchiladas or the Southwestern tuna sashimi or the ensalada de pato—a salad of crispy fried duck breast, sliced and served on greens with pepitas, dried cherries, red onion, and goat cheese. You did save room for dessert, yes? Try the guava empanada or the coconut natilla. The Red Mesa serves lunch Mon through Sat from 11 a.m. to 4 p.m. Dinner is served from 4 to 9:30 p.m. Mon through Thurs and from 4 to 10:30 p.m. Fri and Sat. On Sun, breakfast is served from 9 a.m. to 2 p.m. and dinner is served from 2 to 9 p.m. A sunset prix fixe menu is available Mon through Fri from 4 to 5:45 p.m. $$–$$$.

Skyway Jack's. 2795 34th St. South, St. Petersburg; (727) 866-3217. Look for Humpty Dumpty sitting on a wall, and you'll know you have found Skyway Jack's, an iconic eatery that has been around since 1976. The menu is mostly breakfasts—eggs cooked just about any way you can think of and both salt-cured and country-aged ham—but they also serve salads and sandwiches, chicken pot pie, and more. Named one of Florida's best breakfast spots, Skyway Jack's is open from 5 a.m. to 3 p.m. every day. No credit cards, and watch your step going in. $.

where to stay

Dickens House Bed & Breakfast. 335 8th Ave. Northeast, St. Petersburg; (800) 381-2022, (727) 822-8622; dickenshouse.com. Each of the 5 rooms in this carefully restored and furnished 1912 Arts and Crafts–style home reflects a different aspect of the history of the house, its original owners, and the area. Proprietor Ed Caldwell's breakfasts are equally imaginative—eggs tempura (a poached egg dipped in tempura batter, fried crisp, and served with a light sour cream and wasabi sauce), for instance, and Danish ableskivers (small breakfast cakes) served on sliced apples. Other amenities include an evening wine time and a business center. No pets, and no children under age 9. The Dickens House is within walking distance of waterfront parks and the downtown area. $$–$$$.

The Pier Hotel. 253 2nd Ave. North; St. Petersburg; (800) 735-6607, (727) 822-7500; thepierhotel.com. The Pier Hotel, operating since 1921, gives guests a glimpse into an elegantly appointed yesteryear. The boutique hotel's 33 guest rooms and suites feature period furniture with luxury linens, plus modern amenities such as microwave ovens, refrigerators, wet bars, and Internet access. Guests enjoy a complimentary expanded Continental breakfast and a complimentary beer and wine reception in the evening. Lunch and dinner also are available as is some event space. Children are welcome, but pets must find other accommodations. $$–$$$.

The Renaissance Vinoy Resort and Golf Club. 501 5th Ave. Northeast, St. Petersburg; (888) 303-4430, (727) 894-1000; renaissancevinoyresort.com. A Jazz Age hotel located on St. Petersburg's northeast waterfront, the Vinoy offers a private 74-slip marina, private golf course, salon and day spa, a 12-court tennis complex, and several dining options (see the listing for Marchand's Bar & Grill, above). With its Mediterranean Revival architecture and furnishings to match, it is easy to imagine silent movie stars and baseball legends walking the halls. The Vinoy offers a number of packaged stays—golf, spa, and other packages—as well as other offers. Ask about complimentary off-site parking. No pets. $$$.

gulfport

Back in the 1880s, when competition to grow cities on the Pinellas peninsula was fierce, Hamilton Disston wanted to build a railroad to the tiny town of Disston City. Disston had bought 4 million acres of Florida land—for 25 cents an acre—just after the Civil War, saving Florida from bankruptcy. Then he started building towns—Tarpon Springs was one, Disston City, today's Gulfport, was another. What he really needed was to bring a railroad in to link land and sea transportation lines. Peter Demens was willing to do so, but Disston's board of directors said no. So the railroad went to St. Petersburg (named after Demens's hometown) instead of to Disston City.

Today, Gulfport is a quiet community on Boca Ciega bay, facing St. Pete Beach. We sometimes forget that Gulfport is a beach community, but it is—and it has become known for its somewhat Bohemian arts community. Plus there's dancing at the Casino Ballroom and good eats and more.

Gulfport Chamber of Commerce. 4926 Gulfport Blvd., Gulfport; (727) 344-3711; gulfport chamberofcommerce.com. Stop in for information or order a free visitor guide from their website. The chamber office is open from 9 a.m. to 3 p.m. Mon through Fri.

getting there

From St. Petersburg, take Central Avenue west not quite 2 miles to US 19/34th Street South. Turn left onto 34th Street South and travel south about 1.5 miles to 22nd Avenue South. Turn right onto 22nd Avenue South and travel just over a mile. The Gulfport Chamber of Commerce office is on your left.

what to do

Here's the deal. It's not like there are gobs of official attractions in Gulfport. No theme parks. No big museums. There's a local history museum (see below), where you can learn about the **Gulfport Casino Ballroom** and other local landmarks, and **Clam Bayou Nature Park** (on Miriam Street south of 29th Avenue South), where you can walk the trail or launch a canoe to explore the bay. There's the small **Williams Pier** to fish off of and a small **public beach** area (with restroom facilities), lots of little **shops** (check out Bo-Tiki at bo-tiki.com and Domain Home Accessories at domainhomeaccessories.com), and a laid-back atmosphere that is an attraction in itself.

The first Friday or third Saturday of each month from 6 to 10 p.m., the sidewalks fill with artists, vendors, and musicians. Stores, galleries, and studios stay open, and a good time is most often had by all. Call the chamber office (info above) to confirm the **Art Walk** is happening when you plan to visit. And if you're really adventuresome, check out **The Blueberry Patch** (4923 20th Avenue South) gatherings to celebrate the arts and artists on the 1st, 7th, 11th, and 22nd of each month (blueberrypatch.org). Some things just can't be described, but we'll tell you their slogan is "Peace, Love, and Blueberries!" and you might find anything from open mic nights to lots of imaginative art from repurposed materials.

Gulfport Historical Museum. 5301 28th Ave. South, Gulfport; (727) 327-0505; gulfport historicalsociety.org. If Hamilton Disston had had his way, Gulfport today would rival St. Petersburg in size and prominence. In the 1880s, Disston built Disston City and wanted to bring in a railroad line. Disston's backers refused, and the line went to St. Petersburg instead. Disston City became Gulfport, and Hamilton Disston died a broken-hearted man. Watch the interactive map on the website change from a 1905 version to a modern-day version to see how the town has grown. Learn more about Gulfport at the historical museum, which is open Mon through Fri 2 p.m. to 4 p.m. and Sat 10 a.m. to noon. Admission is free; donations are gratefully accepted.

where to eat

O'Maddy's Bar & Grill. 5405 Shore Blvd. South, Gulfport; (727) 323-8643; omaddys.com. Right on the waterfront and across from Williams Pier, O'Maddy's is known for their St. Patty's Day Party. But year-round they serve up food and drink and music and fun. They know their steaks—the "doneness" chart is succinct—and their calamari salad is colorful and amazing, but their signature item is the "Beef on Weck" or "RBK" or thin-sliced roast beef on a Kimmelweck (rye Kaiser) roll. O'Maddy's is open from 8 a.m. to 3 a.m. Mon through Sat and from 11 a.m. to 3 a.m. on Sun. $–$$.

Pia's Trattoria. 3054 Beach Blvd. South, Gulfport; (727) 327-2190; piastrattoria.com. Pasta—including a lasagna of the day—panini, salads, and fresh-baked desserts come out of Pia's kitchen. Dine al fresco in the courtyard or inside. Lunch is served from 11 a.m. to 4 p.m. Tues through Sat and from 2 to 4 p.m. on Sun. Dinner is served from 4 to 9 p.m. Sun through Thurs and from 4 to 10 p.m. on Fri and Sat. Lovely breakfasts are served from 8 a.m. to 11 a.m. on Sat and from 8 a.m. to 2 p.m. on Sun. $–$$.

where to stay

Peninsula Inn & Spa. 2937 Beach Blvd., Gulfport; (727) 346-9800; innspa.net. Sometimes less is way more. Built at the turn of the 20th century, the Peninsula Inn & Spa offers 11 rooms, furnished in British Colonial style and themed after the South Seas tropics, on its second and third floors. The bottom floor features the Seven Springs Spa, 2 restaurants—Six Tables, which has only 6 tables and serves a prix fixe 6-course meal, and Isabelles, featuring classic Southern cuisine—and a bar. Live music nightly. $$–$$$.

day trip 02

life's a beach—part 1:
clearwater beach; indian rocks beach

More than 35 miles—miles!—of white, sandy, mostly public-access beaches can be found along Pinellas County's coastline. Some are part of manicured resort areas, while others are combed only by the wind and the waves. In this section, we'll visit about 13 of those miles of beaches from Clearwater Beach to Redington Beach. In the next section, Day Trip 03, we'll go from Madeira Beach to Egmont Key—the furthest point south. We'll visit the northern 10 miles, off of Dunedin and Tarpon Springs, in Day Trip 04.

Look also for a listing at the end of Part 2 of this chapter, "Life's a Beach," of spots in the mid-Pinellas area that are worth a side trip—or another trip over the causeway.

Today, we'll meander our way from north to south. Clearwater Beach is home to Winter, of *Dolphin Tale* fame. Sand Key has a jewel of a county park and a ton of high-rise condos and resorts. Belleair Beach and Belleair Shores are there, but don't really have any beach access—but the Belleair Causeway is a popular windsurfing area. Also, charter fishing boats, casino boats, and dinner/sightseeing boats set out from several points in these areas.

Other critters—some of them protected species—make these beaches their homes, not just their playgrounds. Please respect marked and unmarked bird and turtle nesting areas. Remember to properly dispose of all fishing line, cigarette butts, and other trash. Plants, also, are protected and may not be removed or damaged. It is illegal to feed wild animals, including birds.

west day trip 02
Jay B. Starkey Wilderness Park
Land O' Lakes
Howard Park
Tarpon Springs
Lake Tarpon
A. L. Anderson Park
Brooker Creek Preserve
Lutz
Citrus Park
Lake Magdalene
Honeymoon Island State Park
Oldsmar
Caladesi Island State Park
Dunedin
Egypt Lake
Safety Harbor
Clearwater Beach
Clearwater
Sand Key Park
Tampa
Old Tampa Bay
Indian Rocks Beach
Largo
Indian Shores
MacDill AFB
Suncoast Seabird Sanctuary
Seminole
Pinellas Park
Redington Shores
Madeira Beach
Sunken Gardens
North Straub Park
Treasure Island
South Pasadena
St. Petersburg
Gulfport
Lake Maggiore
Tampa Bay
Clam Bayou Nature Park
Boyd Hill Nature Preserve
St. Pete Beach
Ruskin
Don CeSar
Tierra Verde
Skyway Fishing Pier State Park (Northern Side)
Sun City
Port Manatee
Fort De Soto County Park
Egmont Key National Wildlife Refuge
Parrish
N
Anna Maria Island
0 4 8 miles
Palmetto

Note: Most public access beaches and parks charge a parking fee. Restrooms at public parks may not be open on weekdays. Please check each website or call ahead for specific information.

clearwater beach

Clearwater Beach bustles with daytime waterfront activity and nighttime music and parties. Sand Key, just to the south, is the site of high-rise hotels and condos—and a marvelous Pinellas County park with great shelling. To get there, you'll take the very scenic Courtney Campbell Causeway across the top of Tampa Bay, then drive through not-so-scenic mid-Pinellas County all the way to the Gulf of Mexico. It's worth it.

Beach Visitor Information Center. 1 Causeway Blvd., Clearwater Beach; (727) 442-3604; visitclearwaterflorida.com. Located near Pier 60, the Beach Visitor Information Center is open from 10 a.m. to 7 p.m. every day except New Year's Day, Easter, Thanksgiving, and Christmas. Hours may adjust seasonally. Another visitor center is located on the main floor of Surf Style (311 S. Gulfview Blvd.). Their hours are noon to 8 p.m.

Clearwater Beach Chamber of Commerce Welcome Center. 333C S. Gulfview Blvd., Clearwater Beach; (888) 799-3199, (727) 447-7600; beachchamber.com. The chamber's website is another good source for places to go, restaurants, hotels, and more.

getting there

From downtown Tampa, take I-275 South about 5 miles toward Memorial Highway/SR 60 West. Stay to the right and take exit 39/SR 60 West toward Tampa Airport/Clearwater. This is also the exit for the Veterans Expressway, which begins at the end of Memorial Highway. The exit is two lanes. Stay on the inner exit lane. The signs are confusing at this point because there are two ways to get to the causeway. The first sign says "SR60 West to 576/Tampa Intn'l Airport/Clearwater." If you take this exit, follow it around through some airport traffic before ending up on SR 60. Or stay on Memorial and follow the other sign that says "Toll 589 North/Veterans Expwy/Independence Pkwy." Continue about another mile to exit 2A toward SR 60 West/Clearwater. Merge onto SR 60 West toward Clearwater.

Pass through the Rocky Point area and travel over the Courtney Campbell Causeway—about 6 miles—toward Clearwater. Enjoy the drive—the Courtney Campbell Causeway is an officially designated Scenic Highway. Once you reach Clearwater, SR 60 becomes Gulf-to-Bay Boulevard. Follow Gulf-to-Bay Boulevard about 12 miles to Clearwater Beach. Travel over the Clearwater Memorial Causeway toward Clearwater Beach. When you reach the roundabout, you want to be in the right-hand lane. Circle around until you see the PIER 60 PARK sign, then exit the roundabout to the parking area. The welcome center is at the approach to the pier.

where to go

Clearwater Beach Marina. 25 Causeway Blvd., Clearwater; (727) 462-6954; myclearwatermarina.com. Marinas aren't just places where boats dock. At Clearwater Beach Marina, dinner cruises and parasailing and dolphin tour boats dock. There are shops and concessions—and people gather in the afternoon to watch the fishing boats unload the day's catch. The marina office is open Mon through Fri from 8:30 a.m. to 4 p.m.; the fuel dock is open from 6:30 a.m. to 6:30 p.m. every day except Christmas Day. Take the fourth exit out of the roundabout to get to the marina.

Winter's Dolphin Tale Adventure and Clearwater Marine Aquarium. 300 Cleveland St., Clearwater (WDTA); 249 Windward Passage, Clearwater (CMA); (727) 441-1790; seewinter.com. *Dolphin Tale*, a 2011 movie, tells about Winter, a three-month-old dolphin rescued from a crab trap and taken to the Clearwater Marine Aquarium where, against very long odds, she survived with the help of a prosthetic tail. Best value: Buy a general admission ticket, go to Winter's Dolphin Tale Adventure—see the movie and learn about how it was made, visit a touch tank, and more—then take the Jolly Trolley (included in the admission) across the Clearwater Memorial Causeway to the aquarium. There, you can see Winter and many other critters and learn about the marine rehabilitation work. Other options include eco-tours by kayak or by boat and similar adventures. Winter's Dolphin Tale Adventure and Clearwater Marine Aquarium are open Mon through Thurs from 9 a.m. to 5 p.m., Fri and Sat from 9 a.m. to 7 p.m., and Sun from 10 a.m. to 5 p.m. They are closed Thanksgiving and Christmas Day, and they close early on Christmas Eve and New Year's Eve.

Sand Key Park. 1060 Gulf Blvd., Clearwater; (727) 588-4852; pinellascounty.org/park/15_Sand_Key.htm. Part park, part beach, Sand Key Park, a Pinellas County park, is located just south of Clearwater Beach and just over Clearwater Pass. Walk over one of the 9 boardwalks to the beach part, where there are restroom/shower facilities and concessions (food, kayaks, umbrellas/cabanas); look for seashells here. Sand Key's park side has picnic shelters, a dog park area, and a playground. A salt marsh bird nesting area with viewing benches is also part of the park; underwater there's an artificial reef.

what to do

Captain Memo's Pirate Cruise. Clearwater Beach Marina; (727) 446-2587; captainmemo.com. Join this band of brigands as they search for dolphins aboard a 70-foot vessel. They offer daytime and sunset cruises 7 days a week; hours vary according to the season.

Jolley Trolley. (727) 445-1200; clearwaterjolleytrolley.com. The privately owned Jolley Trolley runs from Clearwater Beach up to Tarpon Springs and connects with the publicly owned Suncoast Beach Trolley. The trolley runs from 10 a.m. to 10 p.m. Sun through Thurs and 10 a.m. to midnight on Fri and Sat.

here fishy, fishy

TampaBayCharter.com *lists charter captains, salt-water boat ramps, tide charts, and boat accessible restaurants in the Tampa Bay area.*

Clearwater Marina in Clearwater Beach and John's Pass Marina in Madeira Beach are two main spots to find charter-fishing adventures. One of the main destinations is a hard-bottomed area about 90 miles northwest of Pinellas County called the Middlegrounds area. Most charter boats—also called party boats—leave around midnight. Anglers sleep in bunks, awake at dawn for a day's fishing, then sleep some more on the way back in.

For the ultimate fishing experience, check out the Fisherman's Paradise, *a 385-foot-long by 85-foot-wide several-story luxury hotel on top of a barge, which is anchored several miles off Clearwater. This floating hotel, which launched late in 2011, features resort-style accommodations including a pool and spa, heliport, restaurant-style dining, and more. You don't actually fish from the barge—so plan on making arrangements for a charter captain to be there, too, and to spend your days fishing instead of motoring out to the fishing grounds. Interested? Call them at (727) 441-3474 or e-mail them at info@fishermansparadise.com. Their website is fishermansparadise.com. $$$.*

Suncoast Beach Trolley. (727) 540-1900; psta.net/beachtrolley.php. The Suncoast Beach Trolley runs from Clearwater Beach to St. Pete Beach. The trolley begins running at 5:05 a.m. every day and runs until 10:10 p.m. Sun through Thurs and until midnight on Fri and Sat.

Sunsets at Pier 60. 10 Pier 60 Dr., Clearwater; (727) 461-7732; sunsetsatpier60.com. Pier 60 Park is a Clearwater park with fishing on the pier, snack bar, restrooms, and a covered playground on the beach area. About 2 hours before sundown, buskers—street performers like steel drum performers and living statues—artists, and other vendors gather. The park has a snack bar and restrooms. Sunsets at Pier 60 runs 365 days a year, weather permitting.

where to eat

Bob Heilman's Beachcomber/Bobby's Bistro and Wine Bar. 447 Mandalay Ave., North Clearwater Beach; (727) 442-4144 (Beachcomber), (727) 446-9463 (Bistro); heilmans beachcomber.com or bobbysbistro.com. Bob Heilman's Beachcomber serves classic entrees like the Back-to-the-Farm Chicken Dinner, sautéed fresh chicken livers, jumbo Gulf shrimp—try these bronzed—and, oh, the steaks! Bobby's Bistro features gourmet pizzas, sandwiches, and salads plus char-grilled steak, lamb chops, salmon, and ribs. Both Bob Heilman's Beachcomber and Bobby's Bistro and Wine Bar are open every day of the year. At the Beachcomber, lunch is served from 11:30 a.m. to 4 p.m., and dinner is served from 4 p.m. until whenever. Bobby's Bistro opens at 5 p.m. each day and also is open until . . . $$–$$$.

Frenchy's Rockaway Grill. 7 Rockaway St.; Clearwater Beach; (727) 446-4844; frenchysonline.com. Step off the beach onto the outdoor patio deck of Frenchy's—or vice versa—and enjoy tropical chicken-and-walnut salad served in a tortilla shell, fajitas, fish tacos, steak, and more. Music and dancing, too. Frenchy's Rockaway Grill opens every day at 11 a.m. They close at midnight Sun through Thurs and at 1 a.m. on Fri and Sat. Look for other Frenchy's restaurants in the Clearwater area. $.

where to stay

Barefoot Bay Resort Motel and Marina. 401 E. Shore Dr., Clearwater Beach; (866) 447-3316, (727) 447-3316; barefootbayresort.com. Located near the Clearwater Marine Aquarium and the marina, Barefoot Bay Resort Motel and Marina has 15 rooms and a small apartment, a pool, grill, and laundry facilities. No pets, but children are okay. There is a minimum 2-night stay. $–$$$.

Shephard's Beach Resort. 619 S. Gulfview Blvd., Clearwater Beach; (800) 237-8477, (727) 442-5107; shephards.com. Play in the sun and howl at the moon at Shephard's Beach Resort. Zip around on jet skis by day and do the Wave nightclub by night. Beach Party Sundays and other special events are on the calendar. Dining options include the Shephard's Waterfront Restaurant with a prime rib and seafood buffet (breakfast and lunch buffets are also offered) and the Margarita Grill. No pets. $$$.

indian rocks beach

Indian Rocks Beach has retained much of its small-town beach feel, partly because there are almost no high-rise buildings on the beach side of Gulf Boulevard. There are many public access points, each with a few parking spots. The largest area, however, is the county-maintained beach access park. Across Gulf Boulevard are small shops, restaurants, and land-side parks.

This section includes information about (north to south) Indian Rocks Beach, Indian Shores, Redington Shores, North Redington Beach, and Redington Beach.

Beach Welcome Center. 105 5th Ave., Indian Rocks Beach; (727) 595-4575; beachwelcomecenter.com. Walk through the porthole—you'll know what we mean when you see the door—and into the Beach Welcome Center. You'll find racks of brochures and coupons and friendly people who can give directions.

getting there

From Tampa, take I-275 South toward St. Petersburg. Travel about 12 miles across the Howard Frankland Bridge, and take exit 31 for SR 688 West/Ulmerton Road toward Martin Luther King, Jr. Street/9th Street North. Merge right onto SR 688 West toward the St. Petersburg–Clearwater Airport. Stay on SR 688 West, which becomes Ulmerton Road, and drive about 13 miles across Pinellas County. Ulmerton Road becomes Walsingham Road before crossing the Intracoastal Waterway. After you cross the bridge, take the first left—2nd Street—and then the first right—4th Avenue. Turn right again at Gulf Boulevard, and turn right into the parking lot of the big building on the corner. The Beach Welcome Center is next door and this is their parking area, too (in the back).

From Clearwater Beach, follow CR 699 south to Indian Rocks Beach (about 8 miles).

where to go

Indian Rocks Beach Access. 1700 Gulf Blvd., Indian Rocks Beach; (727) 582-2100; pinellascounty.org/park/07_IRBA.htm. This county-maintained public parking and beach access point has restrooms and showers.

Redington Long Pier. 17490 Gulf Blvd., Redington Shores; (727) 391-9398; tampabay fishingpier.com. Open at 7 a.m. every day of the year, the Redington Long Pier closes at 11 p.m. Sept through Apr and stays open until midnight (2 a.m. on Sat) May through Aug. This privately owned pier has been a Redington landmark since 1962. The pier has a bait and tackle shop, snack bar, restrooms, and benches.

Redington Shores Beach Access. 18200 Gulf Blvd., Redington Shores; (727) 582-2100; pinellascounty.org/park/13_Redington.htm. The beach is about 400 feet wide here. The parking area holds 170 vehicles, and there are restrooms and showers available. No pets. Credit cards require a minimum purchase.

Suncoast Seabird Sanctuary. 18328 Gulf Blvd., Indian Shores; (727) 391-6211 or (727) 391-2473; seabirdsanctuary.com. The Suncoast Seabird Sanctuary is the largest wild-bird hospital in the United States, treating more than 8,000 injured birds each year—that's an average of 20 or so birds each day. Walk through the exhibit areas any time. On Wed and Sun afternoons at 2 p.m., there's a free, guided tour. Admission to the sanctuary, which is open every day from 9 a.m. to sunset, is free; donations are welcomed. There is a small parking area in front, or walk in from the beach.

Tiki Gardens Beach Access. 19601 Gulf Blvd., Indian Shores; (727) 582-2100; pinellas county.org/park/19_Tiki.htm. This county-maintained public access and parking area has spaces for 170 vehicles, restrooms, showers, and a water fountain. A traffic light makes it easy to cross Gulf Boulevard.

where to eat

Guppy's on the Beach. 1701 Gulf Blvd., Indian Rocks Beach; (727) 593-2032; 3bestchefs.com/guppys/home. Seafood—lobster ravioli, anyone?—is the predominant theme at Guppy's, but they also serve beef, chicken, and pork dishes. Located directly across from the Indian Rocks Beach Access park, Guppy's offers alfresco and inside dining. They are open Sun through Thurs from 11:30 a.m. to 10 p.m. and on Fri and Sat from 11:30 a.m. to 10:30 p.m. $$–$$$.

Sweet Sage Cafe and Gift Shop. 16725 Gulf Blvd., North Redington Beach; (727) 391-0453; sweetsagecafe.com. Start the day out right with a Sweet Sage Scrambler or one of their many eggs Benedict variations. Or stop in for a salad, wrap, or sandwich for lunch. Pets are welcome in the garden area and there's even a Doggie Menu just for them. Sweet Sage Cafe is open every day from 7 a.m. to 2 p.m. $.

where to stay

D&W's Sun N Fun. 20116 Gulf Blvd., Indian Shores; (800) 595-6774, (727) 595-3611; sunfun1925.com. Built in 1925 at the peak of the Pinellas land boom, D&W's Sun N Fun once was a beach getaway for a Tampa merchant. Located on the Narrows—a strip of barrier island wide enough for only one row of houses along Gulf Boulevard—this 6-unit guest home gives guests access to a private beach. Read the rate information carefully, as a cleaning fee is charged separately. No pets, but children are welcomed. $$–$$$.

Laughing Lizard Bed & Breakfast. 2211 Gulf Blvd., Indian Rocks Beach; (727) 595-7006; laughinglizardbandb.com. Sleep in one of four remarkably decorated rooms, breakfast on something scrumptious in Lizard Hall, then walk a mere 400 feet to the beach on the Gulf of Mexico. An elevator makes the stay in this 3-story, Key West–styled beach house a breeze. No pets and no children. $$–$$$.

worth more time

Here are a few other points of interest in mid-Pinellas County north of SR 688/Ulmerton Road and south of SR 580.

Bright House Field. 601 Old Coachman Rd., Clearwater; (727) 467-4457; philadelphia.phillies.mlb.com. The Phillies have been coming to Clearwater for spring training since 1948. Bright House Field, built in 2004, seats more than 7,000 people, has a playground area for the young 'uns, and a 360-degree concourse area open to the field. Walk around and see the game from a different perspective. When the Phillies aren't there, their Florida State League team, the Clearwater Threshers, are.

Pinellas Trail. (727) 549-6099, (727) 582-2100 (Park Ranger); pinellascounty.org/trailgd. Running from Tarpon Springs to St. Petersburg, the Pinellas Trail is one of the country's top urban trails. Built on an old railroad corridor, the trail passes through parks, neighborhoods, a couple of downtown areas, and over waterways. Overpasses minimize having to deal with vehicles. The trail guides available on the website show restroom facilities, places to eat, and points of interest.

Ruth Eckerd Hall. 1111 McMullen Booth Rd., Clearwater; (727) 791-7400; rutheckerd hall.com. Ruth Eckerd Hall brings Broadway shows, top-name concerts, and the Florida Orchestra to its stage. The Marcia P. Hoffman Performing Arts Institute provides instruction and performance opportunities in theater, music, and dance.

Safety Harbor Resort & Spa. 105 N. Bayshore Dr., Safety Harbor; (888) 237-8772, (727) 726-1161; safetyharborspa.com. Located on Tampa Bay at the site of natural mineral springs, the Safety Harbor Resort & Spa is a historical landmark and one of the top spas in the country. In addition to 174 guest rooms and suites and the Four Springs Ballroom, the spa has full treatment and fitness areas, multiple dining options, and a tennis academy. Sunday brunch at the spa draws area residents as well as spa guests. $$$.

day trip 03

life's a beach—part 2:
madeira beach; st. pete beach

Today we take in the lower half of the Pinellas County barrier island beaches, starting with Madeira Beach and ending with Egmont Key, an island in the mouth of Tampa Bay.

So what will we see? Well, John's Pass Village on Madeira Beach is a major shopping fun spot. St. Pete Beach is home of the Don CeSar. Fort De Soto has been named America's Best Beach by Dr. Beach; and we know locals who stay in the campground down there and commute to work when spring fever is at its peak.

As before, please keep a respectful distance from wildlife and keep their homes clean. The Suncoast Beach Trolley runs in this area, too—information about it is in the previous chapter.

At the end of this chapter, we will list a few spots in mid-Pinellas County south of Ulmerton Road that are worth considering for a return trip or for a side trip.

Enjoy!

madeira beach

The northern part of Madeira Beach is small-town beachy with a Smuggler's Cove mini-golf that is anything but mini. Go a little farther south and John's Pass Village, with its shops, restaurants, and marina, makes things a little livelier. Kind of nice to have it both ways. This section includes Madeira Beach and Treasure Island, the next town south and home to one of Florida's oldest and longest-running surf shops.

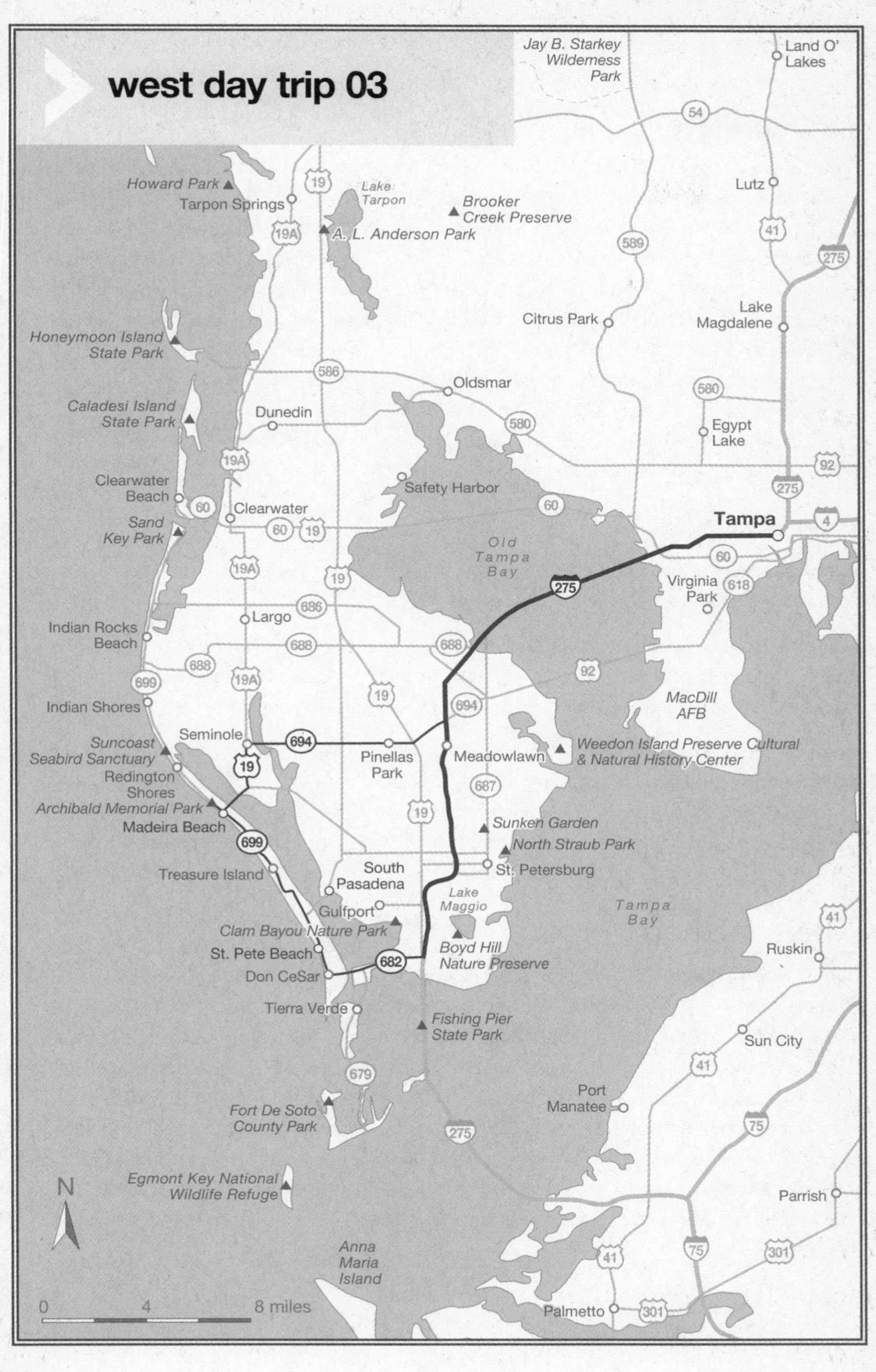
west day trip 03
Jay B. Starkey Wilderness Park
Land O' Lakes
Howard Park
Tarpon Springs
Lake Tarpon
A. L. Anderson Park
Brooker Creek Preserve
Lutz
Citrus Park
Lake Magdalene
Honeymoon Island State Park
Oldsmar
Caladesi Island State Park
Dunedin
Egypt Lake
Clearwater Beach
Safety Harbor
Clearwater
Sand Key Park
Tampa
Old Tampa Bay
Virginia Park
Largo
Indian Rocks Beach
Indian Shores
MacDill AFB
Seminole
Suncoast Seabird Sanctuary
Pinellas Park
Meadowlawn
Weedon Island Preserve Cultural & Natural History Center
Redington Shores
Archibald Memorial Park
Madeira Beach
Sunken Garden
North Straub Park
Treasure Island
South Pasadena
St. Petersburg
Lake Maggio
Tampa Bay
Gulfport
Clam Bayou Nature Park
Boyd Hill Nature Preserve
St. Pete Beach
Ruskin
Don CeSar
Tierra Verde
Fishing Pier State Park
Sun City
Port Manatee
Fort De Soto County Park
Egmont Key National Wildlife Refuge
Parrish
N
Anna Maria Island
0
4
8 miles
Palmetto

getting there

From Tampa, take I-275 South toward St. Petersburg. Travel over the Howard Frankland Bridge and continue south on I-275 South about 20 miles to exit 28. The first sign says exit 28 takes you to Seminole and Indian Shores, which it does, but first you have to pass through Pinellas Park, which is what the next sign says: EXIT 28/SR 694/PINELLAS PARK/GANDY BOULEVARD. Take exit 28 and merge onto Gandy Boulevard, heading west. Within a few miles, Gandy Boulevard becomes Park Boulevard. Continue west about 3.5 miles to Seminole Boulevard. Turn left onto Seminole Boulevard and travel south about 1.5 miles—stay in the left lane, as you will exit left to go right (!) under an overpass to SR 666 West/Tom Stuart Causeway, aka 150th Avenue. Merge onto the Tom Stuart Causeway, go over the bridges, and turn right at Gulf Boulevard. Half a block down on your left is Archibald Memorial Park, Madeira Beach's Gulf hangout since 1934.

where to go

Archibald Memorial Park. 15102 Gulf Blvd., Madeira Beach. This city-maintained beach area has parking, restrooms, and concessions.

Madeira Beach Access. 14400 Gulf Blvd., Madeira Beach; (727) 582-2100; pinellas county.org/park/09_Madeira.htm. This county-maintained beach access has restrooms, showers, and parking for 104 vehicles. The beach is broad and beautiful.

Smuggler's Cove Adventure Golf. 15395 Gulf Blvd., Madeira Beach; (727) 398-7008; smugglersgolf.com/stpetersburg-tampa.aspx. Eighteen holes of mini golf played with live 'gators as part of the mix? Can't get much more beach-kitschy than that. Smuggler's Cove has been rated "Florida's Best Mini Golf" more than once. Open every day of the year from 9 a.m. to 11 p.m. (shortened hours on Christmas Eve, Christmas Day, and New Year's Eve).

where to shop

John's Pass Village. 150 John's Pass Boardwalk West, Madeira Beach; (727) 394-0756; johnspass.com. Shop for beach-wear, shop for souvenirs, or shop for a parasailing adventure or dinner cruise. John's Pass Village has gathered more than 100 shops—Florida Winery, Treehouse Puppets & Treasures, Surf Style, and Spice & Tea Exchange are just a few—restaurants, and other merchants in its turn-of-the-century fishing village. Or just hang out on the boardwalk and watch the charter boat traffic come and go from Hubbard's Marina (800-755-0677; hubbardsmarina.com). Tip: Walk underneath the drawbridge—it's the normal route to get to the beach without crossing Gulf Boulevard—and watch the mechanism that raises and lowers the drawbridge. Check the website for events and special offers.

Suncoast Surf Shop. 9841 Gulf Blvd., Treasure Island; (727) 367-2483; suncoastsurf shop.com. Joe Nuzzo's been selling surfboards and related gear at this spot since 1966, making it one of Florida's oldest and longest running surf shops. Now the Suncoast Surf Shop also sells skateboards, standup paddle boards, skimboards, and more. Plus they rent equipment and give lessons, too. Check the website for the Surfline forecast or call (727) 363-7873. They're open every day from 10 a.m. to 7 p.m. On Saturday, they open half an hour earlier.

where to eat

Lisa's Cafe. 13331 Gulf Blvd., Madeira Beach; (727) 394-2833. Good things come in small packages—and that's the case with Lisa's Cafe. Not a big place, but the decor is thoughtful and the food is not just ordinary—espresso-crusted filet mignon? Eggs Benedict? Oh, yes. Lisa's is open 8 a.m. to 9 p.m. every day. $$–$$$.

Middle Grounds Grill. 10925 Gulf Blvd., Treasure Island; (727) 360-4253; middlegrounds grill.com. Looking for a place a bit dressier than a "walk-off-the beach in your flip-flops" burger joint? Middle Grounds Grill offers a selection of seafood and steak entrees—pasta, chicken, and vegetarian, too—and the wines to go with them. Live music most nights. Middle Grounds Grill opens every day at 4:30 p.m. They close at 10 p.m. Sun through Thurs and at 11 p.m. on Fri and Sat. $$.

where to stay

Barefoot Beach Hotel. 13238 Gulf Blvd., Madeira Beach; (800) 853-1536, (727) 393-6133; barefootbeachhotel.com. The beachside Barefoot Beach Hotel, just north of John's Pass Village, offers 1- and 2-bedroom suite units with kitchen areas. There is a heated pool and free Internet access. Rent a scooter on-site and explore the beach cities. Or the hotel will arrange for limo service. No pets. Parking is free. $$$.

Bilmar Beach Resort. 10650 Gulf Blvd., Treasure Island; (877) 834-0441, (727) 360-5531; bilmarbeachresort.com. Play in the pools or play in the waves at the Bilmar Beach Resort. They also have a mile-long beachside fitness trail and a fitness center in addition to roomy guest suites and studios. On-site dining options include Sloppy Joe's On the Beach (sloppy joesonthebeach.com) and Bazzie's Beach Bar. No pets. Parking is free. $$$.

st. pete beach

To the point—that's St. Pete Beach. They even shortened their name, back in the 1990s, from the cumbersome "St. Petersburg Beach" to the concise "St. Pete Beach." And the point? What part of "beach" did you miss?!

However, if you'd rather bargain-comb than beach-comb, the Corey Avenue Historical District has shops and galleries and restaurants within walking distance of each other. At one end is the Beach Theater, which shows nightly movies.

This section of beach also includes the towns of South Pasadena, Pass-a-Grille, and Tierra Verde, plus Fort De Soto (County) Park and Egmont Key State Park.

Tampa Bay Beaches Chamber of Commerce. 6990 Gulf Blvd., St. Pete Beach; 727-360-6957; tampabaybeaches.com. Go online and view a visitor's guide—or order a hard copy to be mailed to you. Or stop in Mon through Fri from 9 a.m. to 5 p.m. and talk to a real live person.

getting there

From Tampa, take I-275 South toward St. Petersburg. Travel over the Howard Frankland Bridge and continue south on I-275 South about 26 miles to exit 17 toward the Pinellas Bayway (54th Avenue South) and St. Pete Beach. Follow 54th Avenue southwest about 4 miles and across a couple of causeways to Gulf Boulevard. The Don CeSar will be straight head of you as you cross to St. Pete Beach. Turn right on Gulf Boulevard and travel north about 2 miles to the Tampa Bay Beaches Chamber of Commerce office.

From Madeira Beach follow Gulf Boulevard (SR 699) south about 7 miles.

where to go

Beach Theater. 315 Corey Ave., St. Pete Beach; (727) 360-6697; beachtheatre.com. Rocky Horror Picture Show fans, each Saturday night at 11:30 p.m. or so, a live cast, Interchangeable Parts, presents this R-rated and adult-oriented cult favorite. Audience participation is expected. Other shows include first-run movies in the evening. The theater is a holdover from the pre-stadium theater days, so enjoy it for the anachronism it is.

Egmont Key State Park. 4905 34th St. South, #5000, St. Petersburg; (727) 893-2627; floridastateparks.org/egmontkey; Citizen Support Organization: Egmont Key Alliance (egmontkey.org). Egmont Key is the first island ships reach as they approach Tampa Bay from the Gulf of Mexico. The Tampa Bay Pilots Association's base of operations has been on Egmont Key since 1926. There are hiking trails, swimming and fishing spots, and historical ruins to explore on Egmont Key. Access is by private boat or ferry only. Ferry service is currently provided by Tampa Bay Ferry (727-398-6577; hubbardsmarina.com/um/egmont.html), which also rents snorkeling and other equipment. Flip flops are not allowed on the ferry and the sand on Egmont Key can be very hot; thick-soled shoes are a must. All visitors must be off the island by sunset or the park ranger will arrange for a water taxi, at your expense. No pets.

Fort De Soto Park. 3500 Pinellas Bayway South, Tierra Verde; (727) 582-2267; pinellascounty.org/park/05_Ft_DeSoto.htm. Fort De Soto Park, Pinellas County's largest park, consists of more than 1,100 acres on five islands. The park has overnight camping, a historic

boat ramps in pinellas county

For a list of public boat ramps (both fresh- and salt-water access) at nine Pinellas County parks, go to pinellascounty.org/park/parkingfees.htm and scroll to the bottom of the page.

The City of Clearwater's Marine and Aviation web page gives detailed information about the Clearwater Municipal Marina and the Seminole Boat Ramp at the marina (clearwater-fl.com/gov/depts/marine_aviation/index.asp).

The City of St. Petersburg's web page on fishing has information about places to fish, regulations, fishing piers, and boat ramps (stpete.org/parks/fishing.asp).

fort and museum, 3 miles of white sand beach, a boat launch, a canoe and kayak trail, hiking trails, and concession areas. Fish two bodies of water in the same day—one of the park's two fishing piers, each with food and bait concessions, is on Tampa Bay, the other is on the Gulf of Mexico. Tip: As you reach the main ranger office—by the huge flagpole—turn left and follow the road to the end for a really great view of the Sunshine Skyway Bridge.

St. Pete Beach Access. 4700 Gulf Blvd., St. Pete Beach; (727) 582-2100; pinellascounty .org/park/17_StPete.htm. With 235 parking spaces, restrooms, showers, and a water fountain, this county-maintained access area is one of the largest on the barrier islands. Boardwalks carry foot traffic from the parking area over the sand dunes and sea oats and to the sand, sun, and surf.

what to do

Dolphin Landings Charter Boat Center. 4737 Gulf Blvd., St. Pete Beach; (727) 360-7411; dolphinlandings.com. Want to sail away from it all? Check out Dolphin Landings Charter Boat Center for sailing adventures, fishing trips, and other water trips.

Remi's Segway Tours. 4685 Gulf Blvd., St. Pete Beach; (727) 637-2211; stpetebeach segway.com. Aw, c'mon. You know you've wanted to try these things ever since they came out. What better place to ride?

where to shop

Corey Avenue Historical District. coreyave.com. Build a business district in the middle of a mangrove swamp at the height of the Depression? Why not! If you build it . . . In any case, Corey Avenue has been a beach business and shopping center since 1937. Today, accounting offices and grocery stores mingle with art galleries and studios, boutique shops, and salons. Check the calendar for art festivals, open-air markets, and other events.

where to eat

Spinners Rooftop Revolving Bistro. 5250 Gulf Blvd., St. Pete Beach; (800) 448-0901, (727) 360-1811; grandplazaflorida.com/spinners-restaurant.html. Located on top of the Grand Plaza Resort Hotel, Spinners Rooftop Revolving Bistro offers stationary tables or ones that offer an ever-changing view of lower Pinellas County and the Gulf of Mexico. Steaks—Spinners' signature entree is the Brandy Peppercorn Steak, flamed in brandy—and seafood and an extensive wine and specialty drink selection fill the menu. Lunch is served every day from 11 a.m. to 4 p.m.; dinner is served from 4 to 11 p.m. $$$.

Verducci's Pizzeria Trattoria. 7736 Blind Pass Rd., St. Pete Beach; (727) 363-7900. Verducci's serves more than just pizza—Gnocchi Sorrentina is a meatless dish on the must-try list—but the pizzas are famous. They open every day at 4 p.m. Sun through Thurs, they close at 10 p.m.; Fri and Sat they stay open until 11 p.m. Lunch is served part of the year—call ahead. $$.

where to stay

There is a trio of decorative small hotels on Gulf Boulevard that share facilities. ***Note:*** Pets are okay at the Bayview and Bay Palms, but not at the Plaza Beach. Children are welcome at all three locations.

Plaza Beach Hotel. 4506 Gulf Blvd., St. Pete Beach; (727) 367-2791; plazabeach.com. The 39-unit Plaza Beach Hotel is on the beach. $$–$$$.

Bay Palms Resort. 4237 Gulf Blvd., St. Pete Beach; (727) 360-7642; baypalmsresort.com.; Across the street from Plaza Beach Hotel, the 15-room Bay Palms Resort boasts one of the area's largest privately-owned fishing docks. $$–$$$.

Bayview Plaza Waterfront Resort. 4321 Gulf Blvd., St. Pete Beach; (727) 367-2791; thebayviewplaza.com. Next door to the Bay Palms Resort, the 7-room Bayview Plaza Waterfront Resort also has a small fishing pier, plus a fitness room and heated pool. Free wireless Internet, too. $$–$$$.

The Don CeSar, A Loews Hotel. 3400 Gulf Blvd., St. Pete Beach; (800) 282-1116, (727) 360-1881; loewshotels.com/Don-CeSar-Hotel. Built in the 1920s and known as either the "Pink Palace," the "Pink Lady," or just "The Don," the Don CeSar is an icon on St. Pete Beach. Currently part of the Loews Hotel family, the Don features boutique shops on the Garden Level and the on-site Spa Oceana. Camp Cesar provides activities for children, and pets can be pampered with food dishes and pet beds. The Don's 277 rooms and suites are furnished with luscious linens, and dining choices range from the Sea Porch Restaurant to the Chef's Table at the Maritana Grille. Uncle Andy's is a favorite spot for ice cream—even for non-guests! $$$.

worth more time

Florida Botanical Gardens. 12520 Ulmerton Rd., Largo; (727) 582-2100; flbg.org. Part of Pinellas County's Pinewood Cultural Center, the Florida Botanical Gardens has 30 acres of cultivated gardens (herbs, tropical fruits, rose, etc.) and 90 acres of wetland and wooded areas, home to lots of wildlife. Experts at the Pinellas County Extension building, a partnership with the University of Florida, can answer gardening questions. The gardens are open every day from 7 a.m. to 6 p.m. The welcome center and gift shop are open Mon through Fri from 8 a.m. to 5 p.m. Designated picnic areas provide a quiet place for lunch. No alcohol; no bicycles, skateboards, or roller skates. Pets on leashes are permitted, but are not permitted in the natural wooded area. Please respect the quiet of the area. Admission is free.

Heritage Village. 11909 125th St. North, Largo; (727) 582-2123; pinellascounty.org/heritage. A Pinellas County living history museum, Heritage Village sits next to the Florida Botanical Gardens. Almost 30 historic buildings, once part of communities around the county, have been moved to Heritage Village. Take a self-guided tour or join a docent-led tour. During festivals, visitors can see blacksmithing, cane syrup boiling, and other demonstrations. Admission is free, but donations are gratefully accepted. Heritage Village is open Tues through Sat from 10 a.m. to 4 p.m. and on Sun from 1 to 4 p.m. The village is closed Thanksgiving and Christmas Day. Parking just inside the gate is somewhat limited, but you can also park just outside the gate along the fence. Picnic tables are available for brown-bag lunches, and vending machines dispense sodas and snacks.

Raymond James Financial Center Art Collection. 880 Carillon Pkwy., St. Petersburg; (727) 567-5896; raymondjames.com/art/virtual_tour.htm. Turn off SR 688 just over the Howard Frankland Bridge from Tampa and into Carillon Parkway toward the Raymond James Financial Center, and you'll be greeted by a full-size bronze Native American on horseback. Pull into the small parking area and explore the extensive sculpture garden in front of the building. Want to see the extensive art collection inside? Call to request a tour, but remember that this is a private collection at a place of business.

Weedon Island Preserve Cultural and Natural History Center. 1800 Weedon Dr. Northeast, St. Petersburg; (727) 453-6500; weedonislandpreserve.org. Explore Weedon Island Preserve's 3,700 acres on foot or in a canoe or kayak. There are 2 miles of boardwalk and paved trails with observation platforms and tower plus almost 3 miles of unpaved trails. Two well-marked canoe and kayak trails wind in and out of the mangroves surrounding Weedon Island. Canoes and kayaks can be rented on weekends and holidays, or call in advance for weekday rentals. The Cultural and Natural History Center has exhibits, an art gallery, and a gift shop. Weedon Island Preserve is open 7 a.m. to sunset every day. The center is open Wed through Sun from 10 a.m. to 4 p.m. and is closed on holidays.

day trip 04

bagpipes & baklava:
dunedin; tarpon springs

The Scottish Highlands beckon, and we can be there in about an hour's time. Not only that, in the afternoon we can visit Greece—or at least one of the largest Greek communities outside of Greece itself. These two north Pinellas cities, Dunedin and Tarpon Springs, reflect the diverse peoples who have shaped this country. Both have preserved parts of their other-world cultures, and both welcome visitors who want to learn more.

Dunedin, so named by a pair of Scottish merchants in 1882, once was cotton fields, citrus groves, and a major Florida seaport. Today, the town has a number of working artists, galleries, and studios, and the marina provides services to boaters. Across St. Joseph Sound in the Intracoastal Waterway lie two state parks with award-winning beaches and paddling trails.

Tarpon Springs, Pinellas County's northernmost city, grew when natural sponge beds were discovered in the early 1900s. Divers came from Greece to harvest the sponges, and brought their families and their way of life with them. Another state park lies off the coast of Tarpon Springs.

We hear bagpipes skirling and honey-drenched baklava calling our names. . . .

dunedin

Given its name and Scottish heritage, it shouldn't come as too much of a surprise that, from 1956 to 1965, the Professional Golfers' Association of America's national offices were

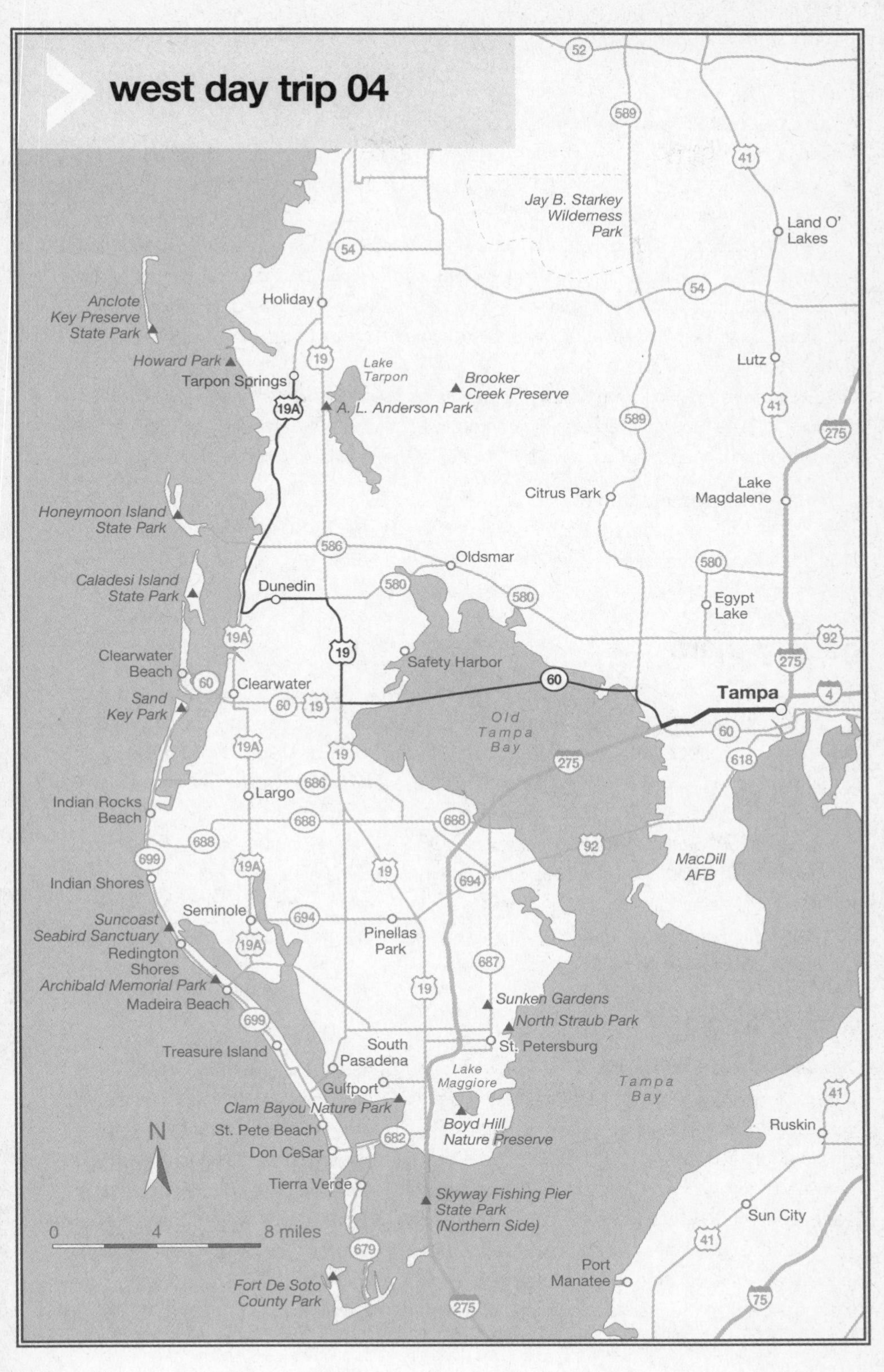
west day trip 04
Jay B. Starkey Wilderness Park
Land O' Lakes
Anclote Key Preserve State Park
Holiday
Howard Park
Tarpon Springs
Lake Tarpon
Brooker Creek Preserve
A. L. Anderson Park
Lutz
Honeymoon Island State Park
Citrus Park
Lake Magdalene
Oldsmar
Caladesi Island State Park
Dunedin
Egypt Lake
Safety Harbor
Clearwater Beach
Clearwater
Sand Key Park
Tampa
Old Tampa Bay
Indian Rocks Beach
Largo
MacDill AFB
Indian Shores
Suncoast Seabird Sanctuary
Seminole
Pinellas Park
Redington Shores
Archibald Memorial Park
Madeira Beach
Sunken Gardens
North Straub Park
Treasure Island
South Pasadena
St. Petersburg
Lake Maggiore
Tampa Bay
Gulfport
Clam Bayou Nature Park
Boyd Hill Nature Preserve
St. Pete Beach
Ruskin
Don CeSar
Tierra Verde
Skyway Fishing Pier State Park (Northern Side)
Sun City
N
0
4
8 miles
Port Manatee
Fort De Soto County Park

in Dunedin. Go back a ways further and we find that the PGA of America leased the city's Donald Ross–designed course in 1944, and in 1945 the course was considered the PGA headquarters. Today, the city-owned Dunedin Golf Club still hosts major tournaments, but it is open for public play, too.

And the bagpipes? The Dunedin Highland Middle School Band and the Dunedin High School Scottish Highlander Band includes pipes and drums—and other instruments—and the City of Dunedin Pipe Band has two competitive units. The Dunedin Highland Games and Festival each April holds a full military tattoo where pipe groups from all over assemble and perform.

Dunedin today, however, is equally known for its downtown art galleries, shops, and restaurants. The Pinellas Trail runs right through town and the marina is just a block or so away, so visitors are as apt to arrive by bicycle, in-line skates, or boat as they are by car.

Dunedin Chamber of Commerce. 301 Main St., Dunedin; (727) 733-3197; dunedin-fl.com. You can't miss the big brick building on the corner of Main Street and Broadway. Stop in for local information. Hours are Mon through Fri from 8:30 a.m. to 4:30 p.m. From Jan through Apr, they also are open on Sat from 10 a.m. to 2 p.m.

getting there

Please read Day Trip 02 in this section for a detailed explanation of getting from I-275 South in Tampa to SR 60 West to the Courtney Campbell Causeway. Once you have crossed the Courtney Campbell Causeway, you are on Gulf-to-Bay Boulevard. Stay in the right lane, and merge right onto CR 611/McMullen Booth Road. Travel north on CR 611/McMullen Booth Road about 4 miles to SR 580/Curlew Road. Turn left onto SR 580/Curlew Road, and travel west about 5 miles. (***Note:*** As you pass US 19, Curlew Road becomes Main Street in Dunedin.) When you reach Broadway Street/US 19A (Alternate 19), turn left. Follow Broadway south not quite 0.5 mile to Main Street. Turn left onto Main Street and the Chamber of Commerce is on your right. Parking is half a block down to the right, next to the train depot that is the Dunedin Historical Society Museum.

where to go

Caladesi Island State Park. #1 Causeway Blvd., Dunedin; (727) 469-5918; floridastateparks.org/caladesiisland. Named America's Number One Beach for 2008, Caladesi Island's western side, accessible by kayak or small boat, features miles of white sand beaches and an unobstructed view of the Gulf of Mexico. The picnic area at Caladesi Island State Park is accessible only by boat or by ferry service (727-734-1501) from Honeymoon Island State Park. The ferry drops visitors off for a 4-hour stay at the marina, where there is a cafe (romantichoneymoonisland.com), restroom facilities, beach access, and nature trails. No pets are allowed on the ferry, but pets are allowed on parts of the island. Overnight on-board camping at the marina is available online at reserveamerica.com.

Dunedin Causeway. This 2.5-mile road leading from Dunedin to Honeymoon Island State Park is a popular windsurfing spot and canoe launch. Public beaches line both sides, and free parking is allowed on the sand close to the road. To sail or paddle over to Caladesi Island, pull off and park on the south side near where the windsurfing rentals set up their wares. Paddle out to the channel, check both ways for boat traffic, then paddle briskly across the channel. Paddle to the sandy beach on the north end, skim over sea-grass flats on the northeast side, or follow the island's east side about a mile south (along the edge of the mangroves) and look for the channel markers leading into the marina. The marina is nestled quite a ways into the interior of the island and is not visible from the causeway.

Dunedin Fine Art Center. 1143 Michigan Blvd., Dunedin; (727) 298-3322; dfac.org. Galleries, classes, and a hands-on children's art museum—the Dunedin Fine Art Center's past exhibits have ranged from the Miniature Art Society of Florida's Annual Competition (almost 1,000 works by artists from around the world) to the National Quilt Museum's biannual art-quilt competition. Gallery hours at the Dunedin Fine Art Center are Mon through Fri from 10 a.m. to 5 p.m., Sat from 10 a.m. to 2 p.m., and Sun from 1 to 4 p.m. A gift shop and a cafe are on the premises.

Dunedin Historical Society & Museum. 349 Main St., Dunedin; (727) 736-1176; dunedin museum.org. Located in the old train depot, the Dunedin Historical Society offers guided tours of Dunedin, living history programs, and museum exhibits in the station. They are open Tues through Sat from 10 a.m. to 4 p.m.

Honeymoon Island State Park. #1 Causeway Blvd., Dunedin; (727) 469-5942; florida stateparks.org/honeymoonisland. Located just across Hurricane Pass from Caladesi Island, Honeymoon Island State Park is more rugged, particularly on the north end, where the waves often get to surfing size. Honeymoon Island State Park has miles of nature trails, swimming and snorkeling areas, a pet beach, and a cafe/concession area. Kayaks and beach supplies can be rented at the concession stand. Rangers conduct occasional guided tours. No overnight camping.

what to do

Dunedin Golf Club. 1050 Palm Blvd., Dunedin; (727) 733-7836; dunedingolfclub.com. Designed in the 1920s by Scotsman Donald Ross, who played Scottish courses and learned his craft there, the Dunedin Golf Club's course is one of the few Ross-designed courses that has retained its original design. Most golfing greats have played here; since 2010, it has hosted the USGA Senior Open Qualifier. It's a city-owned course, open to the public.

where to shop

Celtic Shop of Dunedin. 354 Main St., Dunedin; (727) 733-2200; celticshopdunedin.com. Need to rent a kilt? You've come to the right place—plus you'll find jewelry, food, decorative ware, and more. Celtic Shop of Dunedin is open Mon through Sat from 10 a.m. to 5 p.m. and on Sun from noon to 4 p.m.

Main Street & Broadway. delightfuldunedin.com. Many boutique shops, art galleries, and specialty stores line both Main Street and Broadway and are clustered along neighboring side streets. Pioneer Park, a small green space in the middle of town, is sometimes the site for movies in the park and other events that bring out artists and vendors of various sorts.

where to eat

Cafe Alfresco. 344 Main St., Dunedin; (727) 736-4299; cafealfrescoonline.com. Located on the corner of Main Street and the Pinellas Trail, Cafe Alfresco's sister restaurant, Bon Appétit, is just down the road (150 Marina Plaza, 727-733-2151, $$$). There is no indoor waiting area—when it's busy, people mill around on the sidewalk until a table opens. Menu selections vary from capellini pomodoro to an Asian-influenced sesame salmon. They are open every day from 11:30 a.m. to 9 p.m. $$.

Eli's BBQ. 360 Skinner Blvd., Dunedin; (727) 738-4856. Follow the smoky scent of barbecue north on the Pinellas Trail a couple of blocks to Eli's. Join the line outside the little white building just for pulled pork, sausage, chicken, and ribs. Get your meal—meat, white bread, beans, and slaw—to go, or find a spot at one of the picnic tables under the trees. No dress code, no reservations, no dine-in eating. Cash only, cold canned sodas (no cups, no ice). Eli's is open Fri and Sat from 11 a.m. to 6 p.m. or whenever they sell out. $.

Flanagan's Irish Pub. 465 Main St., Dunedin; (727) 736-4994; flanagansirishpub.net. Irish beer, Irish music, Irish food on the menu. The "Auld Country Traditions" section includes shepherd's pie, bangers and mash, a fisherman's platter, and more. Flanagan's is open every day, usually from 11:30 a.m. until whenever, but check their calendar for hours—they celebrate a lot of festivals and events! $$.

where to stay

The Blue Moon Inn. 2920 Alternate US 19 North, Dunedin; (800) 345-7504, (727) 784-3719; thebluemooninn.com. The amenities of a hotel—heated swimming pool, playground, volleyball, etc.—and the privacy of a B&B. Each of the 9 rooms is on the ground floor, has a mini-kitchen area, and has a private patio that looks out over a shady, grassy area. A Continental breakfast spread is available from 6:30 to 10 a.m. in the common kitchen/dining room. The Blue Moon Inn shares the clubhouse, pool, and other facilities with the Dunedin

RV Resort. Pets are not allowed in the inn. The inn is right off the Pinellas Trail and very near the causeway to Honeymoon Island State Park. $$–$$$.

tarpon springs

Tarpon Springs sits in the northernmost part of Pinellas County where the Anclote River empties into the Gulf of Mexico. Wealthy northerners built winter homes here in the 1870s. Seeing an abundance of tarpon coming into the river to spawn, they named the area Tarpon Springs. By 1887, Tarpon Springs had grown so much it became the first incorporated town on the Pinellas Peninsula. In 1905, sponge divers from Greece came to harvest the sponge beds using techniques not known in this part of the world. For decades, Tarpon Springs was the country's leading supplier of natural sponges.

Today, the influence of Greek culture permeates Pinellas County. Many restaurants serve Greek food; Greek is taught in two of the county's charter schools.

Visitors today go to the Sponge Docks to see the boats and shop. Dolphin cruises leave from the docks, as does the ferry to Anclote Island State Park. But the downtown area has treasures, too. Stop in and see St. Nicholas Orthodox Church, and there's a nice museum full of cars waiting to be drooled over and lots of shops and galleries to be explored.

Tarpon Springs Chamber of Commerce. 111 E. Tarpon Ave., Tarpon Springs; (727) 937-6109; tarponspringschamber.com. Open Mon through Fri from 9 a.m. to 5 p.m., the chamber's offices are located in Artists' Faire Art Gallery & Gifts (see listing below). In addition to being open during the week, the gallery is open from 10:30 a.m. to 5 p.m. on Sat and Sun. Visitors can pick up information 7 days a week.

Tarpon Springs Visitor Center. 100 Dodecanese Blvd. (Sponge Docks); (727) 937-8028. Explore the Sponge Docks (see listing below), but also stop in at the Visitor Center for information on sights to see in other parts of Tarpon Springs. The Visitor Center is open Fri through Sun from 10:30 a.m. to 3:30 p.m.

getting there

From Dunedin, travel north about 10 miles on Broadway/US 19A. Broadway goes through several name changes as it passes through Palm Harbor and other communities. In Tarpon Springs, the name of the road is S. Pinellas Avenue/US 19A. When you reach E. Tarpon Avenue/SR 582 in downtown Tarpon Springs, turn right. The Tarpon Springs Area Historical Society Welcome Center and Museum is about a block down and on the right. There are three visitor centers in town—see above for information about the other two.

where to go

Jolley Trolley. (727) 445-1200; clearwaterjolleytrolley.com. The privately owned Jolley Trolley runs from Clearwater Beach up to Tarpon Springs and connects with the publicly owned bus system. The trolley runs from 10 a.m. to 10 p.m. Sun through Thurs and 10 a.m. to midnight on Fri and Sat.

St. Nicholas Greek Orthodox Cathedral. 36 N. Pinellas Ave., Tarpon Springs; (727) 937-3540; epiphanycity.org. Built in 1942, the Byzantine Revival–style St. Nicholas Greek Orthodox Cathedral is considered one of the most beautiful Orthodox churches in the world. Each Jan 6, the cathedral and nearby Spring Bayou are home to the largest Epiphany celebration in the United States (see Festivals & Celebrations). The church is open to visitors Mon through Sat from 10 a.m. to 4 p.m., and guests are welcome at Sunday services, too.

Sponge Docks. From the downtown area, drive on up North Pinellas Avenue to Dodecanese Boulevard and take a left. Park in one of the (paid) lots at the east end of the docks. The docks lie in the mouth of the Anclote River where it empties into the Gulf of Mexico. Walk the docks or take a dolphin-watching or sponge-diving cruise. There are many small shops and places to eat—be sure to explore some of the side streets.

Tarpon Springs Area Historical Society Welcome Center and Museum. 160 E. Tarpon Ave., Tarpon Springs; (727) 943-4624; tarponspringsareahistoricalsociety.org. Located in the old train depot, the Welcome Center is part visitor information spot, part museum, and part gift shop. They are open Wed from noon to 3 p.m. and Thurs through Sat from noon to 4 p.m.

Unitarian Universalist Church of Tarpon Springs. 230 Grand Blvd., Tarpon Springs; (727) 937-4682; uutarpon.org. American landscape artists George Innes Sr. and George Innes Jr. were winter residents of Tarpon Springs. The Unitarian Universalist Church of Tarpon Springs has the largest collection in the United States of George Innes Jr.'s work. A docent welcomes visitors on Tues from 10 a.m. to 2 p.m. or by appointment.

dodeca . . . what?

Question: *Mathematicians and musicians might figure this one out. How did the Dodecanese Islands in Greece—for which the street along which the Tarpon Springs Sponge Docks lie is named—get their name?*

Answer: *There are 12 islands. A dodecahedron has 12 sides. The dodecaphonic scale has 12 tones. Dodecanese Islands simply means Twelve Islands.*

what to do

Anclote Key Preserve State Park. (727) 469-5942; floridastateparks.org/anclotekey/default.cfm. Anclote Key Preserve State Park—four islands, lying 3 miles off the coast of Tarpon Springs—is accessible only by private boat or by ferry from the Tarpon Springs Sponge Docks (Sun Line Cruises at 727-944-4468 or Sponge-O-Rama at 727-943-2164). Anclote Key, the largest of the four islands, has restroom and picnicking facilities, a historic lighthouse, and a primitive camping area. Overnight campers must arrive by private boat and must call the ranger station in advance. Guided kayak eco-tours are available through Art's Aquatic Adventures (727-686-5968). Pets on leashes are allowed *only* on North Anclote Bar and South Anclote Bar. Bring plenty of water—there is no fresh water on the islands—and some kind of shade. Take all trash out with you—the garbage trucks don't make runs out this far.

Brooker Creek Preserve and Environmental Education Center. 3940 Keystone Rd., Tarpon Springs; (727) 453-6800; brookercreekpreserve.org. Brooker Creek Preserve's 8,000 acres hold miles of equestrian trails and hiking trails. The Environmental Education Center features interactive exhibits, a resource center, some guided hikes, and a gift shop. Overnight parking is not allowed—finish hiking at least an hour before sundown. The preserve is open from 7 a.m. to 1 hour before sunset each day. The center is open Thurs through Sat from 9 a.m. to 4 p.m. Admission is free.

Fred Howard Park. 1700 Sunset Dr., Tarpon Springs; (727) 582-2100; pinellascounty.org/park/06_howard.htm. Part of the park is on the mainland, including picnic shelters and a canoe and kayak launch leading to a loop through the mangroves and to nearby Lake Avoca. A mile-long causeway, along which wave runners launch, leads to an island beach area.

Lake Tarpon. clubkayak.com/cfkt/trips/lake_tarpon.html. One of Florida's top bass and bluegill lakes, Lake Tarpon's 2,500 acres stretch 5 miles south from Tarpon Springs and about a mile east of US 19. Two Pinellas County parks provide picnic facilities and boat launch areas. The two parks are (west side) **A. L. Anderson Park** (39699 US 19, Tarpon Springs; 727-582-2100; pinellascounty.org/park/01_Anderson.htm) and (east side) **John Chesnut Sr. Park** (2200 East Lake Rd., Palm Harbor; 727-582-2100; pinellascounty.org/park/04_Chesnut.htm).

Leepa-Rattner Museum of Art. 600 Klosterman Rd., Tarpon Springs; (727) 712-5762; spcollege.edu/central/museum. Located on the Tarpon Springs campus of St. Petersburg College, the Leepa-Rattner Museum of Art holds a collection of 20th-century art by Abraham Rattner, Esther Gentle, Allen Leepa, and other artists of the period including Pablo Picasso, Henry Moore, Max Ernst, and others. The Leepa-Rattner Museum of Art is open 10 a.m. to 5 p.m. Tues, Wed, and Sat; from 10 a.m. to 8 p.m. on Thurs; and 10 a.m. to 4 p.m. on Fri. The museum is open on Sun from 1 to 5 p.m.

where to shop

Artists' Faire Art Gallery & Gifts. 111 E. Tarpon Ave., Tarpon Springs; (727) 934-2952; artists-faire.com. A cooperative gallery featuring the work of more than two dozen local artists, Artists' Faire Art Gallery & Gifts is located in downtown Tarpon Springs. They are open Mon through Fri from 9 a.m. to 5 p.m. and on Sat and Sun from 10:30 a.m. to 5 p.m. While you are in the area, check out the antiques shops nearby.

Classic Corvettes & Collectibles, Inc. 304 S. Pinellas Ave., Tarpon Springs; (727) 945-1500; classiccorvettes.com. Classic Corvettes & Collectibles, Inc., showcases museum-quality cars, and Classic Car Center, just down the street, restores not-quite-museum-quality cars. The showroom is open to the public Mon through Fri from 9 a.m. to 6 p.m. and Sat from 10 a.m. to 5 p.m.

Halki Market. 520 Athens St., Tarpon Springs; (727) 937-6533. Halki Market sells Greek and Mediterranean food items—several kinds of olives, 23 kinds of olive oil, spices, cheeses, rose petal preserves, pomegranate juice, pastas and pastries, squid, and more. Plus you'll find goat milk soaps made in Tarpon Springs and Aphrodite skin care and cosmetics. They are open every day from 9 a.m. to 5 p.m. On Sun, they open "a little later."

The Sponge Exchange. 735 Dodecanese Blvd., Tarpon Springs; (727) 934-8758; thespongeexchange.com. Located at the sponge docks, the Sponge Exchange used to be where the sponge boats sold their wares to wholesalers—like a livestock auction only with natural sea sponges used in a variety of industries. The Tarpon Sponge Company still anchors the Exchange. You'll also find shops selling clothing, antiques, children's items, home decor, and gift items.

where to eat

Danny K's Alley Cafe. 118 E. Court St., Tarpon Springs; (727) 938-9452. Danny K's sits in the interior courtyard of the downtown Taylor Arcade. Breakfast is served all day, and there's a good selection of omelettes and eggs Benedicts, including a smoked salmon Benedict and a Greek Benedict with gyro meat, tomatoes, and feta cheese plus the Hollandaise sauce. Waffles are made with a malted mix, and French toast can be made with regular, sourdough, or raisin bread. Salads, burgers, Cuban sandwiches, and pita wraps round out the menu. There are a number of vegetarian choices. Danny K's opens every day at 7 a.m. They close Mon through Sat at 9 p.m. and on Sun at 2 p.m. $–$$.

Plaka Restaurant. 769 Dodecanese Blvd., Tarpon Springs; (727) 934-4752; plakatarponsprings.com. Gyros, souvlaki, Greek salads—and burgers and seafood and chicken nuggets, too—Plaka has been serving it up for some 30 years. Yum and yum again. Plaka is open every day from 10:30 a.m. to 8 p.m. They stay open until 9 p.m. on Fri and Sat. $$.

where to stay

Ashley's Victorian Haven Bed & Breakfast. 313 N. Grosse Ave., Tarpon Springs; (727) 505-9152; ashleysvictorianhaven.com. This Victorian 2-story home, built about 1894, was restored by proprietors Barbara and Larry Lawrence and is furnished with antiques from the early 1800s to the early 1900s (except, of course, for the beds). A full breakfast is served each morning. Parking behind the home is abundant and large enough for a rig with a boat trailer. The locked courtyard also shelters guests' motorcycles overnight. No pets and no children under age 13. However, the Lawrences rent a pet- and child-friendly cottage elsewhere in town. $$–$$$.

Innisbrook Resort and Golf Club. 36750 US 19 North, Innisbrook; (800) 456-2000, (727) 942-2000; innisbrookgolfresort.com. Take on Innisbrook's Copperhead Course, or any of the other demanding courses designed by Lawrence Packard. Twenty-eight separate lodges, nestled among pines and oaks, house 620 guest rooms and suites. Fish Lake Innisbrook—tackle and bait are available on site—or check out the charter fishing possibilities, the 11-court Tennis Center, the Indaba Spa, and Loch Ness Monster Pool. Dining options range from a take-out deli and dine-in grill to Packard's Steakhouse. $$$.

day trip 05

way down upon the cotanchobee:

tampa downtown; tampa uptown; tampa sideways west; tampa sideways east

All other chapters in this book have originated in downtown Tampa on the east side of Tampa Bay. In this last chapter, we'll take a day trip from St. Petersburg, on the west side of Tampa Bay, to Tampa and surrounding communities. The City of Tampa extends from the Hillsborough County line in the north to MacDill Air Force Base in the south. Unlike Pinellas County, with its almost 30 municipalities and recognized neighborhoods, Hillsborough County has exactly three incorporated cities: Tampa, Temple Terrace, and Plant City. From its rather humble beginnings, Tampa has grown into a major metropolitan community. It has hosted four Super Bowls and, this past summer, hosted the Republican National Convention. Downtown Tampa is home to the Port of Tampa, the Convention Center, several museums, and Ybor City. Uptown Tampa is where Busch Gardens, Adventure Island, the Museum of Science and Industry, and Tampa's Lowry Park Zoo are located. Go sideways west to see Raymond James Stadium, home of the Tampa Bay Bucs; go sideways east to the Seminole Hard Rock Hotel & Casino, the Florida State Fairgrounds, and more.

And if you're from Tampa? We hope you will read through this chapter, too, and will look at your hometown with touristy eyes. Maybe you'll discover something new, too!

tampa downtown

Downtown Tampa's Curtis Hixon Waterfront Park sits along what early peoples called the Cotanchobee or "Where the Big Water Meets the Land." Spanish mapmakers dubbed it El

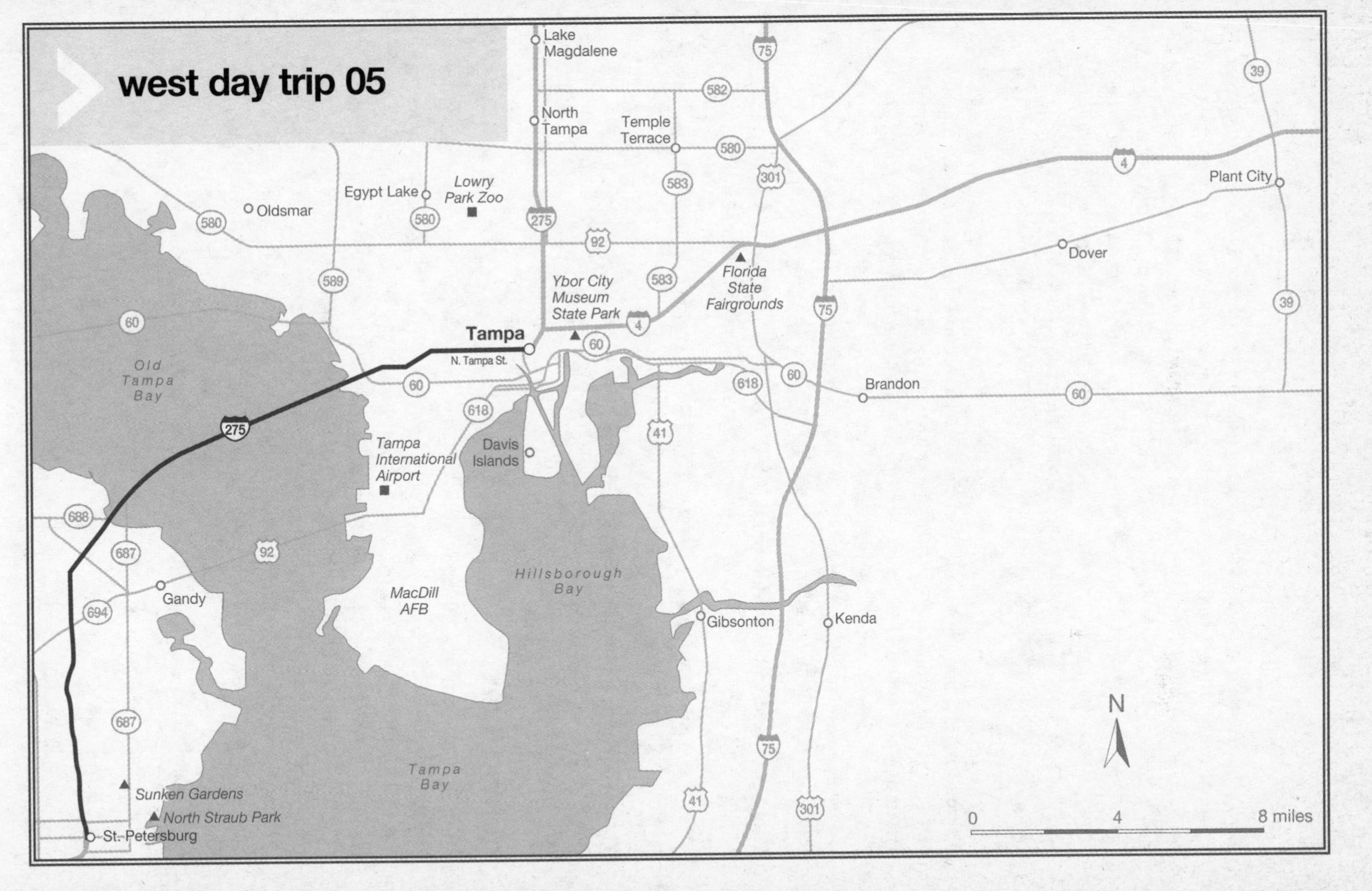

west day trip 05
Lake Magdalene
North Tampa
Temple Terrace
Egypt Lake
Lowry Park Zoo
Oldsmar
Ybor City Museum State Park
Florida State Fairgrounds
Plant City
Dover
Tampa
N. Tampa St.
Old Tampa Bay
Brandon
Tampa International Airport
Davis Islands
MacDill AFB
Hillsborough Bay
Gandy
Gibsonton
Kenda
Tampa Bay
Sunken Gardens
North Straub Park
St. Petersburg
N
0
4
8 miles

Rio San Julián de Arriaga; British mapmakers named it the Hillsborough River, the name it has gone by since then. The Curtis Hixon Waterfront Park area includes the Tampa Convention Center, the Tampa Museum of Art, and more. The park itself offers some green areas and a Riverwalk where visitors can watch the boat traffic. Upriver a bit, the Channelside area—home to the Port of Tampa, Florida's largest port where both cruise and cargo ships dock—is a shopping and nightlife spot; the Florida Aquarium and Tampa Bay History Center are next door. The TECO Line Streetcar System runs from Channelside—and other downtown areas—to Ybor City, another nightlife spot, but with a daytime alter ego well worth a trip across the bay.

Tampa Bay & Company Visitor Information Center and Gift Shop. 615 Channelside Dr., Suite 108A, Tampa; (800) 448-2672, (813) 223-2752; visittampabay.com. Located at the Channelside entertainment complex in downtown Tampa, this Visitor Information Center is near the Florida Aquarium, the Tampa Bay History Center, and more. The center is open Mon through Sat from 9:30 a.m. to 5:30 p.m. and on Sun from 11 a.m. to 5 p.m. Tampa Bay & Company has three other visitor center locations in Hillsborough County.

Tampa Convention Center/Information & Gift Shop. 333 S. Franklin St., Tampa; (800) 448-2672, (813) 223-2752. Hours vary according to Convention Center events.

Plant City Visitor Information Center. 1702 N. Park Rd., Plant City; (813) 754-7045. Open 9 a.m. to 4 p.m. every day except Christmas.

Ybor City Visitor Information Center. 1600 E. 8th Ave., Suite B104, Tampa; (877) 934-3782, (813) 241-8838. Open 10 a.m. to 6 p.m. Monday through Saturday and noon to 6 p.m. Sunday.

getting there

From St. Petersburg, take I-275 North toward Tampa. Travel north, then east, crossing the Howard Frankland Bridge—almost 21 miles to exit 44 toward Downtown East/Downtown West. Stay to the right to take exit 44/Downtown West/Ashley Drive/Tampa Street. Merge right onto Ashley Drive, then move to the left to take the Tampa Street ramp toward the Aquarium-Seaport/SP Times Forum/Convention Center/Harbor Island. Merge from the right onto N. Tampa Street/US 41/SR 685 South and stay on this road for about 0.5 mile to E. Jackson Street (one block past Kennedy Boulevard). Turn left onto E. Jackson Street/SR 60 East/US 41-BR South/SR 685 North. Stay on E. Jackson for about 0.25 mile; take the third right onto N. Morgan Street, travel another 0.25 mile or so, and turn left onto Channelside Drive. There is a parking garage across from Channelside or look for open-air (paid) lots nearby.

where to go

Channelside Bay Plaza. 615 Channelside Dr., Tampa; (813) 223-425; channelsidebay plaza.com. Located on the water near the Port of Tampa, Channelside Bay Plaza has a movie theater complex, some retail shops, and several restaurants and nightspots including Splitsville, Stumps Supper Club, and Howl at the Moon.

Glazer Children's Museum. 110 W. Gasparilla Plaza, Tampa; (813) 443-3861; glazer museum.org. Featuring a number of exhibits designed to help children of all ages learn about their world, the Glazer Children's Museum is open Mon through Fri from 10 a.m. to 5 p.m., Sat from 10 a.m. to 6 p.m., and Sun from 1 to 6 p.m.

Florida Aquarium, Inc. 701 Channelside Dr., Tampa; (813) 273-4000; flaquarium.org. The Florida Aquarium's walk-through environments feature real plants and wildlife—watch otters play, spot 'gators swimming really close up, and see what it's like to be under the sea . . . without getting wet. If you want to get wet, ask about the Swim with the Fishes and Dive with the Sharks experiences. Play in an outdoor water park, or go for an eco-tour on a 49-foot powered catamaran. The Florida Aquarium is open every day, except Thanksgiving and Christmas, from 9:30 a.m. to 5 p.m. On-site food options include a cafe and a cantina.

H.B. Plant Historical Museum. 401 W. Kennedy Blvd., Tampa; (813) 254-1891; plant museum.com. No other Tampa building is as immediately distinctive as the University of Tampa and the H.B. Plant Historical Museum with its silvery minaret-topped roof. Built in 1891, the Tampa Bay Hotel covered 6 acres of land and was 0.25 mile long. Today, most of the building is the University of Tampa. But part of it is the H.B. Plant Historical Museum, open Tues through Sat from 10 a.m. to 4 p.m. and Sun from noon to 4 p.m. except on Thanksgiving Day, Christmas Eve, and Christmas Day. Guided tours begin in the lobby at 1 p.m. Tues through Fri. Call ahead to ask for parking instructions.

Straz Center for Performing Arts. 1010 North W. C. MacInnes Place, Tampa; (813) 229-7827; strazcenter.org. With 5 theaters, the Straz hosts Broadway productions, concerts, plays, and other performances. Park in the Poe Garage and walk across the elevated covered walkway to the center or look for street-level parking lots nearby.

Tampa Convention Center. 333 S. Franklin St., Tampa; (813) 274-8511; tampagov.net/dept_Convention_Center/index.asp. Located on the waterfront, the Tampa Convention Center hosts conventions and gatherings of many sorts.

Tampa Museum of Art. 120 Gasparilla Plaza, Tampa; (813) 274-8130; tampamuseum .org. The just-built Tampa Museum of Art's permanent collections range from Greek and Roman antiquities to contemporary art works in many media, including an eclectic collection of sculpture. Sono Cafe, operated by Mis en Place, offers lunch, La Dolce Vita service (a limited menu for late-afternoon/early evening dining), dinner on Friday, and weekend brunches, plus a full bar. The museum is open Mon through Thurs from 11 a.m. to 7 p.m., Fri from 11 a.m. to 8 p.m., and Sat and Sun from 11 a.m. to 5 p.m.

Tampa Bay History Center. 801 Old Water St., Tampa; (813) 228-0097; tampabayhistory center.org. Located on the banks of the Cotanchobee ("Where the Big Water Meets the Land"), known today as the Hillsborough River, the Tampa Bay History Center puts visitors in the middle of a cattle drive, lets them scull along the Hillsborough River, and invites them to explore other exhibits highlighting 12,000 years of Tampa Bay area history. The Tampa Bay History Center, located near the Channelside Bay Plaza complex, is open every day (except Thanksgiving and Christmas) from 10 a.m. to 5 p.m. Inside the center building are a gift store and a Columbia Cafe.

Tampa Bay Times Forum. 401 Channelside Dr., Tampa; (813) 301-6500; tampabaytimes forum.com. Home of the Tampa Bay Lightning, the forum also hosts other sporting and entertainment events.

The Tampa Theatre. 711 Franklin St., Tampa; (813) 274-8981 (24-hour event info), (813) 274-8286 (business and box office); tampatheatre.org. Built in 1926 by Paramount Studios, the Tampa Theatre was one of the country's most elaborate "movie palaces," with its lavish decor, twinkling stars overhead, and organ music. Today, the Tampa Theatre hosts first-run and classic films, concerts, live theater, children's programs, and other events. Come early to hear the Mighty Wurlitzer Theatre Organ played by a Central Florida Theatre Organ Society volunteer—the way movie music used to sound.

Ybor City Museum State Park. 1818 E. 9th Ave., Tampa; (813) 247-1434; ybormuseum .org or floridastateparks.org/YborCity. Once it was a bakery, with thousands of loaves of crusty bread coming out of its huge brick ovens. Today the building houses the Ybor City Museum State Park. The ovens are still there, and exhibits and movies tell what life was like more than a century ago for Cuban, Spanish, Italian, and Eastern European immigrants. Tour the casitas next door—small homes in which cigar workers and their families lived. The museum is open 9 a.m. to 5 p.m. every day except Thanksgiving, Christmas, and New Year's Day. Some metered parking is available on surrounding streets, or there are two parking garages with a few blocks of the museum—one on 9th Avenue near 13th Street and one at 15th Street and 5th Avenue.

what to do

Skatepark of Tampa. 4215 E. Columbus Dr., Tampa; (813) 621-6793; skateparkoftampa .com. This 8,000-square-foot indoor course—the only one in the Tampa Bay area—hosts worldwide professional and amateur skateboarding championship battles. Skatepark of Tampa also has a 40-foot vert outside, a second indoor area with a bowl and mini-ramp and a 4,500-square-foot beginners' course, a pro shop, and instructors. A lounge area has free wireless Internet and a snack bar. Skatepark of Tampa is open Mon through Thurs from noon until 9 p.m., Fri from noon to 11 p.m., Sat (2 sessions) from 10 a.m. to 11 p.m. and Sun (2 sessions) from 10 a.m. to 10 p.m. Sun from 10 a.m. to 1:30 p.m. is for ages 12 and under only. BMX bikers ride on Wed and on Sun from 7 to 10 p.m. First-timers must bring a parent to sign the waiver—or print it out from the website and have your parent's signature notarized.

TECO Line Streetcar System. (813) 384-6611; tecolinestreetcar.org. The TECO Line Streetcar system covers a good portion of mid-Tampa including the downtown, Channelside, and Ybor City areas.

where to shop

Arnold Martinez Art Gallery. 1909 N. 19th St., Tampa; (813) 248-9572; arnoldmartinez gallery.com. One-of-a-kind artworks in browns and burgundies—painted with coffee, tea, tobacco, and wines. Amazing. Mr. Martinez generally is there Tues, Wed, Fri, and Sat from 10:30 a.m. to 3:30 p.m. or by appointment.

Centro Ybor. 1600 E. 8th Ave., Tampa; (813) 242-4660; centroybor.com. Centro Ybor is home to the Improv Comedy Theater, Game Time, Tampa Bay Brewing Company, Muvico Theaters, and other eat-drink-and-make-merry venues, many of which are open for lunch, too. Small shops throughout Ybor City are nearby.

Downtown Tampa. tampasdowntown.com. Need to find a jewelry store, a bookstore, or an art gallery? Check this website for a comprehensive listing of downtown Tampa's retail sites.

where to eat

Columbia Restaurant. 2117 E. 7th Ave., Tampa; (813) 248-4961; columbiarestaurant .com. Florida's oldest restaurant, established in 1905, Ybor City's original Columbia Restaurant serves Spanish and Cuban dishes, occupies a full city block, and is open every day of the year, Mon through Thurs from 11 a.m. to 10 p.m., Fri and Sat from 11 a.m. to 11 p.m., and Sun from noon to 9 p.m. On Saturday, live jazz entertainment can be found in the Columbia Cafe. Reservations are required for dinner seatings that include the flamenco show. $$–$$$.

Mema's Alaskan Tacos. 1724 E. 8th Ave., Ybor City; (813) 242-8226; memasalaskan tacos.com. Fillings—not just ground beef and chicken; try shrimp or tofu—are wrapped in tortillas and topped with the usual. But the secret lies in cooking the meat and shell together. The menu includes vegetarian items, too. Mema's opens at 11 a.m. each day and stays open until 1 a.m. Sun through Wed and until 3 a.m. Thurs through Sat. Counter service only. Limited seating inside and out. $–$$.

Mise en Place. 442 W. Kennedy Blvd., Tampa; (813) 254-5373; miseonline.com. Savor a luncheon chipotle grilled shrimp, black-bean-jicama-corn salad, and avocado, with a lime-mojo vinaigrette; or select something more exotic from the dinner menu, such as the mustard-pecan crusted rack of lamb or lemon thyme seared tofu. Cheeses, wines, and desserts add the finishing touches. Mise en Place is open for lunch Tues through Fri from 11:30 a.m. to 2:30 p.m., and reopens for dinner at 5:30 p.m., closing at 10 p.m. On Sat, the restaurant is open from 5:30 to 11 p.m. The bar opens at 5 p.m. Tues through Sat. $$$.

where to stay

Don Vicente de Ybor Historic Inn. 1915 Republica de Cuba (corner of 14th Street and 9th Avenue), Tampa; (813) 241-4545; donvicenteinn.com. This historic inn features 16 high-ceilinged guest rooms upstairs, which are furnished with king-size 4-poster or queen-size sleigh beds. Amenities include cable TV, voicemail, broadband access, and a complimentary deluxe Continental breakfast. Free parking for guests is behind the inn. $$$.

Gram's Place. 3109 N. Ola Ave., Tampa; (813) 221-0596; grams-inn-tampa.com. This European-style music-themed hostel—the only one of its kind in the area—offers an inexpensive place to stay in a truly unique setting. Bunk in a co-ed dorm-style room or opt for a more private space. Kids, yes. Pets, outside in carriers only. Bring your own lock and you can use one of the outdoor lockers for extra gear. Parson's Pub (outdoors) is BYOB. Please call after 7 a.m. and before 11 p.m. $.

Tampa Marriott Waterside Hotel & Marina. 700 S. Florida Ave., Tampa; (813) 221-4900, (888) 268-1616; marriott.com/hotels/travel/tpamc-tampa-marriott-waterside-hotel-and-marina. Sitting between the Tampa Convention Center and the Tampa Bay Times Forum, the Tampa Marriott Waterside Hotel is convenient to downtown and the Channelside area. The hotel has 700 guest rooms and suites, a fitness center and spa, 50,000 square feet of meeting space, and its own marina. Dining options include the elegant Il Terrazzo (dinner), the more casual Cafe Waterside (breakfast, lunch, and dinner), Champion Sports Bar (lunch and dinner), the poolside Pool Bar & Grill (lunch), a Starbucks Coffee Bar, and the Lobby Bar. No pets. $$$$.

tampa uptown

Located north of the downtown area, this section of Tampa is home to the University of South Florida and several major attractions.

where to go

Adventure Island. 10001 N. McKinley Dr., Tampa; (888) 800-5447; adventureisland.com. Adventure Island offers slip-slidin' watery fun, a 17,000-gallon wave pool, a sandy beach to lounge upon, Splash Attack fun maze, and an 11-court white-sand volleyball complex. Some rides have wheelchair access. Adventure Island is open from mid-Mar to mid-Oct. At the beginning and end of the season, the park is open on weekends only. The park opens between 9 and 10 am. and closes between 5 and 9 p.m. Call or go online to check their calendar before you visit. Also check dress code and food option information—the wrist-band meal plan is convenient.

Busch Gardens. 10165 N. McKinley Dr., Tampa; (888) 800-5447; buschgardens.com/bgt2. Body-boggling roller coasters, top-quality live entertainment, and one of the largest collections of African animals outside of Africa make Busch Gardens a something-for-everyone destination spot. Some rides are soakers—wear clothing that dries quickly in the sun. Busch Gardens is open from 10 a.m. to 6 p.m. all year. Hours are extended during special events. Look for behind-the-scenes tours, safaris, and more. Dining options include German food, barbecue, and more.

Museum of Science and Industry (MOSI). 4801 E. Fowler Ave., Tampa; (813) 987-6100; mosi.org. With more than 450 interactive permanent exhibits, MOSI (pronounced mosey), is the largest science center in the southeastern United States. Learn about "The Amazing You," including things like intestinal gas and nasal mucous, or ride a counter-balanced high-wire bike on a 1-inch cable 30 feet off the ground. The IMAX Dome Theater, the Science Works Theater, and the Planetarium each offer films and other programs. MOSI opens at 9 a.m. every day of the year. They close at 5 p.m. Mon through Fri and at 6 p.m. Sat and Sun. Check the calendar for special evening programs. Tip: The IMAX Theater's tiered seating can be a bit disconcerting to people sensitive to height. Arrive early and sit in one of the lower rows.

Tampa's Lowry Park Zoo. 1101 W. Sligh Ave., Tampa; (813) 935-8552; lowryparkzoo.com. Explore 8 different habitats containing more than 2,000 water, land, and sky animals at Tampa's Lowry Park Zoo, named the number one zoo for kids by *Parents* magazine (2009). Ride a camel, touch a rhinoceros, or feed a giraffe. The zoo also has 2 water play areas, rides, and a climb-on playground for kids. Or take a pontoon-boat River Odyssey Ecotour on the Hillsborough River. Tampa's Lowry Park Zoo is open 9:30 a.m. to 5 p.m. every day except Thanksgiving and Christmas. Parking is free. Nine different dining options range from snacks to full meals.

University of South Florida Botanical Gardens. 4202 E. Fowler Ave., Tampa; (813) 974-2329; cas.usf.edu/garden. The USF Botanical Gardens cover about 7 acres, including a rainforest area, a temperate forest area, and a wetland forest area. The gardens host a number of workshops, and their website contains information about different kinds of plants and gardening tips. An on-site plant shop and bookstore offer more help for gardeners. The USF Botanical Gardens are open Mon through Fri from 9 a.m. to 5 p.m., Sat from 9 a.m. to 4 p.m., and Sun from noon to 4 p.m. No pets.

what to do

Grand Prix Tampa. 14320 N. Nebraska Ave., Tampa; (813) 977-6272; grandprixtampa.com. You can bat, bungee, go-kart, paintball, or play miniature golf or the games in the

Castle Arcade. Look for package deals and specials listed on the website. The Pit Stop Cafe serves wings, burgers, a variety of sandwiches, soft drinks, and beer. Grand Prix Tampa is open Mon through Thurs from 3 to 10 p.m., Fri from noon to midnight, Sat from 10 a.m. to midnight, and Sun from 10 a.m. to 10 p.m.

where to eat

Mel's Hot Dogs. 4136 E. Busch Blvd., Tampa; (813) 985-8000; melshotdogs.com. Chicago-style, natural casing dogs on poppy-seeded buns are served 12 different ways—plus there are corn dogs and other sausage sandwiches. Mel's is open Mon through Sat from 11 a.m. to 8 p.m. Closed on Sun. $.

Sacred Grounds Coffee House. 4819 E. Busch Blvd., Tampa; (813) 983-0837; sacredgroundstampa.com. Sacred Grounds Coffee House serves veggie wraps, quesadillas, nachos, pitas and hummus, smoothies, coffee, and tea. Check the calendar for days and times of community meetings, open-mike sessions, and live music. Sacred Grounds Coffee House opens each evening at 6 p.m. and closes at midnight Sun through Thurs. Fri and Sat they're open until 2 a.m. $.

where to stay

Holiday Inn Express Hotel & Suites. 2807 E. Busch Blvd., Tampa; (813) 936-8200; tampaholidayinn.com. This Holiday Inn is close enough to walk to Busch Gardens or Adventure Island, but there is also a complimentary shuttle to the parks. Look for package deals on the hotel's website. No pets. $$–$$$.

tampa sideways west

Tampa's west side is where you'll find Tampa International Airport—a place to visit, not just to fly in and out—Raymond James Stadium, and a couple of great shopping malls.

where to go

Tampa International Airport. 4100 George J. Bean Inbound Pkwy., Tampa; (813) 870-8700; tampaairport.com. Take the free airfield tour at TIA and you'll tour the service roads in a minibus, talk to the firefighters at the airport fire department, learn about the runways, and more. Or take a free, 1-hour guided walking tour of the terminal to view the public art program and to learn about the building design. Tours are offered 7 days a week, last about an hour, and participants must be at least 5 years old. Or call to ask for information about the self-guided tour you can conduct yourself any time of day or in the wee hours of the morning. Groups can arrange for a scavenger hunt in the airport terminal. Call (813) 870-8759 to arrange for tours and activities.

Raymond James Stadium. 4201 N. Dale Mabry Hwy., Tampa; (813) 350-6500; raymondjamesstadium.com. Take a tour of the stadium where the Bucs play home games. Walk-up tours begin at 2 p.m. on most Tuesdays, Wednesdays, and Thursdays. Call ahead to be sure a tour has not been pre-empted by other events. Private group tours can be arranged by appointment. A nominal fee is charged, and payment is by cash or check only.

Tampa Bay Buccaneers Headquarters. 1 Buccaneer Place, Tampa; (813) 870-2700; buccaneers.com. The Bucs train here, and some training sessions during the summer are open to the public.

where to shop

International Plaza & Baystreet. 2223 N. West Shore Blvd., Tampa; (813) 342-3790; shopinternationalplaza.com. With more than 200 upscale stores, 16 restaurants and nightspots, and a Looney Tunes Ball Park play area for children, International Mall is a shopping event. The mall generally is open 10 a.m. to 9 p.m. Mon through Sat and from 11 a.m. to 6 p.m. on Sun.

WestShore Plaza. 250 WestShore Plaza, Tampa; (813) 286-0790; westshoreplaza.com. More trendy shops, restaurants, and entertainment options can be found at WestShore Plaza. The plaza is open Mon through Sat from 10 a.m. to 9 p.m. and on Sun from noon to 6 p.m.

where to eat

The View at CK's. 5503 W. Spruce St., Tampa; (813) 878-6500; ckstampa.com. The View at CK's slowly revolves atop the Tampa Airport Marriott Hotel, as guests dine on contemporary-styled sushi, seafood, and steaks. The View's certified Black Angus steaks are specially seasoned then topped with the View's signature chimichurri horseradish butter. The View at CK's serves dinner Tues through Thurs from 5 to 9 p.m., and on Fri and Sat from 5 to 10 p.m. They are closed Sun and Mon. Parking is in the Marriott Hotel parking area (go past the long-term and short-term parking) and will be validated by the restaurant. $$$.

where to stay

Renaissance Tampa Hotel International Plaza. 4200 Jim Walter Blvd., Tampa; (813) 877-9200; marriott.com/hotels/travel/tpaim-renaissance-tampa-hotel-international-plaza. Shop 'til you drop, then drop into bed where you shop at the beautifully decorated Renaissance Tampa Hotel at International Plaza. The on-site, award-winning Pelagia Trattoria serves breakfast, lunch, and dinner. You will also find a full-service business center, fitness center, and pool. No pets. $$$.

tampa sideways east

Clustered around I-4 and SR 60 on the east side of Tampa, you'll find the Seminole Hard Rock Hotel & Casino and the Florida State Fairgrounds. Keep going and you come to Plant City, home of the Florida Strawberry Festival.

where to go

Cracker Country. 4800 US 301 North, Tampa; (800) 345-3247, (813) 621-7821; cracker country.org. Located at the Florida State Fairgrounds, Cracker Country is Tampa's outdoor living history museum. Call to schedule a tour. During February, Cracker Country is open to the public as part of the Florida State Fair.

Dinosaur World. 5145 Harvey Tew Rd., Plant City; (813) 717-9865; dinoworld.net. Come face to face with more than 150 life-size dinosaurs at Dinosaur World just east of Tampa and north of I-4 (exit 17). No scary sounds and no animatronics. Dig in the boneyard, or join a fossil dig and take home 3 authentic fossils. There's also a playground, a museum, and a movie cave.

Florida State Fairgrounds. 4800 US 301 North, Tampa; (800) 345-3247, (813) 621-7821; floridastatefair.com. Home of the Florida State Fair each February, this is also the site of other events all year long. The Bob Thomas Equestrian Center at the Fairgrounds hosts equestrian events.

1-800-ASK-GARY Amphitheater. 4802 US 301 North, Tampa; (813) 740-2446; livenation .com. This open-air facility with covered stage and seating area, plus uncovered open lawn-seating area, hosts rain-or-shine concerts. Traffic can be an issue.

Sun Dome. 4202 E. Fowler Ave., Tampa; (813) 974-3002; gousfbulls.com. Located on the main campus of the University of South Florida, the USF Sun Dome hosts concerts and events of all types.

what to do, where to eat & stay

Seminole Hard Rock Hotel & Casino, Tampa. 5223 N. Orient Rd., Tampa; (866) 502-7529, (813) 627-7625; seminolehardrocktampa.com. The Seminole Hard Rock Hotel & Casino features rooms and suites with in-room sound systems, lots of natural lighting, and oversized bath areas. Nonstop gaming goes on 24/7, but there are also an outdoor pool, a complete fitness center, a Body Rock Spa, and a gift shop. Several dining options include the Council Oak Steaks & Seafood; Floyd's, an upscale nightclub/restaurant; the marketplace-style Fresh Harvest, which features everything from dim sum to pasta; or the Green Room, which never closes. You'll find live entertainment in some of the restaurant areas. $$$.

festivals & celebrations

january

The first weekend in January, the **Dade Battlefield Reenactment** (352-793-4781; floridastateparks.org/dadebattlefield/default.cfm or dadebattlefield.com) explains the events leading to the Second Seminole War, which began here on December 28, 1835. Held on the grounds of the Dade Battlefield Historic State Park, the event includes a reenactors' encampment, showing how people lived at that time. The visitor center at the park includes a museum with historical exhibits.

Held every January 6, the **Tarpon Springs Epiphany Celebration** (727-937-3540; epiphanycity.org) attracts thousands of visitors who line the banks of Spring Bayou and watch while several dozen Greek male teens wait on boats for the Archbishop to bless, then throw, a white cross into the water. A dove is released, the cross is tossed, and the young men dive in after it, hoping for the special blessing awarded to the one who retrieves the cross.

Sample Pasco County's best kumquats and calamondins, small citrus fruits, at the **Kumquat Festival** (352-567-3769; kumquatfestival.org) each January. Munch on kumquat pie, cookies, or bread and check out the car and truck show in a nearby parking lot. An arts and crafts show, a quilt show, wagon rides, and other activities round out this glimpse into rural Florida life.

The **Annual Florida Manatee Festival** (352-795-3149; crystalriverflorida.com/manatee-festival.htm) in Crystal River features boat tours to view the manatees, a Fine Arts Show, children's activities, and live entertainment—even a beer and wine garden with big-screen TVs tuned to sports channels.

Beginning in January and running into March, the **Horse Shows in the Sun (HITS)** hunter/jumper horse show circuit events are held in the Ocala area. For a listing of events and venues, call (845) 246-8833 (HITS main office) or (352) 620-2275 (during show season); hitsshows.com.

The **St. Armands Circle Art Festival** (561-746-6615; sarasotafl.org) is one of the top shows in the country, attracting local artists and those from snowy regions. The two-day festival combines top art with island life leisure.

february

Think what the world would be like without the electric lightbulb—then head to Fort Myers to celebrate this modern marvel at the **Edison Festival of Light** (239-334-2999; edison festival.org). The 3-week celebration begins in January, but ends with a 3-day festival in mid-February. The festival features parades, music, Crafts on the River and a Vintage Market, and more.

The 12-day **Florida State Fair** (800-345-3247, 813-621-7821; floridastatefair.com) held at the Fairgrounds in Tampa each February has a massive midway with games and rides. There are also exhibits from artists, 4-H youth, farmers, and more from around the state.

You don't have to go to New Orleans to celebrate Mardi Gras—the **Lake Wales Mardi Gras** (863-638-2686; lwmardigras.com) is much closer and you can still count on Dixieland Jazz and Zydeco music, Cajun food, and costumes, beads, and parades.

march

The **Sanibel Island Shell Fair & Show** (sanibelcaptivashellclub.com/SanCap_shellshow.html), held early each March since the late 1930s, is the country's oldest shell festival. Hosted by the Sanibel-Captiva Shell Club, the 3-day fair is preceded by several days of "shellabration" as area merchants, parks, and organizations offer specials, speakers, and other events.

Eat strawberries just about any way you like during the 11-day **Florida Strawberry Festival** (813-752-9194; flstrawberryfestival.com) held in Plant City, just east of Tampa. Plus there are top-name entertainers, games, rides, and exhibits.

The **Swamp Monster** (352-596-3757; swampfestweekiwachee.com) makes an appearance—along with a carnival, arts and crafts vendors, musicians, dancers, and food vendors—at the Weeki Wachee Swamp Fest at Linda Pederson Park in Weeki Wachee. No pets; no alcohol.

Bring a lawn chair or beach blanket to **St. Petersburg's Vinoy Park** (727-502-5000; tampabaybluesfest.com), an open-air grassy park near downtown, for 3 days of blues by the bay at the Tampa Bay Blues Festival.

Dunedin's **St. Patrick's Day Street Festival** (727-736-4994; flanagansirishpub.net) features a family-friendly sort of top o' the mornin' along the downtown portion of Main Street starting around 11 a.m. Alcohol is limited to the sponsoring pub's (Flanagan's) property, and the street fest part includes Irish dancing, performances by local pipe bands, and other entertainment.

Mention the **Mount Dora Annual Spring Antiques, Collectibles, and Craft Show** (352-735-1191; mountdoraspringshow.com), to some of us and we're out the door before you can say "good buy."

New Port Richey's 11-day **Chasco Fiesta** (877-424-2726, 727-842-7651; chascofiesta.com), with a Native American Festival and Pow Wow, includes music every night, softball tournaments, foot races, a carnival midway, boat parade, and more. The Native American Festival and Pow Wow includes a dance competition with hefty cash prizes. During the 6-day **Sun 'n' Fun Fly-In** (863-644-2431; sun-n-fun.org), Lakeland's Linder

Regional Airport becomes the busiest airport in the world! Daily air shows, a balloon race, workshops and seminars at the Florida Air Museum, and more bring aviation enthusiasts from around the country to celebrate the wonder of flight. ***Note:*** Because it usually starts near the end of March, Sun 'n' Fun sometimes straddles 2 months. We're listing it in March, but parts of it may occur in April.

april

Pass-a-Grille Beach hosts **Beach Goes Pops** (727-363-0849; beachgoespops.com) with music director and conductor Robert Romanski and 35 or so local professional musicians performing a free outdoor concert for listeners who sit on the beach or set up folding chairs in a paved plaza area.

Winter Park's 10-day **Florida Film Festival** (407-629-1088; floridafilmfestival.com) features more than 150 independent and foreign films—plus speakers, special guests, and lots of food-related events.

The 2-day **Dunedin Highland Games** (727-733-3197; dunedinhighlandgames.com), held the first weekend in April, caps a Scottish Events Week that begins with a Military Tattoo—a gathering of pipe and drum bands from around the area—the weekend before (the last weekend in March). Watch kilted athletes toss the caber—a log about the size of a telephone pole—end over end, and enjoy sheepdog demonstrations, lots of food and drink, arts, and crafts.

may

The 1-day **AsiaFest** (813-864-4500; asiafest-tampabay.com), held in Tampa, celebrates the cultures of as many as 15 separate Asian-Pacific groups living in the Tampa Bay area. Dancers and other performers in colorful traditional clothing fill the St. Pete Times Forum and the plaza outside. Watch the Dragonboat races on the river and enjoy ethnic foods and beverages, arts, and crafts.

Ears to the 3-day **Zellwood Sweet Corn Festival** (407-886-0014; zellwoodcorn festival.com), which features corn-eating contests, live entertainment, carnival rides, games, arts and crafts, and more.

june

Visitors to **John Levique Pirate Days** (727-391-6025), held at John's Pass Village in Madeira Beach, can expect 3 days of skullduggery fun. After a water battle and invasion, pirates parade, then "pillage the village." Jugglers, pirate artists, and other performers provide plenty of entertainment.

Called one of the country's top art festivals, the 2-day **Mainsail Arts Festival** (727-892-5885; mainsailartsfestival.org) in St. Petersburg's Vinoy Park features some 250 juried fine artists from around the country, who compete for more than $50,000 in cash awards.

july

Escape the heat at the **Cool Art Show** (727-892-5202; pava-artists.org), held at the historic Coliseum in St. Petersburg. This juried exhibit features fine art and crafts created in a variety of media from wood to glass, jewelry to watercolors, photography to ceramics, and more.

august

Each August, Lake Placid's **Caladium Festival** (863-465-4331; lpfla.com/caladium) celebrates this shade-loving, pest-free ornamental plant grown in abundance in Highland County. There's an antique and classic car show, arts and crafts, live entertainment, lots of food, and more.

october

The **John's Pass Seafood Festival** (727-391-6025; johnspassfestivals.com), in Madeira Beach, hosts such activities as a fishing expo, an oyster-eating contest, and crab races. Plus there's the juried arts and crafts show that attracts artisans from around the region, a children's Halloween costume contest and trick or treating from shop to shop, and the nonstop live entertainment.

San Antonio's 2-day **Rattlesnake Festival** (352-588-4444; rattlesnakefestival.com), run by R.A.G.E., aka Rattlesnake and Gopher Enthusiasts, features snakes and (gopher) tortoises, live entertainment, an arts and crafts show, the Rattlesnake Run, and the Miss Rattler Pageant—plus food, of course!

The 3-day **Lake Mirror Classic Auto Festival and Auction** (lakemirrorclassic.com) held in Lakeland brings out thousands of visitors and hundreds of classic cars, classic wooden boats, and an amphicar splash-in, where amphibious cars drive on land and in water.

Florida's largest and oldest bicycling event is the **Annual Bicycle Festival** (352-383-2165) held in Mount Dora each October. Events and races for all ages and abilities.

There's games and stuff for kids, live music and entertainment for all. But mostly there's barbecue at the **Fine Swine at the Pit** (fineswine.org) cook-off in Mulberry. There's even a Kids Q Competition—yum!

Spread out a blanket or bring a lawn chair to Coachman Park for the 4-day—free!—**Clearwater Jazz Holiday** (727-461-5200; clearwaterjazz.com) that has featured such top-name artists as Kenny G, Natalie Cole, Zydeco, and the Ramsey Lewis Trio over its 30-year run.

The **Sarasota Pumpkin Festival** (941-706-7605; sarasotapumpkinfestival.com), held at the Sarasota County Fairgrounds, is way more than just a pumpkin patch. Circus-act thrill shows, pumpkin carving and a wall of pumpkins, pony rides, live music, arts and crafts vendors, and more make this fall festival a family favorite.

november

The first weekend in November, Central Florida growers show off their wares at the **Mount Dora Plant & Garden Fair** (352-383-2165). Orchids, roses, herbs, rare plants, and garden decor are among the featured items. A local garden club offers tours of area gardens. Green thumb not required for admission.

Visitors to **Davenport's Quilts and Tea Festival** (863-258-7800; quiltsandtea.com), held the second Friday and Saturday in November, walk or ride in horse-drawn carriages through the historic district to view quilt displays and tea rooms set up at various venues. Plus there's a farmers' market, antiques, car show, entertainment, and more.

Sand sculptors from around the world create amazing, intricate, ginormous sand sculptures on Fort Myers Beach at the **American Sandsculpting Championship Festival** (239-454-7500; sandsculptingfestival.com). Held here for the past quarter of a century, the 5-day festival includes games and music, too.

december

Decorating a 20-room mansion for the holidays is no easy feat. View the results as you tour **Christmas at Pinewood** (863-232-4573; boktower.org), a Mediterranean Revival–style mansion on the grounds of Bok Tower Gardens in Lake Wales. The decorating team features a different theme each year.

The Historic Church Street area in Dade City presents a **Christmas Stroll** (churchstreetchristmas.com). Visitors walk the area and view beautifully decorated homes; listen to carolers, choirs, and other performers; and enjoy hot cocoa and other goodies.

First Night St. Petersburg (727-823-8906; firstnightstpete.com) rings in the New Year with family-oriented festivities along St. Petersburg's waterfront park area. You might find a ragtime piano player at a nearby church, see a ballroom-dance-on-bicycle show in a bank lobby, or make a mask at the Dalí Museum. Fireworks, too!

index

D